Heinz A. Richter
A CONCISE HISTORY
OF MODERNN
CYPRUS
1878-2009

PELEUS
STUDIEN ZUR ARCHÄOLOGIE UND
GESCHICHTE GRIECHENLANDS UND ZYPERNS
BAND 50

IN KOMMISSION BEI
HARRASSOWITZ VERLAG
WIESBADEN

Heinz A. Richter

A CONCISE HISTORY OF MODERN CYPRUS

1878-2009

VERLAG 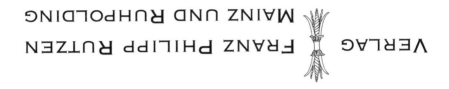 FRANZ PHILIPP RUTZEN MAINZ UND RUHPOLDING

PELEUS
Studien zur Archäologie und Geschichte Griechenlands und Zyperns
Herausgegeben von Reinhard Stupperich und Heinz A. Richter
Band 50

Bibliografische Information der Deutschen Nationalbibliothek
Die Deutsche Nationalbibliothek verzeichnet diese Publikation in der Deutschen
Nationalbibliografie; detaillierte bibliografische Daten sind im Internet
über http://dnb.d-nb.de abrufbar.

Bibliographic information published by the Deutsche Nationalbibliothek
The Deutsche Nationalbibliothek lists this publication in the Deutsche
Nationalbibliografie; detailed bibliographic data are available in the internet
at http://dnb.d-nb.de

Umschlagvignetten:
Umschlagbild: Staatspräsident Makarios besichtigt die Ruine des Präsidentenpalais am 11.
Dezember 1974
Gegenüber Titelblatt: Innenbild einer Schale des Peithinosmalers, Berlin, Pergamonmuseum
(CVA Berlin 2, Taf. 61).

VERLAG FRANZ PHILIPP RUTZEN
D - 83324 Ruhpolding, Am Zellerberg 21
Tel. 08663/883386, Fax 08663/883389, e-mail: franz-rutzen@t-online.de
In Kommission bei Harrassowitz Verlag • Wiesbaden, www.harrassowitz-verlag.de

ISSN 1868-1476
ISBN 978-3-938646-53-3
ISBN 978-3-447-06212-1

CONTENT

THIS BOOK IS DEDICATED TO SOULA. WITHOUT HER PATIENCE AND UNDERSTANDING

IT COULD NEVER HAVE BEEN WRITTEN

Reading experience has shown me for quite some time that the German language has become so exotic that most historians who work on Cypriot history do not know it. Thus research on this topic published in German is ignored according to the principle of *quod non est in lingua britannica/americana non est in mundo*. In order to overcome this obstacle I decided to translate the German text of this "Kurze Geschichte des modernen Zypern" into English so that interested readers may have access to my research results via this short version. Those readers, however, who have command of modern Greek can go directly to the Greek edition of volumes 1 and 2 published by Estia in Athens.

This "Concise History of Modern Cyprus" addresses itself to readers interested in Cyprus who want to learn more than what can be found in guide books or perhaps in newspapers but do not have the time to delve into the history of this island. It is the summing up of my four volume "Geschichte der Insel Zypern" which is 2,667 pages long and was written in seven years. It covers the era from 1878 when Cyprus became British to 1977 when Makarios signed the so-called High Level Agreement and died a little later. I refrained - for the time being - from writing a fifth volume which would bring the story to the present because there has been no substantial development since then. The Cyprus question has been marking time. But in order to help the reader to a better understanding of the development from then to the present this concise history contains a short overview of developments after 1977.

On the one hand my "Geschichte der Insel Zypern" is the continuation of Sir George Hill's classic account of the 1940s and on the other hand it is in its present form the only comprehensive history of modern Cyprus at least in the German language. Originally it was intended as a one volume work but soon it became clear that I was entering totally unexplored territory and in order to explore this adequately a certain epic width could not be avoided. While writing more and more new sources became available e.g., the American FRUS volumes, the delivery of which had been impeded by the CIA. This made it possible to put the narrative on a more and more solidified fundament which increased its quality and the number of pages enormously. Added to this was the fact that I have known many of the protagonists personally since I have been working for 40 years on Greek and 30 years on Cypriot contemporary history. With a lot of them I have been entertaining friendly relations. Thus in my talks with these contemporary witnesses I learned much more than what was written down in the documents. Some of the facts which I described I lived through myself. Only against this broad background it was possible to write the four volumes and this present short version.

The volumes of the long version and the short version describe the genesis and the development of the Cyprus conflict chronologically. Naturally the description focusses on the actions of persons. Makarios and Grivas as well as Clerides left their imprints on the history of the island deeper and for a longer time than comparable protagonists could ever have done in big European states. At the same time it became clear that the history is by far more complicated than that of big states because influence from outside is much stronger. Therefore the narrative must take into consideration developments in and interventions from Athens and Ankara, London, Brussels, New York and Washington.

The Cyprus conflict is the result of British colonial policy in the 1950s designed to repel the ambition of the Greek majority to annex Cyprus to Greece (enosis). The British government played off the two ethnic groups and their mother countries according to the principle of divide and rule in order to keep Cyprus under its control. When in 1956 after the Suez adventure the British position in the Near East collapsed London came to the conclusion that a base in Cyprus would suffice. The result was a state with a limited sovereignty which was rejected by both ethnic groups: the Greeks continued to dream of enosis and the Turks of partition (taksim).

Makarios wanted unfettered independence but was not ready to accept the Turkish minority (18 percent) as equal partners.

These differences inevitably led to a major conflict which broke out in 1963/4 and led to a quasi civil war between the two communities. The mother countries mingled into the conflict. In 1974 the coup by the Greek military triggered the Turkish invasion and the occupation of almost 40 percent of the island and a de facto partition. Since then there have been repeated efforts to find an amicable solution which, however, failed at the intransigence of the one or other side. Since Cyprus' EU membership the Europeans *nolens volens* are involved in this conflict but so far they have successfully managed to bypass their responsibility. The short version supplies the background to the better understanding of this problem.

Essentially the story is based on primary and secondary sources in English, Greek and French from Cyprus, Greece, the UK, the US, France and Germany as well from the UN. Since my original field of research was Greece's contemporary history I had no difficulty in understanding Greece's policy towards Cyprus. At the same time I recognised the differences in the respective political cultures in comparison with those of the mother countries which still are influenced by their Ottoman or Byzantine heritage: their political cultures are clientelistic. In contrast both Cypriot societies are much more europeanised.

When writing the short version I was obliged to reduce the facts to a minimum but the interpretations were retained to a great degree. Naturally the description of many details had to be shortened or completely left aside. Nevertheless, I tried to avoid writing a dry handbook of Cypriot history. The aim was an easy to read fascinating text satisfying all scholarly standards with one exception: I waived an extensive scholarly reference apparatus of footnotes and biblio-graphies. Such an apparatus would have impaired the readability, inflated the text, made the book bulky and expensive. Whoever wants to check a passage quoted or a statement made or learn more details may take the respective volume in his hand. The four volumes match the four chapters of the short version. As the chapters of both editions correspond it is easy to find the location of the item looked for. But there remains the problem of the language, of course.

Finally a word on terminology. I was often criticised in the past not practising "political correctness" i.e. not using the expression "Greek/Turkish Cypriots" when I am referring to Greeks and Turks living on the island even if it is clear that I mean Cypriots of this or that ethnic community. This is a question of style and not of "political correctness". Similarly I speak of "the north" or "the south" meaning the Republic of Cyprus or the "TRNC". Again this is a question of style and not a case of a political denomination on the basis of international law let alone an acknowledgement of the statehood of the "TRNC" by me.

The translation of this short version was done by me but being no native speaker of English it needed some polishing and in this context I want to thank most cordially Anne Cliadakis and Cathy Eve. They did a splendid job.

The Colonial Period

1878-1948

CYPRUS BECOMES BRITISH

In 1878 Great Britain and the Ottoman Empire concluded a Convention by which Cyprus was leased to the British until that distant day in the future when the Russians would move out of Batum, Ardahan and Kars in Armenia, i.e. forever. This Convention, the *Cyprus Convention* as it was soon known, was the result of highly complex developments far away from the island which had begun half a century earlier. In my following exposition I will try to give an outline of the main strands of the story and their interdependence.

There were two main causes which led to the Cyprus Convention: the growing nationalistic unrest among the peoples of the Balkans and the global rivalry of Great Britain and Russia known as the *Grand Game*. But these conflicts were well known all through the nineteenth century and until 1878 had not had any influence on Cyprus. This time, however, it was different. The event, which in 1875 triggered the new development, was one of those periodical peasant revolts against merciless tax farmers in the Ottoman provinces of Herzegovina and Bosnia. In the past the Turks had crushed such revolts easily, but this time there were three new factors which gave this local rebellion an international dimension, namely the pan-Serbian and pan-Slav movements, and Austro-Hungarian expansionism. The Pan-Serbs in Belgrade dreamed of a Greater Serbia including all southern Slavs. The Russian Pan-Slavists wanted to unite all Slavs under the lead of Russia. The Austrians abhorred the idea of a Greater Serbia and therefore aimed at the annexation of Bosnia-Herzegovina. Both the Russians and the Austrians agreed that the Ottoman Empire had to be dissolved; however, they disagreed about the method to achieve dissolution and even more so about the share each of them should get; consequently war was threatening.

The situation was further complicated by two additional facts: The rivalling Austrians and Russians were allies of Germany in the *Dreikaiserbund* and the latter wanted to preserve this alliance. Furthermore, there was Great Britain which wanted to keep the Russians away from the Mediterranean at almost any cost.

In order to avoid a general conflagration, as in the Crimean War twenty years earlier, the Austrians and the Russians together with Bismarck worked out a compromise solution, the so-called *Berlin Memorandum*, which was accepted by the French and Italians as well. But the British refused to approve the compromise.

Until 1874 Britain, under Prime Minister Gladstone, had followed a policy which was known as "splendid isolation". His successor, Disraeli, was an imperialist, i.e. he wanted to expand the British Empire and secure its maritime routes of communications. In his eyes the old European concert of powers controlled by British balance of power politics had been ruined by the creation of Germany. He wrongly distrusted Bismarck's assurances that Germany was *saturiert* [saturated] and rightly suspected the Russians and Austrians of wishing to carve up the Ottoman Empire. In order to cope with this threatening situation Disraeli did his best to sow the seeds of discord among the members of the *Dreikaiserbund* and took measures to keep the Russians away from the Mediterranean and to strengthen the life line of the British Empire through the Mediterranean to India. Moreover in 1875 he brought the Suez Canal under British control by buying shares from the Egyptian Khedive and despatching naval units to the Dardanelles.

In the meantime, the revolt in Bosnia and Herzegovina had escalated into a war between Turkey and Serbia. In the spring of 1876, an uprising of the Bulgarians was crushed by the Turks in such a brutal way that the *Dreikaiserbund* intervened and forced Turkey to conclude an armistice. In December 1876, an international conference was held in Constantinople, during which the Powers exerted considerable pressure on Turkey to initiate reforms, although the

British secretly backed the Turks, enabling them to continue their intransigent policy. Thus, the conference of Constantinople failed.

This meant war. In order to avoid a direct confrontation with the British, the Russians made a last diplomatic effort. In March 1877, Russia, Austria, Germany and Britain signed a protocol asking the Turks to introduce those reforms they themselves had proposed at the Conference of Constantinople three months earlier. The Turks, however, believed themselves to be in a position of strength and rejected the Russian proposal. Thereupon Russia declared war on the Ottoman Empire on 24 April 1877.

The Russians attacked in two directions: in the Balkans and in Trans-Caucasia. Romania consenting, they crossed the Danube and marched towards Sofia. A strong Turkish attack from the fortress of Plevna on the western flank stopped the thrust until December. But in January the fortress surrendered and the Russians advanced rapidly towards the Straits. At the end of January an armistice was signed which allowed the Russians to proceed to Agios Stefanos (today Yeşilköy), a suburb of Constantinople; and on 3 March 1878 the peace treaty of San Stefano was signed.

In terms of British interests this peace treaty was a catastrophe. Among the many territorial changes was the creation of a Greater Bulgaria. The mere existence of this new state, stretching from Lake Ochrida in the West, the Danube in the North, the Black Sea in the East, almost to Adrianople (today Edirne) in the Southeast and the Aegean in the South, was a provocation to all its neighbours and to the Powers. It was clear that this "monster" state could only survive as a Russian satellite, and thus, indirectly, Russia would have become a littoral state of the Mediterranean, a British nightmare.

To make things worse, the Russians gained the Black Sea harbour of Batoum and the strategically important towns of Kars, Ardahan and Bajesid in Armenia. Obviously Russia was moving towards Mesopotamia and an advance towards Alexandretta (today Iskenderun) could no longer be excluded. At the same time the Straits were at the mercy of the Russians. In London the alarm bells rang: this peace treaty threatened Britain's route to India, the Life Line of the Empire. In Disraeli's eyes this treaty had to be completely redrawn.

Ways to minimise the damage for Britain began to be considered when the possibility of a Russian-Turkish war had loomed on the horizon in late 1876. Recollections of the horrible Crimean War excluded any thought of direct armed intervention. Another option had to be found. After intensive discussions among the military, Colonel Robert Home reported: "*England might maintain Turkey at the expense of enormous blood and treasure, but what good would that do? She had better leave Turkey to her fate and seize upon some place that would be of use to her such as the Dardanelles and Cyprus.*" Alternatively, Crete, Egypt, or Rhodes or all three might be occupied. The latter was a radical idea which Disraeli rejected. He and his ambassador in Constantinople, Austen Henry Layard, "*believed that England should support Turkey, aid her by diplomatic pressure to reform in the interests of both Christians and Mussulmans alike and thus continue to guard the route to India by maintaining the Sultan's rule over Constantinople, the Straits, and Armenia.*" But how this could be achieved was unclear.

In early 1877, London demanded Russian guarantees of British interests in the Suez Canal, Egypt, Constantinople, the Straits and the Persian Gulf, but the Russians refused to guarantee Constantinople and the Straits. During the Russian advance into Bulgaria, London, fearing the occupation of Constantinople, toyed with the idea of entering the war, but when the Russian advance was slowed down, the British politicians regained their composure again and started exploring alternatives.

In view of British interests in Asia Minor and Armenia and the safeguarding of the route to India, the best solution seemed to be the acquisition of a *Place d'Armes* in the eastern

Mediterranean. The Straits were quickly dismissed since there were no suitable harbours. After intensive studies of maps, Rhodes and Cyprus were found unsuitable for the purpose and Crete was dismissed because of the rebellious character of its inhabitants. The discussion in Britain procrastinated but when in November 1877 the Russians took Kars, London became nervous once more..

The British Press called for the occupation of Egypt and the conversion of Cyprus into a Gibraltar of the East, from where the British Navy could control the Syrian coast, the Suez Canal and the Straits. Additionally, an old idea resurfaced: the project of building a railway from Alexandretta [now Iskenderun] to the valleys of the Euphrates and the Tigris to Basra and from there to India. The starting point of this second route to India could be protected from Cyprus. When the British learned that the Russians had reached the Straits they dispatched units of the Navy there. Ambassador Layard successfully got the Sultan interested in the railway concept and offered a permanent alliance with Great Britain. In London the new Foreign Minister, Salisbury, liked the idea of an alliance with the Ottoman Empire and the acquisition of a *Place d'Armes* in the region. The question was whether this place would be situated in the Persian Gulf [now Arab] or in the Mediterranean. After analysing all political, geographic, military and commercial aspects, Colonel Home suggested that Cyprus was the most suitable place.

Thus, Britain had returned to a vision which had been formulated 60 years before: *"The possession of Cyprus would give England a preponderating influence in the Mediterranean, and place at her disposal the future destinies of the Levant. Egypt and Syria would soon become her tributaries, and she would acquire an overawing position in respect to Asia Minor, by which the Porte might at all times be kept in check, and the encroachments of Russia, in this quarter, retarded, if not prevented. It would increase her commerce in a very considerable degree:...It is of easy defence; and under a liberal government would in a very short space of time, amply repay the charge of its own establishment, and afford the most abundant supplies to our fleets at a trifling expense."*

In the meantime, diplomatic haggling about the revision of the San Stefano Treaty had begun. Towards the end of May 1878 the Russians signalled that they were ready to withdraw from the Balkans and accept a reduction of Bulgaria's land masse but that they would remain in Armenia. This was used as a pretext by the British to put pressure on the Sultan to conclude the alliance. On 4 June 1878 a secret Defence Alliance, which became known as the Cyprus Convention, was signed. Its central provision was: As long as the Russians occupied those towns it had captured in Armenia, Great Britain promised to help the Sultan militarily in case of further Russian advances in Asia. In return the Sultan promised certain reforms in favour of his Christian subjects *"and in order to enable England to make necessary provision for executing her engagement,...the Sultan further consents to assign the Island of Cyprus to be occupied and administered by England."*

Thus, even before the Congress of Berlin redrew the boundaries of the Balkan countries, Cyprus had, *de facto*, its proprietor changed and since the Russians would hardly move out of Armenia this change was for good. The Cypriots had been no party to this development which had begun as a peasant revolt in Bulgaria and led to a big oriental crisis; they were pawns in this process and – ended as British subjects.

At the Congress of Berlin which lasted from 13 June to 13 July 1878, all the statesmen of Europe met. The results were frustrating for all participants but one: Britain. The big power interests had prevailed; the dreams of freedom of the enslaved peoples of the Ottoman Empire were sacrificed for *raison d'état*. Not one of the Balkan problems was solved, they were only covered up superficially to resurface again in the explosion of September 1914. Bismarck allegedly played the honest broker; in reality he had done his best to keep to the oriental wound open, secretly encouraging the other statesmen to carve up the Ottoman Empire, playing one state off against the other.

Britain succeeded in pushing the Russians back from the Mediterranean and halting their advance in Armenia. Thus, strictly speaking, the reason for the acquisition of Cyprus had become void. And as the Cyprus Convention had up to this point been kept secret, it could have been annulled without creating any noise. But diplomatic processes cannot be stopped abruptly without those involved fearing political damage and loss of prestige. So the final negotiations for the signature of the Sultan under the Cyprus Convention dragged on during the sessions of the Berlin Congress.

On 7 July 1878, the Sultan finally signed the *Firman*, ratifying the Cyprus Convention. In the House of Commons Disraeli justified the acquisition of Cyprus on 18 July: "*In taking Cyprus the movement is not Mediterranean: it is Indian. We have taken a step there which we think necessary for the maintenance of our Empire and for its preservation in peace.*" The British Press reacted in a mixed way: The London *Times* considered Cyprus "*an admirable naval station, whether for the purpose of protecting the Suez Canal, securing a second road to India, or giving this country the requisite authority in its relations with the Porte.*" The *Daily News* was afraid of "*limitless cost, unceasing stress, strain, and danger*" as never before in English history. The Commentator of the *Fortnightly Review* was even more pessimistic: "*An island, two hundred miles long, ravaged by famine, a nest of malaria, with a fatal fever of which it enjoys a monopoly, without harbours, and possessed of a growing population of lepers, is held by Englishmen adequate consideration for an obligation to spend scores or hundreds of millions in defending an empire which either cannot or will not defend itself.*" There were even doubts about the military value of Cyprus. Ambassador Layard believed that the acquisition of a *Place d'Armes* in the Persian Gulf might have been better.

However that may have been, for the time being Disraeli had won a point in that perpetual Russian-British competition known as the Grand Game. For the Greek Cypriots the 300 gloomy years of *Tourkokratia* had ended. It was said that Cyprus was the best administered Ottoman province of the time. This may be so but those who know the facts will agree that of all Ottoman provinces Cyprus was the least badly administered one. In other words, at the end of Turkish domination Cyprus had been run down as never before in its history. With the change to Britain there seemed to be a bright future as a British naval base. A lot of investment capital would flow into the island in the wake of the British building their *Place d'Armes*. Under the benevolent administration of the British, Cypriots would become well-to-do British subjects. If this bright picture did not materialise, this was due to yet another turn of the wheel of fortune of international politics.

Since the construction of the Suez Canal the Egyptian Khedive had been heavily indebted to the British and the French. When he could no longer repay his debts, Egypt's debt-service was put under the supervision of an Anglo-French Commission. In 1879 this Commission replaced the disobedient Khedive with someone more compliant. This triggered a rebellion of the Egyptian army led by Colonel Arabi. Soon he controlled most of the country, but when he refused to repay his country's loan the creditors got active. As the French parliament refused to intervene militarily the British acted alone in 1881. They landed troops in Egypt and beat Colonel Arabi's forces. From now on they were the masters of Egypt. The ensuing Mahdi rebellion in Soudan led to the permanent military occupation of Egypt and the Suez Canal. This development changed the position of Cyprus radically. Having direct control of the Suez Canal and the harbour of Alexandria the British no longer needed Cyprus as a *Place d'Armes*. If they had considered their own interests alone, they would certainly have decided to cancel the Cyprus Convention and hand the island back to Turkey. But apart from the loss of prestige which such a move would have entailed and the difficulties involved in the uprooting of an administration just planted on the island, there would have undoubtedly been a strong feeling in Britain and in Europe against handing back to Turkey a country containing a population of which more than three-quarters were Christians. But there was another aspect strongly supporting the permanent occupation of Cyprus, the Ottoman loan of 1855.

In 1855, during the Crimean War, the Ottoman Empire had secured a loan from England and France guaranteed by the two Governments. In the following years the Turks had continued to borrow heavily and in 1875 the Ottoman debt had reached £200 million. £12 million, half of the Ottoman revenue, was used to pay the interest of the various loans. In 1877 Turkey had to declare itself bankrupt. The British Chancellor of the Exchequer was alarmed because the 1855 loan had been guaranteed by the Government: if Turkey could not pay, the British taxpayer would have had to take over. The British Minister of Finance began searching for a solution which would not lessen his revenue.

And at precisely the same time the discussion about the acquisition of Cyprus began. As early as July the Chancellor of the Exchequer signalled that he would use the Cyprus revenues to redeem the 1855 loan. Later it was explained that the Turkish debt had been the main reason for the acquisition of Cyprus. This seems a little exaggerated, but not too much, if we look at the development of the so called Cyprus Tribute.

SOME BASIC FACTS THEN AND NOW

Before we turn our attention to the colonial period we should take note of some basic facts and the changes which have taken place from then until now.

After Sicily and Sardinia, Cyprus is the third largest island in the Mediterranean. Its size approximates to that of three times Rhode Island in the US. In 1878 its population amounted to 186,000 people, of which, according to the Ottoman millet-system, 72 percent were Orthodox Christians i.e. Greeks and 24 percent Muslims i.e. Turks; additionally there were some Catholic Maronites and some Christian Armenians and some Latins. The Muslims were mainly descendants of those Turks, who had settled in Cyprus after the Ottoman conquest in 1571, at the end of the 16th and the beginning of the 17th centuries. Because of the different religions no assimilation process had taken place. However, among the Muslims were quite a number of the descendants of Greek converts whose ancestors had changed their religion for tax reasons and there were the Lianovamvakoi [linen-cotton], the adherents of a religious blend of Islam and Christianity.

In 1878 Cyprus was mainly rural, with many villages and a few small towns. In 1900 Nicosia had 12,500 inhabitants, according to the entries in Oberhummer's map of the time. Famagusta (9,000), Larnaca (7,600), Limassol (7,400), Paphos (2,600), Morphou (2,500) and Kyrenia (1,300) were really small towns. By the end of the British rule the population had grown to 578,000 people, of which 440,000 were Greeks and 104,000 Turks, i.e. 81.1 percent and 18.9 percent respectively. Of these, 206,000 lived in towns and 368,000 in rural areas. Nicosia, including its suburbs, accounted for 96,000 inhabitants followed by Limassol (44,000), Famagusta (35,000), Larnaca (20,000), Paphos (9,000) and Kyrenia (3,500). By 1974 the population of the island had risen to 600,000 people. In 2006, the inhabitants of Nicosia amounted to 219,000 and those of Limassol 172,000, Larnaca 77,000, and Paphos 51,000. Cyprus had been urbanised.

In 1988 the total population of Cyprus was estimated to be 699,000. In 2006, 771,000 persons lived in the south and, according to a 2001 estimate, 211,000 in the north. The massive increase of the population in the north was caused by immigration from Turkey. However, during the same period about 50,000 Turkish Cypriots emigrated, mainly to the UK. Thus the Turkish Cypriots became, even in the northern part of their own country, a minority.

The two main ethnic groups living in Cyprus differ substantially from their counterparts in Greece and Turkey, the mother countries. Though culturally both clearly belong to the Greek or Turkish speaking world, their Cypriot dialects of the communities are distinctly different from the language spoken in Greece or Turkey. A mainland Greek or Turk did not (and does not) normally understand the dialect spoken on the island not only because of the different pronunciation and syntax but also because both dialects are enriched with words and terms from the other's language. Even though Cyprus had been under Ottoman rule for 300 years, at least the Greek Cypriots, quite in contrast to the mainland Greeks, had never lost the contact with the European world. A rather amusing example from the late 18th century may illustrate this: When a German traveller returning from the Holy Land went ashore in Larnaca he discovered to his great astonishment that the Greek Cypriots wore hats. Of course, this close connection with Europe was strengthened ove the following decades by the British presence and today it is an established fact that both Cypriot communities are much more Europeanised than either Greece or Turkey.

The fact of their different religions inhibited any assimilation of the minority by the majority. This was reinforced by the fact that until 1878 the minority procured the ruling stratum and the majority was governed by them. Thus an ethnic coexistence and two parallel communities emerged which, however, had so much in common that an outside observer would discover a kind of Cypriot identity. However, the internal separative elements were so strong that a true generally accepted identity did not come about. Both communities are aware of their differentness, their so-called Cypriotness, but they are still far away from a common Cypriotness. Analysing the attitudes of both communities to their religions, one discovers significant differences but also much common ground. The Turkish Cypriots are the most liberal or secular Muslims probably in the world. Many of them have not been following the provisions of the Quran and, indee eat pork and know the delights of a good zivania or old brandy. Turkish Cypriot society is an emancipated society; one might even talk of the emergence of a European-ised Islam, to which every kind of fundamentalism or the suppression of women is alien. However, since 1974, due to the immigration of mainland Turks and recently Kurds from Turkey, an authoritarian Islam has been gaining ground even in education and threatens the secular Muslim character of the Turkish Cypriots.

For the Greek Cypriots the road to religious emancipation has been more difficult, of course, because it had been the Church which preserved the Greek identity during the Ottoman rule. The Archbishop of the autocephalous church of Cyprus was, according to the millet system, the leader of his community, the *millet bași*, the *etnarch* in Greek. This high position had its price since the Porte expected the Archbishop to guide his community according to their wishes and e.g. collect the taxes for them. Since the Ottomans conferred more and more power on the Archbishop one could speak of a condominium. At the same time, however, there was an ominous correlation between the height of ecclesiastical wealth and power and the massive exploitation of the population at the beginning of the 19th century. Although the British did not acknowledge the position of the ethnarch, the church remained the biggest landowner on the island and the inhabitants of the rural areas continued to be largely dependent on the church. Thus it is not astonishing that it was Archbishop Makarios III who led the liberation struggle in the 1950s and continued to control the destiny of the island as president. The emancipation process from ecclesiastic paternalism could be said to have only begun after the death of Makarios in 1977. However, what the church lost in the field of spiritual influence over its flock was compensated by its building investments and the creation of a huge economic empire (hotels, banking, KEO).

Strategically Cyprus' geographical position is not as simple as George Hill said in his classical statement: *"He who would become and remain a great power in the East must hold Cyprus in his hand."* From ancient times to the Middle Ages this statement was only conditionally correct. Each Great Power controlling the area occupied Cyprus as well, however, not in order to rule from there but to deny its possession to a potential rival. The only time that Cyprus did not belong to the regional hegemonic power was during the crusades, when the island served as an advance and retreat position of the West. After that Cyprus was again a part of the regional empire of the Ottomans who admittedly took their time to conquer Cyprus as late as 1571. As has been shown, the British interest in making Cyprus a naval *place d'armes* ended when London recognized that Cyprus had no deep water harbour for modern warships. The only time that Cyprus did have real strategic relevance was during the Cold War when the British stationed a number of nuclear bombers there which were the nuclear backbone of the CENTO alliance. The electronic surveillance devices stationed in Cyprus which in the past were used to spy on the Soviet Union and today to eavesdrop on the Arabs are, strategically speaking, irrelevant.

In antiquity the Cyprus economy flourished by mining copper and long distance trade which made the island rich, as has been shown by the archaeological excavations on the island. In the middle ages the product which again bestowed wealth on Cyprus was sugar cane and to a lesser extent cotton. Another source of wealth was the long distance trade when Cyprus again became a fulcrum for the exchange of goods. In Ottoman times agricultural production was reduced to subsistence farming and the maritime trade suffered heavily. In British times mining became important again, for some time, because now copper ores, which could not be smelted in antiquity, became possible to process. More important, however, was the light industry which worked on the basis of local agricultural products. After independence tourism began to boom and thus Cyprus became wealthy again. Recently the provision of services especially in the banking sector contributed substantially to the national income. In 2004 agriculture accounted for 4.7 percent, industry 24 percent and services 70 percent of a GDP of $ 18.371 billions. Thus today Cyprus is a rich country again: in 2006 the BNI per-capita income of the Greek Cypriots was about $ 25,000 (Germany $ 32,689).

After this short survey of important facts about Cyprus we will turn our attention to the colonial period. However, we will not give a chronological description of those 81 years but will elaborate on some important positive and negative developments which have left their imprint on Cyprus.

THE SO-CALLED CYPRUS TRIBUTE

In Article III of the Cyprus Convention London had promised the Sultan to pay the excess of the revenue over the expenditure as a kind of annual leasing fee. There was some controversial discussion about the size of this rent between the Foreign Office, the Porte and the new Cypriot administration. Understandably the Ottomans did their best to inflate this number. Astonishingly, the British accepted the Turkish numbers despite the fact that they well knew that these were highly dubious because the taxes had risen sharply during the years before the conclusion of the Cyprus Convention. They were further informed that a huge part of these taxes had not been paid in kind but in paper money, which was almost worthless compared with the pound sterling. Conservative estimates assessed the real excess to be around £ 65,000 while less cautious estimates believed it to be £ 50,000. Despite these warnings £ 92,800 were agreed upon.

The average revenue of the last five years was assessed as £ 130,000, despite the fact that it was known that the annual revenue before the tax increase had been only around £ 117,000. The annual administrative expenditures were estimated as £ 24,000 over the last five years. This seems plausible because the Ottomans covered only the bare administrative expenditures, which did not even include the salaries of the policemen. Taking this into consideration it should have been clear that the British could not administer the island, let alone develop it. Thus the question arises; why did the British behave in this strange way? The answer is quite simple: Right from the beginning they never intended to pass the surplus on to the Sultan but to use it for paying the interest on the Ottoman bond which had been guaranteed by the British government. In order to find a legal reason the British redefined the surplus as a "tribute" payable to the Sultan which could be used as a compensation for the missing Ottoman payments for that bounced bond. This construction was legally untenable because there had never been a "tribute" in Ottoman times: the Sultan had received the annual surplus of which had of course varied according to the harvest.

There was an additional small problem: the £ 92,800 surplus was higher than the interest which amounted to approximately £ 82,000. The British offered the difference to the Ottoman government, who for understandable reasons rejected the offer, feeling hurt. The Treasury paid the surplus £ 11,000 to a fund later to be used to redeem the Ottoman loan. Until 1907 this fund contained £ 330,000. Properly it should have been £ 370,000, but in 1882 and 1885 the British had used this fund to pay the ransom for two British subjects who had been kidnapped in Ottoman Macedonia.

Pretty soon it was discovered that the difference between the real revenue and the "tribute" was not enough to cover the British administration costs. Only three times between 1879 and 1907 was Cyprus able to raise the sum asked. In view of this situation, the British government understood that it was impossible to increase taxes any further to cover the cost of the administration of Cyprus and decided to grant Cyprus an annual aid of £ 30,000. Until 1907 the British grants-in-aid amounted to £ 857,085, the Cypriots, however, during the same period paid £ 1,799,860 to Britain. This was, in fact, a bargain for the Treasury and the bondholders respectively and their heirs.

As early as 1880 the British High Commisimioner of Cyprus came to the conclusion that the island's revenue was quite sufficient to organise an efficient administration and make the necessary investments in its infrastructure, provided the money remained on the island. The "tribute" went beyond the control of Cyprus and impeded the necessary modernisations. Obviously not even the Governor knew who the real recipients of the "tribute" were. In 1895 his successor complained about the chronic deficit of Cyprus which was caused by the "tribute"; as long as this "tribute" was collected there would be no progress. Even in the House of Commons critical voices were heard, but in 1893 the Chancellor of the Exchequer expressed the opinion that it was no business of the Cypriots whether it was Turkey or the bondholders who received the money. Two years later he stated that he was not ready to finance infrastructure investments in Cyprus with the British taxpayer's money. Even when the relationship between the Ottoman Empire and the British cooled down in the 1890s this political attitude did not change. In 1899 Colonial Secretary Joseph Chamberlain told the Cypriots that even if the British-Turkish negotiations about the bond of 1855 should lead to a change and a lowering of the payment, only the British taxpayer would profit from this, not the Cypriots because in the latter case the grants-in-aid would be cancelled. The climax of ministerial arrogance was the statement of Chamberlain's successor: Though Britain was richer than Cyprus this fact did not oblige London to assist Cyprus. Britain administered the surplus of the Porte and considered conventions as sacred.

In Cyprus the protests against the "tribute" became louder and louder. The Ottoman administration had squeezed the Cypriot taxpayer but oriental inefficiency had left the Cypriots enough to live o. Now British efficiency squeezed the last drop out of the Cypriot lemon. Cypriot sources tell us that in Ottoman times the annual tax revenue had been £ 113,000 but from 1895 this annual revenue had increased to £ 188,000 annually, a rise of 66 percent. Despite this enormous increase the island's administration suffered from chronic lack of money: The following examples of expenditures may illustrate this: road building £ 8,000-10,000, health £ 4,000 and education £ 2,260. In 1893 a Greek Cypriot member of the Legislative Council called the "tribute" "robbery", "seizure" and "piracy". In 1904 the Treasury in London had to admit that Cyprus was the land with the highest relative taxes in the world. Before the First World War Cyprus was the only colony which paid 27 percent of its annual revenue to Britain (a total of £ 2,067,654).

In 1907 a chance for change came when the non permanent secretary of the Colonial Office, Winston Churchill, came to Cyprus, the first government official to do so since the acquisition of the island. The representatives of the Cypriots complained about the "totally heartless policy" of the "tribute", because Cyprus had to shoulder an "entirely foreign obligation" which was the British government's duty. The enormous tax burden prohibited any progress: "'Education did not receive one-fourth of the funds it needs it needed: the construction of public works had not covered even essential needs in roads, bridges, harbours, railways: agriculture, the main source of the country's livelihood, remained primitive, harassed by pests and overtaxed, especially through the tithes: re-afforestation was not carried out: the state of public health was not good and malarious places are to be found not only in the open country but even near the towns: archaeological excavations were not provided from the budget and there was still no Museum: many villages were without mail communication: the salaries of local civil servants and policemen were quite inadequate: local industries remained unassisted while the professional and practical needs of the people were ignored."

Churchill's answer showed that he personally agreed with the Cypriots and he promised to become active in London so that Cyprus would get an annual grant-in-aid. Churchill, however, was a clever politician and when delivering public speeches in Cyprus he watched his language, but having seen the miserable reality he was so indignant that he wrote a long memorandum on the situation of Cyprus and spoke out: "There is scarcely any spectacle more detestable than the oppression of a small community by a great Power for the purpose of pecuniary profit: and that is, in fact, the spectacle which our financial treatment of Cyprus at this moment indisputably presents. It is in my opinion quite unworthy of Great Britain, and altogether out of accordance with the whole principles of our colonial policy in every part of the world, to extract tribute by force from any of the possessions or territories administered under the Crown." At the end of his memo Churchill proposed a change of policy within the context of the 30th anniversary of British rule in Cyprus.

Churchill's memorandum infuriated his superiors in the ministry, who rejoiced when the Treasury called Churchill's memorandum "an insane minute". In 1908 Churchill left the Colonial Office and the "tribute" question again became a backwater. In 1910 the Treasury tried to reduce the annual grant-in-aid which caused considerable unrest in Cyprus because the Cypriots had expected the opposite. Even the Governor protested so violently that his superiors rebuked him. His behaviour came close to being considered disloyalty. The Cypriot protest, however, prompted the British government to renew the annual grant-in-aid to Cyprus from 1911 onwards.

When the Ottoman Empires entered WWI on the side of the Central Powers, Britain renounced the Cyprus Convention and annexed the island. The raising of the "tribute", however, continued. The Treasury now called the "tribute" the "share of Cyprus of the Turkish Debt Charge" and made the Cypriots go on paying. Until this point the Cypriots had paid £ 3,533,136 "tribute" and received £ 1,347,085 grant-in-aid. Thus the Cypriots had paid £ 2,186,051 to the bondholders and relieved the British taxpayer of the same sum.

In 1923 Turkey acknowledged the annexation of Cyprus by Britain in the Lausanne peace treaty. Britain forgave Turkey a couple of debts; among them the 1855 bond. But Egypt and Cyprus were forced to continue their payments because the Ottoman debts were converted into a public debt of those colonies which had to be paid. In 1925 Cyprus became a crown colony. In March 1926 the elected members of the Legislative Council, Greeks and Turks, demanded that the content of the sinking fund, or rather the difference between "tribute" and grant-in-aid since 1914, should be reimbursed; the Cypriots estimated the amount to be a little higher than £ 900,000. This money would be used to establish an agricultural bank and from then on the payment of the "tribute" and the grants-in-aid should end. But new discussions began as late as November 1926.

These new discussions were triggered by the fact that on 24 November 1926 all elected members of the Legislative Council, Greeks and Turks alike, rejected the budget bill for the fiscal year 1927, which still contained the £ 90,000 of the "tribute". The acting Governor (Pop-ham-Lobb) suggested a change to the constitution in favour of the council members nominated by the colonial authorities because they would be certain to vote for the government. At the time a cabinet order would overcome the stalemate.

The Colonial Office analysed the situation: So far the budget bills had passed the Council smoothly because the representatives of the Turkish Cypriots had voted with the government. Thus the government became dependent on the consent of Turkish Cypriots, and this deepened the racial division between them and the Greek Cypriots. A possible policy of divide and rule would be "derogatory to the dignity of the Government". One should not forget that since 1878 Cyprus paid almost £ 200,000 to Britain which had had a damaging effect on the development of the island; thus the reaction of the Cypriots was understandable. But one should not make too many concessions to them because the Cypriots "have an Asiatic mentality, and any such concession would inevitably be regarded as a sign of weakness and would lead us in further trouble." The best solution would be the abolishment of the "tribute" combined with a change to the constitution in favour of the colonial government, but for this the consent of the Chancellor of the Exchequer was needed and, since October 1924, this had been Winston Churchill.

Churchill, however, was confronted by great problems: He had to reduce the huge internal debt stemming from the Great War and the currency had to be stabilized. Churchill introduced stabilisation measures and followed a rigid course of austerity. In particular, he refused to help the Colonial Minister financially which often led to heavy rows between them. In the case of Cyprus, however, he made an astounding exception despite the fact that in the beginning he had steered a tough course.

In November 1927 the Colonial Office warned the Treasury: The situation in Cyprus was serious; if nothing was done, tough measures would be necessary. The Treasury's position that Cyprus was a successor state of the Ottoman Empire and as such responsible for the Ottoman debt was scarcely sustainable because Cyprus had been British for 36 years even before the annexation. Since the Treasury did not answer, the Colonial Office sent a second letter on 14 February 1927 which urgently demanded a reduction of the financial burden on Cyprus. The Treasury's silence had compelled the Colonial Office to administer Cyprus by Cabinet orders.

Finally on 1 March the Treasury answered: A reduction of Cypriot taxes would not be acceptable to the British taxpayers. The Colonial Office should make this clear to the Cypriots. This arrogant answer provoked furious reactions from the civil servants of the Colonial Office: The "Tribute" had then been fixed much too high and if the £ 90,000 had not been assigned to cover the interest of that bounced Ottoman bond it would certainly have been reduced. The theory that Cyprus was a successor state of the Ottoman Empire was absurd and none of the other successor states, neither Palestine, nor Iraq, nor Greece nor Syria had paid anything; Yugoslavia had not even signed the Peace Treaty of Lausanne for that reason. The only ones who paid were the Cypriots, indeed Cyprus had paid more than all the successor states together. Even the colonial government of the island supported the termination of the payment. Winding up the argument the Colonial Office reminded the Chancellor of the Exchequer, Churchill, that he had advocated the abolition of the "tribute" during his visit in 1907.

In early April Governor Ronald Storrs piped up: The calculation of the "tribute" had been totally frivolous. The Turks could only have squeezed the sum they mentioned by spending next to nothing there and allowing everything to run down. There was no one in Cyprus who did not reject the "tribute" completely. The boycott of the Legislative Council was caused by the "tribute". The threat to reduce the constitutional rights of the Cypriots would not bring any result. The wish to get rid of the "tribute" was so great that it could not be suppressed. Only if the "tribute" was abolished could the necessary investments in the infrastructure be made; any further tax increase was ruled out. If the "tribute" were abolished the Cypriot government would have another £ 42,800 which could be taken as a collateral for a bond of £ 700,000 by which the investments could be financed. Storrs presented concrete figures:

In the past 48 years Cyprus paid £ 2,642,648 "tribute", £ 81, 752 of the annual £ 92,800 was used for the interest of the Ottoman fund. The annual surplus of £ 11,048 was used to buy consols (government bonds) and had reached £ 570,900 without interest. He suggested the following compromise solution: 1) The British government should abolish the "tribute" and take over the obligations of the Ottoman debt; 2) It could keep the consols; 3) It could stop the annual grants-in-aid, and 4) Cyprus would contribute £ 10,000 annually to the stationing cost of the British troops. Thus the Cyprus government would immediately have £32,000 at its free disposal to finance the infrastructure.

In early June 1927 the Colonial Office formulated another detailed memorandum full of quotes from Churchill's 1907 report. The Colonial Office expressed the opinion that in view of the huge amounts paid by Cyprus it had the right to expect substantial refunding, at least of the accumulated surplus. One should try and find a compromise. At the decisive cabinet meeting on 20 July 1927, Colonial Secretary Amery presented his proposals and pepped them up by reading long passages of Churchill's 1907 text, which provoked great hilarity among those present. Churchill surrendered.

The solution contained the following points: Cyprus was no longer obliged to pay the annual tribute. The British government promised to take over the interest of the Ottoman bond of 1855. In return Cyprus would abandon its claim on the surplus, which had grown to £ 600,000 in the meantime and contribute £10,000 to the Imperial Defence. This was precisely Churchill's proposal of 1907 and Storrs' of 1927. In order to avoid a precedent Churchill formally refused to abolish the "tribute" but increased the grant-in-aid. In view of the economic situation of Britain at the time this was an acceptable compromise.

Amery informed Storrs about this result and on 18 August he asked him to make it appear as palatable as possible for the Cypriots. He stressed that a £ 10,000 contribution to Imperial Defence was a *conditio sine qua non*; only if this was paid would the grant-in-aid be increased. Further, the Cypriots had to renounce any claim to the surplus. Storrs asked the ministry for permission when informing the Cypriots that he could conceal from them that the British offer was dependent on the renunciation of the surplus. The Colonial Office and the Treasury agreed that he could conceal the linkage and informed Storrs that the agreement could become operative on 1 January 1928.

Storrs invited the members of the Legislative Council, the Mayor, the District Officers, the higher echelons of the administration, the police, and judges as well as many prominent citizens to a special session in Limassol on 31 August 1928. When everyone was assembled he read a carefully worded statement which announced the abolition of the "tribute". He did not mention the surplus with one word but explained that the defence contribution was paid by other colonies as well. Speaking to the audience he stressed his own merits; he had not expected that the "tribute" could be abolished in its entirety. The audience became enthusiastic and cheered Storrs with standing ovations. Afterwards Storrs travelled for a short holiday to Rhodes.

Storrs' speech was printed in English, Greek and Turkish and distributed all over the island. The Cypriots were elated. The Archbishop, who was visiting the Karpas peninsula, sent a letter to Storrs in which he expressed his deep gratitude. The Bishop of Paphos reacted in a similar way. The members of the Legislative Council, Greeks and Turks alike, passed a resolution expressing their deep gratitude which was handed over to Storrs when he returned.

When in October 1927 during the debate on the defence contribution bill the surplus was mentioned in the Council Storrs remained silent and kept the deputies in the dark. He knew that if he told the truth there would be an immediate uproar by all members of the Council and the bill would be rejected. The final consequences were not completely clear but he knew that his position would have been shaky. Faced with this possibility he preferred to obscure the matter and procrastinate. When the deputies refused to let the defence contribution bill pass and the debate came dangerously near the truth, the colonial secretary was sent to the front and he lied to the deputies, telling them that new instructions had arrived from the minister. The Cypriots accepted this argument and let the bill pass. Thus for the moment everything was quiet again, but the problem had not been solved and when Churchill's successor, the Labour politician Philip Snowden revealed in July 1931 that the surplus had been used to redeem the Ottoman loan this caused quite a stir in Cyprus.

This news hit Cyprus like a bomb since it came when Cyprus was already suffering heavily from the impact of the great depression. Storrs was called a hypocrite because as late as March he had promised the members of the Council to make a fuss in London about repayment of the surplus. The nationalists bristled at the "monstrous and immoral disposal of the Cyprus surpluses" and expressed the opinion that only *enosis*, i.e. union with Greece could save the country. Even the acting Governor of Cyprus (Storrs was on leave) protested against the behaviour of the Treasury: There was no moral justification to keep that money. Hopefully the British government would change its mind when the economic situation improved and remove what Churchill had called "a blemish upon imperial policy of a peculiarly discreditable kind." But the Treasury reminded the acting Governor, rightly, that Storrs had provoked the trouble himself because he had not told the Cypriots the truth about the surplus. For the Treasury the case was closed. Storrs' lack of courage, causing his untruthfulness in 1928 came back at him and weakened his position in a critical period.

It should be kept on record here that Britain exploited Cyprus for 50 years for purposes for which there was no legal, let alone a moral, basis. This was only possible because the Cypriots are a peace loving breed of human beings and were glad to live under British rule, in principle. However, the payment of the "tribute" retarded the economic resurgence roughly for two generations.

If the economic upturn did not begin at once this was because of the impact of the Great Depression which hit Cyprus hard. Another cause, the internal exploitation of the peasants by the usurers continued until the early 1940s. Only when this ended later could the economic revival of Cyprus begin. But this topic will be dealt with later.

POLITICAL REFORMS

One of the biggest obstacles for the enforcement of British rule was the clergy and the Greek Cypriot oligarchy. In Ottoman times both had possessed great privileges that made them suspicious, in Governor Wolseley's eyes, because they could only have obtained such privileges by collaborating and becoming a part of the Ottoman system of corruption, suppression and exploitation. This suspicion was not unfounded at all.

One of his first measures was to abolish the church's tax exemption on land. The church was the greatest landowner of the island and so far paid only tithe. Additionally he ruled that from now on violations against canon law would no longer be prosecuted by secular authorities unless they violated British law. Neither the bishops nor their Muslim colleagues would be ex officio members of the advisory bodies of the government. If a member of the clergy committed a crime he would be tried by an ordinary court. Finally, Wolseley prohibited the use of any kind of a State power for the collection of church tax, which caused the church tax to drop by two thirds. At the beginning the clergy offered some resistance but soon the clerics adapted themselves to their new masters and cooperated in the newly created Legislative Council.

The Legislative Council consisted of twelve elected and six ex officio members. The twelve elected members were to be divided in proportion to the population, so i.e. nine Greeks and three Turks. All male Cypriots over 21 years who had paid their taxes were allowed to vote. The legislative period was five years but the Governor had the right to dissolve the Council earlier. Each member had the right to put questions using Greek or Turkish but the protocol and the laws had to be in English. Voting would be conducted according to the majority principle. Since the Turkish members of the Council usually voted with the government there would always be a clear majority for the government. In case of doubt the Governor's vote would decide.

Thus Cyprus had a parliament but it lacked one decisive feature - the right to decide about the budget. No wonder that a contemporary called it mockingly a "toy parliament". Indeed this Council had no legislative authority, no say in matters of the "tribute", the Governor's salary, the the civil servants' pay, all these were London's responsibility. Constitutional changes needed the consent of the British Sovereign. The Governor had the right to agree or reject a bill. The Legislative Council was a mock parliament.

The Greek Cypriots liked the constitution, the Muslims did not. They wanted equal representation in the Council. They had obeyed the British government in almost everything but if the proportional representation were introduced this would lead to a mass emigration of the Turkish Cypriots. In reality the proportional system was a fair suggestion. According to the census of 1881 the Muslims counted for one fourth of the population. Had the British offered the majority voting, as applied in Britain in parliamentary elections, not one Turkish Cypriot would have been elected. In order to avoid this the Colonial Office had originally wanted to introduce a system whereby Christians and Muslims cross voted for a fixed number of proportionally composed double lists. Such a system would have promoted the cooperation of Greeks and Turks and have avoided the drifting apart of the two societies. The Governor, however, had rejected this system and unfortunately he had his way. Thus the religious separation, i.e. the millet-system, was kept and the new system was introduced in November 1882.

Though the Cypriots, in comparison with the British, enjoyed a more democratic voting system, at the same time an over proportional weighting was given to the Tukish Cypriots; a feature which to this very day is creating political headaches. Politics from then on was always measured by how much advantage it brought to one's own ethnic group. This inhibited the development of an inter-communal identity, creating at the same time the leverage for the future divide and rule policy.

The British did not change much of the existing administrative structure. In the towns they introduced municipal councils, but as the elected members of these belonged to the urban upper class, they prevented any direct taxation of their wealthy relatives and instead indirect taxes were raised which were paid by the general public. Consequently the municipalities had only very little money for the water supply and a sewage system and the roads were in a bad condition. In the villages the mukhtar system was kept but was a little democratised by introducing the election of the village headman. This, however, led to the formation of cliques and clientelism. Often the mukhtars were usurers. Thus the same steps towards a clientelistic system were apparently introduced as in Greece in the 19th century.

The British, however, had paid attention to that development attentively because since the 1860s Greece had been a British client state. In Greece the Ottoman administrative system, based on the state monopoly of force, had been destroyed and the clientelistic networks which had come into being during the liberation struggle had taken over. When in 1832 Otto von Wittelsbach became King of Greece, the only existing power structures were those clientelistic networks and he was forced to base his administration on them. However, even when the Greek State was rebuilt it never managed to regain the full monopoly of force. The clientelistic networks continued to exist parallel to the state and when parties come into being these, right from the beginning, were nothing but the fealty of the chief of the respective network. The networks were kept together by the chief's rousfetia (favours) to his followers and that network which was in power had access to state money and was thus able to bind those receiving their patronage more closely. In the course of time the State became a prey to these predatory networks and has largely remained so to this day.

In Cyprus, however, the British were resolved to prohibit such a development. They took pains to keep the whole governmental administration under their close control and moved away from the basis of clientelism by taking action against usury and by abolishing the system of tax farming which was another means of exploitation of the peasants.

The chronic indebtedness of the peasants was another problem which urgently needed a reform. The most productive tax in Ottoman times had been the tithe (harac) which yielded about one third of the island's revenue and was paid by Moslems and Christians alike. Principally it was a reasonable and just tax for an agrarian society because it was raised proportionally to the crop harvest in natural produce. The tithe was paid by the whole village and the village headman and the village elders allocated it to the various families, which could be done arbitrarily. The peasants had to pay the tithe in advance on the basis of estimates and since no peasant had savings, he was obliged to borrow the necessary amount from the local usurers at 25 percent interest. If the estimate had been too high and the crop was bad the peasant was bankrupt. After the harvest the peasant had to sell his crop to earn the necessary money to pay his debt. The wholesale buyers, however, were often the usurers and they levelled down the prices. In other words: the peasants were in the debt trap.

The colonial administration recognised the problem but reacted rather hesitantly because it wanted no quarrel with the Greek Cypriot leadership. In 1897 a Public Loan Fund was set up to supply the peasants with low cost credits, but it did not succeed because it did not have enough funds. Every now and then attempts were made to break the power of the usurers; for example, by the founding of a cooperative credit society but all this did not solve the problem. As late as 1917 the authorities finally decided to tackle the problem earnestly and set up a fact finding commission. In 1919 this commission presented a report which described the existing system in such a way that one is reminded of the situation in Europe in early modern times, when bondage and debt slavery existed. Indeed the usurers exploited the peasants mercilessly.

There were three types of usurers:

The rural usurers were the mukhtars who were the owners of the local shop and some of the few rich peasants who lent money on an interest basis. Their customers were the poorest of the village who could not pay and relied on the state, promising to pay their debts after the harvest in the form of crops. Their land was the security for the loan. As these peasants could not borrow anywhere else they had to accept every condition, making them to be the most exploited by the system. As the risks to the money lenders were rather high with such poor customers, they demanded the highest interest and outstanding debts were collected without any mercy. Thus the land owned by this type of usurer grew considerably.

The urban merchant-moneylender began his career as a shop owner selling things which the peasants could not produce themselves. As the peasants rarely had cash they paid with grain. Thus the creditor became a grain dealer. Though he, too, took the debtor's land as security he was not interested in acquiring or cultivating it. His aim was a constant grain supply at optimal prices for him. He was interested in keeping the peasant solvent. His customers were the well-off peasants.

The third type owned a lot of land himself and had enough money to lend it to other peasants. The debtor gave his land as security in the form of a mortgage pledging to pay his instalments punctually. When he could not pay, his land belonged to the creditor. The money-lender's aim was to get high interest and buy land cheaply. Contemporaries assessed that these creditors owned 5 percent of the land and another 5 percent were burdened by an estate. However, the biggest number of credits, about three fifths of the total number of credits, were awarded among villagers.

Cypriots did not regard money lending as objectionable because there were no other sources. Between 1883 and 1930 almost all members of the Legislative Council were moneylenders but they did not become politicians in order to promote their business. As parliamentarians they demanded the establishment of an agricultural bank despite the fact that they knew that this would ruin their business.

In 1919 on the basis of the commission's report four laws were enacted. The *Usury Law* ruled that the maximum interest rate was 12 percent. The *Merchant and Farmers Law* obliged the merchants to keep precise bookkeeping, and the *Civil Procedure Law* decreed that the property below poverty level could not be forcibly removed. The *Relief of Insolvent Farmers Law* regulated repayment procedures. These laws were well-intentioned but they did not go to the root of the evil. Only the founding of an agricultural bank would bring a real solution.

In 1923 the postwar economic crisis which had hit the island became worse. The number of sales on court orders increased, causing a decline in prices at the same time. The victims were the small farmers who left the rural areas and went to the towns to look for work. This caused a drop in the wages of the unskilled and skilled workers, and the public was aroused by the pauperisation of a great part of the population. The government, however, did little to improve the situation of the indebted peasants. For some months there was talk of establishing a private agricultural bank but this did not work due to lack of money. In 1924 the agricultural crisis reached its climax. The forced sales reached horrifying dimensions and their revenues were so small that the creditors suffered also. In the town the wages dropped further and at the end of the year 1924 *Eleftheria* wrote that life on the island "was hell before the British occupation and it has remained hell under the British administration".

elected. When in January 1923 the new Legislative Council began working it was obvious that those members scarcely opened their mouths and the few elected independents could achieve nothing. The government did not listen to them and the "National Council" was isolated. Another discussion about the right course began. This time the moderates had their way. For them *enosis* was a long term objective but gaining more freedom was the short term objective. But even this change of course had no effect since the Governor stuck to his course making both the "National Council" and the "National Organisation" irrelevant. In 1925 they gave up.

In May 1925 Cyprus got a new constitution as a crown colony. The new constitution was no more than political cosmetics. The number of the Greek Cypriot deputies of the Legislative Council was increased but the combined British and Turkish votes still had the majority. Even if the two communities had cooperated they could not have achieved much because they only had an advisory role. The new constitution made the partition permanent and deepened it. It was clear that the Greek Cypriots would never accept the privileged position of the Turkish Cypriots, and the Turkish Cypriots would stick even more closely to the British in order to preserve their privileges. This would lead to future conflicts and make the development of a common Cypriot identity almost impossible. But this had been the guiding principle of the founding fathers of the constitution: Divide and rule, the old colonial recipe as a basic constitutional principle. One opportunity to overcome the differences between the two ethnic groups was lost, a switch which might have led to a peaceful development was not activated.

In view of the Middle Eastern crisis after the end of WWI, the British government had decided that Cyprus had to remain a part of the British Empire. In order to enforce this course, London sent personalities filled with the spirit of imperialism to Cyprus who regarded the Cypriots as natives and treated them accordingly. They were able to secure their rule with some 50 civil servants and a company of soldiers because the Cypriots are a peace loving breed of humankind who admired the British and trusted them.

In 1926 this changed when Ronald Storrs, a highly educated philhellene, became Governor. He immediately introduced great reforms, of which the abolition of the "Tribute" is the most noteworthy. In his eyes the Greek Cypriots were Greeks. Their wish for *enosis* was disloyal because they were British subjects, but not illegal. He was convinced that in a truly secret plebiscite the majority would vote for Britain, but he was not sure whether this applied equally to the younger generation. In his eyes the Greek Cypriots were taking advantage of the liberal regime. Even the members of the Legislative Council who had sworn an oath of allegiance to the English monarch would break it if *enosis* was on the agenda, only the civil servants were loyal. Despite these considerations he continued his liberal course.

Storrs's policy was supported by a change of power in Athens when in July 1928 Venizelos toppled the conservative government and called elections, which he won resoundingly. Venizelos used his parliamentary majority to make peace with Turkey and conclude a treaty of friendship. But regarding Cyprus, he continued his old course: There was no Cyprus question between Greece and Britain. According to his opinion the Cypriots should solve their problems with Britain on their own. In May 1929 Venizelos advised the Cypriots to strive for reforms and forget *enosis* for the time being.

When in May 1929 Labour won the elections, new hope rose and it was decided to send another delegation to London. This was done and in October 1929 the Cypriot delegates told the Colonial Secretary about their desire for more autonomy and the refunding of the surplus of the "Tribute". They mentioned *enosis* but made it clear that this was a long term objective. The minister reacted in a dismissive way: the time for autonomy had not yet come. The delegation returned to Cyprus and reported their failure. The reaction was typical: the efforts should be intensified.

In January 1930 another political organization was created which was better organised and had only one aim: *enosis*. On the occasion of the Greek national holiday on 25 March an unofficial plebiscite on union with Greece was organized in which three quarters of the Greek Cypriots voted for *enosis*. In August 1930 it became known that the undersecretary of the Colonial Office would visit Cyprus in October. This led to speculation about whether Britain might be ready to transfer Cyprus to Greece. When undersecretary Drummond Shiels arrived he deeply disappointed the Cypriots when he told them that no British government would find a majority in Parliament for the cessation of Cyprus. But Britain was ready to support the culture of both communities. Then he developed a scheme which would have spared the Cypriots a lot of misery had it been realised: *"What would secure our ready sympathy and co-operation would be a Cypriot patriotism rather than one which makes Cyprus a secondary consideration. We do not ask the Greek members to forsake their Hellenic culture, traditions, language and religion which they naturally prize, but only that they should continue to develop these in Cyprus as a constituent part of the British Empire."* At the end Shiels warned them not to exaggerate the opposition against British rule.

No sooner had Shiels left Cyprus than a new discussion started about which course to steer. Some of the leaders talked about a boycott and the founding of parties. The more radical wing dismissed these ideas and secretly founded the National Radical Organization of Cyprus (Ethniki Rizospastiki *Enosis* Kyprou - EREK). Before long this organisation counted 1,200 members throughout Cyprus and penetrated the Greek Cypriot community. It became the centre of all radical forces and the moderates lost influence. EREK became a sort of forerunner organization of the later EOKA which led the liberation struggle in the 1950s.

The creation of EREK triggered a Turkish Cypriot counter movement. The younger generation, who were fed up with the paternalistic rule of the older generation based on the control of the religious foundations (Evkaf), had watched the reforms of Kemal Atatürk enthusiastically. The Kemalist movement was promoted by the Turkish consul in Cyprus, who tried his best to teach the younger generation a Turkish national consciousness but with little success. When the British discovered what role the consul was playing they saw to it that he was withdrawn. By this the British once more succeeded in stabilising the patriarchal system of the Turkish Cypriots but gradually Turkish nationalism spread among the younger generation.

In 1930 Alexis Kyrou, the new Greek consul of Cypriot descent, arrived in Cyprus. Kyrou was a protégé of Greek foreign minister Andreas Michalokopoulos. Of course he knew Venizelos' position on the Cyprus question, but because of his close relation to the minister he believed he could defy this. He believed that an absolute intransigent course would lead to *enosis*. The fate of his Turkish colleague did not impress him. As a born Athenian of Cypriot origin, he was convinced that he knew more about Cypriot politics than the Cypriots, who in his eyes pursued a primitive political course. His condescension was not dangerous, as such, except for the fact that the Cypriots regarded him as the voice of the National Centre. Many Cypriots considered his often totally callow opinions as instructions for action.

According to him, the demand for more autonomy was counterproductive because autonomy was an obstacle on the road to *enosis*. He recommended a tough position towards undersecretary Shiels. Although Michalokopoulos was informed about the escapades of his protégé he only mildly admonished him and allowed him to continue. Even when Kyrou backed EREK and tried to bring this organisation to a course of confrontation Michalokopoulos did not react. London, too, did not take the actions of the Greek consul seriously and rejected Storrs' request for a demarche in Athens. Only when Storrs met Venizelos privately and took the matter up with him, did the latter promise to recall Kyrou. A few days later Kyrou went on his annual holiday and nobody expected him to return to Cyprus.

But even then the tensions did not decrease in Cyprus. There was quite a verbal fight within EREK between the moderates and the radicals about the right course. The dispute in the press between the two wings, the subversive activities of the radicals and the terrible effects of the great depression heightened the tensions further. Under these circumstances the statement of the Secretary of the Treasury, Snowden, about the surplus of the "Tribute" exploded like a bomb. The Cypriot press accused the London government of arrogance, arbitrariness, injustice and contempt for the wishes of the Cypriot population.

When in August it became known that the King had signed the Order-in-Council ratifying the appropriation of the surplus, the members of the Legislative Council were outraged and rejected the budget bill for 1932, forcing Storrs to rule by decree which increased the tension even more. In the following weeks there was a heated debate about the correct course. Some demanded the resignation of the deputies but this would not achieve much, as a similar action had proved in 1920. Others proposed a tax strike and a boycott of British products. Kyrou, who had returned unexpectedly, did his best to fan the flames of political passions.

Things exploded on 21 October 1931 when excited participants of a protest rally decided to march to Government House, located on the southern outskirts of Nicosia. There they met a few policemen but these could not stop them. A huge mass of people assembled on the forecourt of the residence but everything remained calm. Negotiations began between the leaders and Storrs, accompanied by chanting. People were noisy but in high spirits and peace-fully minded. In the meantime night had fallen and this encouraged some hooligans at the back of the crowd to throw stones towards Government House from the hind rows in the dark. The leaders tried to stop this but the teenage hooligans couldn't be stopped. They overturned the cars parked in front of the Governor's residence and set fire to them; a little later the wooden Government House was ablaze.

The burning down of Government House was not a premeditated action. It was the work of 100 to 150 hooligans who ran riot under the cover of darkness. It is improbable that they had been incited by members of the EREK because later nobody gloated about it. The whole episode was unpolitical, but, without the preceding phase of political frustration and the impacts of the Great Depression, it would never have happened. If the police chief had reacted less patiently and had acted earlier he would have spared Cyprus a couple of rather unpleasant years. However, the riots spread throughout the whole island and when the police could not cope with them the military (3 officers and 123 soldiers) were deployed and further troops brought in from Egypt. In order to keep the development under his own control Storrs avoided declaring martial law but announced a limited state of siege and a curfew. In a few days the police and the military restored law and order all over Cyprus. On 23 October six "ringleaders" were arrested, and by 27 October everything was quiet again.

In Athens Venizelos tried to limit the damage: On 23 October he stated to the press that a Cyprus question did not exist between the British and the Greek Governments. It existed only between the British Government and the Cypriots. Until now the Cypriots had conducted the struggle with peaceful methods, which the liberalism of the British considered as legitimate. Now criminal excesses had taken place. Here British tolerance ended and this gave way to the strict enforcement of the law. He expressed his profound regret at the excesses.

In Athens the Foreign Ministry informed the British that Kyrou would be recalled imme-diately. The British Government, however, let the Greeks know that Kyrou was *persona non grata* and his *exequatur* was withdrawn. Venizelos was deeply shocked and ordered his Foreign Minister to apologise officially. But the British stuck to their hard line and told the Greeks that the sending of Kyrou to Cyprus had been a great mistake. Venizelos ended the embarrassing situation by making the following statement in parliament: *"No matter how deep the response which the national wishes of the inhabitants of these islands finds in the Greek soul, it is impossible for the Greek State to undertake support for their realization, or to tolerate that its territory be used to organise a systematic reaction against the peace of these islands. Crucial and more than crucial interests of Greece impose the necessity of undisturbed friendship with Great Britain and with our neighbour, the great Mediterranean power, Italy... In fact we have the right to demand of the Greek inhabitants of these islands that they be less egoistical."* This was the last word in this matter for many years. From now on until the end of WWII Cyprus was not a topic for the Greek foreign policy.

Immediately after the end of the riots Storrs had those six "ringleaders" arrested. He suspected that certain politicians e.g. Bishop Makarios of Kyrenia and the lawyer Savvas Loizides as well as two leading communists were involved. He had them arrested, too, and exiled them to London. On 30 October a letters patent was published in the Cyprus Gazette which abolished the Constitution, the municipal councils and the Legislative Council and transferred the legislative power to the Governor. On the basis of this authority he prohibited the flying of foreign, Greek, flags, reduced the ringing of church bells to a minimum and from now on appointed all mukhtars. Offenders would be punished severely. In December 1931 the Greek Cypriots with the exception of the civil servants were ordered by a new law to pay a special tax of £ 35,000 for the reconstruction of Government House.

Altogether 400 persons were arrested; about 3,400 were charged but only 2,600 were sentenced and of these 2,000 had to pay fines between two and ten pounds. A few received a prison sentence between 6 and 19 months. More deportations were rejected by London on legal grounds. The Archbishop reacted against the church bell regulation by a general ringing strike in order to remind the public of Ottoman times when bell ringing had been totally prohibited; this caused London quietly to drop the bell ringing regulation. The "bell ringing war" led to a smear campaign against Storrs by the press in Greece and when Venizelos tried to stop this the right wing press attacked him. The campaign ended when the effects of the Great Depression hit Greece and led to state bankruptcy. In Cyprus a strict censorship was introduced in October 1931 and each article needed a permit.

In spring 1932 the Colonial Office offered Storrs the Governorship of Northern-Rhodesia, today's Zambia, and he accepted. In June 1932 he left Cyprus. He was the best Governor Cyprus ever had. He had enforced wide-ranging reforms and managed to have the "Tribute" abolished. During the first half of his tenure he successfully improved the life of the Cypriots. Under him, the decades old dream of the peasants to get out of the debt trap was realized by establishing the agricultural bank. He was the first Governor who understood the mentality of the Cypriots and did not regard them contemptuously as natives, but neither did he fraternise. The well known English author and philhellene, Compton Mackenzie, characterised him as follows: *"He was a philhellene by scholarship but not by love."* The impact of the Great Depression on Cyprus and his lack of courage in the case of the surplus led to the explosion of October 1931. When the riots began he did not have any alternative but to do his duty as Governor and restore law and order. But from then on until 1960 Cyprus was governed by decree.

BENEVOLENT AUTOCRACY

Storrs' successor, Reginald Stubbs (1932-33), arrived in Cyprus in December 1932. His first law dealt with censorship. The existing practice of censoring each article had proved to be both pretty inefficient and costly since it needed a lot of personnel. The new method was simple and efficient: Newspapers needed a licence and in order to get one the editor had to submit a bond of £ 500 to the authorities. In case the paper published anything "seditious"or wrong news the licence could be withdrawn and the money was gone. A similar regulation was used with the

Plate 1

Larnaca: Turkish Café at the seafront (Illustrated London News)

Courtyard of the British Consulate at Larnaca (The Graphic)

Plate 2

The British occupation of Cyprus in 1878 (Illustrated London News)

Plate 3

Garnet Wolseley courting Cyprus (Punch 1878)

Plate 4

High Commissioner Sir Garnet Wolseley

Plate 5

Nicosia Victoria Street (Photo Foscolo)

Plate 6

Famagousta: Ag. Nikolaos - Lala-Mustafa-Pasha-Mosque 1875 (Photo Felix Bonfils)

Main street in Limassol in 1878 (Photo John Thomson)

Plate 7

Women spinning and weaving

School in the courtyard of the village church of Kalopanagiotis

Plate 8

Pictorial stamps commemorating the 50th anniversary of British rule 1878-1928

owners of printing presses: From now on they were responsible for the content of their printed material. But censorship was not confined to publications by Cypriots; it applied to the reprinting of articles from the London *Times* or statements by members of parliament. Films and newsreels were also subject to censorship, too. The criteria for censorship were a bit odd: a film showing the wedding of a member of the royal family of Greece was prohibited, whereas films praising Italian Fascism or German Nazism allowed.

Other laws brought the Boy Scout movement under control. Political organizations were prohibited and in order to prevent their tarnished revival as clubs the laws dealing with clubs were expanded. The import of weapons was strictly regulated and even the ownership of hunting weapons was subject to police control.

Another law proscribed the communist party (KKK). The possession of communist literature was threatened with two years' imprisonment. If people were suspected of communist leanings the police were allowed to arrest them, search houses and confiscate printed material without a warrant. The correspondence of communists with foreign countries was also under surveillance, but this measure was not very efficient since a comrade in the main post office found ways to smuggle letters through control. Another field to combat the idea of *enosis* was education. There, too, the influence of the local population was reduced. From now on the Governor was responsible for the appointment of teachers and their salaries; he decided on textbooks and curricula, and controlled the finances of the educational system. By decree he prohibited the teaching of Greek history, the learning of patriotic poems and the singing of similar songs. In order to bring the training of teachers under government control a teacher training institution was added to the Greek and Turkish gymnasium. On 8 November 1933 Stubbs left Cyprus; the Cypriots scarcely remember him.

The new Governor was Herbert Richmond Palmer (1933-1939). Palmer came from the colonial administration of Africa where he had learned the methods of indirect rule through the local notables. During the previous three years he had been Governor of Gambia where he acquired his habit of ruling primitive societies in an authoritarian condescending way. This was true of at least half of the Civil servants, who also came from the west-African colonial service. The Cypriots were treated like natives with whom one had no social relations: Proudly the wife of a high ranking officer said that they had been in Cyprus fourteen years, and never had a "native" inside their house. *"A high legal luminary from East Africa was horrified to learn that he would be expected to shake hands with 'the natives'. 'I understand a white gentleman', he perorated, 'and a black gentleman, though I don't let him touch me; but these betwixts and betweens I don't want to understand.' But these "betwixts" were frequently barristers-at-law, speaking two or three languages."*

Palmer's six-year Governorship is characterised by stagnation. If there were changes in the social and economic field they took place despite him, caused by other factors. A few months before his retirement he had the honour to deliver a speech to the *Royal Central Asian Society* about his experiences in Cyprus. This speech is revealing. He attributed his successful rule of Cyprus to two factors: "The numerous office-holders all over the island [...] *have been selected and not elected.* [... and] *There has existed a certain supervision of the Press which is essential in the interests of law and order."* This reflects exactly the antidemocratic spirit of the time but to hear it from a British official was a bit astonishing. But according to Palmer *"The Cypriots are contented with the results of that régime."* His next insight was sexist and late Victorian racism: In his opinion the Cypriots were *"thoroughly Asiatic and Oriental in outlook and mentality. [...] Several thousand years ago a lady called Aphrodite landed in Cyprus, and the island has never quite recovered. The people of Cyprus make a luxury of discontent and always pretend that they do not like being ruled, and yet, like the lady I have mentioned as a prototype, they expect to be ruled, and, in fact, prefer it."*

His further remarks proved that he had not the remotest idea about Cyprus and his insights into Cypriot society and politics are really preposterous: *"The island must, for the present, be governed and not self-governed. [...] A form of government more on the normal model of colonial government, to which we are accustomed, cannot with safety be initiated in Cyprus until at least a sound British sentiment has been built up."* Obviously Palmer had not understood that he was governing Europeans. It is no exaggeration to characterise his ruling style as close to fascism. In his eyes the wish for *enosis* was just a "chronic obsession" of the urban intelligentsia, the 250,000 peasants were immune to this disease and it was his duty to protect them. Slowly even in the Colonial Office warning voices were heard: *"The Government of Cyprus are becoming more and more autocratic. [...] All this seems to show that the Government are becoming imbued with the political philosophy of Mussolini."*

In May 1936 Neville Chamberlain became Prime Minister. This change was noticed in Cyprus, where three former prominent politicians believed that the time was ripe to send a delegation to London which should try to achieve a change of policy towards Cyprus. The Greek Cypriot press applauded the idea and even the Turkish Cypriot newspaper *Söz* appreciated the plan. The three became delegates and followed the pattern of earlier deputations. They wrote a memorandum in which they complained about Palmer's dictatorial rule and demanded the return to democratic rule. The memorandum was submitted to the Governor in June 1936. When the Governor did not reply in time, the delegates travelled to London and submitted another memorandum to the Colonial Office stressing that the Cypriots considered the present government as authoritarian. Cyprus needed a constitution and its people a say in their affairs in the form of elections.

At the end of July the Colonial Secretary deigned to receive one of them and made it clear to him that the Colonial Office backed Palmer unconditionally and British policy would not change. A Statement in Parliament confirmed this position. The three delegates returned to Cyprus in a rather frustrated mood. When the newspaper *Eleftheria* published the report about their experience Palmer used this as a pretext to suspend its publication for three months. The other newspapers refrained from reporting the story. There were further efforts to influence the Colonial Office, but only as late as July 1939 came a signal that London was considering a change of policy when the new Colonial Secretary said in Parliament: *"The policy of the administration is to work in the direction of more representative government; but this process cannot be hurried, and in my view it must proceed first through a gradual increase of responsibility in local government."* But London did not hurry, the change came during the years of WWII.

Palmer's rule is still remembered in Cyprus as a period of darkness, as a time when freedom was non-existent. Indeed, during his Governorship liberty was at its lowest ebb and repression felt most. The crucial changes in the social, economic and educational sector which began during his Governorship are not attributed to him. They were instigated by other people and realised despite him.

The new Governor, William Denis Battershill, (1939-41) knew Cyprus from his time as Colonial Secretary (1935-1937). He liked the Cypriots and showed it, and they registered his friendly gestures and reciprocated them. In the Colonial Office they expected him to give more freedom to the Cypriots but avoid any new disturbances. The first phase of the war, however, when Hitler overran most of Europe, precluded any greater change. But in August 1941 when Prime Minister Churchill and President Roosevelt proclaimed the Atlantic Charter things began to move: Paragraph 3 of the Charter ruled that *"they respect the right of all peoples to choose the form of government under which they will live; and they wish to see sovereign rights and self government restored to those who have been forcibly deprived of them,"* and in paragraph

6, *"that all the men in all lands may live out their lives in freedom from fear and want."* These were high sounding principles and it was clear that they had also to be applied in Cyprus.

Battershill planned liberalisations from the bottom up to the top. First, communal elections should take place by which town councils and mayors would be established. In order to avoid the revival of the old clientelistic networks Battershill allowed the foundation of parties. The 1931 law prohibiting the meeting of more than five people was repealed. At the same time London sent a specialist from the Ministry of Labour to advise the Cyprus Government on the formulation of a union law, which resulted in a legal framework almost identical to the British trade union laws. The experienced communists pulled the strings from the backstage and soon most of the unions were under their control. They organised the first construction workers' strike in spring 1939 which ended in victory, a first collective wage agreement. In August 1939 the first union congress took place in Famagusta. Working conditions, however, were still dreadful; the average weekly working hours were between 52 and 60 hours. Social insurance was non-existent. The workers were dreaming of an eight-hour workday and 48 hours per week.

When the communists tried to organise the poor peasants in the villages the richer peasants organised themselves into the Pancyprian Agrarian Union (PEK), which later became one of the sources of strength of EOKA. In spring the trade unions united in PSE (Παγκύπρια Συντεχνιακή Επιτροπή - Pancypriot Union Committee). When the British saw how successful PSE was they allowed the Cypriot right to found the right-wing unions SEK (Συνομοσπονδία εργατών Κύπρου). In April 1941, under the leadership of the left intellectual, Ploutis Servas, a new communist party was founded in the village of Skarinou under the name of AKEL which presented itself in theory as revolutionary and orthodox but in reality always steered a reformist course. In November 1941 the 2nd PSE Congress was held. When Governor Battershill left Cyprus in October 1941 the Cypriots had regained their freedom and a say in two important fields: in local government and in economic life. But on the level of governmental politics they were still excluded from power.

WWII scarcely touched Cyprus though the island had been formally at war with Germany since the British declaration of war of 3 September 1939. During the war the British put up two volunteer regiments which took over transport tasks and did this on all fronts. About 25,000 Cypriots of both communities served in the British armed forces. In spring 1941 parts of the first regiment, together with other Commonwealth units, went into operation in Greece. When these were evacuated from the Peloponnese the Cypriots were left behind because only combat troops were evacuated. The same happened when Crete was occupied by German parachutists and mountain troops. The occupation of Crete horrified Nicosia and London, but thanks to the deciphering of the German codes (ULTRA) Churchill knew that Hitler had no ambitions regarding the eastern Mediterranean but was about to attack the Soviet Union.

In January 1943 Prime Minister Churchill visited Cyprus and in a speech he said: *After this war is over, the name of Cyprus will be included in the list of those who have deserved well not only of the British Commonwealth of Nations, not only of the United Peoples now in arms, but as I firmly believe, of future generations of mankind."* These were nice words but the Colonial Office, in a statement to the House of Lords, warned of "unduly haste". This provoked the protest from the London based Cyprus Affairs Committee, which raised concrete demands: The decrees of the dictatorship restricting freedom of speech and assembly, freedom of the press, legalisation of political parties, free and unhampered municipal and rural elections were to be abrogated and the Cypriots to have a voice in the administration of their country.

Towards the end of October 1943 the same committee appealed to the British to apply the principles of the Atlantic Charter in Cyprus, too. This and further statements caused the ministry to send the former Undersecretary in the Colonial Office, Sir Cosmo Parkinson, on a fact finding mission to Cyprus in August 1944. This mission was a failure from the beginning. In order to spare him direct contact with the Cypriots the administration took all sorts of precautions to shield him from the population. Under the pretext that Nicosia was too hot in August he was given accommodation on mount Troodos, far away from the towns. He only met carefully selected people, saw suitable things and he himself refused to talk about *enosis*. The cleverly designed visiting program avoided his seeing the protest demonstrations in the towns. In short, Sir Cosmo's trip simply justified the maintenance of the status quo.

In London, however, there were conflicting positions. The Foreign Office was of the opinion that one was morally obliged to cede Cyprus to Greece because that country had done so much for Britain, but the Colonial Office stuck to its position. In early 1945 the British Government explained its position: Deputy Prime Minister Clement Attlee, who belonged to Labour, stated, referring to Churchill's statement of 1941 in which the latter had said that the Atlantic Charter applied only to Nazi occupied countries and not to the Empire, that no part of the Empire was excluded, meaning Cyprus, of course. Obviously there was no difference between the colonial policy of the Tories and of Labour.

This became more than clear in summer 1945 when the Fabian Colonial Bureau, a kind of Labour think tank, brought forward a memorandum on the future of Cyprus: in the introduction its author and future colonial secretary, Arthur Creech Jones, repeated the arguments of Churchill and Attlee and stated that there were certain colonies, he mentioned Malta, Gibraltar and Cyprus, which for strategic reasons would never be given up. The question was, however, which rights would be given to the inhabitants and which restrictions of their rights they had to accept because of imperial interests. In order to neutralise the wish for *enosis* it was necessary to promote Cyprus economically and give the island autonomy, retaining, however, a few airbases for some time as there were no deep water harbours. The idea of indispensable strategic colonies became the key to Britain's Cyprus policy both for Labour and Tories. It was an attempt to preserve its own standing in the world although it was already understood that the Empire would dissolve.

Therefore nothing changed when Labour won the elections in July 1945. Colonial Secretary George Hall wanted a clear statement that Cyprus would remain a part of the Empire. Foreign Secretary Bevin rejected such a statement because it might have negative repercussions on Greece, which had been totally destabilised since the December 1944 events and was drifting towards civil war. Thus the question remained open until October 1946 when Creech Jones became Colonial Secretary. On 23 October he announced a new course in Parliament: Britain would no longer influence the election of the archbishop. Those exiled in 1931 would be allowed to return. A ten-year-plan for economic development of Cyprus had been worked out, and a Consultative Assembly would be convened which would work out proposals for constitutional reforms so that the Cypriots could participate in the government of the island.

In December 1946 a delegation of Greek Cypriots led by bishop Leontios went to London. The very day they arrived there Attlee announced in the House of Commons that Burma would be decolonised. This raised hopes that the British government might also be generous to the Cypriots. Creech Jones made the delegation wait until 7 February until he deigned to receive them. The Cypriots stated that the vast majority of the population wanted *enosis* and was not ready to cooperate in any model of self-administration. Creech Jones wanted to know whether it would be possible to continue with the constitutional reforms even if *enosis* was turned down. The delegates rejected this, signalling that they were not interested in reforms. Creech Jones ended the meeting with the standard formula that at the moment no change to the status of Cyprus was being contemplated.

While the Cypriot delegation was in London and trying to promote *enosis,* developments influencing world history took place which did not affect Cyprus directly but nevertheless had their effects. Namely, in early 1947 the economic post-war crisis intensified in such a way that Britain felt compelled to reduce some of her imperial obligations: On 14 February 1947 the British government announced that it would transfer responsibility for the Palestinian problem, which was getting increasingly difficult, to the UN. On 20 February London let it be known that India would become independent that summer. A similar development was on the horizon in the case of Egypt. One day later the British Government informed the US State Department that it was forced to end the financial and economic aid it had given to Greece and Turkey since the end of the war. The Americans reacted promptly and took over the role of the British in what became known as the Truman Doctrine.

The imminent independence of Egypt increased the strategic importance of Cyprus for the air force, as the military concluded. From Cyprus one could control the Aegean, the Suez Canal and the terminal of the oil pipeline from Iraq to Haifa and in the Mesaoria, the great plain east of Nicosia, a huge air force base could be built. In view of such considerations it was clear that the security considerations had priority over democratic principle; *Enosis* was no option for British politics.

When the delegation returned to Cyprus it found a different situation. The return of Bishop Makarios of Kyrenia, who had been in exile in Greece since 1931. triggered a huge argument. Makarios hated the communists and was afraid they would win in the Greek civil war. Therefore he was against *enosis*. Additionally, he did not like Leontios for personal reasons. The new Governor's psychological mistakes and the forthcoming election of the archbishop poisoned the climate further. Leontios initially hesitated to stand as a candidate but then allowed himself to be persuaded. When the conservatives put up their own candidate Leontios became the candidate of the left though he himself was no leftist. The election of the electors in May 1947 brought a huge majority for Leontios who was elected archbishop on 20 July.

In early July the Governor invited the Cypriots to nominate candidates for the Consultative Assembly. Leontios turned against this in an encyclical which was read from all pulpits and demanded *enosis*. But quite suddenly the 51 year old Leontios died; *loco tenens* became the 78 year old Makarios of Kyrenia. Thus the power balance was shifted to the right. In August 1947 representatives of the church, of the rightist groups, of the conservative unions and the peasant organization met in the so called ethnarchic council, a consultative organ of the Archbishop, and decided to refuse any cooperation with the government as regards the constitutional reforms. The Cypriots wanted *enosis* only.

The cleavage of the two camps deepened when Makarios ran for archbishop with the slogan "*enosis* and only *enosis*". In mid-December 1947 Makarios was elected archbishop under the name of Makarios II. From now on it was clear that the Cypriot right would boycott even the most liberal British proposals. The left, on the other side, considered any constitutional government better than the hitherto existing ruling by decree. Despite the election boycott of the right the elections for the Consultative Assembly took place. However, instead of 40 members only 18 were voted for, of which eight belonged to the left and six were Turkish Cypriots. The remaining four were independent Greeks and a Maronite. On 1 November the assembly sat for its constituent session with chief justice Edward Jackson in the chair.

On 18 November Ioannis Clerides, mayor of Nicosia, submitted a memorandum with his ideas: Parliament should consist only of elected members voted for in general elections. The minorities should be represented according to their percentage of the population. Parliament should have the monopoly of legislative power over internal affairs of Cyprus. The Governor should issue the laws, with the exception of those which he believed should be voted for by the population. The Governor should be obliged to follow the advice of his ministers. For the time being there would be no Cypriot participation in foreign and defence affairs. The executive was to consist of a ministerial council which would need to command a majority support in the parliament. There would be a minister for Turkish Cypriot affairs elected by this community. This proposal corresponded with the constitutions of Ceylon (now Sri Lanka) and Malta.

The proposal was sent to the Colonial Office but was rejected by the Cabinet. Then the authorities submitted their own constitutional proposals which were published in Nicosia in May 1948. If one compares this proposal with the pre-1931 constitution it is easy to see that the Cypriots would have a greater say in their affairs. In the Legislative Council would no longer be a majority of British and Turkish votes which could block any progress, nor would the Governor have the decisive vote. At the side of the Governor there would be a consultative organ, the Executive Council. Although the Governor was not bound by the decision of this body, the locals were given quite a say by the creation of two quasi ministries. In other words, the Cypriots were offered a limited version of Home Rule, a representative system. The government did not need the confidence (absolute majority) of the parliament and thus this system was not fully democratic, but it was a system which appeared capable of development towards democracy.

The Holy Synod reacted one day later: The proposals were condemned as totally unacceptable and the Synod appealed to the population to remain true to the principle of *"enosis* and only *enosis"* and to boycott possible general elections. The British were accused of promoting communism by having contact with leftist Greeks in the Assembly. The representative of the Turkish Cypriots, Rauf Denktash, on the other hand, fully agreed with the limitation of the right to a say because in this way the rights of the minority were safeguarded. Then he smugly pointed to the misery in Greece caused by the Civil War and said that the Turkish Cypriots were grateful to be under British rule in Cyprus.

On 21 May the decisive session took place. The Turkish Cypriots voted for the constitutional proposals in which they were joined by the two conservative Greeks. The representatives of the Left voted against the proposals and demanded self-government with a responsible government and left the meeting. Jackson adjourned the meeting sine die. In August 1948 the Governor dissolved the assembly which had become meaningless.

The Greek right were jubilant: The danger of an illegitimate solution had been averted. The people had won a double victory, by rejecting the British constitutional proposal and by defeating Communism by definitively condemning their demands for self-government once and for all. The Central Committee of AKEL on the other side announced that the struggle for self-determination would continue in an intensified manner. The slogan *"enosis* and only *enosis"* could not hide the betrayal of the true interests of the people.

The main responsibility for the failure of the Consultative Assembly lies with the Church leadership which steered an intransigent course and obstinately stuck to the position of fundamental opposition. The Cypriot right followed the course of the Church. Both were guided by their strong anti-communism. On the other hand, the decision of the Cypriot left, i.e. AKEL to reject the British constitutional proposal because it did not give enough co-determination to the Cypriots in the end, was a blatant misjudgement. Obviously the Cypriot Left was not experienced enough and its ranks not closed enough to begin a discussion among its members about the path to choose. The failure of the Consultative Assembly meant that Cyprus continued to be ruled by decree until 1960. Thus we may conclude that the failure of the Consultative Assembly was once again one of those lost opportunities which might have given Cyprus a peaceful democratic future.

Since the Greek Cypriots had rejected the British offer for the creation of a self-governing dominion, conflict loomed on the horizon. The question was when and in which form this conflict would break out.

1949-1959

The struggle for Enosis

THE ROAD TO THE STRUGGLE FOR INDEPENDENCE

In 1949 the scenario of Cypriot history changed fundamentally. In Greece the Civil War ended, Greek politics gained more space for manoeuvring and began to show more interest in Cyprus. The global Cold War gained speed, in the African and Asian colonies the anti-colonial struggle set in and in Cyprus Makarios III was elected Archbishop.

The first big transformation was a change of course by AKEL. At the end of 1948 two CC members had visited the chief of the Greek CP, Zachariadis, in his civil war headquarters at lake Prespa on the Albanian-Yugoslav border. Zachariadis had condemned AKEL's advocating home rule and had asked them to change course towards enosis because he would soon enter Athens at the head of his Democratic Army. The leadership of AKEL accepted this brotherly advice and changed the party line accordingly, though the chief of the CPGB, Harry Politt, had warned them that a change of British policy was not in sight, enosis could be achieved at most in the medium term; Zachariadis' ideas were nonsense.

In January 1949 this course was enforced in an extraordinary CC meeting and at the same time the party was purged of all pragmatists and liberals, e.g. Ploutis Servas. At the end of August the VIth Party Congress took place and Ezekias Papaioannou became the new head of the party. Though Papaioannou said that now the party had returned to its Leninist principles AKEL remained a reform oriented force and Papaioannou himself avoided any personality cult. Nevertheless, the character of the party changed because under Zervas the party had become attractive outside its traditional milieu; now it became a conventional communist party with little radiance.

The party congress approved the enosis course and decided to act in this direction. This is astonishing because only a few months previouly the Civil War had ended with a communist defeat. Union with Greece would certainly have led to the proscription of AKEL. The explanation is a little complicated. On the one hand, AKEL was sure that the British would reject enosis and thus it could demand it without risk. On the other hand, AKEL wanted to wrest away the opinion leadership in the enosis question from the Church and the Right. Additionally, it tried to drive a wedge between Athens and London, showing the Greek public that the communists were not the unpatriotic fellows of the government propaganda.

The 1950 plebiscite

The Left's change of course alarmed the Right. The Ethnarchic Council, consisting of the high clerics, some conservative politicians and mayors, had become a haven of anti-communism. Therefore, the Council reacted violently and rejected any cooperation with the communist traitors. AKEL reacted by publishing a "National Memorandum" which demanded self-determination and the holding of a plebiscite on enosis under UN supervision. This memorandum was sent to the governments of the members of the Security Council, to various communist world organizations and parties. It was the first step towards an internationalization of the problem. Until then enosis had only been discussed between the British and the Cypriots re the mother countries. Though it took some time till the UN debated the Cyprus problem, AKEL's initiative got some things moving: the Greek programs of the East European radio stations began to show interest in the Cyprus problem and demanded union with Greece.

The leaders of the Right were alarmed, of course, because AKEL's initiative threatened to wrest away its leading role in the national question. Early in December the Ethnarchic Council met. Its vice-president Bishop Makarios of Kition, the future Archbishop Makarios III, suggested moving forward and organizing a plebiscite of their own under UN supervision. The proposal was accepted and a little later it was announced that the Holy Synod had decided to hold a plebiscite in mid-November. AKEL reacted flexibly, dropped their proposal and disclosed that they supported the plebiscite. Later the Ethnarchic Council made it known that the plebiscite would take place on 15 January 1950. In the following weeks both political camps appealed to the public to participate in the plebiscite. In order to forestall a ban by the governor Makarios informed him in writing about the enterprise and suggested that he himself should organize the plebiscite. If the governor rejected this the Church would organize it. Presumably it was quite clear to Makarios that the governor's answer would be negative, but with this move he gave a whiff of legality to the plebiscite and by informing the British he kept them from forbidding it.

The Turkish Cypriots watched the preparation of the plebiscite with great distrust. Their press demanded that the Governor prohibit its realization. Competing political groups joined forces and on 12 December a mass rally adopted a resolution which sharply rejected enosis and demanded the retention of the status quo. Should England ever give up Cyprus it must be returned to Turkey. The press in Turkey seized the topic and did its best to incite the public, but the Turkish government remained reserved for the time being. But when students demonstrated in all bigger towns the foreign minister piped up and said basically this: Should the status quo of Cyprus change, Turkey would intervene; union with Greece was ruled out for strategic reasons. Thus the plebiscite triggered a Cyprus policy of Turkey.

In Cyprus the Turkish Cypriots on their part began to demand union with Turkey because Cyprus was Turkish. This in turn was made a discussion topic by the press in Turkey and propagated. In January 1950, however, foreign minister Fuat Köprülü rejected the slogan "Cyprus is ours": There was no Cyprus question because Cyprus was British and England was not thinking of transferring this possession to another power. Agitation in Cyprus would not change anything. This statement clearly shows that there were parallel developments in Greece and Turkey: neither Ankara nor Athens were able to control the developments in their respective ethnic groups. Both governments were drawn into the maelstrom of the Cypriot developments, straining their hitherto good relations.

The plebiscite began on 15 January 1950 and ended on 22 January. All men and women over 18 years were allowed to vote. Almost 96 percent of the Greek Cypriots voted for union with Greece. The other four percent were probably civil servants who did not want to risk their jobs. Makarios II informed the Governor of the result. But the answer took a long time coming because in Britain general elections took place in February 1950. Colonial Secretary Creech Jones was not reelected and his successor was a worthy Welsh unionist who was not interested in Cyprus. Thus Cyprus became a topic between the Governor and the ministerial bureaucracy. When London finally replied to the report on the plebiscite it stated that the Cyprus question was closed. AKEL's immediate reaction was the demand to bring the Cyprus question to the UNO. This suggestion horrified Makarios II and he signalled to the Governor that he and his followers would be satisfied if the British obligingly declared that they would cede Cyprus to Greece after 10 years or else one would continue to fight with all legal means.

This British reply equally obstructed a peaceful solution, as the rejection of the constitutional proposal and Home Rule by the ethnarchy had done. On 14 February 1950 bishop Makarios of Kition announced that the ethnarchy would appeal to the UNO and purposely send a delegation to New York, via Athens and London in order to brief the Secretary General on the result of the plebiscite. Thus Athens, the UN, and on British invitation, the Turks became players in the power poker game for Cyprus. The Cyprus conflict slowly became an international trouble spot. The Ethnarchy took over AKEL's policy fearing that the communists might capitalize on this course but the consequences of such a course were not thought about.

As the Ethnarchy rejected cooperation with the left it became clear in the following weeks that there would be two delegations. Additionally, there was a conflict in the ecclesiastical camp about who would take the lead because Makarios II was too old (80) to endure such an ordeal.

Bishop Kyprianou of Kyrenia prevailed and bishop Makarios of Kition had to stay in Cyprus. Thus he got the chance to become the successor of Makarios II, who died at the end of June 1950 quite unexpectedly.

Before the delegation arrived in Athens the British ambassador intervened and told the new Greek government to play down the relevance of the delegation; any other attitude would be regarded as an interference in internal British affairs; besides that, Turkey, too, had an interest in Cyprus. This meant that Britain, as early as that, was ready to apply the divide and rule tactics which it had used for decades with the two ethnic groups on Cyprus, towards the relationship of the two mother countries thus neutralizing Greek ambitions with Turkish ones.

When the Cypriot delegation arrived in Greece the Greek government kept a low profile. Prime Minister Plastiras stated that the Cyprus problem would be solved bilaterally in a friendly manner between Britain and Greece at the appropriate time. In the Foreign Ministry the delegation was warned that an appeal to the UN would make Cyprus an apple of discord in the Cold War between East and West. The delegation did not give up but appealed to the Church and right-wing opposition and its front organizations. The right-wing trade union congress (GSEE) and many members of parliament supported the demands of the delegation. The Greek press assisted by a campaign of banner headlines. The delegation caused such a stir that Plastiras felt obliged to receive them once more but during their meeting he stuck correctly to the previous position.

On 4 July the Greek parliament debated the Cyprus problem. The leader of the opposition, Konstantinos Tsaldaris, who in his capacity as foreign minister as late as December 1949 had characterized a debate of the Cyprus question as untimely, now introduced a resolution supporting the Cypriot demands. Plastiras argued against but the speaker of the house allowed the vote and the deputies passed the resolution which was immediately telegraphed to the Speaker of the House of Commons. It was a typical example of the demagogic behaviour of the Greek Right.

The Colonial Office had watched developments closely and in mid-June the Colonial Secretary stated in Parliament that the Cyprus question remained closed. If this and a few negative remarks about alleged Greek mismanagement in the Dodecanese did not lead to a huff the reason was the outbreak of the war in Korea, demanding unity of the Western camp. At the end of July the delegation continued their voyage to London where the Government kept them waiting in the lobby, so that they left London for Washington at the end of September.

In Washington a high ranking State Department official told them that the Cyprus question was purely a British matter and it was not appropriate to joggle it, in view of the critical international situation. In New York UN officials treated the delegates as private individuals and not one representative of a western state showed any interest in their demand. As it was impossible for them to turn to an eastern block state they returned to Greece, where Sofoklis Venizelos had become Prime Minister. But he, too, fobbed them off with empty promises. On 21 December Bishop Kyprianou returned to Cyprus.

The delegation of the Left encountered similar frustrating experiences. In Athens the government did not allow them to leave the airport. In London they were kept waiting endlessly. In Paris they met Plastiras and asked him to bring the Cyprus question to the UN but he rejected this: The British would transfer Cyprus to Greece at the appropriate time. The delegates should return to Cyprus. In case they managed to bring the Cyprus question into the General Assembly Greece would absent herself from the debate and the voting. The delegates had contacts with the French Left but to no avail. Then the delegates visited Prague, Bucharest, Budapest and Warsaw. With the exception of Poland, all governments maintained a low profile and delegated the visitors' program to a low level. The delegation received some noncommittal promises and nothing more. They did not even succeed in contacting the leadership of the Cominform during their five weeks sojourn in Budapest and when they tried to get a visa for the trip to Moscow the Soviet embassy rejected this. In view of the Korean war Moscow obviously had no interest in Cyprus. Since AKEL chief Papaioannou did not obtain a visa for the US the other delegates travelled alone to New York where they did not achieve anything at all. The failure of delegations showed clearly that at that time Cyprus was not a topic for the West or the East to score with.

The Ethnarchy arrived at characteristic conclusions: Only appeals to the Greek and international public opinion could bring movement into the Cyprus question. Although this first effort to internationalize the Cyprus question had failed, - to use a simile - the genie had left the bottle and nobody had an idea how it could be brought back.

In the meantime there had been personal changes in Cyprus which were to leave their imprints on the history of the island for the next 27 years: On 28 June Archbishop Makarios II had died. Followers of Bishop Makarios of Kition proposed him as successor. The only other candidate was Bishop Kyprianou of Kyrenia but he was abroad with the delegation. When it was rumoured that AKEL was supporting the candidature of Kyprianou the loco tenens, the suffragan bishop of Salamis, sent an Encyclia to all parish priests to delete all communists from the electoral rolls. Thus the result of the election was secure: on 16 October bishop Makarios of Kition was elected Archbishop Makarios III and ethnarch.

Makarios' First Steps
Before we turn our attention to the career of Makarios it seems reasonable to make some remarks on the role of the monasteries and bishops of the Greek-orthodox church. Christian monasteries are places of seclusion and asceticism. In the realm of the Greek-orthodox church, however, they are cadre schools of the high clergy because the higher echelons were reserved for celibates or widowers. Greek orthodox parish priests are married, as is well known. Whoever has the ambition to become a bishop must enter a monastery. In Ottoman times bishops were not only clerics: According to the millet system religion, and not ethnicity or language, was the decisive criterion for the allocation of the population. Thus the orthodox Church and its clergy in Cyprus became the bearer of national identity and its propaganda. The Archbishop became the Ethnarch. Originally the office of the Ethnarch had been an Ottoman invention, which was conferred upon the archbishop by *berat* of the Sultan. The last archbishop with a berat had been Sofronios II, who held this office from 1865 to 1900. Strictly speaking this office had come to an end when the British took over Cyprus, but the Cypriot church did not pay any attention to this legal problem and de facto sustained this office and all archbishops continued to be primarily ethnarchs, i.e. political leaders and only secondarily spiritual leaders; such was Makarios III. In view of this fact Makarios must be seen and judged primarily as a politician, but this the politicians in London never apprehended.

Makarios was born on 13 August 1913 as Michael Christodoulos Mouskos, in a mountain village east of Paphos. The family was not well off and young Michael had to help his father in his farm work. Nevertheless, he was so good at school that his teacher suggested sending him to a secondary school. As the family did not have the money for that his teacher suggested that Michael should apply to be a novice at Kykko monastery. The Abbot examined the boy intensely and accepted him as a novice in 1926. He passed the three year monastery lyceum so successfully that the Abbot sent him to the three years lyceum in Nicosia. In 1938 he was ordained deacon and assumed the name Makarios (beatific). In the same year the monastery conferred a scholarship on him to study theology at the university of Athens. In 1942 he finished his studies but as Greece had been occupied by the Axis forces he could not return to Cyprus and remained at the University studying law. During the occupation years he earned his living as a deacon at the renowned Ag. Irini church in Aiolou-Street in the Centre of Athens. After the end of the war he remained in Greece and prepared for his ordination, which took place in 1946.

A few months later he received a scholarship from the World Council of Churches to study theology at the University of Boston, where he arrived in the autumn of 1946. Besides theology he attended classes in religious sociology. In 1948 the higher Cypriot clergy managed to have him elected bishop of Kition in absentia. Makarios gave up his studies and returned to Cyprus in 1948 to assume his new office. Quickly he was elected head of the four person ethnarchic bureau, which had the task of coordinating the struggle for enosis. After the death of Makarios II, he was elected archbishop at the age of 37, after a four month backstage fight. In his enthroning speech he promised the people to work without rest for union with Greece.

Makarios rejected Communism, as most Greek clergymen did, but he was no militant anti-communist, which was astonishing because he had watched the communist excesses in Athens towards the end of the 1944 December events (Dekemvriana). He understood that enosis could only be achieved if both political camps in Cyprus cooperated to realize this aim. Moreover, it was clear to him that via AKEL he could obtain support from the Eastern block. Later he was even ready to cooperate directly with AKEL. The Greek Left's resistance against the Axis occupants served as a kind of model for his own future armed struggle.

In September 1949 Makarios visited Athens. He learned that, on the one hand, the Greek Government was not ready to challenge its good relations with Britain and, on the other, that the Greek public had not the slightest idea about the problems of Cyprus. Therefore, it was necessary to organize a big public relations campaign so that the public would put pressure on the Government. The same was true on an international plane, i.e. without broad international backing, especially in the UN, union with Greece could never be achieved.

During his stay in Athens Makarios met the retired officer Georgios Grivas, whom he had met once in 1946. Grivas was born on 23 May 1898 in Nicosia, but grew up in the village of Trikomo, where his father was a corn dealer and money lender. From 1909 on he attended the Pancyprian Gymnasion in Nicosia. When World War I broke out he wanted to become a soldier and successfully applied for acceptance to the Athens military academy. He participated in the Asia Minor campaign as lieutenant. After training at the École Superieure de Guerre in Paris, he became captain in 1926 but promotion to major came as late as 1938. Grivas despised the unstable Greek republic and appreciated it when General Ioannis Metaxas set up a fascist dictatorship together with King George II on 4 August 1936. In the Greek-Italian war in the winter of 1940/41Grivas was a member of the staff of the 2nd Division. After the surrender to the Wehrmacht on 20, or rather 23 April 1941 Grivas returned to Athens.

Because Grivas was a fanatic anti-communist and an equally fanatic royalist, participation in one of the big republican resistance movements was excluded. It is not surprising, however, that he did not join one of those right wing groups but founded his own group which he called X (Chi); he wanted to be in command. X was an anti-communist combat unit whose aim was to save the fatherland from Communism. In order to achieve this Grivas did not even hesitate to cooperate with the German occupants and have his groups armed by them. But for the British, too, this right wing combat group was a potential ally in their fight against the left resistance and thus they, too, supplied arms to Chi. When the Wehrmacht withdrew from Greece, Chi counted about 250 men. During the December events (Dekemvriana), Grivas and Chi fought at the side of the British against the Left.

The peace treaty of Varkiza, which ended the Dekemvriana, envisaged democratic conditions in Greece, but the opposite happened. A counter-revolutionary wave hit Greece which reversed the existing balance of power. Towards the end of 1945 the Greek Right was in power and the Greek Left in jail or was hunted down. Grivas contributed substantially to this process. In the following months Chi spread throughout the country and in 1946 Grivas could announce proudly that his organization had 200,000 members. Chi penetrated the state, especially the security organs on all levels, even the General Staff. Slowly a state within the state came into being which became increasingly influential. This power structure the Greeks call *parakratos*.

This *parakratos* terrorized different minded people and political murders were on the daily agenda. Chi became one of the factors contributing to the outbreak of the Greek Civil War. Only with great difficulties did the liberal Prime Minister Sofoulis manage to cut down the might of Chi, but the structures of the *parakratos* survived until the 1960s. After the end of the Civil War Grivas tried to build a political career but he failed because of the Greek clientelistic system: Grivas could offer no rousfetia. Slowly he became embittered, worked on a theory of guerilla warfare and waited for a new chance, which was offered to him by Makarios a little later.

The beginning of the Korean War enhanced the British decision to keep Cyprus and in this they were supported by the Americans. The new Greek Prime Minister, however, stressed that Greece was striving for enosis. Makarios was delighted about this and when he visited Athens in March 1951 he demanded that Venizelos bring the Cyprus problem to the UN. Venizelos, however, rejected this because of the general political situation. The Greek press had reported Makarios' presence in Athens and students for whom the 37-year-old Makarios was an identification figure organized a demonstration in Syntagma Square. Makarios addressed them from a balcony of the hotel Grand Bretagne and demanded - for the first time in public - that the Greek Government should bring the Cyprus problem to the UN. Venizelos, who was present, reacted reservedly.

When the British reacted angrily, Venizelos submitted a proposal which was supported by all leading Greek politicians: If Britain were ready to cede Cyprus to Greece Athens would be prepared to accept British bases not only in Cyprus but in Greece proper as well, which might even have extraterritorial status. Should the British Government not be able to act accordingly at this moment, a promise that the Cyprus question would be solved within a certain period of time on the basis of self-determination, would suffice. Both suggestions were reasonable and advantageous for the British and implicitly excluded an appeal to the UN. Had London accepted this proposal the future of Cyprus would certainly have been peaceful but London reacted arrogantly, rejecting: Athens should see to it that the agitation for enosis stopped. The Americans admonished more reserve.

Parallel to these political talks Makarios had contact with a group of Cypriots living in Athens around the brothers Savvas and Sokratis, who were planning to set up an underground revolutionary organization and start an armed upheaval. Grivas was to take over the lead because he had experience in underground work. Makarios agreed and therefore Grivas travelled to Cyprus in July 1951 to reconnoitre the situation. In August Makarios and Grivas met in Nicosia. Grivas suggested a double strategy: small partisan units should operate in the Troodos mountains and saboteurs should assault military targets. Makarios did not rate the success of the first highly and believed that acts of sabotage would make the British give in. However, no decisions were taken.

Even in 1950 the Turkish Government had announced its conviction that there was no Cyprus question. However, the student demonstrations in Athens triggered similar ones in Turkey and when the Turkish press joined in, the government felt that it should take a stand. In April 1951 the Turkish foreign minister declared that Turkey had a say in the Cyprus affair because of geographical vicinity, historical connections and the Turkish minority. Should the status of Cyprus change, this could not be done without Turkish participation, but the Turkish government attached great importance to its good relations with Athens.

In Cyprus the agitation for enosis died down in the second half of the year. In Greece, however, there was total political instability. The coalitions came and went almost in a weekly rhythm. In order to secure anticommunist stability, US ambassador Peurifoy intervened and took care that the former marshal of Greece, Alexandros Papagos, became chief of the right wing. Though Papagos' party became the strongest in the elections of 9 September 1951 he was not ready to enter a coalition with Venizelos' liberals, so the political instability continued.

In Britain there were also elections. The new Prime Minister became, once again, Winston Churchill, who was 77, and colonial Secretary Oliver Lyttleton and Foreign Secretary Anthony Eden. This Tory Government steered a rather tough course on the Cyprus question. When the Greek Government, in order to quieten the nervous public, made a statement in the UN about Cyprus, the British began to put pressure on Athens. Eden used a NATO meeting in Rome in November 1951 to tell his Greek colleague, Evangelos Averof that the British Empire was not for sale. A Cyprus question did not exist.

Eden's well staged outburst signalled two things: first, from now on London spoke with one voice because the Foreign Office had taken over the lead. Second, Eden did not even think of giving a millimetre on the Cyprus question. The Greek Government had behaved improperly and had been scolded accordingly and now knew what London's course was. Of course, he knew that his message would be passed on to Makarios and he hoped that his hard line would induce the Archbishop to steer a more moderate course.

Thus in 1951 those personnel changes had taken place which were to shape developments in Cyprus for the years to come: Makarios, who aimed at enosis determinedly but was flexible in the choice of his ways and means; Grivas, who only knew the road of violence and Eden, who insisted totally inflexibly that Cyprus had to remain British. The Greek Government played a role but it was slowly losing its control over the development. The Americans on the other side wanted to prevent the emergence of another trouble spot. As neither side was ready to compromise a slow process of escalation toward the armed conflict began.

The search for the right course

In 1952 two developments began: on the one hand the armed struggle was prepared and on the other hand an attempt was made to bring the Cyprus question to the UN. Already in 1951 Grivas had stressed the importance of a militant youth organization and Makarios had reacted by founding the PEON (Pankypria Ethniki Organosi Neoleas - Pancypriot National Organization of the Youth) which appealed to the urban youth. The rural youth were organized in the youth organisation of the farmers union PEK and there was still the Christian youth.

The leaders of PEON applied the well known recipes of youth organization of totalitarian states, Fascist or Communist: there was an admission ceremony with oath and mystic rituals. Obviously the leaders appealed to youthful romanticism and idealism and put over to the youths the feeling that they had a right to have a say and to act, which was very attractive for young people in the gerontocratic society of Cyprus. The teachers supported these efforts because they, too, advocated union with Greece. In the history lessons they taught the pupils a rather condensed version of Greek history whose focal point was the glorious antiquity and the eternal Greece. The priests filled the young souls with similar teachings. The parents accepted this indoctrination approvingly. The future fighters of the liberation movement EOKA were recruited from these youth organizations.

In spring 1952 Makarios visited Lebanon, Syria and Egypt to gain the support of these states in the UN. In June he appeared in Athens in order to induce the Greek Government to bring the Cyprus problem to the UN. When Foreign Minister Venizelos rejected this Makarios threatened to make this refusal public. Venizelos countered that he would not allow Makarios to control Greece's foreign policy. When Averof reminded Makarios that the Greeks of Istanbul would probably pay the bill, Makarios replied that these were doomed anyway. In an interview with the state radio Makarios attacked the Greek leadership frontally and called them impostors.

This interview set a new benchmark: Makarios had dared to strike such a note and had spoken in the name of the nation, presenting himself as the incarnation of the will of the people. This interview was a challenge to the political leaders of Greece and signalled a quicker pace to the British. Generally speaking, Makarios had succeeded in imposing his claim for leadership on the Cyprus question on the Greek side.

Besides these talks in public Makarios had confidential talks with the committee which was preparing the armed struggle. They informed Makarios about the state of their preparations but no decision was taken. Later Grivas came again to Cyprus where he stayed until February 1953. During these months he visited PEON and gained the impression that there would be enough recruits for his liberation troops. At the same time he realized that the rules of international law concerning partisan warfare could not be complied with and thus the death penalty threatened his future fighters when caught. Parallel to this Grivas began to build up the logistic infra-structure with the help of a functionary of the peasant organization (Azinas).

From October 1952 to February 1953 Makarios was in New York. This visit was not very successful because he did not manage to meet the UN grandees. His contacts in Washington were on a similar level, also. Makarios recognized that progress in the UN was only possible if the Cyprus question was put on the agenda of the UN by a member government of that body.

In October 1952 the Greek government changed. In March 1952 Ambassador Peurifoy had pressed Prime Minister Plastiras to make a law providing the application of the majority voting system in the next election. Now, under a pretext, the Greek parliament was dissolved and Papagos gained 49 percent of the votes but 82 percent of the seats. From then on until the early 1960s the Greek right dominated the country. On the Cyprus question, however, Papagos tried to continue the course of the previous governments.

The already good relations between Athens and Ankara seemed to become even better in 1952. Both countries entered NATO in February and in April the Turkish Prime Minister Menderes and his foreign minister visited Athens. In June the return visit of the Greek royal couple took place. Even the Turkish press restrained itself. As in Greece the control of their kin in Cyprus slowly slipped out of Ankara's hands.

In Cyprus the Turkish Cypriots had watched the rapprochement of the mother countries mistrustfully. As early as 1950 the first voices were heard asking for the union of Cyprus with Turkey, but the great majority still advocated the status quo and the Turkish Government reacted very reservedly. During the Greek-Turkish honeymoon in 1952 even the querulous Turkish press refrained and only mildly reminded the Greek side that the friendly relations could be marred by encouraging the enosis movement. It would be better to let the Cyprus question rest. But now the weight shifted towards those asking for union with Turkey. This change was caused by alterations of British policy during those years: When the British began to withdraw from their positions in the Near East the Turkish Cypriots began to have second thoughts as to whether the British would not give up Cyprus, too. Seen in this context, union with Turkey seemed to be the only way to avoid enosis which was no promising perspective for the Turkish Cypriots. There only remained the question of whether the leadership of the Turkish Cypriots could enforce this course on Ankara and when. The triggering element was clear: the appeal to the UN. In the eyes of the Turkish Cypriots this was the beginning of the end of the British domination. Thus a fatal automatism came into being: if Athens yielded to Makarios' pressure and brought the Cyprus problem to the UN the good relations with Ankara would be ruined and the Turkish-Cypriots enabled to force their political demands on Ankara.

The first Greek British clash

In January 1953 the Prime Minister said to the British ambassador in Athens that he could not go on with his non-committal course on the Cyprus question indefinitely and thus the friendship between Greece and Britain would be endangered. In order to avoid this Britain should give Cyprus a liberal constitution and promise the population a plebiscite in two or three years by which they could realize their right to self-determination. In return for this Greece would offer Britain bases in Cyprus, Crete and on the mainland. Papagos wanted a legally binding agreement by which the Cyprus problem would disappear within a reasonable period of time.

Since London's reply was not as brusque as before, it was decided to raise the issue with Eden during his visit to Athens in April. But Eden became seriously ill and thus the planned meeting took place as late as 22 September 1953. When Papagos touched on Cyprus Eden let him finish his statement but his answer was extremely offensive. Papagos left, deeply hurt, saying that from now on the Greek Government would act according to its wishes.

Much has been speculated about Eden's behaviour. The fact is that Eden had deliberately misbehaved. Striking such a note towards the 70-year-old Prime Minister of Greece was simply improper and at the same time revealing. It was a typical example of imperial arrogance towards the chief of a client state who was to be rebuked. The often heard excuse that Eden's outburst was caused by his bad health and his habit of throwing tantrums is not convincing. Eden knew quite well what he was doing and this is proven by his later behaviour.

Unfortunately, the content of their conversation found its way into the Greek and Cypriot press, forcing the government to act. On 15 October the Greek foreign ministry sent a formal note with three proposals to the British embassy in Athens: The British should repeal all illiberal laws promulgated after 1931. A liberal constitution should be issued immediately and in two years a plebiscite was to be held under international supervision. If this was not granted the Greek Government reserved its right to a free hand.

From mid-November 1953 the Greek Government slowly got accustomed to the idea of bringing the Cyprus problem to the UN. At the end of November the Greek foreign ministry let it be known that from now on Papagos was in charge of the Cyprus question. He was still in favour of a solution resulting from bilateral negotiations, but he would look for another solution if the British did not accommodate. Again Eden rejected this proposal arrogantly, and Papagos reacted in January 1954 saying that Greece would bring the case of Cyprus before the UN.

After his return to Athens in February 1953, Grivas began working out plans for the rebellion. Typically for a staff officer without any experience in partisan warfare he tried to cover all eventualities in his plans. He wanted to lead a war of attrition against the British, wearing them down to the point where they would surrender. Grivas understood that due to the morphology of Cyprus a large scale guerilla war was excluded and that the main emphasis had to be on sabotage. The attacks of the partisans would have an auxiliary character diverting the forces of the adversary. Cypriots working for the British would be neutralized and heavily punished. Greek propaganda efforts would assist this struggle. He worked on instructions for hit-and-run attacks, the creation of hiding places, the organization of passive resistance, protest demonstrations and the printing and distributing of leaflets. Special groups should exterminate persons who might endanger the struggle.

In March 1953 Makarios was informed on the state of the preparation but reserved the last word for himself. Grivas agreed. The Greek Government ordered Grivas to keep quiet; diplomacy still had priority. The official relations between Athens and Ankara were still very friendly but in the Turkish press opinions were voiced saying that if something changed in the status of Cyprus it ought to be given back to Turkey. It slowly became clear that the friendly bilateral relations were influenced by British policy in Cyprus; if Britain applied a divide and rule policy towards the mother countries, catastrophe was certain.

The appeal to the UN
In 1954 the strategic importance of Cyprus in the eyes of the British was increased by several factors. In the past years the British position in Iran had been lost after the Anglo-Iranian Oil Company (later BP) had been nationalized. In March 1954 Nasser came to power by a coup and terminated the agreements with the British, forcing them to evacuate the Suez Canal zone. In 1953 Yugoslavia, Greece and Turkey had concluded the Balkan Pact and negotiations began with Iraq and Jordan which in 1955 ended in the Bagdad Pact, which became the CENTO Pact when Pakistan joined in. All these necessitated a strong military presence of the British resulting in the conclusion that the regional headquarters had to be set up on British soil and the only English property was Cyprus.

As London understood that the Greeks would be pressed by the Cypriots to bring the Cyprus Problem to the UN sooner or later, a double defence line was built up. On the one hand the British tried to quieten the Cypriots by offering them a greater say in their affairs. Accordingly the new Colonial Secretary, Henry Hopkinson, stated in Parliament in early February 1954 that the constitutional offer of 1946 was still in force. On the other hand, London tried to forestall a debate in the UN by cooperating with the Americans and the Turks. In mid-March Eden said in the House of Commons that Britain was not ready to discuss the status of Cyprus. This infuriated Papagos who stated publicly that if the British Government continued to reject bilateral negotiations he would bring Cyprus to the UN.

London did not worry much about the Greek threats and continued to give Papagos the cold shoulder. In early May Papagos issued a kind of ultimatum: If London had not begun negotiations by 22 August the Cyprus case would be brought to the UN. Again the British Government rejected discussion about the status of Cyprus. At the end of June 1954 London corroborated its position: the British Government was ready to concede to the Cypriots the right of self-government but not self-determination. On 26 July 1954 the British Cabinet stated more precisely: Cyprus had to remain British; the constitutional proposal of 1946 would be replaced by another one with less self-administration and the 1931 Sedition Law would be reinstated. One day later the inexperienced new Colonial Secretary let himself be provoked by questions in the House and made the following fatal statement. *"It has always been understood and agreed that there are certain territories in the Commonwealth which [...] can never expect to be fully independent."* When his predecessor added that a cession of Cyprus to Greece would undermine the south-eastern flank of NATO and would lead to a massive lowering of the standard of living in Cyprus, this statement was considered worse than that of Hopkinson.

Both statements were no slips of the tongue but they signalled a tougher course. Hopkinson's statement was broadcast in Cyprus by the state radio and at the same time the promulgation of the new constitution was announced. If one compares the 1954 constitution with that of 1882 one comes to the conclusion that the latter had been an example of liberalism: in the Legislative Council provided for by the new constitution the ex-officio members and those appointed by the government had the absolute majority. The Governor put the Sedition Law in force again and introduced an absolute censorship of the press. But this did not hinder Makarios from preaching against the dictatorial methods and demanding enosis. When the British press criticised these methods the Governor backpedalled a bit. On 22 August an enormous crowd assembled at the Faneromeni-Church in the centre of Nicosia. Makarios attacked the British measures vehemently and ended his sermon asking those present to swear a holy oath to fight with him for the national aim and not to submit to force, the aim being "enosis and nothing but enosis."

Under normal circumstances the British would have been obliged to arrest Makarios at once because he had violated the Sedition Law but they wanted no martyrs for the enosis movement. They did not understand that by their inactivity they became paper tigers in the eyes of the Cypriots. Makarios had won his first victory over the colonial power.

As early as 20 August 1954 the Greek Government had filed the motion in the UN which stated that the principle of self-determination should be applied in the case of the population of Cyprus as well. Self-determination, of course, meant enosis. In the following weeks the British, in a great diplomatic effort behind the scenes, tried to hinder the Greek demand from coming on the agenda, at the same time trying to force the Americans to join their course. But on 23 September a majority of the General Committee agreed to put the Greek motion on the agenda. Now the British tried, again in vain, to make the General Assembly postpone the voting on the motion. Now London returned to manoeuvres behind the scenes, trying to find a majority for a postponement of the discussion. In mid-December the British managed to win the necessary majority.

But this was a kind of Pyrrhic victory: the British won a temporary victory over the Greeks but it was clear that the Cyprus Problem would come back on the agenda of the UN and as they themselves had blocked a compromise solution by enforcing an illiberal constitution they strengthened those forces aiming at a solution by force. The British blockade in the UN had another negative consequence because Turkey entered the discussion: *"Cyprus historically, economically, ethnically and geographically was a continuation of the Anatolian Peninsula. [...] The so-called Cyprus Issue was entirely artificial and was kept alive by widespread propaganda."* The demand for self-determination meant annexation, which violated the Treaty of Lausanne and here Turkey had a say, as well. The British were delighted about this "strong stuff".

The Greek side was deeply disappointed because it had naively believed that the problem would be solved in the UN, but another attempt would be made. As the Americans had supported the British in the UN there were violent anti-American demonstrations and riots all over Greece organized by students. In Cyprus, too, there were demonstrations but only when the pupils of the Pancyprian Gymnasium marched to the American Consulate did clashes with the police occur. These student demonstrations were rather difficult for the police to cope with because in the first row young girls were marching. Nationalists of both communities provoked the first inter-communal clashes. At the end of 1954 the governments in Athens and Ankara slowly lost control over the conflict; they were pushed forward by the agitated public in both countries who were incited by the chauvinist agitators. This mechanism produced a feedback and thus tensions escalated.

In March 1954 Grivas succeeded in bringing through a first weapon transport to Cyprus, another one followed in October. On 9 November Grivas went ashore at the village of Chlorakas, north of Paphos, and went to Nicosia. In the following weeks he recruited the first 19 saboteurs who all came from the ranks of OXEN and the other right wing youth organizations and the youth of SEK. He deliberately selected youths because they were prepared to risk their lives and defied death, i.e. Grivas misused their enthusiasm, idealism and naive credulity. Their leaders were only a few years older, following the principle that youth leads youth.

Target practice was excluded because the authorities would have learned about it. Grivas decided that the future fighters would learn this when attacking the British. The youths were divided into small groups which were ordered to prepare plans for the first sabotage actions. Until the end of the year Grivas was waiting for Makarios' order to begin the struggle, but this order did not come.

Count Down to Rebellion

The preparations of the armed struggle were rather slow; weapons, ammunition and explosives were missing. The previously mentioned functionary of the farmers association, Andreas Azinas, managed to buy the necessary items with money given to him by Makarios. At the same time he built up a secret channel of communication between Athens and Nicosia. After his return from Athens in January 1955 Makarios met Grivas and Azinas. Makarios informed them that Papagos, too, was for the armed struggle and suggested they begin on 25 March, the Greek National Holiday. Azinas was afraid that the British might learn about their plans and suggested an earlier date. Makarios, however, left the decision to Grivas.

On 13 January 1955 Azinas learned from Athens that the kaiki Ag. Georgios was on its way to Cyprus transporting the weapons and the explosives he had bought. The load was to be put ashore at Chlorakas. Azinas informed Makarios but was warned by him that the British were aware of the trip. Indeed Makarios had informants in the colonial administration and the police. One of them had told Makarios at the end of 1954 that the British were well informed about the preparations of the rising, and British agents in Athens had learned at the beginning of January that soon a boat full of weapons would sail to Cyprus. Obviously they had heard the rumours circulating in Athens, which was not astonishing because many persons were involved and few things remain secret in Athens. Ag. Georgios became a victim of talkativeness and not of a sinister conspiracy, as is still claimed today.

While Azinas was in vain trying to stop the Ag. Georgios, the British navy and air force observed its course. When the crew brought the cargo on land the police were waiting for them and the "reception committee" and arrested them all. Captured documents betrayed Azinas, who escaped to Greece and continued his studies. On 31 January 1955 Makarios and Grivas met at the Nicosia branch of the Kykko monastery (metochi Kykkou). Makarios criticized the lack of secrecy and forbade all partisan actions for the time being. The sabotage teams should be very careful not to hurt any human being and such actions should begin after the trial of the Ag. Georgios case.

The trial began on 17 March but after a few days the court decided to transfer the case to the Court of Assizes. This court dealt with the case in early May 1955 and passed relatively light sentences despite the fact that in the meantime the EOKA struggle had begun. Obviously the British side wanted to induce the Athens Government to practise greater restraint and the Cypriots to abstain from further escalating the violence.

Governor Armitage had followed developments closely and recognized what was brewing. In his eyes the crux of the Cyprus Problem was the close relationship between the Greek Government and Makarios. If one succeeded in driving a wedge between them the danger of an upheaval would be reduced considerably. In order to achieve this one should grant the Cypriots self-administration based on a liberal constitution and seek the consent of Athens. Colonial Secretary Lennox-Boyd considered this proposal so good that he submitted it to the Cabinet. In mid-February he spoke to Eden about it but the latter rejected it radically. For Eden this proposal was a kind of appeasement policy leading to a weakening of the British position in the Near East. Additionally Eden wanted to succeed Churchill as Prime Minister and believed that, therefore, he should show no weakness.

Lennox-Boyd, however, did not give up and told Armitage to get in contact with Makarios. Via intermediaries Armitage contacted Makarios who in turn was interested in a peaceful solution. A secret meeting was agreed upon in the Metochi Kykkou for the end of February 1955. Armitage understood that he needed London's permission for this rendezvous. Therefore he briefed Lennox-Boyd who in turn informed Eden. The Foreign Secretary reacted absolutely negatively: it was inconceivable that the Governor would go to Makarios' territory like a petitioner with his cap in his hands and beg him for help.

In mid-March a second effort failed and when Armitage suggested that one should stop the extremists via Papagos, Eden exploded and asked Armitage to report personally in London. At a meeting of ministers and high ranking civil servants Armitage was demolished. On 23 March 1955 he returned to Cyprus and noticed that the revolt was about to begin. In desperation he tried to save the situation, suggesting that the Government make a statement in the House of Commons about Cyprus. But the Foreign Office rejected this definitively. Thus a doomed fate took its course.

In the meantime Grigoris Afxentiou, a student and reserve lieutenant of the Greek army had joined Grivas. He knew where to find explosives, buy weapons on the black market and how to construct bombs. The organization of EOKA progressed but not fully, according to Grivas' ideas who was very often infuriated by the lack of discipline. The basic structure was the cell system completely centred on him. Communication went by couriers and the district leaders had to submit written reports on a weekly basis in which they informed Grivas about their past actions and future plans. At the same time Grivas ordered Polykarpos Georkatzis, a former clerk of the board of trade, to create a kind of intelligence organization. At another meeting of Makarios and Grivas on 7 March they agreed that the revolt should start after the 25th of March when British vigilance was declining. First targets were the Nicosia radio station, and the British Headquarters in the Wolseley barracks. In other towns public buildings should be attacked..

On 21 March the preparations were finished. Grivas wrote a revolutionary proclamation in which after an appeal to God, he likened the coming struggle to fighting at Marathon, Salamis, Thermopylae and those battles of 1821. He signed the proclamation as Dighenis, his nom de guerre from now on. On 30 March at the final meeting with his district commanders he read the text aloud; all were moved by the pathos of the text and even its author was moved to tears. He embraced each of them and wished them good luck. With a view to his future memoirs, Grivas put his diary and some other documents in two glass jars with a screw cap and gave them to a confidante who buried them in his garden.

1955: THE BEGINNING OF THE REBELLION

The first phase of the armed struggle April - August 1955
The first EOKA strikes took place in the night of 1 April 1955. With the exception of the destruction of the radio station by Markos Drakos, all other attacks were not very successful. As the young saboteurs had no experience the actions were amateurish. At the end of April Makarios ordered Grivas to interrupt all actions for political reasons. Grivas used the pause to organize the gymnasium students. He ordered the establishment of EOKA youth groups under the name of ANE (Alkimos Neolaia EOKA - Fighting Youth of EOKA) in all secondary schools. Its tasks were to demonstrate, distribute leaflets, write slogans in blue colour on walls, serve as couriers and spies, throw incendiary bombs and supervise British agents. Whoever proved himself successful was accepted by EOKA. When the director of the Pancypriot Gymnasion protested against this kind of youth work Grivas threatened him; Makarios, however, did not object.

At the end of May Grivas suggested an escalation of the struggle methods. So far force had only been applied against inanimate objects. Now Grivas wanted to extend it against persons as well in the form of hit-and-run operations. In early June Makarios agreed and in mid-June the first attacks against premises frequented by British soldiers and on police stations began, but there were no deaths because the assailants hesitated to kill people. In order to overcome this Grivas called the policemen traitors who could be killed without scruples. After that there was an attack on the police headquarters of Nicosia with a time fused bomb where people were killed, but many EOKA fighters still hesitated to kill in cold blood. Therefore, Grivas ordered Georkatzis to set up special indoctrinated execution squads to liquidate traitors. At the same time Grivas managed to recruit informers in the police but he could not hinder the British from doing the same in the ranks of EOKA.

The Cypriot Left had watched the developments suspiciously. AKEL's leadership, too, wanted enosis but only in theory because its realization would have led to an immediate ban on the party. For AKEL union with Greece would only have been acceptable if democracy had ruled in Greece and no ban threatened. But since this was far away in Greece AKEL preferred the maintenance of the status quo. This, however, could not be said publicly because it would have alienated the Cypriots so the party continued to pay lip service to enosis.

On the other side of the political spectrum EOKA-circles let it be understood that they did not want AKEL to participate in the struggle for enosis. Participation, on the other hand, would have meant giving up AKEL's traditional cooperation with the Turkish Cypriots, to subordinate itself to the ethnarchy if not actually Grivas himself; which, of course, was excluded because of the latter's anticommunist past and present leanings. The founding of a competitive organization was excluded as well since this would have led to rivalries and clashes between the two political camps. Additionally, the communists rejected the individual anarchic terror and considered partisan warfare impossible on an island. They continued to believe in mass struggles.

In view of this situation the party opted for a course of neutrality. This, however, exposed AKEL to the accusation of treason to the national cause which can be heard to this day. Later AKEL practised self-criticism and admitted that it had made a mistake but in reality there was no reasonable alternative. The party was confronted with a classic dilemma: Each decision was wrong as it led to negative consequences for the party. When the chief of the Greek CP, Zachariadis, disclosed the identity of Dighenis in a radio transmission from Roumania the relations between Grivas and AKEL were thoroughly poisoned. A few young hotheads like Vasos Lyssaridis, later chief of the Socialists, left the party and joined EOKA.

During those weeks important developments took place outside Cyprus which had their impact on the island. In London, Eden succeeded Churchill as Prime Minister and Harold Macmillan became Foreign Secretary. In April England joined the Bagdad Pact and at the end of the month the Bandung Conference met. In early May the Chief of the Empire General Staff, Field Marshall John Harding, stated that Cyprus as a whole was necessary for the military. The Tories were the victors of the parliamentary elections on 26 May 1955. In early May the Federal Republic of Germany was accepted into NATO and a few days later the Warsaw Pact came into being. All this needed Eden's attention and he therefore left the Cyprus Problem to Macmillan and Lennox-Boyd.

The assaults in Cyprus and the certainty that the Greeks would bring the Cyprus Question to the UN again induced the Foreign and Colonial office to search for a solution. When they exchanged their opinions it became clear that the Colonial Office intended to grant Home Rule to Cyprus by enacting a liberal constitution and including self-determination as a long-term perspective. The Foreign Office preferred influencing Athens and Ankara. Finally, the two ministers agreed to call together a tripartite conference including Britain, Greece and Turkey which would work out a solution on the basis of these joint proposals of the two ministries. In addition to the concept of the Colonial Office the Foreign Office suggested integrating the two mother countries by creating a kind of condominium. This solution would hinder the Greeks from bringing the Cyprus Problem to the UN. It is obvious that here Greek ambitions were to be neutralized by Turkish ones; it was a classic case of divide-and-rule-policy this time applied to play off the mother countries against each other. Additionally, London planned to force the solution on the Cypriots.

Ankara readily accepted the invitation to this conference since it implied that Turkey would gain a say in Cyprus. The Greek Government immediately recognized that this manoeuvre would stop the approach to the UN and that it was a piece of divide-and-rule-policy. If one accepted the invitation one recognized the right of Turkey to have a say implicitly; if one rejected it one could be accused of being intransigent, the good relations with Turkey would be endangered and the Greek position in the UN weakened. In view of this dilemma Athens refused to participate. When Makarios heard about it he demanded that Athens immediately file an application to the UN to put the Cyprus Problem on the agenda.

At the beginning of July 1955 Lennox-Boyd travelled to Cyprus in order to create the impression to the world public that the Cypriots had a say in the future negotiations. He was the first Colonial Secretary ever to visit Cyprus. During their conversation on 9 July Makarios made it clear to the minister that he considered the conference a crooked approach leading to an impasse. When Governor Armitage wanted to know from Makarios whether he could imagine a solution to the conflict on the basis of a liberal constitution and the promise that the right to self-determination would be applied in the future, when the international situation permitted such a move, Makarios replied that such an offer could be discussed; he could imagine such a solution. This proposal corresponded with the earlier Greek proposals. But the Cabinet had committed Lennox-Boyd to the conference and thus another opportunity for a solution passed. When Lennox-Boyd did not react to Makarios' offer the Archbishop gained the impression that the British were steering an intransigent course.

On 11 July 1955 Lennox-Boyd returned to London, and Makarios flew to Athens. At a press conference in Athens Makarios said that without Cypriot participation no decision about Cyprus could be taken. The Cyprus Problem was a bilateral matter between London and Nicosia. A solution could only be found by bilateral negotiations and not by involving third parties. The right place to find a solution was the UN and not the tripartite conference. Greece should bring the Cyprus Problem to the UN before the conference. Makarios said the same to the Greek Government, which promised to do this on 20 August, i.e. two days before the deadline for application, in case the conference did not yield any satisfying result or had not begun at all.

In London the Cabinet fixed the beginning of the conference on 29 August and informed Ankara and Athens about this. Foreign Minister Stefanopoulos pointed out to Macmillan when they met in Paris that this late date forced the Greek Government to submit the Cyprus case to the UN. Macmillan replied that he considered this a great mistake which would affront the British people and their Parliament. Stefanopoulos asked Dulles for help but even the US Secretary of State could not prevail against the intransigent Macmillan. In the meantime Makarios once more spoke to the Athenian Press: he had not succeeded in his effort to make the Greek Government change course. The conference was a trap, a manoeuvre to stop the application to the UN and to make the whole affair so complicated that no solution could be found. The Cyprus Problem was not a problem between Britain, Greece and Turkey. The Cyprus Problem was a question of self-determination. He would not accept any result of the Tripartite Conference if it ignored this fundamental right even if Athens signed it.

When, due to these open words, the Athens public began to boil with rage the Greek Government retreated and announced that on 25 July it would submit a motion at the UNO to place the Cyprus Problem on the agenda. Nevertheless it signalled a readiness to compromise: should the Conference produce a constructive result it was ready to abandon the idea of a UN resolution. But London continued to turn a cold shoulder.

The Tripartite Conference 29 August - 7 September 1955

It was Macmillian's aim to play off the Greeks against the Turks in such a way that they would quarrel and block each other and Cyprus would remain British. There was no diplomatic preparation of the topics to be discussed at the conference. It was clear that the Cypriots would have no say. The conference was solely the concern of the Foreign Office, or rather Macmillan, and behind him was Eden. The Colonial Office played no role. Macmillan made the Cabinet take the decision that even mentioning the word self-determination was excluded. On 15 August he informed the Cabinet of his ideas: after his own opening statement Greece and Turkey were to present their cases and a committee was to be formed which would take note of the differing positions and fix them in writing. Then the conference would adjourn and only then would the British plan be presented. Should the conference fail before that it would be because of Greek-Turkish contradictions and not because of British intransigence. The Cabinet agreed. Thus the course was clear. Self-determination was no longer a topic.

The conference began on 29 August 1955 in Lancaster House. On 30 August Macmillan spoke, one day later Stefanopoulos and on 1 September the Turkish foreign minister, Zorlu. Macmillan's speech contained the well known British positions. Stefanopoulos declared that the right to self-determination could not be denied to the Cypriots forever. Should it be granted, however, Greece was ready to grant full minority protection to the Turkish Cypriots and give bases to the British. Zorlu demanded to retain the status quo. In case this was changed Cyprus had to be returned to Turkey. Eden was highly pleased by this statement. In the following days personal talks took place.

On 6 September 1955 two important things happened. In London Macmillan presented his constitutional plan stating agreement not to agree about the international status of Cyprus. He therefore proposed to adjourn the conference after the introduction of the constitution. The Cypriots could participate at that meeting. Stefanopoulos principally welcomed Macmillan's proposal but criticized the rather undemocratic way of presenting the new constitution and the withholding of the right to self-determination. Zorlu, on the other hand, wanted to know whether England did really accept the right to self-determination which Macmillan denied. On 6 September the first anti-Greek pogrom took place connected with the Cyprus problem which had been diligently planned beforehand by chauvinist forces and certain government circles around Zorlu and Menderes.

At the final meeting on 7 September Stefanopoulos regretted that the Greek views had not been considered. Nevertheless, he would submit the British proposals to the Greek Government. According to Zorlu Athens was responsible for the messy situation. Each change in Cyprus meant a revision of the Lausanne Treaty, a destabilisation of the balance and endangered good relations. Athens should withdraw the demand for self-determination. Where the Greek demands led to had been seen the day before in Istanbul, he added cynically. But Zorlu rejected the British proposal as well. Thus the Conference was at its end and Macmillan declared it interrupted. A little later a negative reply arrived from Athens.

The British side had successfully played off Ankara and Athens so that they mutually blocked each other on the Cyprus question. But the hope that this enabled Britain to keep up the status quo while laughing from the side-lines was deceptive because Turkey, as the pogrom in Istanbul had shown, followed a new course serving Turkish interests only. The British had succeeded in bringing the Turks into the game but from now on they could no longer control them. Moreover they did not understand that neither Athens nor Ankara was controlling its ethnic group. Eden's and Macmillan's policy made the Cyprus Conflict more complicated than it had been, because from now on it was linked to the minority problem. Whenever there were inter-communal conflicts in Cyprus the Greeks of Istanbul would pay the bill.

On 23 July 1955 Greece's representative at the UN had requested the Secretary General to put the right to self-determination on the agenda of the General Assembly. The Americans originally intended to keep out of the matter and even criticized the pogrom but following British pressure they changed their attitude. Secretary of State Dulles informed Stefanopoulos who reacted embittered. On 21 September the General Committee dealt with the Greek request. A slim majority accepted the Greek motion, but the General Assembly rejected it. The reason for the American behaviour can be found, on the one hand, in the special relationship with Great Britain and, on the other, in the strategic considerations of Washington within the containment policy: in Dulles' eyes Turkey was more important for the security of the free world than Greece, since Turkey was the link between NATO and the Bagdad Pact and thus he took a realpolitik decision. With this decision, however, the Americans lost their innocence on the Cyprus question.

In Athens the waves of indignation rose high. Under normal conditions Stefanopoulos should have succeeded Papagos when he died on 5 October 1955, but the King insisted on Konstantinos Karamanlis as new prime minister. The opposition spoke of a royal coup but on 12 October the Greek parliament confirmed Karamanlis in his new office overwhelmingly.

Escalation of violence and the Makarios-Harding talks

During Lennox-Boyd's visit to Cyprus the Chief of the Imperial General Staff Field Marshal had been there, too, in order to have himself briefed on the security situation and advise the Government. On his recommendation the number of policemen was increased and their equipment improved. Before the rebellion the police had counted 1,397 constables, of which 850 were Greek and 508 Turkish Cypriots and 29 British. Additionally, he proposed to build up a Special Branch. As there were not enough qualified policemen a Special Constabulary was set up consisting mainly of Civil Servants of the colonial administration who took over the guard service and patrol duty. Most of them were Turkish Cypriots. To this an Auxiliary Police Force was added which soon counted 1,000 men. The members of this unit received some short training and were responsible for routine police work. The majority of them were Turkish Cypriots, too.

In September 1955 a paramilitary unit, the Mobile Reserve, was established which, with the exception of the officers, consisted exclusively of Turkish Cypriots. The officers possessed experience in fighting guerillas from Palestine, Kenya and Malaya. The members of this unit received special training in breaking up urban riots. Some were trained in encircling and search operations. In 1956, 70 percent of the police force consisted of Turkish Cypriots, only 15 percent were Greek Cypriots. It was clear that this constellation would lead to conflicts. Old good neighbourly relations between the two ethnic groups were torn down and hatred began. The divide-and-rule policy of the British caused the first inter-communal clashes which led to the Cypriot civil war.

The new Special Branch consisted of loyal Cypriots of both communities who had excellent knowledge of persons and localities, which the normal policemen were lacking, and thus they operated very successfully. Constant traffic controls were a means to reduce the radius of activity of EOKA and to arrest wanted fighters. When in autumn, after the failure of the Tripartite Conference, EOKA increased its activities, Governor Armitage suggested deporting some clerics, he was thinking of the bishop of Kyrenia and not of Makarios, whom he believed to be harmless. Lennox-Boyd agreed that this was the right means at the appropriate time. Though Armitage was rather successful London began to think about replacing him.

The efficient work of the Special Branch caused Grivas to withdraw to mount Troodos and order attacks on the police. Georkatzis, at 23 years old, had formed his first killer team out of adolescents. This team tried several times, in vain, to kill Inspector Irodotos Poullis, a member of the Special Branch who was responsible for the supervision of the communists. On 18 August 1955 the team finally succeeded in tracing and shooting Poullis in the back, killing him. The killers fled, but one of them, Michalakis Karaolis, a government employee, was caught. Similar attacks were tried but did not succeed. When the Cypriot radio denounced these deeds as political terrorism, Grivas justified them by comparing them with attacks by partisans.

When on 17 September the "Battle of Britain" day was celebrated at the RAF base at the airport, a group of youngsters turned over an Army jeep on Metaxas Square (today Plateia Eleftherias), forced their way into the British Institute and set fire to the library. As the authorities did not react properly the library burned down completely. On 23 September imprisoned EOKA members managed to flee from Kyrenia castle, their jail. Some of them were caught again but P. Georkatzis and M. Drakos managed to go into hiding. This reminded Lennox-Boyd of Palestine and he decided to replace Armitage. He offered him the governorship of Nyasaland (today Malawi) and Armitage accepted grudgingly. He had been a good governor. If London had listened to his advice to promise the Cypriots self-determination in a few years there would have been a peaceful development. But Armitage had collided with the two grandees of British politics, Eden and Macmillan and had to pay for this. Macmillan's policy of making impossible universal application of the right to self-determination differed only semantically from Hopkinson's "never".

The new Governor was Field Marshal Harding, who was close to his retirement. Harding had made an exemplary military career and accepted the new office under the condition that he would always have direct admission to the Prime Minister and that he would do the job for two years only. Harding was instructed to keep Cyprus come what may. London gave him carte blanche for the methods applied but self-determination could be no option. In order to achieve this, Harding intended to introduce self-administration by releasing a liberal constitution, and to talk to Makarios. Harding did not understand at this moment that these two aims mutually excluded each other.

At their first meeting on 4 October, Harding informed Makarios about his ideas and asked him to cooperate in the preparation of the Constitution, so that soon a parliament could be elected which would be fully responsible for the internal affairs of Cyprus. Self-determination, however, had to be adjourned but could be discussed after the Constitution was launched. Makarios countered: London should recognize the Cypriots' right to self-determination as the basis of the solution to the problem. After that he would be ready to participate in the working out of the constitution. London and Nicosia should fix the date for the realization of self-determination in a conference. With this statement Makarios had shifted his ground but Harding said he had to consult London. Indeed both positions were closer than never before. Everything depended on London's answer but Eden and Macmillan remained stubborn: Harding was only authorized to talk about self-administration. London would fully support him, should it come to a breach. Thus Harding had no room for manoeuvring at all. The only option left was armed repression.

At their next meeting on 11 October, Makarios assured the British that he was totally unhappy about the situation and Harding replied that he felt the same way. It was obvious that the two would have found a solution if London had allowed them to. Probably in order to make Eden give way a bit Harding asked for permission to deport certain clerics. Without thinking about the consequences Eden agreed, determined the Seychelles as place of exile, and added that from now on a plane would be kept ready constantly. Nevertheless Eden made a small change of course stating that it was not the position of the British Government never to grant self-determination but not now. If the situation permitted one could talk with the Cypriots about it.

Karamanlis informed the British that he would accept each solution to which the Cypriots agreed. The Turkish Government, on the other side, did not agree with Eden's formula but accepted it as a fait accompli. In order to sweeten the bitter pill for the Cypriots London decided to carry through an economic development program of a considerable size in order to win over the population. Harding himself had three aims: First, he wanted to find a political solution by negotiating with Makarios. Second, he wanted to defeat Grivas and EOKA militarily and, third, he wanted to win over the population by a suitable economic development program.

On 15 November 1955 Harding gave Makarios the not-never-but-not-now-proposal in writing and announced the development program amounting to £ 38 million. Such a program had worked excellently in Kenya and Malaya against the communist guerillas, but it could not be applied in Cyprus because here the adversary was the bourgeois middle strata of society sympathizing with EOKA. Makarios remained sceptical because in his eyes it was the old program, only more nicely wrapped, only. Harding considered the program as serious. He could not imagine that the politicians would do that which Makarios was afraid of and that they would even abandon him if they considered it opportune. He did not understand the reason why Makarios rejected the offer and became embittered, after all, he had fought for its acceptance in London.

In Athens, on the one hand, the Government was appalled by Makarios' rejection but, on the other, it regarded the double negation formula unfortunate because it would not be understood, and said so to the British. Makarios, however, began to think in a different direction: perhaps complete independence was the right solution. During a lengthy exchange of opinions between Athens and London the Greeks tried to persuade the British to change the formula and decide on a precise date, but Eden rejected this, using Ankara as an excuse. Karamanlis was not happy about this answer but nevertheless he tried to persuade Makarios to be more flexible. Had he urged Makarios to accept the British formula, the latter might have moved, maintaining that he had given in to pressure from the National Centre. But without clear backing from Athens he did not risk a confrontation with his nationalist hotheads. Obviously, even at the end of 1955, there was still a chance for successful negotiations provided the British side moved away from their gridlocked positions.

Shortly after his arrival in Cyprus Harding had restructured the security forces. A central headquarters was set up in Nicosia coordinating the activities of the administration, the police and the military. Analogous institutions were created on the district level. Safeguarding of towns and communication channels had priority. In December 1955 Harding had more than three brigades, i.e. more than 12,000 men at his disposal, among them elite units. The Judiciary formed a Special Court exclusively in charge of EOKA cases, operating, however, on civil procedural law. On 26 November Harding proclaimed a state of emergency. On the basis of his new authority Harding could accelerate the legislative process by issuing laws in Cyprus without London's participation. In due course he released 76 emergency regulations. Among them was a law extending the death penalty to firing a gun at human persons, and the production and transport of weapons and explosives. In order to reduce juvenile rioting a whipping law was enacted which threatened the delinquents with birching. This law, however, was counterproduc-tive because the castigated youth was regarded as a hero and victim of the colonial authorities by his comrades. Additionally, it strained the inter-communal relations because the castigating policeman was in most cases a Turkish Cypriot.

The rights of habeas corpus were restricted: an arrested person could be kept in police custody for three weeks without seeing an examining magistrate. The freedom of assembly was reduced and political strikes were prohibited. The press was censored. The ringing of church bells was forbidden. There were collective penalties. All these measures were ineffective but people were angered and pushed towards EOKA. Another law prohibited the hoisting of Greek flags on school buildings. The pupils enjoyed hoisting a new flag each day, thus ridiculing the security forces removing them. On 28 October 1955, the second national holiday of Greece commemorating Mussolini's attack on Greece in 1940, demonstrators and security forces clashed and when precisely on this day Karaolis was sentenced to death the waves of indignation rose really high; There were demonstrations of pupils and heavy riots. Bombs and assassination attempts killed 11 soldiers in November and December.

In the Troodos mountains Grivas prepared partisan warfare. Imitating the Greek resistance during WWII, he let his fighters build a headquarters near Kakopetria at Spilia in the northern Troodos mountains from where he intended to direct the partisans' attacks on the British. As the British concentrated their efforts on the security in the towns Grivas' men could operate almost undisturbedly and attack single lorries on a secluded road.

Following the pupil demonstrations the secondary schools had been closed; this, however, was absolutely counterproductive, because the students could concentrate on the flag war, the demonstrations and the organization of further student groups. The flag war continued until autumn 1956. Teachers who had come from Greece were expelled from Cyprus. Grivas, on the other side, ordered the students to control the patriotism of their teachers, which they did with great pleasure, of course. From Athens the Greek radio added fuel to the flame and incited the pupils even more. Many of those tuition-less pupils were receiving lessons from EOKA in the art of bomb throwing and how to attempt assassinations. The murders committed in Famagusta were exclusively the work of secondary school students. On 4 December 1955 rioting pupils attacked the post office at Lefkonoiko and set fire to it. Some of them were arrested but most escaped. The village was collectively punished to pay for the reconstruction. There was talk of schoolboy terrorism.

In early December the British undertook a first cleansing operation against Grivas and his 30 partisans near Spilia. In the beginning the partisans tried to resist, but soon they were on the run. It became clear that partisan warfare was impossible in the Troodos mountains with its many forest roads. Troodos was not Pindos. Whenever the attacked fought back the attackers lost, as this example shows: On 15 December the group of Markos Drakos attacked an army jeep near ancient Vouni. The driver was mortally wounded but the other front seat passenger, major Brian Coombe, managed to steer the car into the roadside ditch, grasp his submachine gun and attack the partisans, wounding three of them. When he ran out of ammunition, he crept back to the jeep and fetched the driver's gun. Now the attackers tried to outwit the major, two of them pretending to surrender, but Coombe discovered the machine gun behind some rocks and shot one of the snipers. The other - Markos Drakos - escaped wounded. The two others did surrender. Coombe guarded his prisoners until help arrived. The killed partisan was a distant relative of Makarios, Charalambos Mouskos.

Though Charalambos was from Paphos, Harding allowed him to be buried in Nicosia provided not more than 50 persons participated in the funeral. But when his corpse was transported to Nicosia hundreds knelt at the roadside of the villages passed. Flowers were thrown on his coffin. Makarios himself held the memorial service in the Faneromeni church. The interment had the character of a hero's entombment with thousands participating. The local police officer misinterpreted this totally and dispersed the crowd with teargas. Harding's well meaning gesture had been turned into the opposite.

On 14 December 1955 Harding committed a capital mistake when he outlawed AKEL and had the leaders arrested. AKEL verbally was pro-enosis but really it was not interested in it. Objectively only Grivas benefited from this stroke because until then there had been a rule that where AKEL was strong EOKA was weak. The reason for Harding's mistake was a misinterpretation of Makarios' position. Harding believed that Makarios was under pressure from the right and the left. He believed that the Makarios relieved from left pressure would be able to face the pressure from the right. Harding did not understand that Makarios was the spiritual leader of the rebellion. The AKEL ban was counterproductive in all respects.

1956: VIOLENCE AND COUNTERVIOLENCE

Towards the political impasse, January - July 1956
During the NATO-Summit on 14 December1955 in Paris, Secretary of State Dulles and Macmillan had induced their Greek colleague, Theotokis, to influence Makarios to continue his talks with Harding, which was successfully done. Macmillan, on the other hand, had promised that the double negation in the solution formula would be removed. Thus on 9 January Harding and Makarios met secretly and Harding presented the new formula which differed only in verbal cosmetic from the not-never-but-not-now formula. Makarios rejected this and Harding promised to consult London. As Dulles, too, had piped up Eden made another cosmetic change. At their next meeting on 13 January Makarios criticized the new formula but remained ready to compromise. Harding, however, gained the impression that each time he submitted a new formula Makarios presented new demands. In view of this situation Harding considered it best to go to London for consultations.

His talk with Eden ended in a massive row. Eden wanted to keep the Cyprus Question open until decisions had been taken on the future Near East policy. Harding rejected this harshly and the Colonial Office, demanding the release of a liberal Constitution, supported him. When the Americans, who wanted an election victory of Karamanlis, put pressure on Eden, too, he agreed to other cosmetic changes in the formula but these should be linked with a written statement by Makarios stating that he accepted the formula and would do everything to end violence and disorder. After the end of violence one could talk about a constitution.

On 26 January 1956 Harding informed Makarios about the new formula and the statement expected from him. Makarios observed that the formula and constitution could not be separated and added some basic principles which had to be realized in the constitution. Harding wanted Makarios' answer by 1 February. Makarios understood that in this case he could not take a decision on his own. At a secret meeting Grivas considered the British proposal a trap but ordered a temporary cease fire. The Ethnarchic Council was vehemently against but other organizations left the decision to Makarios. On 2 February Makarios replied: He regarded the formula not satisfactory but agreed to it in order to bring peace to the island provided certain democratic principles regarding the sovereignty of the people would be accepted. Thus Makarios had shifted ground again and was ready to accept the formula provided the British committed themselves regarding the Constitution. Harding had the impression that Makarios wanted a solution.

In London, however, Eden was under strain from his own party. The Tories had crushingly lost a by-election. Voices were heard demanding the resignation of Eden, cutting him to the quick, because Eden did not have the thick skin politicians usually have. Additionally, his health was weak. When the Americans gave him to understand before his visit to Washington that they did not regard him as an equal partner Eden was reminded of the American behaviour during the conference of Yalta and decided to steer a tough course on the Cyprus Question.

In this situation the Labour backbencher Francis Noel-Baker offered his help. Noel-Baker was an expert on Greek politics and spoke Greek fluently. He knew Makarios and other Cypriot politicians personally from earlier visits to the island. After consulting his cabinet colleagues Eden agreed that Noel-Baker should act as go-between and told him so. In the beginning Harding reacted very reservedly and full of distrust but Makarios received Noel-Baker cordially.

In the following days Noel-Baker managed to smooth the waves and on 14 February Harding sent a letter to Makarios accepting almost all his constitutional proposals provided violence ended. He expected Makarios to call an end to violence and unrest the moment he announced the solution formula.

Thus Harding, too, had shifted ground but there remained two critical points: the responsibility for public security was to remain with the Governor and the formulation that there would be an elected majority in the future parliament was not unambiguous. It did not say anything about the size of the two ethnic groups and it might have resembled the pre-1931 situation when the representatives of the Turkish Cypriots always voted with the British. And there was Grivas demanding a full amnesty for all EOKA-fighters, including those in jail. During a conversation between Makarios' secretary Kranidiotis and the second-in-command of the colonial administration, Reddaway, it became obvious that the Cypriots regarded the constitutional proposals as binding and demanded an amnesty. Harding agreed with the first, but had scruples with the second.

Makarios gained the impression that the negotiations were stalling and rang up Noel-Baker, who had returned to London and asked him to come to Cyprus again. Noel-Baker agreed and obtained the approval of Eden and Lennox-Boyd. Eden even offered to fly to Cyprus as soon as Noel-Baker had negotiated an agreement. Unfortunately, Noel-Baker considered the presence of Lennox-Boyd enough. Thus he unwillingly discharged Eden of his obligation to stick to his present opinion. When Noel-Baker arrived in Nicosia he quickly understood that Makarios was searching for a solution. At the meeting on 24 February 1956 Makarios, Harding and Noel-Baker came very close to a solution by keeping certain demands in abeyance, giving the other side the chance to give in in a face saving way. According to the agreement with Eden and Lennox-Boyd he informed the Colonial Secretary, who prepared to fly to Cyprus. But on 25 February Makarios almost ruined the solution by tabling new demands not noticing that he had overplayed his hand.

In the meantime Eden had changed his opinion and instructed Lennox-Boyd to steer a tough course, thus narrowing his room for general manoeuvring considerably, but on the constitutional question totally. Makarios, on the other hand, insisted on proportional representation but trusted Harding's promise that nobody would be executed. Lennox-Boyd agreed and informed London. Eden, however, rejected proportional representation because the Turks would reject it. At their second meeting Lennox-Boyd went as far as the maximum of Eden's concession. Makarios, however, pushed his luck further and tried to squeeze some more concessions on the question of the amnesty. But Lennox-Boyd rejected this and thus an agreement was impossible.

Recalling Makarios' original position had been enosis-and-nothing-but-enosis, it becomes clear that he had shifted ground considerably during the talks with Harding. His mistake was his constant trying to reopen the sore and his inability to grasp when he had to stop. Eden, too, had given way a little bit by moving away from Hopkinson's "never" to "not-never-but-not-now", but from here on he became stubborn and allowed only cosmetic changes. The failing of the Makarios-Harding talks is again a station on the long track of missed opportunities of Cypriot history.

Thus Harding and the British had only one option left: the use of force. In order to avoid popular riots when arresting Makarios, they waited until 8 March 1956 when Makarios intended to fly to Athens for consultations with the Greek Government and waited for him at the airport. A group of soldiers escorted him to a waiting military plane. A little later other clerics were brought who had been arrested in Nicosia. The plane brought the deportees to the Seychelles, according to plan.

Reactions in Cyprus were restrained because of the presence of a huge number of security forces. In Greece, however, the waves of outrage rose high when the plane from Cyprus landed at Hellenikon without Makarios. For days student demonstrators and security forces collided. The Government recalled the Greek ambassador in London to report and announced that it would submit the Cyprus Question to the UN. Washington was displeased with the British action. In London, Parliament discussed the Cyprus question for five hours on 14 March 1956 during which the Opposition attacked the Government vigorously. Though Noel-Baker kept the secret of his mission his criticism was clear. In the House of Lords debate on 15 March, criticism was straightforward.

On 14 March the representative of Greece at NATO raised the Cyprus issue. Secretary General Lord Ismay did not exclude an arbitration by the Alliance, and Harding, too, considered this a good idea, but Eden was against it. He did not even think of changing his course. In the House of Commons he stated that new negotiations were excluded as long as violence continued in Cyprus. Harding, on the other hand, knew that the military option would not lead to a solution and therefore developed a plan of his own: Cypriot nationalism could not be placated by vague promises. The decisive question was how long Britain really needed Cyprus for strategic reasons. A way had to be found to bring about the change in sovereignty (i.e. enosis) acceptable to the three states involved. This could be achieved within NATO. There had to be an interim period of about ten years. If there was agreement on this a liberal constitution could be introduced. Thus Harding had arrived at exactly the same proposals which Armitage had suggested during Lennox-Boyd's visit in July 1955. They had been discussed, Makarios had accepted them but Lennox-Boyd had rejected them. Harding's plan was feasible but needed London's authorization.

Eden, who had a part of his parliamentary faction on his back, rejected the proposal on 17 April stating in the House of Commons that there would be no talks as long as violence ruled in Cyprus. Two days later Lennox-Boyd confirmed this but announced the dispatch of Lord Radcliffe as Constitutional Commissioner to Cyprus.

On 15 April 1956 the Privy Council rejected the appeal for clemency and thus only the Governor could prevent the execution of Karaolis, but Harding believed that clemency helped the terrorists and would demoralize the security forces. There were protests in Britain and the Greek Foreign Minister asked Dulles to intervene. But the Secretary of State knew that the British would stand firm and therefore did not intervene. The British stalled the execution until the end of the NATO Summit in Bonn in early May, but on 7 May 1956 Karaolis, who had killed a policeman, and another young man, Andreas Dimitriou, who had shot at an Englishman without hitting him, were hung in the Central Prison in Nicosia. In order to avoid occurrences like those at the funeral of Mouskos and to prevent their graves becoming a place of nationalist pilgrimage and worshipping they were buried in a separated inner court of the prison. This became common praxis with most killed EOKA fighters so that 13 of them found their last rest there. The Cypriots called these graves "fylakismena mnimata" (imprisoned graves). Today they are the destination of school excursions.

In Greece heavy riots took place on the eve of the executions. The police even used guns against the hooligans; thus there were 4 dead, 165 heavily and 100 lightly wounded. The opposition was outraged and G. Papandreou demanded the resignation of the Karamanlis Government. The British Government was not impressed by the protests in Greece and around the world. Nicosia remained rather calm due to the heavy presence of security forces: the Cypriots mourned in a quiet way. In Athens pressure on the Government continued and on 21 May a three day war of words began in the Greek parliament, at the end of which Karamanlis sacrificed Foreign Minister Theotokis, asking him to resign. He was succeeded by Evangelos Averof.

Karamanlis and Averof agreed that they should steer a tougher course on the Cyprus Question, at the same time watching possible consequences for the Greek minority in Istanbul. Makarios had to be brought back and the problem itself to the UN. Karamanlis agreed with

Averof's proposal to establish contact with Grivas, but left the realization to Averof. It became clear that from now on Averof would have the main say in the Greek policy towards Cyprus. His first measure was a change of personnel in the Greek consulate. The new Consul General became the experienced diplomat Angelos Vlachos, who had served in Istanbul and Ankara.

In London on 14 May 1956 Parliament debated Cyprus for the fifth time within 18 months. It was obvious that the Government did not know how to get out of the cul-de-sac into which it had manoeuvred itself by the deportation of Makarios. On 1 June Eden added fuel to the flames by stating in a speech at Norwich that oil transports from the Near East could not be protected properly without the possession of Cyprus. In Athens, Karamanlis commented sarcastically that: now one knew the real motives of the British. In Nicosia, however, Harding recognized the fact that a military victory was impossible if the British did not succeed in winning over the majority of the population. Therefore, he decided to go to London to push through his April proposals. At the same time the Ethnarchy signalled that it was ready for compromise.

From 1 June on, Harding tried his best to find supporters for his plan; he talked to Members of Parliament, high ranking soldiers, journalists, presenting his ideas. Even the Chiefs-of-Staff agreed. On 6 July Dulles made it known that the Cyprus Question was not a British problem but troubled the Western Alliance. Eden reacted nervously: Military successes had been achieved in Cyprus and more would follow. Indeed there had been inter-communal clashes, and the Turkish Cypriots rejected enosis radically. Another 250,000 of them lived in Turkey, influencing public opinion; where Eden took this number from remained his secret. Making more concessions might lead to war. Only the possession of Cyprus guaranteed the unhindered flow of oil from the Near East. When Eisenhower and Dulles discussed Eden's reply, the idea came up whether the two ethnic groups could be resettled. How far the British-Greek relations had deteriorated was shown by the fact that on 13 June 1956 Greece filed a motion at the UN to put the Cyprus Problem on the agenda of the General Assembly, reasoning that the British had made Cyprus a huge concentration camp and were leading a war against the Greek Cypriot population. London's only aim was the safeguarding of its oil interests.

Renewed American pressure led to a little change of British policy: Lord Radcliffe would be sent to Cyprus to prepare the constitution. The new constitution would provide a two-chamber system. The first chamber would be composed proportionally to the strength of the ethnic groups, the second would consist of an equal number of Greeks and Turks. In about ten years' time one could discuss a possible transfer of sovereignty in cooperation with NATO. Before, however, submitting this plan to the Americans, the Turks should be consulted. This was done on 18 June 1956 and the Turkish Ambassador rejected the idea of an interim period. Should the British ever give up Cyprus this would annul the Lausanne Treaty and endanger the Greeks of Istanbul. He preferred a resettlement of the population with ensuing partition. Foreign Minister Zorlu rejected the British proposals totally.

On 19 June the Americans were informed about the proposals officially. Dulles did not think much about it. In his opinion this plan would make the Cyprus Problem more complicated. The integration of Athens and Ankara served only one purpose: the perpetuation of British rule in Cyprus. Obviously Dulles recognized the divide-and-rule tactic of the British, so did Prime Minister Menderes, but he went one step further: If the status of Cyprus and thus the Lausanne Treaty changed, Turkey would claim Western Thrace and the Aegean islands and one would have to talk about the Greek minority of Istanbul and the oecumenic Patriarchy. NATO could not act as arbitrator in case of inter-communal clashes. Thus Menderes unveiled the long-term strategic plans of the Turkish leadership. It is amazing that precisely at this time the Foreign Office began to think about ethnic cleansing in Cyprus. Though these ideas were rejected by all those involved, there is an unwritten law that a thought once articulated comes up again and gains life.

All through, Harding had done his best to convince Eden to accept his plan. But Eden rejected even a modified version. In Harding's eyes each constitutional proposal not linked to a clear termination of the application of the right to self-determination was useless because it would increase the Cypriots' mistrust of British intentions. Apparently, the Americans did not understand this because they congratulated Eden. From all this one gets the impression that from the beginning Eden planned to outmanoeuvre Harding, the Greeks and the Americans; he provoked a Turkish "No" hoping to keep the status quo forever.

This policy was totally unrealistic, as became visible a little later when Lord Radcliffe returned from his fact-finding-mission presenting ideas, like Harding and Armitage had done. But Eden, Lennox-Boyd and Foreign Minister Selwyn Lloyd believed in the military solution, hoping that Harding would crush EOKA. If London had had any doubts about the wisdom of their course, these were wiped aside when the Egyptian head of state, Nasser, announced that the Suez Canal Company had been nationalized. But before we turn our attention to this new situation a retrospect on the EOKA activities during the first six months of 1956 is necessary.

Increase of violence during the first half of 1956

Grivas was now 58 and remarkably fit for his age. He covered great distances on foot in all weather and needed little sleep outdoors. As the British were constantly chasing him and his men he had to change his hiding place every now and then. All in all, there were 43 partisans in the Troodos area divided into 6 groups. In the Pentedaktylos range another 10 guerillas were active. 220 fighters divided into 47 groups operated in the towns and 750 in groups of 75 in the villages. The real fighters numbered 273 who had 100 guns. Most of the urban fighters were part-time fighters who had a regular job. Most of the village activists had shotguns.

In order to reduce pressure on him and the groups in the mountains and to disturb the Makarios-Harding talks Grivas instigated the students of Nicosia to organize wild demonstrations as a kind of diversionary operation. The students reacted enthusiastically and looked for opportunities to attack policemen or British soldiers. On 26 January 1956 they occupied the Pancyprian Gymnasion and threw stones from the flat roof at the approaching security forces. These countered with tear gas and the pupils fled. The Government closed the school for an undefined period, which the pupils considered as extra-holidays, using the additional spare time to instigate pupils of 14 other schools. The pupils attacked primary schools, destroyed the furniture, threatened the teachers and called on the pupils to act against the British. The flag war was intensified. In late spring 1956 only 81 schools out of 499 primary schools worked. Radio Athens did its best to incite the pupils. Besides hooligan actions, the youths murdered alleged traitors and members of the armed forces.

Grivas ordered "hit-and-run"-operations. The fighters should throw bombs, organize ambushes, commit acts of sabotage and shoot adversaries. Among the first blows was the blowing up of an aeroplane by a time bomb. The plane was torn to pieces but there were no dead since the departure had been postponed. Another coup was aimed at Harding. A bomb with a time fuse was placed under his bed but the coolness of the night delayed the chemical detonator. Thus the bomb was discovered only when the beds were made next morning and was exploded by experts in a sandy dimple. During the second half of March the assassination attempts on British (5) and Greek "traitors" (6) increased. Among them was a really ugly one in a church in Kythrea where an alleged traitor was shot in front of the congregation and his four children. When it became known that he had been no traitor, EOKA claimed that the British secret service had committed the murder.

Plate 9

Aerial view of Govenment House before its destruction

Ruins of Government House on 7 November 1931

Plate 10

Bellapais Abbey

Cloisters of Bellapais Abbey

Plate 11

Famagousta: Caravansary

Famagousta: Market

Plate 12

Agriculture: ploughing with traditional wooden implement

Plate 13

Women's work: transporting rocks for road building

Women's work: breaking rocks for road work

Plate 14

Asbestos mine at Amiantos in Troodos

Plate 15

Transporting ore using mules

The first locomotive and its crew

Sifting the copper ore

Plate 16

View from the ancient theatre of Soli, in the background the CMC loading facilities

Striking miners of the Cyprus Mining Corporation in 1948

Many killers tried to minimize their risk. A typical example was the murder of the Chief of the Special Branch, Kyriakos Aristotelous, on 10 April 1956. As on duty he was accompanied by bodyguards, the killers had no chance. When, however, Aristotelous wife was delivered of a child in hospital, the proud father visiting her was shot in the clinic. When the public bristled at this cowardly murder Grivas retorted by a leaflet justifying the murder verbosely. Every now and then EOKA killers attacked Turkish Cypriot policemen, killing some. The Turkish Cypriots interpreted this as attacks on their community and hit back. Thus the Cyprus conflict acquired a new dimension: the colonial conflict between the British and the Greek Cypriots widened into inter-communal conflict. So far EOKA had attacked only Turkish Cypriot policemen but it was a question of time when violence would escalate. These first inter-communal clashes caused the security forces to separate the inimical ethnic groups by barbed wire. This line of separation was the predecessor of the later Green Line dividing Nicosia to this day.

In May 1956 the first mopping-up operation against the guerillas in the mountains began, using helicopters and search dogs. Within a short period of time the Kyrenia mountains were purged. The mopping up of the Troodos mountains was done systematically from North to South by a step by step encirclement operation. Though Grivas managed to escape, in June it became clear to him that most partisan units had been smashed. Thus he ordered a temporary cease fire in the mountains and he himself fled to Limassol where a well disguised hiding place, including an underground bedroom was waiting. Indeed, the whole infrastructure built with great labour had been destroyed. Grivas' idea of a GHQ in the mountains from where he could direct the struggle had proved a chimera. Many EOKA cadres had been caught and important documents had fallen into the hands of the British. Only two groups were left, that of Markos Drakos, south of Lefka, and that of Grigoris Afxentiou, in the eastern Troodos near the Machairas monastery.

In this context the big fire in Paphos Forest caused by British mortar fire must not be forgotten. This fire killed 21 British soldiers and 70 suffered heavy injuries. EOKA did not succeed in killing one British soldier in combat because there was none. In reality EOKA avoided direct clashes and, only in two cases, cornered EOKA fighters defended themselves to the end. One cannot compare EOKA activities with the fighting of Greek partisan units in WWII. EOKA was a town guerilla organisation with juvenile death squadrons.

On 3 June two juvenile killers attacked British soldiers swimming near the Dekelia base and killed one of them, wounding a second. On 25 June there was an especially ugly murder. A young shop owner belonging to the Special Constabulary, doing guard service and patrol duty, wanted to meet his fiancee at noon break. EOKA killers shot him in the back. The photograph showing his bride sitting on the road curb in a striped white dress staring desperately at her dead fiancé appeared in the world press.

The building up of the Special Branch made great progress and in the urban areas a well functioning net of informers had been created. But in the countryside, in the partisan areas, this did not work. In order to overcome this lack of information an interrogation specialist who had experience from the struggles in Malaya and Kenya, was brought to Cyprus. He and a lieutenant of the Gordon Highlanders apparently beat the information about EOKA mountain hideouts and logistics out of the captives. When this became known, the two officers were court-martialled and sacked. Radio Athens produced the wildest rumours about the horrible British torture methods. Objectively it may be stated that the police respected the legal framework and torture was the absolute exception. The comparison with Malaya and Kenya shows that in Cyprus the British contained themselves. There was no military rule, no martial law, there were no drumhead courts martial, no mass executions, no hostage taking and shooting. Apparently they knew that Cyprus was a colony inhabited by Europeans where such brutal methods would have provoked protests on the national and international level.

In July 1956 another chance for the solution of the Cyprus Problem came when the new Greek consul general, Angelos Vlachos, arrived in Nicosia. Averof had ordered him to search for a solution and make EOKA accept a cease fire. After that the Ethnarchy should authorize the Greek Government to negotiate a solution with the British, provided Makarios agreed. The Ethnarchy consented and Grivas, too, accepted the proposal provided he could announce the cease fire from a position of strength. Averof agreed and in early August Grivas ordered his activists to organize riots, to throw bombs and attempt assassinations.

In the meantime Vlachos formulated the text of Grivas' future cease fire proclamation. Grivas signed it and had it distributed as a leaflet. The population was relieved beyond description. Harding, too, reacted positively at first, but his military advisors characterized Grivas' offer as a stratagem to gain a breather after his heavy losses and to prepare new attacks. Harding accepted these arguments and reported to London accordingly. There in view of the Suez crisis, they were for a tough course asking EOKA to surrender within three weeks. A limited amnesty was offered to the fighters: a life-long exile in Greece or, if they remained in Cyprus, legal persecution and punishment, even death threatened them. Grivas reacted with a leaflet saying that victors do not surrender and ordered his district leader to resume fighting.

Though the population was tired of the constant violence and counter-violence, it had its pride. The demand to surrender was ridiculed: a donkey was set free in the middle of Nicosia carrying on its sides and back placards saying "My Marshal I surrender". This photo showing a donkey ready to surrender appeared in the international press. The mockery of the Cypriots ridiculing Harding strengthened their self-confidence and their readiness to persevere. When no EOKA fighter surrendered, a kind of pride in the young people of EOKA developed and people began to identify with them, even when, again, the first bombs exploded on 29 August.

More futile efforts to find a political solution, August - December 1956

As was mentioned before, on 26 July 1967 Nasser nationalized the Suez Canal. Eden saw a chance to stabilize his position by steering a tough course planning an attack on Egypt, together with the French. In this, Cyprus played a major role as command and logistics centre. Thus it was hardly astonishing that the Greek peace initiative failed. Eden's intransigent position was strengthened by an event in Cyprus: on 21 August 1956 those two glass jars with a screw cap, which Grivas had given to a trusted friend on 30 March 1955 who had buried them in his garden, fell into the hands of the British..

Special Branch had arrested one of Grivas' messengers and through him they traced a certain Andreas Lazarou, a watchmaker who was one of Grivas' distributors of orders. They offered him two alternatives; detention camp or cooperation with generous help in building up a new existence in Britain. Lazarou, having a sick wife, four children and high debts, accepted and from then on supplied the British with copies of Grivas' letters to his district commanders. Lazarou knew that Grigoris Loukas had buried diaries and told this to the British who offered Loukas a huge sum of money, a new identity and existence outside Cyprus. He accepted, betrayed the hiding place of the jars, got the money, flew with his wife out to England. Lazarou, however, was unlucky: During an interrogation of the randomly arrested Georkatzis by the Special Branch, they showed him a photocopy of a letter he had sent to Grivas. Georkatzis immediately understood that the only person besides him and the messenger who had touched the letter had been Lazarou and had him shot by one of his killers.

Instead of keeping the find secret and evaluating Grivas' diary and persecuting the persons mentioned, London decided to publish extracts of the diary as a white paper, probably believing because of the Greek initiative, that the final victory was at hand. The diary contained details about the cooperation between Grivas and Makarios justifying *post festum* the deportation of Makarios. The white paper appeared in September under the title *"Terrorism in Cyprus. The*

Captured Documents". Quite in contrast to the usual sober white papers this publication looked trendy. Besides Grivas' diary it contained some impressive photos, letters, orders, memos and compromising quotes of Makarios. In Cyprus the Cyprus Mail serialized the diary. Grivas was taken aback but maintained that it was a forgery by the British, which nobody believed. In Cyprus the publication caused a wave of arrests of all persons mentioned in the diary.

In Washington the Government watched developments in Cyprus with growing worry and Dulles thought it time to interfere and help to find a solution acceptable for all three states. Dulles asked his special assistant Julius Holmes to develop a concept on the basis of which a comprehensive plan was formulated and presented on 13 August 1956: a solution must be found before the UN debate. In Cyprus supervised elections should take place for a constitutional assembly which should work out a constitution on the basis of Radcliffe's proposals. In order to integrate Turkey, the Constitution should contain certain basic features, e.g. the rights of the Turkish minority, should be predefined. Foreign and defence policies should remain in the competence of the Governor, who in the case of internal unrests should cooperate with NATO's high command. An amnesty should be proclaimed and violence should end. As soon as the Constitution was finalized Cyprus should get home rule, based on it. Makarios was to be integrated in the solution and should return. London should bindingly declare before the elections that after 10 years a plebiscite would be held on the following four topics: 1) Enosis, 2) Local autonomy under the Greek Crown, 3) Full independence, and 4) Self-administration within the Commonwealth. Certain parts of the island should remain British military bases forever. The protection of the minority should be guaranteed by an agreement of the three states. A US representative should "sell" the plan to the three Governments.

This plan was reasonable and acceptable to the Cypriots. Surely Makarios would have agreed and so would Athens and consequently Grivas. Ankara could not have rejected a joint American-British initiative. The decisive question was now whether the Americans could make the British accept it. But because of the hardened position of the British this appeared doubtful. Nevertheless Dulles asked Holmes to make the plan palatable to the three governments.

Holmes's talks in London, unsurprisingly, met with little success. London was thinking of filing a motion against Greece in the UN in order to postpone the debate on Cyprus or to have both motions removed. After weeks of haggling, the British Government agreed to Holmes' mission, provided the discussion was confined to self-government on the basis of a liberal constitution and the right of self-determination was principally acknowledged but postponed for an indefinite period. Thus Holmes had a green light for further exploratory talks.

On 4 October Holmes met Averof in Athens. Averof was ready to compromise and developed ideas very close to those of Holmes. A common paper was worked out which Holmes would submit to the British. Karamanlis promised that the British could keep their bases forever even if the Cypriots should vote for enosis in the plebiscite after 8 years. Thus the Greeks unknowingly accepted Holmes's original plan.

On 6 October Averof and his Turkish colleague, Settar Iksel, met. Averof said that the Greek Government would accept every solution assented to by the Cypriots and added, jokingly, even partition. Iksel answered earnestly that a partition along the 35th parallel would be the best solution because both sides would get an equal share. Averof rejected this, laughing, but Iksel did not understand that Averof's answer was a rejection and reported to Ankara that the Greeks offered a partition. In Ankara the Government agreed that partition was the best solution and stretched feelers towards London to find out British opinion on that.

On 7 October Holmes informed the British about his talks in Athens and the Greek offer, which corresponded with his own ideas. His dialogue partners were evasive and Eden showed himself bewildered by this American intervention and refused to meet Holmes. Finally on 25 October the parliamentary Undersecretary in the Foreign Office, Nutting, condescended to receive Holmes and give him a rejection of the Greek proposals. It became obvious that the British did not want negotiations. Rather frustrated, Holmes flew to Ankara on 27 October where he was kept waiting, too. On 29 October he learned that Israeli forces were attacking Egypt and that on 1 November British and French forces joined the attack.

On 2 November, finally, Menderes received Holmes and expressed the hope that an early solution to the Cyprus Conflict would be found. The Foreign Minister, on the other side, brusquely rejected the Greek offer. It was obvious that they were playing the game of the good and the bad cop. On 3 November 1956 Eden rejected the UN request to stop the attack, thus morally enabling the Soviets to attack Budapest and flatten the Hungarian rising. On 9 November international pressure led to an armistice in Egypt and on 13 November Holmes had the last conversation of his mission in London. It became clear the British policy towards Cyprus was in disarray. The Holmes mission failed because its prerequisite, a joint British-American effort in Athens and especially in Ankara, was ruined by the Suez adventure of the British and because Ankara had taken a liking to the idea of partition.

On 12 November Radcliffe presented his constitutional proposals: power should be shared between the Governor and the elected parliament and the government responsible to the latter. The Governor would be responsible for foreign and defence policy and the inner security of the island, and be a kind of Head of State enacting laws. The Government, with a Chief Minister appointed by the Governor, should come out of parliament. A minister for Turkish affairs should belong to the Cabinet. The activities of the Governor and the Government should be coordinated by a Joint Council consisting of the Governor and his deputy, the Chief Minister and his deputy, the minister for Turkish affairs, a representative of the British armed forces, the Legal Secretary and the Attorney General. Radcliffe rejected equalization of the two ethnic groups because it was against democratic principles if 18 percent of the population had the same weight as 80 percent. He envisaged a reinforced protection of the minority as a solution. Compared with the earlier constitutions, this one was liberal, but the Government still had too much power; it was a typical colonial constitution.

Radcliffe's proposal offered a viable solution if it had been realized. But when Radcliffe submitted his proposal to Lennox-Boyd on 12 November the latter said that it would be published in due course. Meanwhile, a conflict had broken out between the Foreign and the Colonial Office. The FO considered it reasonable to mention a possible partition in the Constitution in order to get the Turkish consent. The CO wanted an early acceptance of the constitution by the Cypriots and a postponement to self-determination to a distant time. At the end of November Lennox-Boyd gave in a bit but the FO insisted that the Turkish Cypriots, too, had a right of self-determination of their own. Lennox-Boyd yielded and on 3 December he put forward a text to be published together with the Radcliffe Plan. The text contained a passage on double self-determination and thus implicitly on partition. The Cabinet decided that Lennox-Boyd should fly to Athens and Ankara to sell the new concept to the Greeks and Turks.

On 13 December 1956 Lennox-Boyd informed Athens of his intention to declare that self-determination, if ever granted, should enable both communities to decide freely over their future status. Karamanlis reacted frostily because this meant partition. No Greek Government could agree to such a demand without being toppled at once. Lennox-Boyd, however, remained bullheaded and added that rejection meant a deterioration of British-Greek relations; Karamanlis did not doubt that. The Foreign Office was very indignant about Karamanlis' behaviour which they considered *"ungracious and ungenerous and very stupid"*.

Lennox-Boyd was not impressed by the Greek rejection and travelled on to Ankara. During a talk with Menderes on 16 December he stated that a change of sovereignty was not intended for the time being. Menderes suggested partitioning the island right away. Lennox-Boyd considered this impracticable at the moment but promised to ask the Cabinet to formulate the reference to partition more clearly. This meant that Lennox-Boyd was ready to promote the Turkish partition demand in London. After his return Lennox-Boyd changed the wording of the declaration, thus the decisive sentence read: *"When the time comes [...] it will be the purpose of Her Majesty's Government to ensure that any such exercise of self-determination should be effected in such a manner that the Turkish Cypriot community, no less than the Greek Cypriot community, shall, in the special circumstances of Cyprus, be given freedom to decide for themselves their future status. In other words: Her Majesty's Government recognise that the exercise of self-determination in such a mixed population must include partition among the eventual options."*

On 19 December 1956 Lennox-Boyd told Parliament that the Radcliffe proposals would be published as a Command Paper and read out the above statement. When Labour MPs attacked him he fought back with exactly the arguments Ankara had been using for some time. Further, he denied that his statement contained a proposal. Lennox-Boyd's statement contradicted the proposals of Radcliffe who had strictly rejected partition and it had a binding character since it had been made in parliament.

Lennox-Boyd's statement was rejected by all parties in Athens. From Nicosia Vlachos warned that this statement would revive the Greek-Turkish conflict and bring it into the Aegean. The British had hoped that the Americans would support them but Washington, grasping the real consequences, distanced itself from the British position to the great displeasure of the British. The Turkish Government appreciated the statement, of course. By Lennox-Boyd's statement partition (taksim) became an integral part of Turkey's Cyprus policy followed openly and offensively. Zorlu went even as far as to assert that Lennox-Boyd had promised him personally an early partition. Makarios, on the other hand, rejected the constitutional proposals, also.

Lennox-Boyd's statement is a kind of turning point in the development. From now on the 18 percent minority became a community with equal political rights. This reduced the number of possible solutions to four: continuation of British rule, condominium, partition and independence. As a condominium would have been impracticable and partition would have required ethnic cleansing, these two were excluded. Thus only two options were left: the continuation of the status quo or independence, as Averof recognized clearly. Lennox-Boyd's declaration was the last element of Britain's divide-and-rule-policy. For tactical reasons another demon was allowed to leave the bottle without thinking of the consequences, which were catastrophic, indeed.

The climax of violence in autumn 1956

Autumn 1956 in Cyprus was characterized by renewed violence. One name excelled especially, that of the journalist Nikos Sampson. He stemmed from a bourgeois family from Famagusta. As a youth he was like any typical teddy boy of the time. After the end of school he became "correspondent" of the Times of Cyprus and when the unrests began he was always searching for the ultimate headline. Later he went to a Greek newspaper. Some say reporting violence did not have enough kick for him and, therefore, he joined EOKA and became an active member. In spring and summer 1956 he participated in the execution of some "traitors". He apparently impressed his superiors so much that they made him leader of a killer team at the age of 21.

This team consisted of three young men and two young women who were transporting the weapons under their skirts to the place of the assassination. There they handed the weapons over to the killers who gave them back after the attack. Then the group dispersed in all directions. This group organized a spectacular liberation operation with some dead in Nicosia hospital. Precisely planned attacks against unarmed Englishmen and some "traitors" followed. Allegedly Sampson, the journalist, showed up after the assassination and took photos of the dead. In mid-September the team shot a British army doctor in his car waiting at a traffic light for green. At the end of that month they attacked three British policemen in plain clothes shopping in Ledra-Street and two were killed, one survived wounded. In September 20 human beings were shot by the killers, among them 10 British, 8 Greek Cypriot "traitors" and 2 Turkish Cypriots. The number of violent attacks totalled 285 in September and 129 in October when another 20 people were shot, 6 British soldiers and 14 Greek Cypriot "traitors".

Grivas knew that the days of partisan warfare were numbered and that the assassinations by the killer teams disgusted the public, therefore, he tried to influence the public politically by founding the PEKA (Politiki Epitropi Kypriakou Agonos - Political Committee of the Cypriot Struggle). PEKA tried to infiltrate all clubs, associations, brotherhoods, guilds, and professional associations. The chief of PEKA Nicosia was the lawyer Tassos Papadopoulos, the future president of the republic.

The security forces reacted in a tough way by imposing a curfew over Nicosia in order to search the town, and by operation Sparrowhawk British units purged the Kyrenia mountains of the last partisans. Grivas reacted by changing his hiding place, moving to the house of a certain Marios Christodoulidis on the outskirts of Limassol. There he had a working room on the ground floor and in the basement the ultimate hiding place, the entrance being under the kitchen sink.

When the British attack on Egypt began Grivas believed that the final victory was at hand and ordered an intensification of the terror. In November 416 acts of violence occurred killing 15 soldiers, 4 civilians and 10 Greek Cypriots and 1 Turkish policeman. Booby traps on roads caused ugly head wounds. Radio controlled bombs under the road were used to blow up lorries transporting troops. In the towns the killers were at large, Sampson excelling particularly, allegedly killing more than a dozen people. Increasingly the killers were looking for so-called soft targets, i.e. British civilians working in Cyprus or pensioners spending the evening of their life there. As many of these attacks took place in Ledra street, the main shopping street of Nicosia, it acquired the sad name "Murder Mile".

Harding reacted to the increasing terror with sharpened repression. He flew to London to get a sharpening of the emergency laws, at the same time demanding a political solution: the Radcliffe proposals should be published quickly. But the minister responsible, Lennox-Boyd, did exactly the opposite. In Cyprus a Central Intelligence Wing had been set up in which the security forces of the police and the military cooperated closely. Small anti-guerilla units were formed out of Cypriot policemen, mainly Turkish Cypriots, but also some Greek Cypriots, members of the Special Branch and Military Intelligence. Their methods to gain information were rather efficient, but often not compliant with the rules of police work or the Geneva Convention.

The local interrogators often used tough methods close to torture. But often these were not necessary because many arrested youths talked readily when offered an alternative to the death penalty for carrying a weapon. These methods conflicted with all traditions of British justice but they yielded results. The increasing successes of the security forces made Grivas insecure; he suspected treason. As the British had set free the interned AKEL members, Grivas arrived at the mad conclusion that the "treason" was their work and ordered his killer teams to attack the communist "traitors". From now on the assassination of AKEL members had priority. If the wanted "traitor" was not found the killers attacked family members. Grivas' fear of treason became pathological. Now he even suspected EOKA members who managed to flee British custody. From now on flights had to be permitted by Grivas. During that time 15 persons were murdered, 13 Greek "Traitors" and 2 British. The acts of violence decreased from 416 to 96. The struggle within the Greek Cypriot community began to look like a civil war.

In January 1957 Sampson was arrested and made a full confession when he was interrogated. In court he revoked the confession, saying he had been tortured during interrogation. Since the prosecution had no other proof the case was lost. Another indictment because of illegal possession of weapons led to a death sentence. The 1959 amnesty promulgated when independence came saved Sampson from the gallows.

In the same month the end of the last partisan groups came. Georkatzis and his two companions were caught in northwestern Troodos because of treason. On 19 January Markos Drakos clashed with a British patrol and was shot. With his 24 years he was one of the oldest EOKA fighters. Afxentiou had managed to withdraw with his group to the eastern Troodos in the vicinity of the Machairas monastery. Again there was treason and a British anti-guerilla unit was able to trace his hideout in the mountain flank near the monastery. A Greek speaking officer asked Afxentiou and his comrades to surrender. Afxentiou ordered the latter to give up, which they did. He refused to capitulate and fired at the British from his hiding place. When a British officer succeeded in throwing a hand grenade into the stronghold it was quiet. The British sent one of Afxentiou's comrades, named Afgoustis Efstathiou, into the hiding place to pull out the dead Afxentiou. But Afxentiou was alive and in an upsurge of feelings Afgoustis decided to stay with his chief and for the next hours they defended the stronghold. Finally, pioneers poured gasoline into the crevices above the hiding place. When it was set ablaze Afgoustis fled the stronghold but Afxentiou remained. At the post mortem it was discovered that Afxentiou had not been killed by the fire but by a bullet fired at short range. With his death partisan warfare ended forever.

At the time of his death Afxentiou was 28 and, after Grivas, the oldest fighter of EOKA. The circumstances of his death made him a martyr of the EOKA struggle. Contemporary propaganda and later literature, romanticized his death and lifted him to the pantheon of the heros of the Greek nation. Today Afxentiou's (reconstructed) stronghold is a national pilgrimage place.

In January 1957 there were 161 acts of violence and 14 persons were killed (5 British, 8 Greeks, 1 Turk). In February the number reached 259 but murders decreased (4 British, 2 Greeks, 1 Turk) and in March there were only 4 assassinations (1 British, 3 Greeks). EOKA was so weakened that Grivas ordered a temporary cease fire. When the UN passed resolution 1013 and Vlachos pressed him hard, Grivas declared a unilateral armistice.

1957: INTERNATIONALIZATION AND INTERNAL CONFRONTATION

International policy searching for a solution formula

The year 1957 began with a change of the *dramatis personae*. In London Eden resigned as Prime Minister and Macmillan succeeded him. In Athens Karamanlis decided to send an ambassador to London again, choosing the diplomat and poet Georgios Seferiadis (Seferis). Georgios Pesmazoglou, who had been a friend of Atatürk was sent to Ankara, and Dimitrios Bitsios took over the Cyprus desk in the Greek Foreign Ministry.

Lennox-Boyd's December statement made it clear to Averof that clinging to the demand for self-determination would lead to partition. The only way to avoid this was a change of paradigms in Greece's Cyprus policy: The partition demand could only be defused if one agreed to it on the principle that the majority of all Cypriots agreed to it. Additionally, one had to win American support or at least neutrality. Developments inducing the British to give up Cyprus should be prevented at all cost. Thus one must take a hard line with Grivas stopping the intercommunal clashes that were beginning. Grivas had to be forced to an armistice.

In Ankara Prime Minister Menderes declared partition the only solution; Turkey needed a military base on Cyprus. In view of the impending Cyprus debate in the UN, Washington began thinking which course to take. A policy of blockade as of two years before was unthinkable. Dulles suggested one should influence the UN debate in such a way that no unacceptable resolution came about. London was told that the US expected the British Government to resume talks with Makarios and other Cypriot leaders and seek a solution based on self-determination. London reacted indignantly: Should the Americans vote against the British motion in the UN this would be interpreted as an unfriendly act. Obviously British nerves were on edge due to the American attitude during the Suez Crisis. In view of the almost hysterical British reaction Dulles decided to back pedal, advising a Turkish delegation to show moderation during the UN debate. When Dulles and Averof met the latter behaved in a statesmanlike manner: one had to survive the debate without creating irreparable damage. They should avoid insulting each other, and the negotiations between the British and the Cypriots should be resumed.

As will be remembered on 14 March 1956 Greece had tabled a motion to have the Cyprus Question put on the agenda of the General Assembly. On 12 October London had submitted a counter-motion accusing Athens of supporting the terrorists in Cyprus. On 14 November the General Assembly decided to have both motions dealt with in the First Committee on 18 February 1957. The debate began on that day and ended after ten sessions on 22 February. The arguments brought forward were repetitions of well known positions and accusations. The NATO and Bagdad Pact states supported the British-Turkish position, the states of the Warsaw Pact and the Arab states backed the Greeks. Finally Resolution 1013 was agreed calling all states involved to seek a solution within the framework of the UN Charter, expressing the hope that negotiations would be continued soon. On 26 February 1957 the General Assembly supported this with 56 yes votes and one abstention.

But when the states involved interpreted the resolution it became obvious that the old differences continued: Greece understood that the demand to continue the negotiations meant that the Harding-Makarios negotiations should be resumed. The British and the Turks were of the opinion that this meant the continuation of the tripartite negotiations.

Averof and Karamanlis believed that on the basis of resolution 1013 a solution to the Cyprus Problem could be found, provided Makarios participated. But this meant that he had to be released and this could only be achieved with American help. During a conversation with the US Ambassador, Karamanlis stressed the importance of including Makarios in a solution. Averof believed that the British, too, were looking for a face-saving solution. He hinted that his thoughts were moving towards an independent Cyprus and that he guessed that Makarios' thoughts were moving in the same direction. In other words: from March 1957 enosis was no longer a solution option for Greece.

Not only did the Greeks move but NATO as well. In the past there had been several proposals to solve the Cyprus Problem within the framework of NATO but those always failed because of American or British objections. But when NATO Secretary General Lord Ismay made another advance in February 1957 the British Government at first reacted hesitantly, but on 15 March London agreed to a mediation. Since Macmillan had become Prime Minister he had befriended the thought that an airbase on Cyprus would suffice for British strategic interests and that the Greeks and Turks could partition the island. After some backstage manoeuvring, Lennox-Boyd said in the House that the British Government accepted Ismay's proposal and was ready to set Makarios free provided he came out against EOKA violence before being released. Grivas and his fighters would be granted safe conduct to Greece.

In the beginning the Greek Government rejected mediation, fearing this might lead to another Tripartite. The Turkish Government, however, reacted positively, believing it could push through partition. Meanwhile, Makarios had been informed about the development and had shown himself ready for compromise. The Cabinet in London decided to set Makarios free by an act of grace. Makarios stated that he was ready to continue the bilateral negotiations with the British as Resolution 1013 demanded. This, however, was not what the British expected but they decided to continue the course decided upon and Lennox-Boyd announced that Makarios would be set free to go everywhere except Cyprus. Makarios replied that without returning to Cyprus he would not negotiate with the British. The negotiations about Cyprus had to be bilateral.

On 13 April Makarios arrived in Athens, where he was welcomed enthusiastically. From the balcony of the Hotel Grande Bretagne he spoke to a huge mass of people in Syntagma Square. He underlined the right to self-determination of the Cypriots. Neither the oil of the Near East, nor the defence needs of the Free World nor Turkish opposition could hinder the realization of self-determination. The crowd was enthusiastic about his charismatic performance. Makarios had become the identification figure of the Greek nation, the champion of the struggle against colonialism and imperialism. At this moment he was the undisputed hero of the nation and for the young generation almost a kind of pop star, but for the politicians he became a problem, if not a danger.

The Turkish Government did not like the whole development. Menderes wanted partition which he hoped to push through with British help on a Tripartite basis. It was obvious that the Turkish Government had committed itself to partition and nothing else. When it learned that Makarios would soon arrive in Athens, it warned the Greek Government against possible concessions to Makarios in tones which usually are common between states close to war. Averof retaliated warning Ankara against renewed assaults on the Greek minority and submitted the matter to the NATO Council, which promptly advised moderation. The Americans were worried because they considered neither enosis nor taksim a practicable solution and developed a plan of guaranteed independence within or outside the Commonwealth about which a plebiscite would decide.

When this plan was submitted to Menderes he rejected it vigorously: Turkey could not agree to an independent Cyprus. The only feasible solution was partition. Evidently Ankara was fixed on partition. As this could not be realized, the danger arose that a short circuit reaction could induce London to withdraw from Cyprus, as had happened in Palestine when the British had fled head over heels, leaving behind the conflict provoked by their divide-and-rule-policy. In the case of Cyprus this would not mean a total pullout but a withdrawal into the bases.

Lennox-Boyd's statement that Grivas would get safe conduct to Greece meant that the latter would have to give up the struggle, but Grivas was not ready to do this on his own. The only ones able to order him were Makarios and Karamanlis. But Karamanlis hesitated because an intervention might have cost him the parliamentary majority, and Makarios was afraid to talk to Grivas as ethnarch ordering him to stop the struggle. Thus they both appealed to Grivas though they knew that Grivas did not listen to appeals. Since Lennox-Boyd's December statement they understood that enosis no longer existed as an option. The only feasible solution acceptable to all sides was self-administration with a perspective of independence because there had not yet been any major inter-communal clashes nor EOKA excesses against the Left. But Makarios and Karamanlis lacked the courage to enforce this solution. Thus another occasion for a reasonable solution passed by and Makarios accepted that the struggle would continue. From now on Grivas determined the direction of developments almost uncontrolled.

Makarios, however, tried to stay in the game with the help of the Americans and tried by letters to make the British cooperative threatening otherwise to start a PR campaign against the alleged torture of EOKA prisoners. But the British gave him the cold shoulder: London was not ready to negotiate with Makarios any more. Makarios was no longer a player in the Cyprus poker game. A Cyprus solution would be found in negotiations between London, Athens and

Ankara without Cypriot participation and enforced upon the Cypriots. Neither Makarios nor the Athens Government understood that the number of solution options had been reduced to two: partition or independence.

Psychological warfare

Bacon, quoting Plutarch, knew *semper liquid ha'p'orth* and Goebbels allegedly said that a lie must be big enough to be believed. Since 1956 and growing in spring 1957 the British had been confronted with this situation when Greek nationalists in Cyprus and Greece unleashed a propaganda war aiming to undermine the moral integrity of the British. The main slanderer was radio Athens. Its propaganda transmissions invented ever increasingly wild imaginary stories.

The accusations concerned conditions in the detention camps and the alleged torturing during interrogations. On the basis of the Detention of Persons Law of July 1955, in November of that year an internment camp had been erected at Kokkinotrimithia, about 13 kms west of Nicosia. In June 1956 another camp was set up at Pyla. The Law entitled the Governor to send suspects directly to those camps without participation of the judiciary. In the camps there was a cross section of the nationalist part of Cypriot society: lawyers, clerics , teachers, civil servants, worker and peasants. The youngest inmates were 15 the oldest 70. The camps were desolate and the sanitary equipment mediocre, but there was no forced labour or a kapo system. Food was sufficient but dull. The detainees could write to their relatives and be visited by them. The barracks had roofs of corrugated iron which made them ovens in summer and refrigerators in winter. In day time the inmates worked, took exercise, stayed outside, chatted or read. The biggest problem of the camps was the deadly boredom. Among the detainees were those who the courts had not found guilty. Propaganda styled the camps a new Buchenwald or Dachau and this propaganda lie circulated outside Cyprus as well. Radio Athens embellished its transmissions with horrible details which had occurred - in the Nazi camps.

Already in 1956 Britain was accused of permitting torture. The accusations did not differentiate between the circumstances of the arrest of a person and the subsequent interrogation. In the first case it was normal to apply force because only a few had themselves arrested without resisting. As long as the arrested person was in the hands of the regular Police from the Military nothing happened to them. However, the six special interrogation teams formed out of specialists of the military and the Special Branch, among them many Turkish Cypriots, often seem to have applied force, the Turkish Cypriots doing the dirty work. The interrogators applied the principle of carrot and stick: he who spoke was rewarded, he who remained silent received his deserts. Many of those who opened their mouths claimed later that they had been tortured, but this was often a lame excuse. There were two interrogation centres, one in Omorfyta, north of Nicosia and the other in Platres, on mount Troodos, the latter being notorious. As there was never an official investigation and only few reliable testimonies exist the real extent is not known.

Harding seems to have known nothing or little. In summer 1957 he considered it appropriate to counter torture charges by publishing a white book. It was admitted that there had been cases of brutality while arresting people but the accusation of systematic torture during interrogation was denied. Harding stated that he had intervened in the only case known to him and had the culprit removed from the ranks of the army. The white book described individual cases, trying to prove how baseless the accusations were, but the argumentation does not appear fully convincing. Makarios countered by publishing a kind of white book, too, trying to prove 30 cases of torture. But all these cases have one thing in common - inadequate verifiability. The few cases which can be verified show that the authors either did not have precise knowledge or were deliberately distorting facts. It is not known whether Makarios was informed about the "inaccuracies". The aim of this documentation was exclusively its propaganda effect.

The accusations, however, had far reaching consequences: the longest parliamentary debate ever held on Cyprus on 15 July 1957. The torture campaign was a continuation of the EOKA struggle by means of propaganda, and this was by far more effective than those attacks in the mountains or the assassinations in the town. They hit the adversary in the centre of his power as the parliamentary debate and the reactions of the press proved.

Tridominium-Plan, NATO-Initiative and UN Debate

In April 1957 minister of defence Sandys visited Cyprus to inform himself about the military situation and needs. He came to the conclusion that two British enclaves, one for an air force base and one for a monitoring station and propaganda radio station, transmitting towards the Arab world, would be enough to meet the obligations from NATO and the Bagdad Pact. Partitioning the island was impracticable since about 150,000 persons would have to be resettled. This analysis was a kind of bankruptcy declaration of British Cyprus policy. To partition the island under these circumstances meant war between the mother countries and collapse of NATO's southeastern flank.

After a complicated opinion forming process, Macmillan presented a new plan on 8 July 1957 hoping this would be acceptable to all sides: The British bases at Akrotiri and Dhekelia excepted, the rest of Cyprus was to become a Tridominum of London, Athens and Ankara. The future Governor stemming from a fourth state should be elected by the three powers. There were further highly complicated constructions, presuming perfect international cooperation and the assistance of the US and NATO. But as a first step Macmillan need the acceptance of all British ministries and institutions, which was achieved at the end of July after a lot of haggling.

On 26 July Macmillan decided on the further procedures: In September a conference would come together in which the three powers, the US and NATO Secretary General Spaak would participate. But only the Americans would be briefed about the plan roughly. At first the Conference would discuss possible solutions, when, realizing that the Cyprus Problem was in a cul-de-sac, he would present his plan which would appear as the only logical way out. Dulles rejected official participation but was ready to send an expert observer; Spaak, on the other hand, signalled agreement. Thus London informed Athens and Ankara.

Because of their experience with the Tripartite Conference of 1955 Karamanlis and Averof distrusted the British and on 9 August refused to participate in a conference which was not diligently prepared. On 16 August the Turkish Government informed the British that they could not participate in a conference before the parliamentary elections on 16 October. Thus the Tridominum Plan was dead.

A plan developed by Spaak had a similar fate. In the beginning of June Spaak had suggested a guaranteed independence on a certain date. The US should be one of the guarantor powers. The Foreign Office rejected the plan but the Colonial Office found it interesting. Ankara rejected it outright and treated Spaak as a non-person for some time. Averof, on the other side, appreciated Spaak's plan. For some time Spaak's initiative was pushed aside by Macmillan's Tridominum Plan but when it was off the table it resurfaced. In October Karamanlis agreed to guaranteed independence with full minority protection. But Ankara again stalled asking equal rights for its community. Spaak's plan suffered a coup de grace when the British suggested putting the future NATO bases on Cyprus under Turkish administration. Thus six months' efforts finding a solution had been shipwrecked.

On 12 July Greece had put forward a motion that the Cyprus Problem should be put on the agenda of the UN General Assembly. The motion consisted of two parts; in the first part the application of Cyprus' right to self-determination was demanded, but the second part, under the influence of Makarios, tried to bring the torture campaign to the UN. There was the danger that because of the second part the whole motion would be rejected. After some haggling behind the scenes in which the US and Canada played a major role, the General Assembly decided on 20 September to accept the modified Greek motion and sent it to the First Committee. After further talks Makarios agreed that the second part be dropped but he insisted that the text of the future resolution should contain a reference to the realization of self-determination, i.e. enosis. The final version of the Greek resolution text deplored that there had been no progress in Cyprus since resolution 1013 of February 1957. The situation was described as dangerous and a solution on the basis of the principles of the UN Charter urgently necessary.

In the debate which began on 9 December 1957, 28 states participated. The arguments brought forward were more or less the same as during the debate of February. On 12 December 33 states voted for the, again modified, resolution, 20 against and 25 abstained and sent it to the General Assembly where it passed with identical votes. Thus Resolution 1013 remained in force, which meant little. Averof understood clearly that a solution could only be found outside the UN.

On 15 December 1957 the regular NATO Council meeting took place in Paris. This time however, in view of the aggravation of the arms race the heads of government of the NATO states appeared. Averof learned that Menderes intended to table the Cyprus Problem and Spaak, too, wanted to refer to it in his opening speech. Requested by Karamanlis, Averof took the matter up with Spaak: If Menderes spoke about Cyprus this would lead to a big quarrel in the Council and between the states involved afterwards. In this case Karamanlis would demand an official debate of the Cyprus Problem. Should Spaak refrain from mentioning the Cyprus Problem and Menderes restrain himself he himself would only touch the topic briefly. After some diplomatic seesaw all agreed to Averof's proposal. Cyprus did not become a topic of the summit.

At a meeting between Dulles, Averof and Karamanlis, the latter expressed the opinion that the Cyprus Problem should be solved. The US should intervene. Spaak had told him that the British were ready to grant independence to Cyprus but the Turks were against it. Couldn't the Americans influence the Turks? Dulles replied that the US was ready to help all sides by appealing to reason. If all states involved formulated their ideas in writing a compromise could be worked out. Obviously Dulles was not up for burning his fingers on this topic. What was said during the subsequent talk between him, Menderes and Zorlu is unknown because the related documents were not released by the State Department. In view of the continuing Turkish intransigence on the Cyprus Question one may safely assume that Dulles had not spoken out. Thus at the end of 1957 it was clear that neither the UN nor NATO had succeeded in bringing new movement to the stalled situation in Cyprus.

Grivas' attack on the Left

Grivas' unilateral armistice held until 28 October 1957, Greece's second national holiday. Meanwhile EOKA's political front organization, PEKA, tried to strengthen its hold on the population. New youths were recruited for the next round of the underground struggle. At the end of summer the ranks of EOKA were full again and the fighters were waiting for the order to attack. The relative quietness prompted Harding to ease the control measures, to suspend the obligatory death penalty for carrying and firing of weapons and throwing bombs, Sampson was among the beneficiaries, his death sentence being converted to lifelong imprisonment.

AKEL had watched the activities of EOKA with distrust and rejected this kind of struggle. In April 1957 the CC of AKEL practised self-criticism: EOKA had been assessed wrongly and its activities deserved respect. However, a solution could be brought about only through negotiations between London, Makarios and representatives of the Cypriot people (including AKEL). Obviously AKEL tried to come closer to Makarios. AKEL had about 4,000 members and PEO 25,000. Since the release of the leading cadres AKEL had tried to rebuild its previous position within Cypriot society in local, union and social affairs.

Grivas had watched this with growing distrust and ordered PEKA to fight AKEL politically. When he saw that he had little effect against the well organized and experienced communists he ordered an attack on them. In August 1957 an ugly smear campaign began against the Left, accusing them of treason and collaboration with the British. The British secret service had its fingers in the pie as well and did its best to increase the confrontation. Towards the end of August the first punitive actions began. Masked EOKA members appeared in numbers in the villages, attacked the local PEO office, and beat up the functionaries and members. In pamphlets the most absurd allegations about leading AKEL cadres were put forward, meaning that Grivas intended to begin a general attack. A little later numerous murders of left "traitors" occurred.

From Athens Makarios watched this development with growing concern. After the first round of murders, leading AKEL cadres among them, the mayor of Limassol and PEO secretary general visited him to complain. Makarios appeared anxious because the attacks on the Left would lead to a split in the Greek Cypriot camp. He appreciated the growing strength of AKEL as it was a counter-balance to Grivas, who acted more and more independently. Here began the cooperation between Makarios and AKEL which later played an important role. Makarios advised Grivas to be less aggressive towards the Left. Grivas threw a tantrum and announced that he saw no reason why "traitors" should be protected by a Communist trade union card.

During the whole liberation struggle EOKA killed 23 members and relatives of AKEL members. From the point of view of AKEL these were political murders. Up to the present day the association of former EOKA fighters rejects this and refuses to examine the cases. The events happened 50 years ago and there were no files. Tassos Papadopoulos, who led PEKA and who was, together with Grivas, responsible for these murders, rejected any fact finding in 2002 and AKEL, for reasons of actual day-by-day politics, did not insist.

Grivas steered an "independent" course not only against the Left but he also tried to force his course upon the Greek Government and Makarios. At the same time he prepared himself and his organization for a fight with the Turkish Cypriots and in this he was supported by nationalist circles and clerics. Makarios came under pressure from two sides: The Cypriot nationalists tried to pin him down to enosis and the Greek Government tried to make independence palatable to him. The attitude of the nationalists is not astonishing because they did not have information about the real situation. The Greek Government, on the other side, could not enlighten or scold the nationalists because this would have led to attacks by the Greek hardliners and the opposition. This narrow room for manoeuvring of the Greek Government and Makarios enabled Grivas to start the struggle omnium contra omnes.

Change of Governor
On 4 October 1957 Barbara Castle, deputy chairwoman of the Labour Party, announced at the annual party conference in Brighton that her party would grant Cyprus self-determination if Labour won the elections. This statement pulled the rug out from under Harding's feet. He had managed to stabilize the situation in Cyprus, having smashed the guerilla groups and crippled the killing teams to such a degree that Grivas announced a unilateral armistice. He had consolidated the morale of the police and security was no longer the concern of the military. In other words: Harding had fulfilled Eden's mission.

But since Sandys' visit, he knew that it was British policy to withdraw to the bases and reduce the numbers of British troops considerably. He was further informed that Grivas would soon begin with new attacks. Though he would be able to break up EOKA militarily again a final victory was impossible. A political solution had to be found. When he took over the governorship he had promised Eden that he would hold the office for two years. Observing now how his hard fought successes were gambled away by the politicians, his frustration grew more and more and by the end of September 1957 he began thinking about resigning. Castle's statement caused him to inform Lennox-Boyd about his tentative resignation in early October. Lennox-Boyd accepted the resignation and the Governor of Jamaica, Hugh Foot, was designated as his successor. When he bid farewell to the chiefs of the security organs he said that there was only one solution, the political one. Though Harding refrained from public critique, privately he said to US Consul Belcher that Macmillan and the other minister had handled the Cyprus Problem like a spare time matter.

His successor, Foot, knew Cyprus as he had been Colonial Secretary from 1943 to 1945, at times deputizing for the Governor. He knew the Cypriots intimately. When he had informed himself about the existing situation he found the following four elements of a solution: a cooling down period of four or five years; ending of the state of emergency; return of Makarios; negotiations in Cyprus with the leaders of the two ethnic groups; guarantee, that the solution found must be acceptable for both sides. Self-determination should no longer be a topic. These were ideas, not a plan. Lennox-Boyd agreed that Foot should submit a plan based on these ideas. The question was now, whether Foot could overcome the deadlock.

1958: FURTHER SEARCH FOR A SOLUTION AND INTERNAL CONFLICTS

The Foot Plan

Right from the beginning Foot's ideas met with resistance from all sides, but that did not impress him much, since he was sure that his ideas would convince the doubters. But Foot took over his office when the character of the Cyprus Conflict was changing again: it had begun as a colonial conflict, had been changed into an international conflict by the British machinations and was now turning into an ethnic conflict. The question was whether Foot would be able to adapt his ideas to the new situation.

Foot began by making gestures commanding the respect of both communities: on 13 December 1957 he strolled almost alone through the old town of Nicosia and talked to the people. Later he rode with a tiny escort through villages. He visited the internment camp at Kokkinotrimithia and set 100 inmates free. He met representatives of the Church, visited a monastery, talked to the leadership of the Turkish Cypriots. These gestures impressed the simple people but not the leadership and the administration and the security forces were also rather sceptical. At the end of December Foot believed he had grasped the situation and flew to London to get the green light for his plans. During his talks with Lennox-Boyd and Foreign Secretary Lloyd, both told him that at the end of the interim period partition of the island had to be offered as a solution option as had been announced on 19 December. The Colonial Committee, however, agreed with Foot's ideas.

The final decision was to be taken on 6 January 1958 by the Cabinet. But on this day some Minister resigned, making Cyprus a minor case. Lennox-Boyd repeated his known position containing partition as an option. Since he was afraid that Ankara might create difficulties, the Cabinet decided to send the Foreign Secretary there, accompanied by Foot, and later to Athens in order to sell the plan. This would be a difficult task because Ankara had distrusted British policy since the liberation of Makarios and the appointment of Foot, who was considered a Philhellene.

At the end of December 1957 Foreign Minister Zorlu stated to Küçük publicly that Greeks and Turks on the island could no longer live together, partition was the only solution and that each hit of EOKA would be retaliated. Although the Turkish Government officially demanded partition it would have been content obtaining a military base from where it could have interfered. Politically it wanted a federal solution as a first step towards partition and this as quickly as possible. Thus the Foot plan, with an interim period, had no chance.

When on 9 January the British Ambassador informed Zorlu about the Foot Plan he reacted angrily: If Foot intended to talk with Makarios, too, he needn't come to Ankara. Turkey insisted on partition. Later he demanded the cession of a military base and a treaty of double self-determination. London should call together a Tripartite Conference and, in case Athens refused to participate, negotiate with Turkey bi-laterally. Turkey had made a great concession accepting partition; properly Cyprus had to be given back to Cyprus. Prime Minister Menderes talked in a similar way to President Eisenhower, twisting historical facts even more and characterising his intransigent demands as a compromise solution. Menderes was conscious of the strategic importance of his country for the Americans and was sure that no doubt the Americans would give the Turks their head.

Meanwhile Foot had returned to Nicosia, asking himself whether Lloyd could achieve anything in Ankara. On 24 January 1958 Lloyd, invited by Turkey, flew to Ankara for talks with the Turkish Government about Cyprus. There the Turkish Government finally agreed that Foot could come as well. What followed reminds one of Hitler's treatment of certain Foreign Ministers from the Balkans. Since one could not directly humiliate Lloyd, the Turks made Foot the target and kept him almost locked up in the British Embassy; he even had to ask for permission to take a stroll. Occasionally he was allowed to participate in the talks between Lloyd and Zorlu, the latter proving to be an absolutely ruthless politician.

But these humiliations were not all. Openly Ankara ordered its kin in Cyprus to riot. Obediently the Turkish youth rioted in the same way as their Greek counterparts had done and the Turkish Cypriot policemen looked on. The British had to use the military to restore law and order. At the end 7 Turkish Cypriots were dead, 12 soldiers, 28 policemen and 14 firemen were hurt. When Lloyd asked Zorlu to stop the riots, the latter replied that the Turkish Cypriots were not under his control but under that of the Turkish military, but he did not hide the fact that he had ordered the start and the end of the riots. Instead of protesting sharply against the Turkish military's intervention in the internal affairs of a British Crown Colony, Lloyd backed off, thus encouraging Zorlu to make even tougher demands.

When the British Government showed readiness to make further concessions Zorlu pressed on: The Turkish Government wanted the partition of Cyprus, if London did not agree it had to reckon with the joined resistance of the Turkish Cypriots and Turkey. Küçük, who had at the same time been in Ankara, announced triumphantly after his return to Nicosia that half of Cyprus would become a Turkish province and did not even exclude a war between Turkey and Britain. Though this was a total exaggeration, it showed the thoughts behind the scenes in Ankara. Ankara knew that they were in the stronger position.

Foot felt that he was absolutely out of place and, without the tiniest farewell gesture from the Turkish side, flew back to Cyprus. Now Menderes deigned to receive the British Foreign Secretary in the presence of Zorlu. A scene followed reminding one of the reception of Chamberlain by Hitler on the Berghof. The Foot Plan was dead. Zorlu had recognized the Achilles' heel of British policy in Cyprus, its total dependence on the Turkish Cypriot police and misused this mercilessly. Moreover, he knew that for strategic reasons neither the British nor the Americans would risk a break with Ankara.

The meeting at Ankara meant a paradigm shift. From now on Ankara was one of the players in the poker game for Cyprus but it was in control, having the better cards. Foot stated in a letter to Lennox-Boyd that Ankara could cripple British policy at any time by simply ordering police inactivity. Ankara's control mechanism was the underground movement of TMT, to which we will come later.

Under normal circumstances it could have been expected that Foot, after this personal humiliation, would resign, but for this step he lacked inner strength. He was a successful civil servant flexible enough to make the turn and adapt himself to the new conditions. From now on he would cooperate more closely with the Turkish Cypriots. This in turn provoked Grivas to a war of leaflets against Foot but because of Athens' pressure the armistice held, still.

From 10 to 12 February Lloyd visited Athens accompanied by an unwilling Foot, who considered his participation as counter-productive. The Greek Government showed itself flexible but rejected Lloyd's proposal to set up a Turkish base in Cyprus and to convene a Tripartite Conference. A meeting between Makarios and Foot did not yield any political result but they came closer personally.

After his return to Cyprus, Foot, together with Reddaway, developed a new plan which resembled the Tridominum Plan. According to this plan the status quo should be maintained for about 15 years, Greece and Turkey having a kind of supervision of Cyprus. The negotiations should be terminated. Thus the British could act on their own. Macmillan had himself informed and asked Foot to work out details. In May 1958 Macmillan announced that soon a new plan would be brought forward. In order to keep Grivas from beginning bigger actions, Foot sent him a letter via intermediaries, appealing to him not to renew violence and suggesting a personal meeting. Grivas rejected the latter but ordered a stop to sabotage.

The Macmillan Plan
The new plan was a mixture of Harding's partnership program and the Tridominum plan. Athens and Ankara were to send a representative to Cyprus who should cooperate with the Cypriot Government. The Government was to be representative, but the two ethnic groups could handle their communal affairs on their own. All Cypriots would have Greek or Turkish citizenship besides the British one. There would be an interim period of 7 years in which the partnership model would be tried. The Constitution should be worked out jointly. Each ethnic group should have a house of representatives with full legislative power over its own communal affairs. Cyprus as a whole was to be ruled by a Council, presided over by the governor, composed of the representatives of the mother countries and six elected ministers, four Greek and two Turkish Cypriots. The Governor would be responsible for internal security, foreign and defence policy. The representatives of the mother countries would have the right to have bills checked by an independent court. A precondition for the application of the plan was the cessation of violence. As soon as violence ended the British would lift the state of emergency and allow the banished to return.

The comparison of this plan with the Radcliffe Plan and the constitutional offer of 1948 shows that the Cypriots would obtain less rights. There was not even a Chief Minister. The Greek Cypriot majority would be levelled in the decision taking bodies. Macmillan had elegantly sailed around the dangerous cliffs. He had managed to free himself from the December 1956 declaration (double self-determination) and thus avoided immediate partition and postponed the final decision for seven years, but at the same time the December statement remained in force. In a situation favouring Turkey, partition could be achieved. The Tridominium concept was a continuation of the old divide-and-rule game on a higher level. Macmillan knew that the Greeks would never accept a British-Turkish condominium and sooner or later would grudgingly accept the Tridominium. Under the attractive disguise of partnership, the continuation of British rule was taken care of by the Macmillan Plan. The winner of the plan would have been the Turks and the Greeks the clear losers.

Of course the British Government tried by intensive diplomacy to have the plan accepted but with little success. Makarios had invited the mayors of the six big towns, the bishops of Kyrenia and Kition and another 15 leading personalities to Athens to discuss the plan. On 20

June, after intensive debates, the Cypriots rejected the plan because it interfered with the right to self-determination and increased the cleavage between the ethnic groups. But Makarios was ready to discuss a really democratic constitution. One day later Karamanlis rejected the plan, declaring, however, that he was ready to participate in well prepared negotiations, but tripartite negotiations were excluded.

In Cyprus, Denktaş, deputizing for Küçük who was abroad, expressed the opinion that the Macmillan Plan was a step in the direction of enosis. On 28 June Menderes' reply to Macmillan became known, rejecting the Plan because it did not imply partition. Thus the states concerned rejected it but uninvolved states, e. g. the NATO states, found it to be good and public opinion in Britain considered it practicable. Even the Labour leaders refrained from criticism, as was shown during the debate in Parliament on 26 June 1958. Though there were diplomatic efforts to save the Plan, all failed because of Turkish intransigence. Macmillan's Plan seemed to have died.

But all of a sudden the tide turned when on 14 July 1958 in Iraq the military took over and a republic was proclaimed. The new government declared its withdrawal from the Bagdad Pact. Jordan, having thrown out the British two years before asked for British help and the Lebanese Government called the Americans. The coup in Iraq fundamentally changed the threat scenario for Turkey: in the West Bulgaria, in the North the Soviet Union, in the East Iraq and in the Southeast the UAR Syria. Ismet İnönü who had close contacts with the armed forces, warned the Government during a secret session of the parliament not to overstretch. Menderes panicked and turned round: After a meeting of the remaining members of the ruined Bagdad Pact in London on 29 July he met Macmillan secretly.

He declared himself ready to accept the Macmillan Plan fully provided there were no changes at all. In this case he would cooperate with the British, stop violence in Cyprus and abandon partition and the demand for a military base. Macmillan pointed out to his visitor that he had to reserve his right to discuss Greek suggestions and possibly accept them, but he would keep the Turks informed. Menderes urged Macmillan to apply the Plan without changes and conduct only mock negotiations with the Greeks. It was agreed to meet again the following day. As Menderes was pressed for time - his return flight was imminent - he accepted Macmillan's proposals. Now the Greeks had to be persuaded.

In order to achieve this Macmillan flew to Athens on 7 August 1958 to conduct talks with Karamanlis. At their first meeting they agreed on two basic points: the ending of violence and an interim period of seven years with a provisional solution without prejudicing the final solution. At the second meeting Karamanlis pulled apart the Plan, characterizing it as the worst of all ever submitted. Macmillan was adamant because he knew the Turks would reject any concession made to the Greeks. He promised, however, to make an effort in Ankara to push through as many as possible of the Greek requests for change. It was obvious that the content of the results of the Athens talks was rather irrelevant for Macmillan. For him it was decisive that world opinion noticed that he talked with Greeks. Typical of this attitude was the fact that Macmillan refrained from telling the Greeks that the Turks had principally accepted the plan because this might have led to bigger demands from the Greek side.

In Ankara the Turkish leadership had overcome its panic and had returned to its old intransigence. When Macmillan arrived on 9 August in Ankara the reception was splendid, but during the talks Zorlu behaved arrogantly, presenting such exaggerated demands that Macmillan left the room one time, totally infuriated and returned only after a great effort on the part of his companions. The Turkish side insisted that the plan had to be applied precisely; only then would it cooperate. The consequences of a non-application were not mentioned but they were clear. When Macmillan left Ankara on 10 August 1958 he had achieved nothing.

Macmillan's visit to Ankara was a total failure. The Turks had made it clear to him that they were not ready to modify any part of the plan. Should Macmillan not modify the plan the Greeks would reject it. Should he modify it the Turks would stall. Thus modifications could be made only with the greatest caution. But before the Prime Minister rose to this challenge he visited Cyprus on 11 August for a few hours.

On 12 August Macmillan reported to the Cabinet, which decided to continue with the application of the plan, but make some changes. The representatives of the mother countries should no longer sit in the Governor's Council but should have the characters of ambassadors with an advisory function. The idea of a double nationality was dropped as well as the reference to a condominium as a final solution. A common elected representative institution was mentioned as a possibility. These changes met the Greek demands halfway in minor matters but the decisive question of the presence of a representative of the Turkish Government Macmillan did not raise, knowing that in this case the Turks would reject the plan. In order to sweeten the bitter pill of the small concessions to the Greeks, Macmillan envisaged official recognition of existing illegal self-administrative authorities in all towns; he even planned separate municipal councils for both communities. The plan was to be realized soon so that the representatives of the Governments could be appointed on 1 October.

By a show of reinforced diplomacy Macmillan tried to push the plan through but the Greek Government continued to reject it, though offering negotiations. The Turkish Government accepted provided the right to a double self-determination was put down in writing, which Macmillan rejected. In Washington it was recognized that the plan could be pushed through against the will of the Greeks and with Makarios rejecting it totally. The latter had announced he would bring the case to the UN. Even the Colonial Office was sceptical about enforcing the plan in this way.

British policy, which had brought the Turks into the game to neutralize Greek ambitions by Turkish ones in order to stay in Cyprus forever, had arrived at a point where this policy began to reverse. The British would once more fight EOKA and probably beat it again but not defeat it once and for all. At some time British public opinion would demand an end to the struggle. As long as the British fought back they were dependent on the Turkish Cypriot police, and in order to keep them on the British side the Turkish Government had to be kept in good humour. Thus the British fought to clear the way of the Turks for partition.

On 7 September the first preparation for the realization of the Macmillan Plan began. Registers of voters were compiled, despite the fact that it was clear that only the Turkish Cypriots would vote. On 9 September Grivas announced the end of the armistice, and on 18 September the American vice-consul, who had just arrived, was shot at and heavily wounded. EOKA's next round of violence began.

The beginning of the inter-communal clashes
As early as summer of 1955 Küçük's party was renamed *Kıbris Türktür Partisi* (Cyprus-is-Turkish-Party). From that time a close relationship existed with organizations in Turkey carrying the same name (*Kıbris Türktür*). Since 1956 Küçük, with the approval of Menderes, preached partition of the island. In September of that year the first important underground organization VOLKAN, was founded. When EOKA killed the first Turkish Cypriot policemen, VOLKAN took revenge. In May 1956 the *Times of Cyprus* wrote that ethnically motivated violence was a fact in Cyprus. When in 1957 radio Ankara issued the slogan that Greeks and Turks could not live together, VOLKAN did its best to adduce evidence by instrumentalizing the Turkish Cypriot mob. The security forces turned a blinf eye to the ensuing riots. Turkish Cypriots who did not agree with this course were threatened or even attacked. In September 1957 the riots assumed such proportions that the authorities outlawed VOLKAN.

In the meantime, however, a new underground organization called TMT (Türk Mukavement Teşkilati - Turkish Resistance Organisation) had been set up. Its commander was Lieutenant Colonel Riza Vuruşkan of the Turkish army. TMT's emblem contained the Grey Wolf (Bozkurt) and its aims were: 1) Fight for the security of life and property of the Turkish Cypriots; 2) oppose EOKA; 3) discourage attacks on the Turkish Cypriots; 4) ensure the security of the Turkish community and fight communism; 5) strengthen the bonds between the Turkish Cypriots and the mother country and fight for union with Turkey. Officially Rauf Denktaş, who had been state attorney until then, became the political advisor of Vuruşkan. In reality Denktaş had a position within TMT resembling that of a political commissar in the Soviet Red Army.

While TMT structures were being built up in Cyprus the military in Ankara set up a support staff with branches for coordination, training, supplies, telecommunication, weapons, and logistics. Many regular officers and reactivated reserve officers were sent to Cyprus under the disguise of "school inspectors, teachers and imams" where they took over leading positions in TMT. There is little doubt that the British were informed about this.

Comparing the structures of TMT with those of EOKA one discovers great similarities. There were cells and youths were recruited. But there were decisive differences: the leading cadres were trained military who took care of discipline and unconditional obedience. TMT, too, punished treason by death. Qualified members were sent to Turkey for military training, and the Turkish General Staff assisted the organization with the supply of weapons. TMT managed to get the Turkish masses under its control. Turkish Cypriot riots were no schoolboy riots with willful riots and confrontations with the security forces; these riots were assaults on the Greek Cypriots and destruction of their property, the inhabitants being expelled. This was the beginning of the ethnic cleansing practised later on a larger scale. The most decisive difference, however, was that TMT always remained under the close control of Ankara. Denktaş was no Grivas steering an independent course almost outside Athens' control. TMT was Ankara's instrument to push through its aims.

In early summer 1958 TMT ordered its people to break off any contact with the Greek Cypriots and not to speak Greek any more. Obviously TMT tried to deepen the ethnic cleavage and incite the two communities against each other. At the same time EOKA and TMT began to attack the Cypriot Left, AKEL and PEO, who were considered traitors. Cultural centres of the Left were destroyed and its members terrorized. About 1,500 of 3,692 Turkish Cypriot PEO members defected. Leading cadres were murdered.

When on 7 June 1958 agents provocateurs of TMT exploded a bomb at the press office of the Turkish embassy, the riots began. Bands of Turkish Cypriot youths entered those parts of the old town of Nicosia inhabited by Greek Cypriots, attacked the Greeks, plundered and destroyed shops; two persons were killed and dozens wounded. There were street battles. On 8 June the riots spread over the whole island. Radio Ankara took pains to inflame the mood to boiling. On 11 June the riots reached another climax when in Nicosia 30 houses were burned down by the mob and the riots spread to the villages. The composed British reaction was astonishing, only on the next day a curfew was imposed on the Turkish quarter of the old town. Criticism of the security forces was rejected by Foot.

12 June 1958 became known in Cypriot history as the Gönyeli (Kioneli) massacre day. On 11 June British security forces had arrested a group of Greeks near the mixed village of Skylloura who wanted to attack their Turkish neighbours. Next day they were to be brought to Nicosia but at the city's outskirts the commander of the transport received the order to set them free. Shortly behind the village of Gönyeli, the convoy stopped and the military let the Greeks go and told them to march to their village 12 kilometres away. This was the usual praxis to cool down the tempers. But on the way the group walked into a Turkish ambush. Nine were slain,

the others escaped death because the commander of the British transport unit stopped the massacre. The ensuing official inquiry found no culprits.

The riots of June were the work of the leadership of the Turkish Cypriots and Ankara. They were the "proof" that Greek and Turkish Cypriots could not live together. The allegation that they had been provoked by EOKA terror against the Turkish Cypriots is erroneous, because until then there had been no EOKA victims among the Turkish Cypriots, except a few policemen. Even after Gönyeli the murders continued with a short interruption. Towards the end of 1958 the conflict took a new form: TMT fanatics terrorized Greeks in certain suburbs of Nicosia and Limassol in such a way that they fled with bag and baggage. Simultaneously a new TMT controlled migration movement of Turkish Cypriots towards the north of the island began. This was the beginning of what is today called ethnic cleansing.

Grivas understood that the flight of the Greeks had to be stopped otherwise a de-facto-partition threatened and he ordered his people, in leaflets, not to run away from the Turks but to stay and fight. The result were chaotic days following the principle of revenge and counter-revenge. By the end about 100 people had been murdered senselessly, and 170 had been seriously injured. The numbers of victims on both sides were almost equal. In July, however, 44 Turks and 28 Greeks lost their lives. The murders were executed in incredibly brutal ways and the victims were unarmed. Had the security forces not intervened, the number of dead would have been much higher.

Foot wanted to crack down on TMT but the commander of the security forces knew that an EOKA attack was imminent against the British and accepted the logic that the enemy of my enemy is my friend. If the British attacked the Greek Cypriots, the Turkish Cypriots would accept some arrests of their people. Thus on 22 July almost 2,000 Greek and 58 Turkish Cypriots were arrested. Not one EOKA activist was among the Greeks. The Greeks were locked up for many months while the Turkish Cypriots were discreetly set free after a short while. On 23 July TMT was outlawed, but not one of its well known leaders was arrested. Küçük and Denktaş had been informed about the action.

This action embittered the Greek Cypriots and Foot lost all credibility in their eyes. For them it was clear that the British and the Turks were working together for the partition of the island, and the publication of the Macmillan Plan strengthened this impression. Salvation could only come from EOKA. Unwillingly these actions intensified the control of EOKA over the Greek community.

Final activities of EOKA

All along Grivas had been living in his hiding place in Limassol. Over the months he lost his sense of reality and developed a bunker mentality reminding us of the last days of Hitler underneath the Reichskanzlei. He relied on the reports of his subordinate commanders, and as these knew his choleric temperament they reported to him what they believed he wanted to hear. Failures caused him to throw a tantrum. His loss of reality took on grotesque features. Thus he asked Athens to resign from NATO. Via the bishop of Kition he bombarded Athens with messages full of misinterpretations, magniloquent pieces of advice and senseless demands. When at the beginning of August Averof and Makarios informed him about the Macmillan Plan he replied utterly arrogantly: *"The Cyprus problem will not be cleared up by palavers between London, Athens and Ankara. Historic times demand historic decisions."* Slowly Grivas became a burden on the policy of Greece.

In October 1968 Grivas ordered EOKA to attack the British again. But the new generation of EOKA fighters did not have the stamina of those of the first round. Since the British soldiers had become cautious, Grivas' fighters were looking increasingly for soft targets for their assassination attempts and their bombings and ambushes were not carried out in personal attacks but by radio or cable control. Moreover, Grivas could no longer control the carrying out of his orders and his inferiors interpreted them according to their taste. A military code of honour was unknown to them, thus women became targets, too, a fact which Grivas rejected on principle.

In October 1958 EOKA killed 31 persons (16 British among them 4 civilians, 12 Greeks and 1 Turk. The ugliest murder was committed on 3 October 1958 in Famagousta when the wife of a sergeant and mother of five children was killed. She, her daughter and a German lady friend were shopping downtown for her daughter's bridal dress. When they left the shop two youths came from behind and shot at the two elder women. The mother died on the spot, her friend was heavily wounded but survived thanks to a Greek pharmacist who rendered first aid. The daughter was able to take cover behind some cars and thus escape the killers. The perpetrators were never caught. Grivas alleged in a leaflet that British agents provocateurs had committed the murder.

If the number of lethal attacks decreased in November this was the result of the security forces' new tactics. British civilians were taught how to shoot and received guns. Women were allowed to do their shopping only at certain hours when the streets were supervised by soldiers. More efficient was a curfew, especially designed for youths from whom the killers were recruited. They were allowed to leave their houses go to their work place and even there they were not allowed to leave the buildings. This was controlled by soldiers watching from flat roofs, balconies, entrances and gardens. These solders wore boots with rubber soles and could move noiselessly. They had the right to fire at all offenders. Additionally there were night patrols controlling the curfew. The risk for the killer teams became so big that the assassination attempts stopped completely in December.

The security forces succeeded in breaking the communication system of EOKA and a growing number of captured EOKA fighters were ready to blow the whistle. Kyriakos Matsis, one of the first fighters of EOKA, became the victim of treason. Matsis was 32 years old. On 19 November soldiers encircled the village and began to search house after house for Matsis' hiding place. The house where the soldiers knew that Matsis was hiding was searched several times but only when a soldier probed the joint between the tiles with a bayonet was the trap door discovered leading to Matsis' cellar hiding place. The soldiers asked Matsis to surrender but he refused; he told his two companions to climb up and surrender. The two youths came out and gave themselves up. They reported that Matsis was heavily armed and would try to escape. The soldiers threw a smoke-bomb into the hiding place and when Matsis did not come out they threw a hand grenade, which killed him immediately. In order to avoid demonstrations like the one at the Mouskos burial, Matsis' corpse was brought to the Central Prison in Nicosia where he was buried in the court of the imprisoned graves beside his comrades. The house where the hiding place had been was blown up.

When in October the new round of terror began Governor Foot asked the United Kingdom's counter-intelligence and security agency, the MI5 for help. The agency sent an expert to Cyprus who analysed the situation and expressed the opinion that Grivas could be found by analysing the captured documents and observing the movements of certain people. In January 1959 the MI5-Chief himself came to Cyprus accompanied by that analyst. Within a few weeks additional MI5 experts localized the hiding place of Grivas. Though Grivas, warned by someone, managed once more to escape, his persecutors were on his heels, as he himself admits in his memoirs. However this may be, Grivas' claim that he could have continued the EOKA struggle for an unlimited period is wrong. His juvenile killer teams were immobilized by the curfew. His partisans were hunted down. And it was a question of time before MI5 would have traced his new hiding place, thus at least obliging him to flee again. Thus the second round of violence was moving towards defeat. If this did not happen it was to the fact that a political solution was found above Grivas' head.

Renewed confrontation in the UN and the road to the solution
As we already noted, the British Government decided in early September 1958 to begin with the preparations for the realization of the Macmillan Plan. The Greek Government on the other side tried to stop this by two diplomatic efforts I. E. in NATO and the UN trying to enlist American support. As early as 15 August Athens asked the UN to put the Cyprus Problem on the agenda of the General Assembly. In September Averof flew to New York and managed by intensive lobbying to have the Cyprus Question debated on 28 September.

Simultaneously from Athens Karamanlis made an effort to bring the problem to the NATO Council, arguing that the sending of an official representative of Turkey to Cyprus might lead to a withdrawal of Greece from NATO. Secretary General Spaak was alarmed and suggested convoking a tripartite conference with participation of the two Cypriot communities under NATO auspices, where he himself would present a plan. Karamanlis agreed and Averof affirmed that in this case Greece's UN motion would be withdrawn. The British side, however, remained intransigent.

On 24 September 1958 Spaak submitted a plan similar to Macmillan's Plan but containing decisive improvements: Besides the two houses of representatives there was to be a central parliament, the Governor's Council should have a clear Greek majority consisting of him and the two presidents of the houses of representatives. An equalization of majority and minority was for him out of the question but the latter should receive guarantees. The Greek Government agreed with Spaak's proposal and signalled that Makarios, too, approved it. The British Government, however, obstinately clung to the application of the Macmillan Plan. American pressure made London declare its readiness to participate in the conference suggested by Spaak, and the Turkish Government announced that instead of sending a representative to Cyprus the Turkish consul would take over that function. Spaak was afraid that the Greek Government might reject this.

In the meantime, invited by the Ethnarchy, Barbara Castle had gone on a kind of fact-finding-mission. On 15 September she met Makarios in Athens. During their conversation Makarios made a sensational concession: *"I am ready to accept an independent Cyprus provided this cannot be changed neither by union with Greece nor partition nor otherwise except the UN approves such a change."* Such an independence guaranteed by the UN would not hinder Cyprus from staying in the Commonwealth. The rights of the Turkish minority would be determined by negotiations. The British Government together with representatives of the Cypriots should work out a constitution which should be in force for an interim period. Obviously Makarios had understood that there was only one alternative left: Independence or partition. During her talk with Karamanlis the following day the latter confessed to be totally astounded by this step of Makarios', but agreed. However, he doubted whether the British Government would accept it.

In Ankara Castle was told that Macmillan had accepted partition in writing. Should Britain give up Cyprus it must be given back to Turkey as a whole. Castle gained the impression that Macmillan had duped Parliament. In Cyprus she talked with Foot and the leaders of the Turkish Cypriots, receiving the impression that the latter demanded partition. After her return to Athens she recommended to Makarios that he make his renunciation of enosis and his proposal of independence known to her. This was done, and the British Government rejected it immediately because it feared trouble with Turkey. In his zeal to please Turkey, Lennox-Boyd went as far as calling Cyprus an offshore island of Turkey, in his speech at the Tory Party Congress. Obviously he wanted to torpedo Spaak's Conference Plan and Makarios' independence. In this he succeeded partially because Karamanlis withdrew his promise to participate in Spaak's conference. Thus Spaak's Plan was finished. The only way to stop the realization of the Macmillan Plan was the UN.

In the meantime Makarios came under fire from the Greek and Greek Cypriot nationalists insisting on enosis. In order to get out of the line of fire, on 22 November he claimed that he had made the independence proposal on American advice. But independence, however, did not exclude union with Greece, which might come later, but he was not sure whether the British bases could remain on the island. This statement provoked a strong worded denial from the State Department and the British and the Turks interpreted Makarios' statement as a proof of his duplicity and trickery. In reality this was a typical example of Makarios' tactic to take the wind out of his opponent's sails by paying lip-service to enosis. After a stormy conversation between Averof and Makarios the latter denied his statement: he had been misunderstood. Makarios did not understand that thus he was gambling away his credibility while at the same time making the other distrustful.

The debate in the First Committee lasted several days and the arguments brought forward were almost the same as in earlier debates. At the end a resolution submitted by Iran was adopted which implied a defeat for Athens. By this resolution Ankara became, under international law, an equal player in the poker game for Cyprus and the acknowledgment of the "legitimate aspirations" implied even partition. Thus Athens had not succeeded in stopping the Macmillan Plan in the First Committee. The question was now whether this could be achieved in the General Assembly. Information reaching Averof was depressing: on the horizon a two-thirds majority for the position of London and Ankara began to show. In this situation something incredible happened: While Averof was talking to some journalists in a corridor, Zorlu addressed him suggesting a private meeting the next day. Averof agreed provided the Iranian resolution was not put to the vote. Zorlu agreed and during the next hours the text of a milder resolution was worked out behind the scenes. On 5 December 1958 the new resolution was voted for and on Saturday 6 December Averof and Zorlu met in the empty UN building.

Zorlu said that the British had played off the Greeks against the Turks in order to keep Cyprus. Recently they had pinned their hopes more on Turkey as the Macmillan Plan showed. Turkey wanted partition, but as the Greeks rejected partition vehemently and Ankara wanted friendly relations with Greece and the Greeks and the Greek Cypriots had accepted the idea of a guaranteed independence, it was time to search for an amicable solution.

Averof agreed with Zorlu's analysis almost completely but there remained the question which form independence should have. Zorlu replied that in order to make the British accept their plan they should be allowed to keep their bases. As there were two ethnic groups on Cyprus, certain areas of public life had to be organized differently; he mentioned education, religion, family law, and civil status law. In all other areas ways to share power had to be found. The bigger community should be ready to give the smaller community more than a proportional share of power. In some areas the two groups should be equal and in others a relation of 6 to 4 could be imagined. In the towns there should be separate municipalities. For security reasons Turkey needed a military base in Cyprus.

Averof rejected the latter because it would undermine the sovereignty of a Cyprus republic. Then he pulled apart the argument that Cyprus was necessary for Turkey's security and suggested that for the future Republic of Cyprus a status of neutrality, like Austria, would be appropriate. Averof saw no problem in granting the Turkish minority over-proportional rights, and agreed to a separation of education etc. as Zorlu had proposed, but he rejected the idea of separate municipalities because that would be the beginning of separation. Instead separate communal authorities should be created. As a way out Zorlu suggested the creation of a federal republic. The decisive point for him was that the old friendly relations between Greece and Turkey would be re-established. He proposed that they should inform their Governments and Makarios about their talk. They could meet again at the next NATO Council session in Paris and continue their secret talks. The British should not hear anything about their talks, otherwise they would fail. If they negotiated bi-laterally and did not allow outside interference they could talk honestly and openly. Averof gained the impression that Zorlu was talking on behalf of Menderes and that the Turkish side had discussed and planned the topic in all details.

The reason for this Turkish volte face probably was Turkish security considerations: the Bagdad Pact had collapsed, and Iraq was approaching the UAR which maintained close relations with the Soviet Union. The Kurds in Turkey and Iraq spoke of creating a state of their own. Since the end of November Khrushchev's Berlin ultimatum threatened the Western Alliance. A Greek withdrawal from NATO could not be excluded if a fait accompli was created in Cyprus. Additionally Parliamentary elections were imminent in Britain and in NATO a majority was for Cypriot independence. In view of this situation, Ankara opted for a practicable solution.

The main topic of the annual winter meeting of the NATO Council from 16 to 19 December 1958 was the rejection of the Berlin ultimatum. The private meeting between Zorlu and Averof on 15 December was not noticed. Averof and Zorlu worked out a number of basic principles: Turkey and Greece would conclude an agreement about the independence of Cyprus excluding enosis and partition. A treaty of alliance should link the new state to Greece, Britain and Turkey. The sovereignty and territorial integrity of Cyprus should be guaranteed by an agreement. Another treaty was to guarantee the abidance of the constitution. Cyprus should become a republic with a unitary House of Representatives and two Communal Chambers responsible for religious and cultural matters of the two Communities. The Vice-President of the Republic had to be a Turkish Cypriot who should have a veto in matters of foreign and security policy. Details should be negotiated later.

On 17 December 1958 Averof and Zorlu informed their slightly irritated British colleague, Lloyd, that they wanted to talk to him about the fate of a British colony and he had not slightest idea what they were talking about. A meeting was agreed upon for 18 December. At that meeting Averof and Zorlu assessed that the Cyprus Problem could only be solved if the island became independent and the British gave up all rights of sovereignty. They could retain two military bases of a reasonable size. Lloyd was taken aback by the idea that Britain would no longer have a say in Cyprus. While the British were squirming, negotiations between Athens and Ankara were running at high speed.

In the middle of January 1959 Averof and Zorlu met again in Paris. As there was almost total agreement a meeting of the Prime Ministers was agreed upon. Makarios showed himself content with the results of the negotiations so far. On 2 February there was another meeting in the vicinity of Athens Airport. Averof wanted to know, on behalf of Karamanlis, whether according to Zorlu's and Menderes' opinion official negotiations could begin. Simultaneously. the last conflicting points were solved. Zorlu once more tried to get Greek approval for a Turkish military base. Averof, understanding Zorlu's motives, rejected this again. Though not all open questions had found a solution, Averof and Zorlu agreed that the last round between the Prime Ministers could begin. On 3 February Ankara gave the green light, and it was decided that these negotiations should begin in Zurich on 6 February 1959.

THE TREATIES OF ZURICH AND LONDON

The negotiations in Zurich

Both delegations arrived in Zurich on 5 February. The delegations were rather small, consisting of the Prime Minister, the Foreign Minister and a few high ranking diplomats. The Greek delegation had the impression that the Turkish Government meant business. There was no representative of the Cypriots.

The negotiations proper were done by the Foreign Ministers. There was no protocol. These negotiations were far less relaxed than those between Averof and Zorlu because now the results were binding. Though the topics were the same, now the details had to be fixed and it happened every now and then that the devil was in the details. There were two rounds of negotiations, one in the morning and one in the afternoon. As soon as a result was achieved the diplomats put it into the final wording of the treaty. The Prime Ministers staying in their hotel suites, were constantly kept informed about the results. When it happened that they disagreed with a formulation, they sent the text back to the Foreign Minister to re-negotiate it. But the teams came closer humanely: on one of the days Karamanlis had a fever attack; a concerned Menderes visited him in his suite and asked after his state of health.

One of the most difficult topics was the renewed demand for a military base for Turkey. When the Greek side continued to reject this Zorlu suggested the establishment of a joint British, Greek and Turkish headquarters. The Greek side agreed but now the question arose about the number of troops stationed on Cyprus. Since the two Foreign Ministers could not find an agreement this problem was put to the Prime Ministers. Karamanlis suggested a relation of 900 Greek to 600 Turkish soldiers and officers. Menderes demanded an increase by 50 and received it. Thus this thorny problem was solved.

Another hot topic was the character of the future state. The Turkish side demanded a federal structure which the Greek side rejected because it might have led to partition. The solution found took all anxieties into consideration: Cyprus was to become an independent republic with a president. The new republic should have the right to become a NATO member and both Prime Ministers promised to promote this as much as possible.

Altogether three treaties were worked out: The first contained the basic structure of the Constitution which will be analysed separately. In the second, the Treaty of Guarantee, Greece and Turkey guaranteed the independence of Cyprus. An economic integration into another state was excluded, as was a direct or indirect partition of the island. Activities calling for enosis or taksim should be prohibited. A Treaty of Alliance should protect the independence and territorial integrity of the new state. Should there be riots in Cyprus the guarantors should consult each other and then have the right to intervene with the only aim of restoring the *status quo ante*. The same Treaty regulated the stationing of the military contingents of the mother countries.

Besides these three fundamental agreements on the setting up of the independent Republic of Cyprus, which were published after Great Britain had entered the agreements as well, there was another secret "gentlemen's" agreement between Karamanlis and Menderes which was never published. In it the two Prime Ministers promised that they would support Cyprus' membership of NATO. The Zurich solution averted partition inherent in the Macmillan Plan. The Zurich agreement was, in the existing circumstances, the best possible solution. Now Makarios' and Grivas' approval had to be obtained. If this succeeded the end of the conflict was at hand.

On 11 February 1959, after his return to Athens, Karamanlis informed Makarios about the results of the negotiations. Makarios declared his approval of everything but wanted to have a say in the question of the size of the future British base, which was accepted by the Greek side. On 12 February Makarios informed Grivas and the Bishop of Kition by letter: the Zurich agreement was the maximum that the Greek Government could get. Having only just been informed, Grivas already began to obstruct. On 12 February Karamanlis informed Makarios that the British agreed to a conference of five including the Cypriots. Again Makarios agreed with the results achieved but wanted the assent of his compatriots.

During his talks with representatives of the Greek Cypriots on 13 February he encountered strong misgivings and began to dither. A discussion of many hours followed which came to the decision that Makarios should travel to London and should denounce the agreements if he could not improve them. During a talk with officials of the Greek Ministry for Foreign Affairs it was obvious that Makarios was totally insecure. In the evening Karamanlis was able to steady

Makarios so much that he declared he would take a final decision on 14 February. This he did, at the same time announcing that he would take those Cypriots with him to London. Obviously Makarios intended to make them share responsibility. Grivas remained silent, he was insulted and ignored.

The negotiations in London

Averof and Zorlu arrived in London on 11 February in order to brief the British Government about the results of the Zurich negotiations. Macmillan had realized in the meantime that his plan could not be pushed through and was ready to accept almost everything provided the British could keep their bases. After he had been informed about the content of the Zurich agreements, he had the new course accepted by the Cabinet. Lloyd at first wanted to have a say in formulating the constitution but gave in. On 16 February all texts were agreed upon and could be signed. Thus the Prime Ministers of Greece and Turkey as well as Makarios and Küçük were invited for the final conference in Lancaster House in London on 17 February.

The Greek Cypriot delegation arrived in London on 15 February. In the morning of 16 February Makarios informed the delegates about the state of affairs, asking them to voice their opinion. The huge majority of those present argued against accepting the Zurich agreement but at the end of the discussion each of them declared that he would follow Makarios' lead whatever he decided. Makarios made it clear to them that they had only an advisory function and that he would decide according to his conscience. When Averof heard of Makarios' renewed dithering he sent two diplomats to browbeat him and the delegates.

The British Government, too, did not trust Makarios' oral assurances, not totally, and considered it possible that the Archbishop could make the conference fail at the very last moment. Therefore, they considered it wise to make Makarios sign a paper declaring that he agreed to the Zurich agreements. Foot was asked to obtain such a declaration from Makarios. The Archbishop signed the paper at once, noticing that the paper's wording was not unambiguous.

On the morning of 17 February the Greek Cabinet once more gave Karamanlis full freedom of action with Makarios and the Cypriots and the Prime Minister flew to London. The conference began in the late morning. Lloyd stated that the Zurich Agreements were a fundamental one on which to build the final solution. Zorlu spoke of the revival of Turkish-Greek friendship and hoped that the communities on Cyprus would develop the same spirit of cooperation. Makarios claimed some caveats. Denktaş, deputizing for Küçük, declared agreement. Lloyd adjourned the conference until the next day.

Averof informed Karamanlis, who had arrived in London, about Makarios' attitude. Karamanlis made Makarios and his advisors come to the Greek Embassy and accused him of breaking his word. Makarios admitted this, invoking his conscience. Karamanlis exploded: Makarios made the Greek Government look ridiculous. If he wanted to continue the struggle in Cyprus he would have to look for other allies. Karamanlis said this and left the room in a fury. Averof understood that Makarios was trying to win over the majority of the Cypriot delegates and suggested another meeting next morning. At this meeting all Cypriot delegates were present. Averof explained to them the importance of the agreements. In the ensuing discussion it became clear that the majority of the delegates were for acceptance. When the vote was taken 27 voted yes and only 9 voted no; among them were Tassos Papadopoulos, Vasos Lyssaridis and the representatives of PEO/AKEL.

The continuation of the conference had to be postponed to the afternoon because Menderes' plane had had a terrible accident when landing at Gatwick and the Prime Minister was in hospital. Lloyd stated that the three Foreign Ministers had agreed. Now it was the Cypriots' turn to give their opinion. Makarios spoke first and began to pick the agreements to pieces.

Everybody was horrified. After Makarios, Denktaş stated that precisely these points which Makarios had criticized were indispensable for the Turkish Cypriots. Changing them was impossible; if one began changing, the whole Agreement would collapse. He had told Makarios in the morning that the Cyprus Republic would be created by all the agreements. The Agreements recognized the rights of both peoples and provided compromises where conflicts might appear. On the basis of this new order a Cypriot nation could certainly come about, but until this happened both sides had to make sacrifices and show understanding. The Turkish Cypriots were ready for this.

Averof stated that Greece stood by its word; for the Greek Government the Zurich Agreements were binding. The Cypriots had accepted that Makarios decide for them, and he had been constantly informed by the Greek Government and had agreed to each step. A period of quietness followed. Makarios asked for half an hour's interruption of the conference. When the Conference continued Lloyd asked Makarios whether he accepted the agreements as the foundation of the final settlement. Makarios avoided a clear answer and continued to do so. Finally, he gave them to understand that he might agree but not then. Lloyd adjourned the Conference until the next morning.

Makarios came under fire from all sides. His compatriots asked him to sign. Labour leader Gaitskell pressured him. Queen Frederica implored him on the telephone. Finally, he gave in and informed the Greek Government that he would sign the Agreements. This he did at the last meeting of the conference on 19 February. At the ensuing reception by the Greeks, Makarios went up to Karamanlis and said: *"'Well Prime Minister, did you ever really imagine that I was not going to sign?' 'In that case,' expostulated Karamanlis, 'why did you cause us so much trouble?' 'I had my reasons,' answered Makarios, beaming with pleasure."*

Makarios' reasons are of a complex nature. It is certainly right that he did not want to shoulder responsibility alone and wanted to have a majority of the Greek Cypriots behind him. But since the voting, he knew that he had it. In his ensuing behaviour there is an element of lust for bargaining and bluffing, as his petty games show during the second plenary meeting. But again he overplayed his hand and if Averof had not intervened the Conference would have broken down. Additionally, he could not put up with not taking the centre stage and only playing a walk-on part. With his public resistance he could satisfy his ambition and signal to his critics that he had fought hard. Should something go wrong he could lay the blame on Athens. He had just bowed to Athens' diktat. With his resistance at the conference he had already begun creating myths and won the interpretative control over the Zurich and London Agreements: he or rather the Cypriots, were the victims of a Machiavellian policy of Averof and Karamanlis toward Cyprus.

It was not only Makarios who was playing petty games, but Grivas as well, who for weeks played hard to get before accepting the Agreements. Only when on 8 March 1959 Foot announced a general amnesty for all EOKA members did he declare the struggle ended. When he heard of the honours waiting in Athens for him, he struck the pose of Sulla who had humbly withdrawn from the public eye after the end of his struggle, but everybody knew that Grivas took those honours for granted and it was clear that he would mingle in politics, which unfortunately had ugly consequences for Cyprus.

When on 1 March 1959 Makarios returned to Cyprus the exaltation was boundless. It is said, that over 200,000 people were in the streets to receive him. Unfortunately, he did not state clearly in his first speech that the solution was final and that any effort to change it would lead to a new catastrophe. He did not have enough courage to say so, but perhaps he himself did not understand it at that moment. In Athens and London the Governments were relieved that finally a solution had been found.

Balance
At the end of this chapter a tally of the victims of those three years is necessary. According to EOKA about 250 members lost their lives. 134 of them died in accidents or violence within the organization. About 100 were killed by the British; among them are the 9 executed. EOKA killed 104 members of the British armed forces. Between 1 April 1955 and 31 December 1959 360 soldiers lost their lives in Cyprus due to accidents, "friendly fire" or forest fires. Most of them would have stayed alive if they had not been in Cyprus, but to add them to the victims of EOKA is an exaggeration. The number of wounded soldiers was 601. The police had 51 dead, among them 12 British, 15 Greek, 22 Turkish and 2 other policemen. 206 policemen were wounded. Among the 288 civilian victims of EOKA were 26 British, 203 Greek, 7 Turkish Cypriots and 2 others. 288 civilians were wounded. During the inter-communal clashes 60 Greek and 55 Turkish Cypriots lost their lives. 98 Greeks and 86 Turks were wounded. According to Grivas EOKA counted about 1,000 members including PEKA and other activists. In 2005 22,000 former fighters of EOKA were decorated with a medal. These must have included all who had participated in the struggle by throwing stones or shouting slogans. This inflationary tendency of the member numbers reminds us of similar phenomena in postwar France when the number of former résistants increased enormously. Such a wondrous augmentation can apparently not be avoided. However, the heroization of the EOKA fighters on all levels of education is critical because it strengthens the existing nationalism and the more so since, on the Turkish Cypriot side, a similar phenomenon can be observed heroizing TMT fighters. The courageous performance of individual EOKA fighters deserves respect but the action of the organization as a whole had severe consequences discriminating against the Left as traitors and is the cause for the inter-communal conflict. Additionally, it led to a brutalization of both societies and an irritation of the sense of right and wrong for quite some time. And the real aim of the struggle, enosis, was not achieved.

1959-1965

The Destruction Of The Republic

The haggling for British Sovereign Bases

The Zurich Agreement had been a classical octroi of Athens and Ankara. The London Agreement included the leaders of the Cypriot communities but only, to keep their scope for trouble making as narrow as possible. Strictly speaking the London Agreement was also forced on the Cypriots. The London Agreement is more comprehensive (8 parts) but basically it does not differ much from the Zurich Agreement. In its final part the contractors agreed to realize the Constitution and the Agreements as quickly as possible, at the latest by 19 February 1960. By then the future President and Vice-president should have been elected.

In order to initiate the transfer of sovereignty, several commissions were set up. In Cyprus a *Joint* (Constitutional) *Commission* was to work out a constitution based on the Zurich Agreement. This commission was to consist of two representatives of the Greek and the Turkish community and two legal advisers sent by the Greek and Turkish Governments.

In Cyprus the *Transitional Committee* would prepare the transfer of sovereignty to the future independent Republic of Cyprus. Its members were the Governor, the two leaders of the ethnic groups, i.e. Makarios and Küçük, and a number of other Greek and Turkish Cypriots in proportion of 7 to 3. Certain members of the Transitional Committee would take over administrative and ministerial functions of the Government as soon as possible making, them de facto ministers.

In London another *Joint Committee* should be created which soon became known as the *London Joint Committee*. It was composed of representatives of the three Governments and of the two Cypriot communities. Its task was to prepare the final texts of the Agreements and subsidiary agreements and, among the latter. the agreement about the British bases. During the negotiations in Zurich the British bases had not been a topic. Zorlu and Averof had agreed that the British should obtain bases and had been convinced that it would not be difficult to find a mutually acceptable solution. In the London Agreement the bases had been mentioned and roughly described. The description, however, did not say anything about their size or borders and nothing at all about whether Cypriots might live in these extraterritorial areas. This impreciseness became a source of massive quarrels invoking prestige and principles.

Macmillan wanted either to lease an airport on long duration or have it under British sovereignty like Gibraltar. He would probably have been content with a minimum area but he had to consider the hardliners of the Tory faction who abhorred giving up Cyprus. In order to satisfy the Tory hardliners the area of the bases had to be maximised. This would ex post justify the sacrifices of the past four years. For Makarios on the other side the talks about the bases were the opportunity to log on to the negotiations. The only negotiable clause of the London Agreement was that of the bases and Makarios was determined to achieve the maximum on this point in order to gain a victory for himself.

Already at the first meeting of the London Committee on 23 March 1959 it became clear that the ideas of the two sides were far apart. The British wanted 170 square miles inhabited by roughly 16,000 Cypriots. Since the Cypriot negotiator, Rossidis, demanded that the bases should consist mainly of uninhabited land, the meeting was adjourned until April. When Minister of Defence Sandys visited Cyprus and met Makarios on 24 April, the latter demanded that the bases' area should not exceed 36 square miles and that not one Cypriot village should be included. During the following months both sides moved so little that the British suggested calling a conference of all those involved in London in January 1960.

The conference was fixed for 16 January 1960 but from 14 January onward talks with the Cypriots would take place. Makarios understood that he would encounter the same situation as precisely one year before. Again a solution should be found within a given time frame and again he stood alone against all others. But this time Makarios was determined not to accept an octroi and this time he had, indeed, better cards in this new game of poker: he was not pressed for time because he was ready to postpone independence. The decisive fundamental basics of a solution had been found in 1959 and the interests to those involved had been included. The problems now at stake were of no great interest for the mother countries. Thus they would not apply much pressure on him though they would side with the British, who were obliged to try to comply with the temporal requirements of the London Agreement and decolonise Cyprus on 19 February 1960. But this could only be achieved if Makarios agreed.

The arguments put forward during the conference were almost the same as those which had been produced during the last months. Makarios pushed his luck and when he got something accepted he at once tried to achieve something more in another field. On 18 January the Conference adjourned for one week. The Greek and Turkish Governments retired from the Conference because they had had enough of the haggling. But now a new alliance formed: the representatives of the two ethnic groups began to put forward joint demands. On 29 January it was obvious that the Conference had failed but that the negotiations between Makarios and the British would continue.

The new British negotiator was Julian Amery, who was as cunning a negotiator as Makarios. During the next months these two bargained about the size of the bases and that of the financial aid as though in an Oriental bazaar. Makarios obstinately demanded an area smaller than 100 square miles and Amery tenaciously wanted to stay above 100. In April they haggled about 4 square miles. When after one year of enervating negotiations they agreed upon 99 square miles Makarios opened another front, fighting for the precise line of the border and the financial aid.

Finally, on 30 July 1960 they agreed: The British grant-in-aid would be £ 14.34 million. Makarios had achieved the maximum in a rather weak position because of his negotiation skills. But to a certain degree his success was caused by the wish of the other side to get rid of the Cyprus Problem under reasonable conditions and their inability and lack of will to steer a tough course. Whether the British really needed the bases is questionable, perhaps in the context of the CENTO-Pact. The Americans, on the other hand, were of the opinion that the military weight of Cyprus had increased. The airports on Cyprus were a kind of fallback position in case the Air Force Base in Adana should be lost. Indeed, a little later the RAF base in Akrotiri became a takeoff and landing place for U2-planes. There was even a discussion whether heavy US and British bombers should be stationed there to attack the Soviet Union with nuclear bombs in case of a war. Most valuable for the Americans were the eavesdropping stations on Troodos, listening to the southern Soviet Union and the Arab world.

The Constitution

As has already been mentioned in Cyprus a Joint Committee was established to work out the constitution of the future republic on the basis of principles contained in the Zurich and London Agreements. Within a short time this committee, due to its task, became known as the *Constitutional Committee*. It consisted of legal experts of differing expertise; among them, as the neutral Swiss legal expert, Marcel Bridel. The Greek and Turkish Cypriots were represented by two delegations headed by G. Clerides and R. Denktash, both lawyers. As these two persons played a central role in Cypriot politics for many years they shall be introduced here in a more detailed manner.

Glafkos Clerides, son of the well known liberal politician I. Clerides, was born in 1919. At first he attended the *Pankyprio Gymnasio,* but in the last term he crossed over to the *English School* to prepare for his studies in England. In 1936 he began to study law in London. When World War II broke out he volunteered for the RAF, participated in bombing raids over Germany and in 1942 he became a prisoner of war there. After WWII he continued his studies at King's College and Gray's Inn in London until 1948 and in 1951 he became Barrister at Law. Between 1951 and 1960 he practised law. He was a founding member of EOKA but remained legal and defended EOKA defendants. Now he was designated minister of justice.

Rauf R. Denktash, son of a well known judge in Paphos, was born in 1924. He, too, graduated from the English School, worked as an interpreter, judicial employee and teacher. Later he went to London and studied Law at Lincoln's Inn. After the exam he returned to Cyprus in 1957 and practised law. In 1948 he was one of the representatives of the Turkish Cypriots in the Consultative Assembly and member of the *Turkish Affairs Committee*. In 1949 he became state attorney and after 1955 he participated in the prosecution of EOKA members. In 1957 he resigned and began a political career. He was one of the founders of TMT, the Turkish Cypriot equivalent of EOKA.

The Constitutional Committee began its work on 20 April 1959. In order to speed up its work a four headed subcommittee was set up which was to discuss details. On 6 April 1960 the draft constitution was ready. It had 198 articles with about 40,000 words and five pages with annexes. It was one of the longest and most verbose constitutions of Europe. When the British tried to have some changes made the Turkish Government rejected this flatly. Obviously the process begun in Zurich was continuing: the British were losing their influence on the developments in Cyprus more and more. Decisions were made by Ankara and Athens. After some hesitation London came to terms with its fate confining its criticism to semantics and linguistics.

After the successful end of the bases negotiations the representatives of the Cypriots and the mother countries signed the last amendments on 6 July 1960. On 14 July all texts dealing with Cyprus becoming an independent state, in the form of a Command Paper and the bill granting independence, were submitted to Parliament. On 29 July Parliament passed the bill in the third reading, and on 3 August Queen Elizabeth ruled by an *Order-in-Council* that the Constitution would come into effect on 16 August 1960.

Article 1 shows clearly that the Constitution had a two community character stating that the independent and sovereign Republic would have a Greek President and Turkish Vice-President elected by the two communities. The Human Rights Catalogue is far more detailed than that of most other European constitutions partly because it is a verbatim copy of the European Human Rights Convention. Obviously the authors tried to meet all eventualities and preclude violations. Restrictions of rights should be allowed in precisely described exceptional cases. Some of the articles contain noteworthy regulations e.g. Article 9 a detailed prescription for social welfare, Articles 11 and 12 classical principles of law, making Cyprus a state under the rule of the law. Article 23 acknowledged the right for a redistribution of the land which, however, was not applicable for the biggest landowner in Cyprus - the Church. Another article recognized the autonomy in wage bargaining of the Unions.

The President of the Republic, always a Greek Cypriot, is the head of the state and the Vice-President, always a Turkish Cypriot, is the vice head of the state. The President and the Vice-President represent the Republic, the first acting, the latter being present. Horizontal and vertical power sharing is prohibited, thus neither the President nor Vice-President can be a minister, deputy or member of the communal chamber or mayor of a town. If the President is abroad or incapable of executing his duties, the President of the House will act for him, in the case of the Vice-President the Vice-President of the House will perform this duty. The President of the House is always a Greek and the Vice-President a Turk each being elected by the deputies of their community. Thus the Cypriot Presidential system differs from all other such systems where the Vice-President always represents the Presidents. The President and the Vice-President are the highest representatives of their communities. They cannot act responsibly for the other community because this would violate the principle of bi-community.

Plate 17

Makarios as novice at Kykko-Abbey

Beginning of the EOKA struggle
Heroic Grivas monument at Chlorakas

Plate 18

Gouvernor Fieldmarshal John Harding

Separation of the two communities: creating the "Green Line" in the old town of Nicosia

Plate 19

Makarios, Kranidiotis, Harding, Reddaway and Paschalidis

Noel-Baker, Harding, Kranidiotis, Makarios and Lennox-Boyd

Plate 20

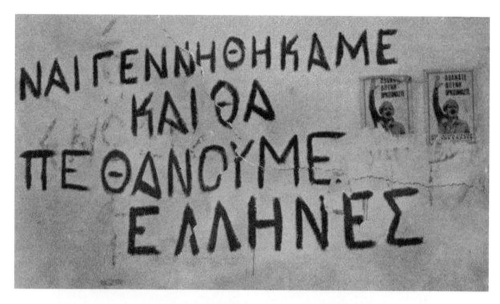

Grafitti: "We were born Greek and will die Greek"

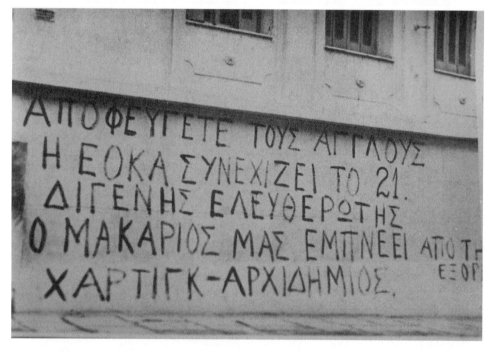

Grafitti text approximately:
"Keep away from the English. EOKA continues the struggle of 1821. Dighnis our liberator. Makarios inspires us from his exile. Harding assassin."

Plate 21

Place of execution in the Central Prison

Plate 22

Fylakismena Mnimata (Imprisoned graves)

Arrested school boys

Plate 23

Mass arrests

Conducting a car check

Plate 24

Looking for hidden weapons

A village round up

The President and Vice-President are not only the double head of the state but they are heads of the government as well, assisted by a Council of Ministers. The Ministers need not be deputies. One of the following three ministries must be administered by a Turkish Cypriot: Foreign, Defence or Finance. Decisions of the Council of Ministers must be taken with the absolute majority. Ministers are not responsible to the House but they can be sacked by the President or the Vice-President depending on their ethnic origin. The President and the Vice-President have an absolute and suspensive veto right on decisions of the Council of Ministers and the House on questions of Foreign and Security policy as well as budget laws.

Looking at the clauses dealing with the President and the Vice-President one is inclined to call the latter a Co-President and to talk of a bi-communal construction of the Executive. The usual hierarchy of a presidential constitution is replaced by an equality. Both Presidents are the guardians of the interests of their communities. This construction can function well if there is mutual trust but in the case of a conflict the two Presidents can hinder the proper functioning of the government or paralyse it.

The Legislative has a bi-communal character. It consists of the House of Representatives and the two Communal Chambers. The House has the legislative competence in all cases except those expressly reserved to the Chambers. The number of deputies is 50; 70 percent are elected by the Greeks and 30 percent the Turks of Cyprus. Each Cypriot above 21 has the right to vote and each Cypriot over 25 can be elected to an office. The election period is five years. The Chamber is responsible for religion, education, culture, civil status, communal affairs, such as welfare and sports, communal taxes and fees. These provisions deepened the cleavage between the two communities.

Especially problematical was the separation of the educational system because it prolonged the separation introduced by the British: The mother countries could continue to send teachers, professors and clerics as well as schoolbooks, to Cyprus. Naturally the new state could not publish Cypriot textbooks for the two communities because of financial reasons but whoever knows the Greek and Turkish textbooks of those years is well acquainted with the fact that the textbooks for teaching the native language and the history books were full of extreme nationalism. The development of a Cypriot identity was extremely impeded because the books and the "imported" teachers implanted a Greek or a Turkish identity with matching nationalism and the concept of an enemy, thus keeping alive the dreams of enosis and taksim even in the new republic. Education and culture were affairs of the ethnic groups, the state of Cyprus had no say in these important fields.

The constitutional articles dealing with the civil service provided a relationship of 70:30 of Greeks and Turks. The Republic was to have an army of 2,000 men of which 60 percent were Greek and 40 percent Turkish Cypriots. The 70:30 rule should be applied to the 1,000 men of the security forces (police and gendarmery). The commanders of the armed and security forces could stem from different communities but their deputies had to be from the other.

Separate municipalities with elected councils were to be set up in the five big towns. After four years the President and the Vice-President were to investigate whether this separation should continue or not. Changes of the articles containing the clauses of the Zurich Agreement were excluded. The Treaty of Guarantee and Alliance were part of the constitution.

The main objective of the constitution was the prevention of a new conflict. The way to achieve this was the strengthening of the bi-communality on all levels by making great concessions to Turkish Cypriots lifting their influence far beyond their real strength (18 %). Politically they were no longer a minority; *de jure* they were not yet equal but *de facto* they were. For the Greek Cypriots this was too much to accept. They let it be understood that they intended to change this. The Turkish Cypriots were happy with the result and regarded each effort to change suspiciously. Thus the necessary prerequisite for a proper functioning of a constitution, i.e. good understanding, trust and good will did not exist, and thus the republic based on this constitution was doomed. However, it was not the complicated constitution which led to the failure of the Republic of Cyprus but the lack of Cypriots identifying themselves with it.

The problem of the separate municipalities

Since the inter-communal clashes of early 1958 the Turkish Cypriot side had aspired towards separate municipalities. The British had watched this with a benevolent eye as is proved by the Macmillan Plan. When the preparations for the application of this plan began in late summer of 1958, a Municipal Commission was created under a former civil servant of the colonial administration in Cyprus, Brewster Surridge, to work out proposals. On 12 December the Surridge Commission submitted its proposals.

There were no doubts that separate municipalities were possible but very expensive: There would be two mayors, two city directors and two administrations. Some towns had grown so big that these offices needed full time civil servants. If the administration were divided neither side could afford the expenses. The already existing double market halls were absurd. As the disadvantages of a separation of municipal administrations outweighed by far the advantages, they should have been rejected. But there were feelings of hatred between the two communities caused by their nationalisms. However, neither this nor any opinion poll among the Cypriots were the reason to recommend separation but only the argument of the Turkish Cypriot leadership claiming that the majority of the Turkish Cypriots could no longer live together with their Greek compatriots. Separate municipalities could at best be realised in the five towns only. Surridge considered them an *"administrative nonsense but a political necessity"*. But as we have seen, they were part of the Zurich and London Agreements and became part of the constitution.

The Greek-Turkish rapprochement had only little impact on the climate in Cyprus because there the separatist activities relied on the Turkish Cypriots playing the active role. The Turkish Cypriot leadership stuck to its course of separate municipalities, but there were two distinctly different positions. Küçük played the generous and cooperative role whereas Denktash acted as the hardliner and intransigent. At the same time they were rivals in the leading of the Turkish Cypriot community, Denktash aiming at replacing Küçük at the top. Both, however, were acting in close contact with the Government in Ankara.

After their return from Ankara in March 1959 it became clear that Ankara approved the separatist course. The aim was to divide the two communities in each field and to create ethnically homogenous settlements. Turkish Cypriots living in mixed villages were encouraged to move to the town and settle down in the Turkish quarters; Greeks living there were browbeaten so that they moved. Another means of separating the communities was the economic separation: TMT enforced a boycott of all Greek goods and services. Denktash ordered the creation of a Turkish chamber of commerce, agricultural cooperatives and unions. The few remaining Greeks became victims of chicanery so that they left. It became clear that the Turkish side was aiming at an ethnic reallocation.

When at the end of March 1959 Makarios stated that the separate municipalities did not mean separate quarters and their establishment was only a trial, Küçük insisted on geographical, and not only functional separation. In April a compromise came into sight. Makarios hoped that by concessions he might induce the Turks to give up the thought of separation. In May he suggested the following: Separate municipalities should be set up in the five towns elected from their community no matter where they lived and operate independently from each other but there should be no geographical separation. They should have the right, e.g., to tax their community and repair the roads under their control. A coordinating committee should be responsible for comprehensive tasks such as city cleaning. Municipal facilities should be used jointly.

The Greek mayors blocked this and the Turkish Cypriot separatists, under the lead of Denktash, demanded huge areas under their control. At the end of August the talks about the Constitution and the separate municipalities stalled. Thus Ankara intervened, and by mid-September the situation had relaxed so that Makarios and Küçük declared their agreement with a temporal law recognizing the Turkish Cypriot municipalities so that these could collect the municipal dues and taxes. On 13 October this law was released and the tense situation relaxed but on 18 October the so-called Deniz incident again blocked any progress.

Internal developments in Cyprus in 1959
When Makarios returned to Cyprus on 1 March 1959 he found a most difficult political situation. In both communities the radicals had the say and were armed. The Greek Cypriots continued to dream of *enosis* and the Turkish Cypriots of *taksim*. If the development were to stay peaceful the radical forces had to be disarmed. On the Greek side this problem was solved as early as March when EOKA laid down its weapons, Grivas left the island and the prisoners and internees were released. On the Turkish side Küçük announced that TMT did not have any weapons, which was untrue, of course. At the same time there were some brawls over posts in the future Republic.

On 2 April 1959 the names of the future ministers were announced. The three Turkish ministers were middle aged men (36, 44, 50) with work experience. The list of the seven Greek ministers perplexed even experienced observers. They were solely former EOKA activists, all very young and had, with the exception of Clerides, no professional experience. Interior Minister T. Papadopoulos was 24, Labour Minister P. Georkatzis 27, and G. Clerides was the oldest at 39 years. No wonder that there were jokes about Makarios' children's choir. The explanation of Makarios' decision is rather simple: He did not want any experienced elder competitors in his Government who might have challenged his monocratic style of ruling; after all he himself was clueless in many political fields. The young inexperienced political newcomers would nod through all his decisions or do everything he ordered. Thus he could mildly outshine them.

Makarios did not only appoint former EOKA fighters to cabinet posts but he placed them in the administration, the police, the military and later even in the diplomatic service. The whole reminds one of the well known spoils system in US politics. There should be no frustrated former EOKA fighters who might intrigue against him, all should feel obliged to him. After independence there would be a power vacuum and he was determined to fill this with persons dependent on him. Thus he created a kind of fealty oriented towards him and kept together by his favours; it was the beginning of a kind of clientelism. The question remained whether he would succeed by this in gaining the support of the radical followers of Grivas. Additionally questionable was the fact that he did leave out the Cypriot Left, i.e. AKEL and PEO (union); had he integrated them he could have built up a counter weight to the EOKA faction. Apparently Makarios did not consider this necessary at this point.

During those weeks there were continuously small inter-communal incidents showing that there were still tensions under the peaceful surface. Though Makarios and Küçük made efforts to reconcile the two communities, Denktash continued his separatist subversive activities endorsed by certain circles in Ankara. Thus in May the president of the National Student Federation of Turkey, Jelal Hordan, came to Cyprus to build up a Turkish youth organization called "lightning groups". In September the Turkish Government ordered his return, since his activities endangered the rapprochement with Greece.

It is possible that Grivas did intend after his return to Athens to lead a private life but when he returned from his holiday and noticed that he was no longer at the centre of public attention he began to listen to the whisperings of certain politicians of the opposition. He did not understand that these wanted to exploit his popularity for their purposes. Additionally, frustrated Cypriot nationalists belonging to the clique of Bishop Kyprianos of Kyrenia and former EOKA fighters visited him and criticised Makarios' course. Thus in summer Grivas piped up, continuously criticising Makarios regarding the British bases and in September he opened a political bureau, thus entering the political arena.

At the same time Grivas' relations with the Greek Government deteriorated. In an interview with a Canadian journalist Makarios stated that it would be a grave mistake if Grivas entered politics because he did not understand politics. Grivas felt provoked and when the Greek Right encouraged him he went as far as stating in an interview that he believed himself capable of leading Greece to new glory. His relations with Karamanlis became frosty. Visitors from Cyprus tried to influence him in their direction: followers of Makarios admonished more restraint, and the super-nationalists did their best to incite him. At the end of July 1959 Grivas saw dark forces at work: he told visitors that he was ready for another fight. A little later he denounced Makarios' treacherous cooperation with the British, the Turks and the Greek Government and declared war on him. On 29 July he dissociated himself from the Zurich and London Agreements. In Cyprus Bishop Kyprianos said in a sermon that with God's help Grivas would soon be prime minister of Greece and then freedom would come to Cyprus. Especially fanatical nationalists founded a new underground movement (KEM - Kypriako Enotiko Metopo - Cypriot Front for Enosis), which began a leaflet war against Makarios and the Greek Government.

All this was not very important for the time being but it showed that there were forces in Cyprus which rejected the solution found and hoped that they could use Grivas against Makarios by appealing to his excessive vanity. The political Right of Athens recognized that Grivas' naivety was the appropriate means to agitate against the Government without risking anything themselves. The game of those forces went on all through summer but when Grivas' tones became shriller in autumn Makarios saw that he had to act. Via middlemen a meeting between him and Grivas was arranged in Rhodes in early October. During this meeting Makarios brainwashed Grivas by his eloquence. The communique published on 9 October spoke of full conformity of opinion. At a social reception Grivas assured that from now on he would support Makarios.

Apparently the months long quarrel between Makarios and Grivas was over and mutual trust had been restored. But the real reason for the quarrel, the implementation of the Zurich and London Agreements, had not ended and could lead to another conflict. Makarios had managed to repair Grivas' self esteem and make him quiet temporarily. The meeting of Rhodes was a win on points and would protect him against attacks from this side for the time being. Thus he could concentrate on the urgent internal problem.

As was mentioned before, on 18 October the so-called Deniz-affair began. During the night of 17 October the captain of the British minesweeper *Burmaston* discovered a motor kaïki steering towards the Karpasia peninsula. When the boat was stopped two crew members tried to flee with a rubber dinghy. The kaïki was identified as Deniz, registered at Izmir. When the British sailors searched the boat they found another man on board and a cargo of 75 cases. At the same time they noticed that the vessel was sinking because the last crew member had opened the sea valve. Nevertheless, the sailors managed to search the boat and found that it was very well equipped. They brought two of the 75 cases on board the *Burmaston*. When they were opened they discovered 1,248 rounds of British infantry ammunition from WWII; the total cargo had been about 600,000 rounds. After that the two fleeing men were caught and all three were brought to Famagousta and handed over to the police.

The ammo smuggling trip of the Deniz was the first really big one of a series which had begun in 1958 after the first inter-communal clashes. Then TMT recognized that they did not have nearly enough weapons and the Turkish Government had agreed to the smuggling. Since then small vessels had transported small amounts of weapons and ammo to Cyprus. After some time, however, it turned out that the necessary quantity could be brought to Cyprus in this way. Therefore the Turkish Ministry for Foreign Affairs gave the money to buy Deniz and the military modernised the communication equipment and supplied the crew. The cargo stemmed from army stocks. When the kaïki was stopped Ankara ordered, by wireless, the sinking of the boat. Afterwards it was claimed that the boat had been hunting dolphins. Denktash, as political commissar of TMT, was informed about the details; it is not known whether Küçük knew what was really going on. The fact is that from now on TMT was the decisive force within the Turkish community and Denktash was the political master of TMT. The Deniz crew were taken to court but after the judgement they were deported to Turkey by the British.

There was some agitation caused by the Deniz affair but the beginning of the election campaign replaced it in the headlines. On 31 October Makarios had the election law published: there should be six electoral districts according to the six administrative districts with a Greek and a Turkish list. Each Cypriot citizen, men and women alike, over 21 should have the right to vote. The Greeks would elect the President and the Turks the Vice-President. Elections would take place on 13 December 1959.

Probably Makarios had assumed that there would be no rival candidate but by his lone decisions and the appointment of former EOKA activists as ministers he had upset the whole older generation of politicians. After quite some haggling on 17 November T. Dervis and I. Clerides founded a new party the *Dimokratiki Enosis Kyprou* (Democratic Union of Cyprus). Ioannis Clerides (father of the Minister of Justice, Glafkos Clerides,) told Makarios that he would abstain from candidacy if Makarios reorganised his cabinet after the elections of the House of Representatives, taking the ministers from the members of the House. Clerides was under the impression that Makarios had accepted his demand but in reality Makarios insisted on his presidential right to choose the ministers at will.

Thus on 26 November Clerides announced his candidacy: He had hesitated long whether he should undergo this stress at the age of 73 but he felt obliged to the island. Makarios published his election program and AKEL announced that it would support Clerides. Thus the fronts were clear and the election battle began. Both sides organized mass rallies in the town which were well visited and peaceful. But in the villages the situation was different; there the representatives of the Democratic Union were not received well. There were cases where their representatives were beaten up and stones were thrown at their cars. The villagers made Makarios' election tour a triumphal procession. The left wing union PEO advertised Clerides and its right wing counterpart SEK praised Makarios. The forces fighting for Makarios called themselves the Patriotic Front. Küçük, on the other side, announced that as there was no rival candidate an election was not necessary.

On 1 December 1959 Governor Foot lifted the AKEL ban. On 3 December the Commissioner of Nicosia appointed Küçük Vice-President of Cyprus. On 8 December the date for the parliamentary elections was fixed for 10 January 1960. The actual presidential election was a quiet affair. About 238,900 women and men were entitled to vote. They did this in 370 polling stations in the six districts. The number of the urban voters were 58,438 and the rural voters counted 180,441. About 95 percent of those entitled to vote did so. 144,501 people voted for Makarios. Clerides received 71,758 votes. More town dwellers voted for Clerides, the villagers preferred Makarios. The rural votes and the votes of the women led to Makarios' overwhelming election victory. There were villages with not one single vote for Clerides.

When the counting of the votes was finished and Makarios' victory was sure the church bells were rung, fireworks were displayed and the people danced and shouted until they lost their voices. Makarios delivered a speech calling an end to fanaticism and antagonism and for cooperation with the Turkish Cypriots. Küçük applauded the election result and hoped for trustful cooperation with Makarios. Thus Makarios' and Küçük's positions had a democratic legitimation.

Internal development until independence in August 1960
On 8 December 1959 it had been announced that the election for the House of Parliament would take place on 10 January 1960. On 19 December the Government published the election bill: Cyprus was again to have six electoral districts of which each would send a certain number of Greek and Turkish deputies to parliament. When voting the elector could vote for a certain candidate or a group of candidates. Whoever reached the absolute majority was elected. The future parliament should have 50 seats, 35 Greek and 15 Turkish seats. The municipal elections would take place one week later. AKEL denounced the bill as undemocratic because it made election alliances necessary.

In spite of its criticism AKEL began negotiations with Makarios' *Patriotic Front*. Apparently the leadership of this party offered AKEL five seats, i.e., of the 35 possible candidates it would nominate only 30 and leave the rest to AKEL. Thus with the help of AKEL's votes the Front would defeat the *Democratic Union* easily and could control AKEL to a certain degree. Though there was a small row within the Patriotic Front against this alliance, this quieted down rather quickly when it became known that the Turkish side wanted the elections to take place after the Constitution had been finished and published. The Patriotic Front denied that it had an alliance with AKEL, this was a malicious fabrication of the Democratic Union. As Clerides recognized that despite all denials there was an agreement between the Patriotic Union and AKEL, reducing the election chance of his own party to zero he announced that his party would not take part in the election parody. Makarios disclaimed any knowledge of this.

When the elections were postponed public attention turned to the bad economic conditions of Cyprus. Originally it had been planned that independence would come on 19 February 1960 but the haggling about the British bases postponed this date further and further. As the beginning of British financial aid was linked to the independence date, difficulties began. Planned building projects could not start and projects under construction had to be interrupted. The result was massive unemployment in the building sector. The reduction of the British troops and the transfer of many colonial civil servants to other places in the Commonwealth reduced the demand and hit the merchants hard. Agriculture, too, had problems because in winter 1959 it had not rained and the crop was withering in the fields. Added to this were corn diseases and attacks by pests. An unexpected rain in March, however, saved the peasants at the last moment.

In May the unemployment number rose to 10,000 and according to PEO there were 8,000 families who had absolutely no money and did not know how to feed their children and pay their rent. On 15 March the *Times of Cyprus* wrote that "*the British are using the plight of the unemployed as a means of forcing an agreement on their own terms [...] To obtain concessions by turning the economic screw on those who have no say in the negotiations is something that could not be forgiven.*" One could not understand why the grants were withheld.

The impression that the British were using the economic misery as a lever in the negotiations became stronger when Foot spoke about an imminent economic catastrophe which could only be avoided if the negotiations came to an end quickly and the Republic was founded in summer.

The grants could not be given before independence. In June the misery reached such proportions that the left and right wing unions threatened to organize together a general strike. Even the employers were ready to help to stop the misery of the masses.

When on 1 July 1960 the bases agreement was signed, it was announced that Cyprus would receive in the next years about 14 million pounds in grant. Thus, finally, a solution to the unemployment became visible on the horizon since the work on the building projects was resumed. But in the meantime another problem had shown up.

The Zurich Agreement had determined that the relation of Greeks and Turks in the civil service would be 70 to 30 but that the quantitative realisation depended on the practicability. This clause had been included in the Constitution. The Turkish side wanted this clause to be applied at once. The Greek side argued that on the Turkish side there were not enough qualified personnel for the middle and higher posts in the administration, which was doubtlessly correct. In the police sector, where the Turks were over-represented, a compromise was found on the 60:40 relation but in the civil service a conflict developed which quickly escalated verbally. When Bishop Kyprianos of Kyrenia added fuel to the fire by stating that enosis would come soon Denktash hit back appealing to the honour of the Turkish Cypriots. In the following weeks the exchange of blows continued. By the end of June Denktash threatened with an intervention of Turkey if the 70:30 relation was not realised.

But the new Turkish Government under General Gürsel, who had forcefully taken power on 27 May 1960, had no interest in the continuation of the conflict and ordered the Turkish Cypriot leadership to come around. On 4 July Makarios and Küçük met and agreed that the 70:30 relation should be realized within five months after independence. A joint committee was to find a solution to the question whether the relation should be applied generally or to each individual department. Thus the necessary compromise was achieved which, however, mortgaged the future republic.

On 1 July 1960 the agreement on the military bases was initialled and on 5 July the interim cabinet decided that the elections for the House of Representatives would take place on 7 August. On 25 July I. Clerides, the leader of the Democratic Union, refused to participate in the election. Thus the Patriotic Front was the only party running for election. In the future House only the Front and AKEL would be represented. On 10 July Governor Foot announced that independence would come on 16 August. Cyprus would be regarded as an independent member of the Commonwealth until the time when the future parliament would decide to stay or leave. On 12 August AKEL decided to put up no candidates of its own and confine itself to the five promised seats. On 20 July the nomination process for candidates began: on the Turkish side there were no rival candidates in the electoral districts of Nicosia, Kyrenia and Larnaka. Thus the candidates were declared elected without actual voting the next day. As there were independent rival candidates in Limassol and Famagousta, the voting took place. On the Greek side, with the exception of Paphos, there were independent candidates and candidates of a newly founded party of former EOKA fighters. Among the five AKEL candidates were AKEL Secretary General Ezekias Papaioannou and PEO boss Andreas Ziartidis. Minister of Justice G Clerides, Makarios' personal physician V. Lyssaridis and the lawyer Lellos Dimitriadis (the future mayor of Nicosia) were among the candidates of the Patriotic Front. AKEL appealed to the independent candidates to withdraw their candidature which did not have any chance but cost everybody a lot, but this happened only in Paphos. Thus there was no voting in Paphos; the candidates were declared elected.

Election day was quiet, almost dull as the *Times of Cyprus* remarked because the day-long ban on alcohol induced many people to leave the town and go to the mountains or the seaside.

Since the election victors were clear from the beginning only 64 percent went to the polls. On the Turkish side 74 percent voted. Of the 30 deputies of the Patriotic Front 20 were former EOKA members. The result was that the House neither contained the pro-Grivas-elements nor those who were against the Zurich agreement. The independent candidates, with the exception of one, lost their bail (75 pounds) because they did not win one fifth of the votes.

On 6 August it was announced that, with the exception of Kyrenia, the independent candidates had withdrawn their candidature for the Communal Chamber, thus all candidates of the Patriotic Front were declared elected. On the Turkish side all independent candidates had given up their candidacy. Thus only in Kyrenia elections took place and the poor independent lost his 75 pound bail. In this way the future Republic had elected legislative organs.

A little later Makarios reshuffled his cabinet: Only two of the Greek ministers remained in office (P. Georkatzis and T. Papadopoulos). The Turkish Ministers kept their office. Spyros Kyprianou became the new Foreign Minister. Georkatzis changed to the Ministry of the Interior and Papadoulos became Minister of Labour. The 53-year-old A. Arouzos was the senior member of the Cabinet and Stella Soulioti was the first Cypriot woman to be a minister (Justice).

Spyros Kyprianou, born in 1932 in Limassol, was at 28 years old probably the youngest foreign minister the world had ever seen. He had studied economics at the City of London College and law at Gray's Inn. In 1952 he had become secretary to Makarios and in 1954 he became the chief of the London branch of the Ethnarchic Council and enlightened the British public about the situation in Cyprus. Additionally, he represented the ethnarchy at the UN in New York. In 1959 he had participated in the Zurich negotiations and in 1960 in the London negotiations.

Stella Soulioti (b. 1920), stemming also from Limassol, was the daughter of a lawyer and member of the Ethnarchic Council who was ennobled for his services to the Crown. In WWII she worked in the governmental office of enlightenment from 1939 to 1942 and then she joined the RAF female auxiliary corps ending as captain. After the end of the war she studied law in London and in 1951 she began to practice law in Limassol. She was the first Cypriot woman who studied law and opened an office of her own.

After Amery, Makarios and Küçük had agreed about the size of the base and the financial grant, the final texts were initialled by the representatives of the UK, Greece and Turkey on 6 July 1960 and one day later they were published as the 222-page Command Paper (Cmnd. 1093). In the following days the necessary three readings in Parliament took place, and on 29 July the House of Lords also passed the law. Thus the way for independence on 15 August 1960 was open.

By 12 and 13 August politicians and journalists had come to Nicosia to participate in the independence ceremony. Labour sent Tom Driberg, Lena Jeger, Kenneth Robinson and Francis Noel-Baker who in the past had engaged themselves for Cyprus. From Greece admiral A. Sakellariou came and a representative of Grivas. Küçük had invited four representatives of Turkey and a conservative MP (Patrick Wall) who had always promoted the interests of the Turkish Cypriots. In the meantime, Governor Foot bade farewell to many people and institutions.

At noon on 14 August the colonial government arranged an official luncheon at Ledra Palace Hotel for 200 invited guests, among them the diplomats. By 23.30 hours cars with ministers, diplomats, deputies of the House of Representatives and the Communal Chambers had arrived at the building of the ministerial council, today's parliament building. The crowd assembled in the big conference room, today the chamber of the House of Representatives. A little later all present stood up to greet a small procession of dignitaries led by President Makarios. Küçük, the representatives of Greece and Turkey and Governor Foot followed. When he arrived the police band in front of the building played "God Save the Queen". A few minutes before midnight a fanfare signal was heard and Sir Hugh Foot read out the royal proclamation bestowing independence on Cyprus and constituting the Republic. Precisely at midnight a battery fired a 21-shot salute. The Republic was born.

After this the representatives of London, Athens and Ankara and the two communities signed those agreements which they had initialled over a month ago on 6 July. The signing took almost an hour. The whole time the police band played lively melodies. At 1:30 Governor Foot and Lady Foot gave a reception at Government House to say goodbye to the diplomats. After that Foot directed a radio speech to the population of Cyprus, whishing them well for the future.

By 7.30 personal friends and guests appeared in Government House to bid the Foots farewell. At 8 o'clock Makarios, Küçük and the cabinet members showed up to wish the Governor and Lady Foot bon voyage. Foot paced a guard of honour of parachutists and drove to Famagousta. Originally Foot had planned a high grade symbol-laden farewell with a ceremonial lowering of the Union Jack in Nicosia and a rather theatrical changing of the guard in Famagousta, but the Greeks did not play along. Thus poor Foot had to do without a withdrawal with flying colours. In Famagousta the family sat down on canvas chairs while Foot paced another guard of honour. After that he and his family went aboard the frigate *Chichester* while a salute was fired from the walls of the old fortress. Not even a military band had appeared. A bagpipe lament was heard. It was a melancholic, undignified end of British rule but at least a humiliating expulsion like that from Palestine twelve years previouly had been avoided. Neiter were the Cypriots in a mood to celebrate.

In Nicosia on the first morning of freedom the elected deputies went to the chamber where they were sworn in and Glafkos Clerides was elected Speaker and a Turkish Cypriot Vice-Speaker. After that Makarios and Küçük appeared in front of the building where they were received by a guard of honour of the police and the gendarmery. The new flag of the Republic was hoisted for the first time: A golden map above two olive tree branches. The Greeks went to the Faneromeni church where Makarios celebrated a Te-Deum. In his sermon he promised to work for the well being of the Cypriot people. It is unknown what Küçük did during this time.

In the afternoon the first Greek and Turkish troops of the military contingents arrived in Famagousta. The Greek soldiers had a friendly welcome. The press photo with that kneeling old man with his cap in his hands welcoming the young solders went around the world. The soldiers went to their quarters without any incidents. The Turkish Cypriots had appeared in great number to welcome the Turkish soldiers enthusiastically but here, too, were no incidents. While the Turkish Cypriots celebrated, the Greek Cypriots were in sinister mood. There were no celebrations, no parades, no processions, no bell ringing and no dancing to welcome independence. The new state was not what the Greek Cypriots had dreamed of, i.e. *enosis*.

However, for the first time in Cypriot history a power ruling the island had transferred the control of the island to the inhabitants. Centuries of foreign domination had come to an end. But the solution found was not a real one, it was a pseudo solution because it did not remove the internal conflicts but allowed them to continue to exist below the surface, even worse, it institutionalised them by integrating them into the Constitution: The inter-communal conflict became permanent, supervised by the guarantors. The 1960 solution achieved only the stabilisation of the Western Alliance by settling the conflict between Greece and Turkey provoked by Britain. But even this was not final because the next unrest in Cyprus would inevitably draw the mother countries into the conflict. The Cyprus conflict and the relations between the mother countries behaved like a system of communicating pipes; the Greek Cypriots and the Greeks of Istanbul were the sufferers.

Only the British and the Americans were pleased by the result. The British could keep their bases and these were important in two ways during the Cold War: It was an advanced RAF base from which air force attacks against the Middle East and the southern Soviet Union could be flown. Even with nuclear bombs. And the bases in Cyprus became the western centre for electronic eavesdropping in this part of the world which even the US could use on the basis of a cooperation agreement with Britain.

1960-1962: THE PEACEFUL YEARS

Old and new problems
The founding of the Republic did not remove any of the existing problems, quite the contrary; some were aggravated because when trying to solve them the inherent conflict broke out vehemently. The Greek Cypriot side considered the waiving of *enosis* as a huge concession and many could not come to terms with this. For them independence was a transitional station on the way to *enosis* which had to be prepared by constitutional changes. For the Turkish Cypriots, independence meant waving *taksim* and they were resolved to defend their rights and privileges fighting tooth and nail even if this was impracticable or provoked conflicts. The mutual distrust was so deep that the two sides were rarely ready to compromise. The poverty of the Turkish Cypriots did not interest the Greeks who considered it self-inflicted. Thus they were not ready to yield anything to them. With some good will and a little tactfulness unnecessary tension could have been avoided.

When in 1958 Makarios recognized that the alternatives were partition or independence, he opted for the latter and signed the London Agreements in 1959. By signing the Cyprus Treaties on 16 August 1960 independence became permanent according to international law. Perhaps he had some inner misgivings but he understood that with his signature on the treaties the die was cast for independence. The problem was that he did not dare to admit this publicly because it would have caused an explosion. Makarios knew quite well that he had to use very cautious tactics because even his own followers were hot-blooded, undisciplined and often difficult to control. It was impossible to discipline the nationalists, though Makarios made rhetorical concessions and statements sounding as if he was aiming at *enosis*. But these tactical manoeuvres made to quieten the radicals were taken at face value by the Turkish Cypriots. The adherents of partition considered them proof of their suspicion that Makarios was heading for *enosis*.

And from Greece Grivas suspiciously observed developments in Cyprus. Each departure from striving for enosis was treason in his eyes and as his word weighed heavily with the radical wing of the former fighters a split of the national camp threatened. At the same time Makarios could not afford an alienation of AKEL. This precarious balance of power forced Makarios to steer a tactically motivated zigzag course between the various camps; his policy resembled a ride on the back of a tiger. It is not astonishing, therefore, that at times Makarios became a driven person trying to offer delaying resistance and thus to avoid wrong developments, or at least to slow down or mitigate them.

Though Makarios had accepted independence he was not prepared to accept the equal partnership between the Greek and Turkish Cypriots enforced upon him by the Constitution. His aim was to preserve independence and increase the rights of the majority, i.e., he wanted to overcome the restrictions of the Zurich and London Agreements. If he had applied a long term policy of confidence building measures with the Turkish Cypriots he might have succeeded, but Makarios thought tactically and not strategically.

But the Turkish Cypriot side, too, was split. Dr Fazil Küçük was an affable person. He belonged to the elder generation of Turkish Cypriot politicians who had grown up in the time of peaceful coexistence of the two communities and were ready for cooperation provided their interests were respected. But Küçük, too, was under pressure from the radical Turkish Cypriots around Rauf Denktash and had to compromise; besides that the political leaders of Turkey were watching him and these, too, were not speaking with one voice. Thus he was obliged to use tactics and tricks and his room for movement was rather limited, as well. In the last analysis he, too, had to face the same problems as Makarios, because he was also riding a tiger. Generally speaking the relations in 1961 and 1962 were relatively relaxed. Makarios and Küçük dealt gently with each other, and in parliament a lot of bills were passed without any problem. Smaller cases of friction and conflict existed nevertheless.

This conciliatory course was supported by the mother countries. The new Turkish leadership exerted a moderating influence on the stirrers of the Turkish Cypriot community. Ankara attached importance to good cooperation but rejected tendencies to Cypriotisation, i.e., to a formation of a Cypriot identity. The Cyprus treaties forbade agitation for *enosis* and *taksim* but not cultural and political events praising the Greek and Turkish character. Both sides should remain in their parallel societies because only in this way could Ankara hope to maintain its influence in Cyprus. In order to achieve this it was necessary that the Constitution not be revised.

As during the interim period, several controversial topics dominated the development. The 70:30 relation and the separate municipalities continued to cause conflicts. Added to this was a controversy about the armed forces of the Republic. Another conflict arose from the constitutional clause that in tax questions separate majorities of the communities were necessary in parliament. The problem of the separate municipalities and their territorial delimitations was the thorniest topic because in this conflict Turkey became a direct player in the Cypriot poker game.

As will be remembered, Makarios and Küçük had agreed in July 1960 that the 70:30 relation in the civil service was to be realized within five months after independence and a joint committee should work out the modalities. This committee managed to submit its report even before independence and recommended the setting up of a mixed commission which would regulate the recruiting. But when this commission could not solve the basic problem of lack of qualification, a chronic conflict developed lasting until 1963. Although there was some progress it was too slow. The continuous conflict made Makarios put this problem on his 13 points list of constitutional changes. But this problem could have been overcome with a little good will without changing the Constitution.

The future army was to have 2,000 men and consist of 60 percent Greek and 40 percent Turkish Cypriots. In 1961 the House passed the necessary bill to set up two battalions of 600 men altogether at first. The Greek ministers wanted mixed units and the Turkish ministers sepa-rate units. Apparently the first did not like the thought of bigger separate units under a Turkish minister of defence. The Council of Ministers decided on a mixed army with a majority vote but Küçük insisted on separation and asked the Cabinet to discuss the topic once more.

Inevitably this provoked a conflict. The Greek side wanted mixed units down to the platoon (30 men) and the Turkish insisted on ethnically homogeneous companies (150 men). In September the minister of finance stated that the army could not have more than 700 men due to lack of money. Küçük vetoed the cabinet decision and Makarios stopped the whole enterprise. The 300 men, mainly officer cadets, recruited so far remained on duty for the time being. Among them were 150 Greeks, all former EOKA activists, who later became instructors of the illegally set up militia created by Georkatzis. When Makarios put this problem on his 13 points list this topic was closed.

Article 78 of the Constitution ruled that each tax law needed a simple majority of the deputies of each community. This meant that a bill passed by the Cabinet with the consent of the Vice-President and all Turkish ministers and passed by the House with a majority of Greek and Turkish deputies could be stopped if it did not find a majority in the separate voting, i.e. 8 Turkish deputies could block such a bill even if 42 deputies voted for it. This clause had been included in the Constitution in order to prevent the majority from taking advantage of the minority on tax questions. But now it had the effect of an additional Turkish veto which might be used as political leverage. But for the time being the colonial law was to be applied until a new law was worked out on the basis of Article 78.

If the revenue of the two communities had been big enough to cover their expenses a compromise might have been found, but in 1962 91.9 percent of the income tax revenue was paid by the Greek and only 8.1 percent by the Turkish Cypriots. The whole tax revenue of the Turkish community amounted to 80,000 pounds. The expenses for the specific tasks of the communities (education, culture, religious matters, civil status) were 3 million pounds on the Greek side and 800,000 pounds on the Turkish side. Both sides needed grants from the Government, the Greeks 1,6 million pounds and the Turks 400,000 pounds. For the Greek side this was no problem because the Greeks were rich enough, but for the Turkish Cypriots this was a problem because they were simply too poor. This meant a revenue allocation.

The Greek side was of the opinion that this allocation should be proportional to the population. In this case the Greek Cypriots would have received 80 percent and the Turkish Cypriots 18 percent. This attitude inhibited the insight that in a state with two communities there must be a revenue allocation between the richer and the poorer part of the population. As for the Turkish side, the 18 percent was far too little so it developed the idea that in this case, too, the 70:30 relation should be applied. In order to be on the safe side and to ensure that its financial problems were solved indeed, it made its consent to the income tax increase dependent on the acceptance that it would be allocated according to the 70:30 principle.

Within a short time the two sides were hopelessly at loggerheads. Finally, on 18 December 1961 after long negotiations, the Government submitted a new income tax bill to the House which had passed Cabinet unanimously, i.e., with the consent of the Turkish ministers. Denktash, however, feared a convergence of the two communities by a compromise and ordered his followers in the House to torpedo the bill in the separate voting. Therefore there was no legal basis for the raising of taxes. During the next months the two Communal Chambers passed tax laws, thus increasing their political weight. The result was that the two communities drifted further apart. Although a partial solution was found in the general tax laws so that foreign investors were attracted and enough means were collected to continue the five-year-development plan, the state of affairs was unacceptable in the long run.

Finally in November 1962 the hardened fronts moved when G. Clerides submitted a compromise proposal. Before the compromise was realised on 8 February 1963 the Supreme Court ruled that the old colonial law was no longer in force. Thus the Republic did not have any tax law in force and thus no revenue.

The situation became even worse when no solution was found on the question of the separate municipalities. The Turkish side stubbornly insisted on the territorial separation of the respective quarters and the Greek side rejected this equally obstinately. On 10 February 1961 Makarios submitted a compromise: in the five towns there should be two Municipal Councils and a coordinating committee but no geographical separation. The citizens would pay their taxes to the respective administration. Küçük agreed but Denktash was not satisfied and put pressure on Küçük who gave in and linked the solution of this problem with the 70:30 relation and the tax question. Makarios rejected this linkage as illegitimate and informed the ambassadors of the guarantor powers.

Inaccurate information made Makarios gain the impression that Ankara might make concessions on the question of the separate municipalities. He did not understand that the administrative separation of the communities had been *conditio sine qua non* for Ankara's consent to the Zurich and London agreements. Ankara rejected the methods of the separatists because they endangered the *status quo* but was not prepared to accept the reduction of the Turkish Cypriots to a minority. The Zurich and London Agreements guaranteed an equal partnership.

During his visit to Ankara at the end of November 1962 Makarios tabled the blocking tactics on the tax question of the Turkish Cypriots and met with the understanding of the Turkish Government promising that they would use their influence. When Makarios spoke about the separate municipalities his dialogue partners rejected any change in a diplomatic, friendly but definitive way . Makarios did not grasp that this was a warning. He had registered Turkish flexibility on the question of the army and the separate majorities and probably assumed that in the end Turkey would be flexible in the question of the separate municipalities. He did not understand that the separate municipalities were an essential part of Turkey's Cyprus policy. The positive impression of his visit to Turkey made him continue his course without acting with necessary caution.

After his return the negotiations continued without any result because the separatists stuck to their intransigent course and so did Makarios. On 31 December 1962 the breakdown came when the Turkish Cypriot side rejected another prolongation of the old colonial tax law. Makarios reacted by reactivating another colonial law. This law authorised the Government to declare each district an "Improvement Area" and erect an "Improvement Board" which took over the administration of the district. The Government declared the five-town "Improvement Areas" and initiated steps to have them administered by the "Improvement Boards". Makarios declared that in view of the situation the constitutional provisions concerning the separate municipalities were not applicable. As long as the Turkish side rejected unified municipalities there was no other solution but to abolish them. He regretted this but from now on the Government would take over the functions of the municipalities. Albeit the Turkish ministers in cabinet tried to stop this law on 10 January 1963 it passed with a 7 to 3 vote.

In Athens the Government was appalled by Makarios' action. On 1 January 1963 Karamanlis told Makarios not to carry things to the extreme. On 5 January the Turkish Ambassador in Athens protested against Makarios' behaviour: Should the Cypriot Government dissolve the municipalities forcibly then the Turkish Government would consider this a violation of the Constitution and as a case for the Treaty of Guarantee. Obviously Turkey was threatening with an intervention. At the same time it became known that Küçük, after his return from consultative talks with the Turkish Government in Ankara, had announced that he would submit this case to the Supreme Court.

Makarios rejected the accusation that the erection of the Development Boards violated the Constitution. Besides, the whole affair was an internal matter for Cyprus. In Ankara Foreign Minister Erkin repudiated this in turn: Turkey had the right to a say in this matter because of the Constitution and the Treaty of Guarantee. The Turkish Government would not tolerate any violation of the Treaties nor any reduction of the rights of the Turkish Cypriots. According to Erkin Makarios was trying by "crafty logic" to present the Turkish Cypriots as the culprits. Apparently Makarios still did not understand that Ankara was not prepared to give up the partnership principle agreed upon in Zurich despite its readiness to compromise on the question of the separate majorities. Thus Makarios was entering a dangerous slippery path.

In the following days the Improvement Boards which had been appointed by the Government began to take over control of the municipalities. Their chairmen announced that the municipalities should go on working but the Boards would direct them. Indeed, the takeover of the administration went rather smoothly; there were even some Turkish Cypriot Board members. On 24 January the Ministry of the Interior ruled that from now on all movable property and real estate of the towns and their sub-organizations belonged to the Republic. This was the legal lever to bring municipal property illegally occupied by the Turks, such as the market hall in the old town of Nicosia, back under the control of the municipality. This was a first step to dissolve the Turkish Cypriot municipalities.

In the evening of 25 January 1963 a bomb exploded outside the Bayraktar mosque situated on the Constanza bastion. The damage was small but inside the mosque another explosive charge was found which had not been exploded. Since this mosque had been the target of an attack in March 1962 by *agents provocateurs* it was immediately suspected that this attack, too, was the work of provocateurs. This impression was intensified when well organized demonstrations took place in Istanbul within a few hours. The explosion was a warning to the Greek administration. Although Küçük and Denktash contained themselves at first, a little later aggressive tones were heard. On 30 January G. Clerides, Speaker of the House, and R. Denktash, chairman of the Turkish Communal Chamber, filed an action at the Supreme Court: Clerides wanted to have the legislative activities of the Chamber banned and Denktash wanted to have the work of the Improvement Boards stopped.

In the next weeks there were numerous "summits" between Makarios and Küçük which brought no results. By mid-February Clerides and Denktash were asked to work out a compromise solution. Here for the first time Clerides' ability to find compromises even under the most difficult circumstance became obvious. In this case they suggested that the separate municipalities should resume their work controlled by the coordinating committees. The Turkish municipalities should have at their disposal a certain fixed amount. On 31 December 1963 Makarios and Küçük should meet and decide on the abolition of separate municipalities and the transfer of their competencies to the coordinating committees thus establishing united municipalities. In the case of differing opinions of the President and Vice-President the case should be submitted to the presidents of the Constitutional Court and the Supreme Court. Their decision should be binding. The decision should be published stressing that it was in line with the Constitution.

This concept worked out by Clerides and Denktash was reasonable; it would have removed the decisive stumbling block of the Republic by an acceptable compromise and spared Cyprus a lot of misery. Makarios accepted the proposal but Denktash had second thoughts and refused a final agreement by absenting himself from the negotiations. It is improbable that Ankara was behind this manoeuvre. It was Denktash who torpedoed the solution.

In early March the Constitutional Court began its hearings. From Athens Averof warned Makarios that Ankara might resolve to intervene. But Makarios could not be intimidated. On 27 March he declared that a separation of the municipalities was impossible. If the Turkish side did not accept the proposals the status quo had to prevail. The question of the municipalities was an internal affair of Cyprus and the treaty of guarantee did not confer a right of intervention on the guarantor powers. Should there be an intervention he would appeal to the UN. Obviously Makarios wanted to bring the Cyprus Problem to the UN again. As Cyprus was a member state it could directly appeal to the UN: moreover Cyprus' position had been strengthened there since it could count on the support of the non-aligned states, the former colonies, the Commonwealth states and the Eastern block.

On 31 March 1963 Makarios added fuel to the fire by a speech on the eve of the anniversary of the beginning of the EOKA struggle: The state created by the Zurich and London Agreements was not the aim of the struggle. The aim of the Cypriot people was still enosis and the Agreements were only a starting point for new efforts. Denktash considered Makarios' speech irresponsible and dangerous; it violated the Cyprus Treaties. He accused him of trying to abolish the Constitution in order to achieve enosis. Makarios was not impressed and added more fuel to the fire: the Greek Cypriots were an integral part of the Greek nation. The Republic was a new state but had not created a new nation. The organisation of separate municipalities was impossible and the respective articles of the Constitution inapplicable.

When Ankara reacted irascibly and the Americans admonished it, Averof warned Makarios. When Makarios evaded, saying that the situation was harmless, Averof and Karamanlis budged: The security of Greece was precarious and a break with Turkey could have dangerous conse-quences for the Oecumenic Patriarchate and the Greek community in Istanbul. Even interna-tional treaties offered enough protection. They expected responsible behaviour. Should Makarios try to abolish the Cyprus treaties as a whole or in part, Athens would dissociate itself from this publicly. These were clear words which did not allow interpretation and they made an impact because during the next weeks until the resignation of the Karamanlis Government in July 1963, it remained quiet on the constitutional front.

On 25 April 1963 the Supreme Court pronounced that judgment on Clerides' and Denktash's cases: both laws were declared unconstitutional. During the voting it became visible that the two Cypriot judges geared their decision to the position of their community and not to the constitution. Foreign observers spoke of a "complete deadlock" and of chaos. Renewed pressure from Athens and American admonitions made Makarios resume his "summit talks" with Küçük, and on 7 May he submitted a fully elaborated proposal for an interim period: In each of the five towns a board should be set up, the members of which should be appointed by the President and the Vice-President and their number was to be proportional to the size of the community. The board was to have at least 4 members but not more than 15. The members of the board should elect a chairman and a deputy who were to be appointed by the President and the Vice-President respectively. These boards were to take over the function of the old municipal administrations. The market halls were to be managed jointly and each community would have a budget of its own. With this proposal Makarios had made great concession to the Turkish Cypriot side.

But now it was Küçük who played the intransigent by stating that the proposal was unconstitutional. In order to avoid administrative chaos Cabinet decided - the Turkish Ministers voting against - that the District Officers should take over the administration of the town on the basis of the "Street and Buildings Regulation Law". In principle this was the same procedure as the "Improvement Boards" which the Constitutional Court had declared unconstitutional. Küçük vetoed it. Obviously the negotiations over the separate municipalities had reached a deadlock. Neither side was ready for compromise. The Turkish Government supported their fellow countrymen. The Greek Government had distanced itself and rejected the abolition of the Cyprus treaties, or parts of them but did not exclude a change to individual articles of the constitution. These changes, however, should be made amicably. Under these circumstances it was clear that Makarios began to search for a way out.

Among Makarios' considerations were an appeal to the UN and the replacement of the treaties of guarantee and alliance by one with the UK. This, however, was rejected by the Lord Privy Seal Edward Heath and the Foreign Office. During a talk between Foreign Minister Kyprianou and Commonwealth Minister Sandys the latter rejected secret negotiations behind the backs of Turkey and Greece. He suggested that Makarios should discuss this topic with High Commissioner Clark. The relatively inexperienced Foreign Minister interpreted this statement as a green light; in reality, however, it was a polite rejection. This interpretation is strengthened by the fact that when Kyprianou had a first talk with Clark after his return to Nicosia the latter declared he had received no instructions from London but he was ready to listen to Kyprianou's ideas and, after consulting London, comment upon them, but absolute privacy had to be ensured.

When by the end of May Kyprianou presented his ideas to Clark the latter considered them logical but was afraid that Turkey might react allergically. When Clark informed London about them the answer was that they were against any change to the Cyprus Treaties. At the most some small constitutional changes were possible. Clark passed this answer on to Kyprianou and Makarios in such a friendly way that they gained the impression that although the British were against a change to the Cyprus Treaties they would not object to constitutional changes. And they did not grasp that Clark had warned them to be cautious. Had this warning been voiced by a diplomat of the Foreign Office it would have been clearer, but Clark was no diplomat used to implying foreign policy factors in his considerations but a colonial administrator of the Commonwealth Relations Office, the former Colonial Office.

The already tense situation was worsened because Greece and the UK went through an internal crisis: on 10 June Karamanlis resigned after a violent clash with Queen Frideriki. Panagiotis Pipinelis became the new Prime Minister. Karamanlis left Greece and went to Paris in exile. On 18 June the Profumo scandal caused Prime Minister Macmillan to announce his resignation which took place on 18 October 1963.

No sooner had Karamanlis resigned when Makarios told Clerides to work out a paper with constitutional changes. Clerides tried to make Makarios understand that this was too early. But when he recognized that Makarios had decided to act, he advised him to wait until the Greek elections and the change of Government and the ensuing consultations had taken place. In the meantime foreign constitutional experts should be consulted about the right of unilateral action within the frame of the Treaties of Guarantee and Alliance, especially regarding the military contingents of Greece and Turkey. Besides that, Makarios should talk to High Commissioner Clark and find out whether Britain was really prepared to support the constitutional changes. Makarios accepted Clerides' proposals and thus the latter travelled to London to consult the famous constitutional expert, Sir Frank Soskice. Soskice declared himself ready to render his expert opinion in this case.

In Cyprus Makarios used every opportunity to talk about the necessity of constitutional changes. In August the acting High Commissioner warned London that Makarios was ready to act unilaterally and even to accept bloodshed but unfortunately because of the governmental crisis, this effected nothing. The new Greek Prime Minister, however, warned Makarios: he should under no circumstances act unilaterally and should take his time. Makarios replied evasively and continued his policy.

By the end of August it was clear that Makarios was not impressed by the ever clearer warnings from Athens, Washington and London. He had a target for which he was wilfully heading. Objections did not impress him; he believed he could neglect the possible danger from the Turkish Cypriot side and was convinced that there would be no Turkish intervention because it might have provoked a Greek-Turkish war. The "gambler" in Makarios was obviously gaining the upper hand and he was playing hazard. The only ones who might have stopped Makarios with a sharp shot across the bows were the British and the Americans. A clear public statement by the British Government could have stopped an approaching catastrophe. But the British policy was split: the Foreign Office wanted to intervene but the Commonwealth Relations Office rejected this.

By mid-September 1963 Makarios became even clearer: A constitutional revision was a necessity; the rights of the Turkish minority would be respected properly. He was determined to proceed. The revision of the Constitution was an internal affair of Cyprus and he recognized no right of intervention of the so-called guarantor powers. A Turkish forceful intervention would be an act of aggression which would not only interest Greece but the UN also. Apparently Makarios was ready to hazard a Turkish intervention but considered it improbable.

But this was a total misinterpretation because, after the overthrow of Menderes and Zorlu and their death by hanging, Ankara's Cyprus policy was not controlled by changing ministers but by the director general of the Foreign Ministry, Turan Tuluy. He said to a British diplomat that Makarios' unilateral action could produce a favourable climate to push through the Turkish separation plan which had been developed as *ultima ratio*. The Turkish Government did not plan a military intervention but Turkish weapons would be sent and volunteers would find their way to Cyprus to help their brothers, the Government officially disapproving of this, of course. The Turkish Cypriots had been instructed that under no circumstances should they begin the fight. The Turks would not fire the first shot. This plan would be realized the moment Makarios dissolved parliament, thus beginning with the revision of the Constitution.

This information reached London but was not heeded in the run-up to the formation of a new Government. In the decisive phase nobody paid any serious attention to developments in Cyprus. Thus Clark became the decisive figure. In September he submitted proposals which were accepted by the British Government: Makarios should be restrained from unilateral actions. Turkey should be persuaded that some constitutional changes were necessary. Makarios should be induced to submit fair and reasonable proposals for changes to the Turkish Cypriots. Representatives of the guarantor powers should informally meet with the Cypriots to approve these changes. Had these proposals been submitted in May they would have had a chance to be accepted, but in the meantime the situation had changed radically and this plan had a chance only if all acted rather quickly. But this did not happen because Clark returned to Cyprus as late as mid-October from his holiday in Britain.

By the end of September, general elections had been called in Greece and the Pipinelis Government had resigned and a service Government had taken over which prepared the elections. This change in the Greek leadership meant that until the elections and the forming of the new Government Greece was incapable of action. Additionally there was a danger that Cyprus would become a topic of the election campaign with dangerous repercussions on the island itself.

When Clark arrived in Nicosia on 21 October 1963 he found out that during his four months absence the relations between Makarios and Küçük had deplorably worsened and the Turks had totally lost confidence in Makarios. Instead of analysing diligently, Clark went to work. He informed Makarios that Commonwealth minister Sandys agreed with constitutional changes. Makarios should submit proposals. Sandys was prepared to discuss these during his visit to Cyprus in early December. Makarios agreed and suggested that Foreign Minister Kyprianou should discuss these proposals with Clark while they were being formulated. Complete confidentiality was agreed upon; only Clark, Makarios and Kyprianou would be informed. Clark informed his ministry and asked for a green light, which came on 5 November under the condition of absolute privacy. The question was now whether Clark would be able to bring Makarios to show moderation.

Makarios' 13 points

Makarios entrusted Clerides with the elaboration of a catalogue of constitutional changes. Clerides warned him that this could lead to great troubles but Makarios insisted. Clerides worked out a comprehensive paper and passing it on to Makarios he again warned him that Turkey would never accept such far reaching constitutional changes because they destroyed the basis of the Zurich and London Agreements. Makarios pushed the objection aside. When Makarios showed Clark the paper the latter said that it should be reduced and concentrate on the most burning problems. Makarios gained the impression that Clark saw the affair very positively. In order to push forward he set up a committee consisting of Clerides, Minister of Justice Soulioti, Labour Minister Papadopoulos, Constitutional Court Judge Triantafyllidis and

Attorney General Tornaritis, ordering them to make the necessary selection and work out a well balanced document with explanations for the proposals of the constitutional changes.

On 10 November 1963 the result was presented to Makarios who passed it on to Clark. It was a list of 13 points. The most important changes were: the vetos of the President and the Vice-President should be abolished. The Vice-President should be able to deputise for the President. The two speakers of the House should be elected by the whole parliament. The separate majorities of laws should be abrogated. The separate municipalities should be replaced by jointly elected organs composed proportionally to the population. The ethnic separation of courts and security forces should end. The civil service was to be composed in proportion to the population. The Greek Communal Chamber was to be dissolved, as was the Turkish, but this was not said *expressis verbis*.

In his report to the Ministry Clark characterised these proposals as reasonable but he did not point to the critical points. Probably it was clear to him that the proposals regarding the veto, and the separate municipalities would lead to violent reactions in London. Supposedly he hoped to defuse these problems during his talks with Makarios and Kyprianou so that they would become acceptable. However this may have been, the responsible officers in the Foreign Office were "taken aback". But as this was the headache of the Commonwealth Ministry they criticised the text only mildly. Because Sandys was preoccupied with other problems he did not interest himself in Cyprus; thus Clark had plenty of rope.

During the following days Clark revised the text of the proposals as a personal favour to Makarios. He made great efforts to avoid formulations which might cause Turkish allergic reactions. It can be assumed that Clark told Makarios that this was a personal favour, that he was acting in a personal capacity. Clark did not understand this was irrelevant for the Greek side because for them he spoke for the British Government. This was a well known phenomenon. In the Greek world statements by British representatives, no matter whether they were diplomats, or soldiers were always interpreted as the opinion of the British Government. Additionally there were no negative reactions from London, a fact which Makarios interpreted as a green light and the more so since Clark assisted him. According to Clerides, Makarios was convinced that the British Government backed him and thus went on. On 29 November Makarios handed over the final text of his 13 points to Küçük and the Ambassadors of Greece and Turkey.

Since the 13 points play a major role in the history of Cyprus we will try and find an answer to the questions whether it had been necessary to suggest constitutional changes at this point and which aims Makarios really had. Clerides presented convincing answers in his memoirs: The Council of Ministers worked impeccably, so did the judges, the Highest Court, the civil service and the security forces. The President and the Vice-President cooperated smoothly, promulgating the laws of the House or the decision of the Council of Ministers. The vice-presidential veto had been used once in connection with the army but the Greek side had been pleased with this. The issue of the separate municipalities could have been solved by simply implementing the constitutional provisions and examining them after the period of five years, as provided by the Constitution. The implementation of the 70:30 ratio in the civil service was progressing satisfactorily so that there was no need for a constitutional amendment. The courts functioned well despite the separation according to the communities. The question of the election of the two Speakers of the House was absolutely no source of conflict. The abolition of the Greek Communal Chamber made sense because education would have come under the control of the Ministry of Education. Generally speaking there was no urgent need for a change to the Constitution. Makarios' 13 points were mistimed.

Makarios' mistake was a wrong assessment of the international situation: in Greece there were two weak interim governments which Makarios could neglect. Even when G. Papandreou became Prime Minister he did not pay much attention to him but hoped for support. The crisis in the British Government was welcome to him because it hindered a timely intervention. Further, he certainly knew that the Turkish Government had been shaky since the municipal elections of 17 November. All this encouraged him to submit his 13 proposals.

Makarios still had two targets: unfettered independence and reduction of the privileges of the Turkish Cypriots. Enosis was no option for him. His verbal commitments were lip service to keep the radical nationalists quiet. Makarios' foreign policy aimed at the abolition of the treaties of alliance and guarantee in order to get rid of the right of intervention of the guarantor powers. In internal politics he wanted to make the Turkish Cypriots a privileged minority and reduce the excessive rights given to them by the Constitution.

The 13 points were a deliberate provocation designed to create a small controllable crisis. The danger of a unilateral Turkish intervention was small - according to his assessment. He assumed that the British and American Governments would exert pressure on Turkey and thus the Turkish Government would give in and the Greek Government would consent. The pressure would be applied at the annual NATO meeting in Paris on 8 December 1963. In case this stratagem would not function he could go to the UN where he could expect a huge majority from the non-aligned states and the former colonies.

However, the hope for British support was a total miscalculation because the Foreign Office managed to keep Sandys from an active Cyprus policy of his own and thus the initiative fell back to the Foreign Office. When on 22 November 1963 President Kennedy was murdered in Dallas the ability of the Americans to act was reduced momentarily. The Greek Government did not think much of the 13 points, as Foreign Minister S. Venizelos admitted. On 2 December Prime Minister Inönü announced the resignation of his government and in Athens the resignation of the Papandreou government was on the horizon. Thus Makarios' foreign policy scenario began to flounder.

When in the morning of 30 November Makarios gave the memo with the 13 points to Küçük the latter had a quick look at it and was appalled by its length, but with a grim sense of humour he said that enosis would have been better than this. However, he promised to check the proposals thoroughly and work out counter-proposals, which would take roughly a week. Makarios and Küçük agreed to keep everything secret.

Until 5 December privacy was observed but on this date an indiscretion happened when S. Venizelos disclosed that Makarios had sent proposals for a revision of the constitution to the three guarantor powers. It is unknown whether Venizelos committed this blunder deliberately or carelessly. But when the Athens News Agency published details, the Turkish Government had the perfect excuse to reject Makarios' 13 points. On 6 December the Turkish Government informed the Americans that it would reject Makarios' proposals. Although the Americans advised moderation, new indiscretions added fuel to the flames.

On 13 December it became known in Nicosia that Küçük was still working on his counter-proposals but Denktash spoke out: If Makarios violated the Constitution he actually dissolved the Republic. In this case the Turks were free to found their own state or to join Turkey. It was here that this formula was used for the first time which was to become one of Denktash's standard arguments for the next decades. With Makarios' 13 points the Greeks had dissolved the Republic unilaterally. On the morning of 16 December Makarios received a sharp answer from the Turkish Government to his 13 points. When he had read them he sent the memo back to the Turkish embassy. In order to stop the rumours afloat about the 13 points he had the full text published on 18 December.

On 15 December Dean Rusk and his Turkish colleague, Erkin, met in Paris at the NATO meeting of the Foreign Ministers. Erkin stated that if Makarios did not respect the Constitution Turkey had to intervene together with the other two guarantor powers or unilaterally. In the extreme case Turkey would demand partition. Rusk passed this on to Kyprianou when they met on 20 December and advised him to show moderation. Obviously, the State Department was not interested in being drawn into the Cyprus Conflict. Cyprus was a British headache.

On the same day the representatives of the guarantor powers met in the Greek Embassy. Erkin was in the chair. The communiqué published afterwards was vacuous but apparently it was decided that Erkin would advise Küçük to resume the talks with Makarios provided they move in the frame of the Constitution and did not aim at its overthrow. Makarios announced that he would ask the UN to check the treaty of guarantee. But before this happened a petty incident caused an explosion in Cyprus. The controlled crisis which Makarios had provoked in order to push through his aims got out of control.

On the way to civil war

When Makarios made his change of course towards constitutional changes in spring 1962 this triggered a power struggle between the moderates and the radical separatists. Speeches by Makarios and Minister of the Interior Georkatzis praising enosis were grist to the mill of the separatists. In order to torpedo the slightest chance for a compromise and to inflame the mood to boiling they organized demonstrations in the towns. The explosions on 25 March 1962 at the Omeriye mosque in the walled city and the Bayraktar mosque on the Constanza bastion added fuel to the fire though they did not do much harm. Immediately after the explosions suspicion arose that these had been the work of the separatists because the execution was similar to the explosion at the birthplace of Atatürk in Thessaloniki in 1955, which triggered the pogrom in Istanbul and the explosion at the Press Office of the Turkish Consulate in Nicosia on 7 June 1958 which led to the inter-communal unrest of 1958. Therefore, Georkatzis immediately suspected that the Turkish extremists had laid the bombs. A little later he had unambiguous proof that the explosion had been the work of TMT. Anyhow, the situation was soon calm again.

The moderates among the Turkish Cypriots were afraid that this could be repeated. On 27 March 1962 the journalist Muzafer Gürkan, who advocated inter-communal cooperation went to the Turkish Embassy in order to ask Ambassador Dirvana, who was considered a moderate to intervene with the leadership of the Turkish Cypriots in order to avoid a greater crisis. But the Ambassador was absent and thus Gürkan spoke with the Press Attaché Mehmet Pamir who was at the same time resident of the Turkish Secret Service. Allegedly Pamir told Gürkan that Denktash was behind the explosions. Afterwards Gürkan visited Georkatzis to inform him about this. Georkatzis had the conversation taped secretly. This conversation and remarks by Gürkan and his colleague Ayan Hikmet to representatives of the foreign press that the Turkish Cypriot leadership insisted on the erection of separate municipalities because their aim was partition of Cyprus infuriated TMT in such a way that they decided to silence them and Dr Ihsan Ali. On the night of 23 April the death sentence of TMT was enforced on the two journalists when they were executed by TMT killers: Hikmet was shot when he was asleep and Gürkan when he parked his car in front of his house.

During the following weeks the police investigated the explosions and the two homicide cases. On 10 May *Cyprus Mail* reported that on the eve of the explosions three Turkish Cypriot policemen in mufti had been seen near the Bayraktar mosque. Two days later an explosives expert of the British army stated that the explosive charges had been placed in such a way that they would cause as little damage as possible. On 21 May there was a sensation when Georkatzis told the investigating commission about the existence of the tape and played it to them. Georkatzis added that he had further information proving that the explosions had been the work of the Turkish side. Gürkan's widow testified that Denktash had threatened the two journalists with death if they went on with their work. Denktash denied the accusations and counterattacked, stating that the explosions were the work of Georkatzis and the tapes were faked. As nothing could be directly proved the investigation ended here. Two voices which had advocated cooperation between the two ethnic groups in their newspaper had been silenced and from now on the separatists had the say.

In early 1962 Makarios ordered P. Georkatzis, T. Papadoulos and G. Clerides to set up a secret defence organisation with a staff, local commanders and weapon caches. The first volunteers came from the ranks of former EOKA members and the cadres of the Cypriot army, most of whom had belonged to EOKA, too. These men were loyal to Makarios but more loyal to Georkatzis. Communists were not accepted. As not all former EOKA fighters accepted Georkatzis as their leader Vassos Lyssaridis and Nikos Sampson were authorized to set up their own companies of armed men. The extreme Grivas adherents organised a very small group, as well. The Georkatzis force allegedly counted 500 men and this number had grown to 1,800 by the end of 1963. Makarios welcomed the split into several competing groups because thus he could control them.

As the former EOKA fighters had only experience in underground fighting it was clear that in the case of a clash with TMT led and trained by military professionals of the Turkish army they could not persist. Thus the new organisation needed training by professionals, i.e., Greek officers. These could only come from the Greek contingent (ELDYK). In order to get the support of these officers who strictly observed the letter and the spirit of the Treaty of Alliance and did not interfere in the internal affairs of the Republic, the organisation was brought to a strictly anti-communist line. It was hoped that by this the support of the right wing officers would be obtained. That is what happened, indeed. The chief of the operations and reconnaissance department was a certain major Dimitrios Ioannidis, who in 1973 replaced Georgios Papadopoulos as dictator of Greece and ordered the coup d'état against Makarios in summer 1974. Ioannidis was on especially familiar terms with Sampson. According to Makarios he and Sampson were even thinking about the annihilation of the Turkish community.

Since the organisation was a kind of continuation of EOKA, Georkatzis, as chief took over certain attitudes of Grivas: Grivas had assumed the *nom de guerre* "Digenis", now Georkatzis followed suit calling himself "Accretes". Both names stemmed from a Byzantine hero ballad of the 10th century. Grivas had signed his orders "The Leader, Digenis"; Georkatzis signed "The Leader, Akritas". Those involved tried to find a catchy name for the organisation but did not succeed in finding something suitable and thus the organisation became known as the *organosis*. The second in command of the *organosis* was T. Papadopoulos.

The Organisation had a double task. It should be able to subdue a TMT rising and repel a Turkish invasion until help came from Greece. The training of the officers by Greek officers took place in private houses. Manoeuvres and weapon exercises were held in remote areas of the island. In December 1962, a two-day staff exercise was held in Troodos successfully. When in summer 1963 the Greek Government fell, the *Organosis* began to recruit openly. Trained members of the Organisation and civil servants recruited men in the villages, mainly in areas inhabited by Turks. Companies of 100 to 130 men were formed and trained. In December, 1963 the *Organosis* allegedly had 5,000 fully trained fighters and another 5,000 men with varying training. The necessary weapons came from Greece. One of the main organizers of this smuggling was Colonel Georgios Papadopoulos, the future dictator of Greece.

The Turkish-Cypriot side, too, prepared itself for the coming clash. Officers of the Turkish contingent (TOURDYK) trained the leading cadres of TMT. As there were no spacious Turkish settlement areas where unobserved training would have been possible, a great part of the military training took place in Turkey. The cadres of the Turkish paramilitaries came from TMT, the police and Cypriot army. As in 1958 the commanders were Turkish army officers. The C.-in-C. was a Turkish colonel with the *nom de guerre Bozkurt* (wolf).

Since autumn, 1963 both sides had been preparing the clash. But there was a decisive difference: While the Greek Cypriots and the *Organosis* were on their own and could only conditionally expect help from their mother country, TMT was sure of active Turkish help. Turkey was even ready to accept that the first deaths would be Turkish Cypriots. This would allow them to fool the world that the Turkish side was only defending itself. Ankara instructed the Turkish Cypriots accordingly. By the end of 1963 it was only a question of time when the explosion would take place.

One of the most controversial documents of the history of modern Cyprus stems from this period, the so-called Akritas plan. The Turkish side and some foreign authors supporting them allege, until today that the aim of this plan was the annihilation of the Turkish-Cypriot community. This allegation was so often repeated by Denktash that even the Greek Cypriots believed it. No one took the trouble to check the original text for this though the text had been published even as a UN document (S/12722), it was not easily accessible. Even when G. Clerides published the text in his memoirs in 1989, thus declaring it authentic, this did not change the interpretation - obviously nobody cared to read the text because everybody believed he knew the content.

If one reads and analyses the text, it becomes clear that it is a kind of secret circular of Accretes (Georkatzis) to the commanders of the *Organosis*, describing the tactics followed so far and those to be applied in the future. The first part of the paper contains a description and interpretation of the foreign policy manoeuvres of Makarios during the last months, the aim of which was to abolish the treaties of Guarantee and Alliance - and implicitly the right of Turkey to intervene - and to reach the unlimited right to self-determination. As this term was not defined simple members of the *Organosis* could gain the impression that self-determination meant - as during the time of the struggle for independence - enosis. Makarios, however, perceived self-determination as unfettered independence. Whether Georkatzis understood this cannot be proved by the text. The ambiguity should keep members still dreaming of enosis in the ranks of the *organosis*.

The second part of the paper dealt with the tactic of how to avoid an intervention by Turkey if a change of the Constitution was pushed through. The aim described here was clearly the abolition of the equal partnership and its replacement by the concept of a privileged minority. The paper analysed possible gradual reactions on differing forcible actions of the Turkish side. This part shows an excessive overestimation of the Greek abilities, but nowhere does one read anything about an annihilation of the Turkish Cypriots. The Greek actions should neither provoke the other side nor should they be forceful. In case of an incident one should react with legal means. Twice the text stresses *expressis verbis* that one did not intend to suppress the Turks and certainly not kill even one. In case of a major military attack by Turkey enosis would be declared unilaterally - probably to draw Greece into the conflict.

Ultimately the so-called Akritas plan explains Makarios' foreign policy to the members of the *Organosis* in the forefront of the 13 points and points out the possible consequences and secret intentions of this policy. The political part is fully based on Makarios' thoughts whereas the tactical parts reflect the thinking of Georkatzis. Obviously the latter was ready to risk a confrontation. But not one word can be found on the annihilation of the Turkish Cypriots. The inherent aim of the so-called Akritas plan is the termination of the equal partnership between the Greek and the Turkish Cypriots and the enforcement of the principle of a Greek Cypriot majority and Turkish Cypriot minority.

Only once is enosis mentioned as an aim which must not be mentioned under any circumstances and its purpose is clearly to keep the old EOKA members faithful to the *organosis*. It is not known whether Georkatzis himself was behind this tactic but the acidity of his polemics against the adherents of Grivas at the end of the paper suggests this assumption. Hence the plan was published by the press close to Grivas in 1966 and thus disavowed.

Unlike the Greeks, the Turkish separatists wanted to abolish the state created in 1960. In spring, 1962 Denktash wrote a paper stating that the Zurich and London Agreements had been accepted as an interim solution because the rights of the Turkish Cypriots had been recognized according to international law. One would profit from the mistakes committed by the Greek side and if they tampered with the Constitution, trying to abolish it, then one gained full freedom of action again and could proceed towards partition of the island. Those Turkish Cypriots who wanted a compromise had to be stopped or silenced. But Denktash did not develop concrete ideas about how the separation would look.

In September 1963, however, Denktash produced these concrete ideas: In 1964 Makarios would try to push through constitutional changes and abolish or revise the Zurich and London Agreements. Though Turkey had the right to intervene, even unilaterally, in the case that the Constitution was abolished, the result of such an intervention would only be the return to the *status quo ante*. Such an intervention would cause trouble with the UN and raise world public opinion against Turkey, therefore it would be counterproductive. For this reason the Turkish Cypriot side should take their fate in their own hands and set up a Turkish Cypriot Republic. The hitherto Turkish Cypriot Vice-President would become President, recognised by the Turkish Cypriots and a Government, consisting only of Turkish ministers would be formed. The mother country would recognize the new Government which in turn would ask Turkey for help thus causing the motherland to intervene. The members of the House and Communal Chambers would form a new parliament of the Turkish-Cypriot Republic and proclaim a Turkish Republic. The mother country would immediately conclude a commercial and help agreement thus making help from Turkey legal. It is here that this scenario was developed for the first time which was realised in a slightly modified way in 1974. The aim of the separatists was to set up an independent Turkish Cypriot Republic. In the whole text there was not one word about union with Turkey.

Thus in autumn 1963 both communities were ready to abolish the order established by Zurich and London. The Turkish Cypriot side spoke with one voice; the opposition fell silent after the murder of the two journalists. From now on Denktash determined the course and this aimed at separatism and secession. He planned an independent state and in order to achieve this he was ready to use force and destroy the existing Republic, i.e., to do precisely that which he and the propaganda of his separate state later accused the Greek side of doing.

The Greek side spoke with multiple voices. The nationalist extremists continued to dream of union with Greece and wanted to abolish the Cyprus Republic. Makarios and the moderates wanted to keep the Republic but to get rid of the external chains caused by Treaties of Guarantee and Alliance and revise the Constitution. Makarios wanted to use diplomatic negotiations to achieve his aims. With a different political constellation in Ankara he might have succeeded, as the negotiation of 1968 proved when the Turkish Government was prepared to accept concessions roughly corresponding to the 13 points.

For Makarios the use of force was only an eventuality in case of a Turkish attack. It was no option to achieve a political aim. The problem was that there were forces on the second level prepared to apply force. It is the tragedy of Cyprus that this was true on both sides and thus the civil war was programmed.

1963-1964: THE CIVIL WAR

The 1963 Christmas riots and the London Conference in January 1964

By mid-December 1963 the tensions between the two camps had risen so far that the tiniest provocation sufficed to trigger an explosion of violence. This happened at about 2 o'clock in the morning of 21 December 1963 when a police patrol stopped a car with Turkish Cypriots near the red light district of old Nicosia to control their ID-papers. But they refused to show their papers. A loud angry exchange of words followed attracting quite a number of Turkish Cypriot residents. Someone out of the crowd fired at the policemen who fired back and withdrew, waiting for reinforcements.

This, strictly speaking, was an insignificant incident, however, it triggered the unrest everybody was afraid of because now both sides mobilised their paramilitary forces and deployed them in Nicosia along the perimeters of their respective quarters. As the guards manning the front line were nervous and inexperienced they fired at anything that moved during the night. The leadership of the Greek paramilitary asked Makarios to release the weapons which had been under lock and key so far. But Makarios hesitated because he rightly feared that the Greek paramilitary might start a general attack on the Turks leading to numerous deaths which would provoke an intervention of Turkey. As during the day of 22 December the firing diminished, the victims of the night before could be buried without any incidents. At the same time there were indirect contacts between the two sides via the representatives of the UK and the US. Makarios spoke about setting up a commission of enquiry. Obviously he had not yet understood that the civil war had begun.

In the night of 22 December new shooting occurred. Cars with armed Greeks drove through the town firing on everything that moved. Inversely the Turkish Cypriots fired at police cars on patrol. In one case the policemen stopped, took cover and fired back. A Turkish Cypriot was killed, another badly wounded, and three Greek civilians were wounded by bullets. From other cars shots were fired at all lighted windows, causing the people living there to turn off the lights. From minarets and the roof terrace of the Saray hotel Turkish Cypriot snipers fired at passers-by and passing cars. The shooting spread to the mixed suburbs in the north and the west of Nicosia. Most Turkish policemen left their posts and defected to the Turkish quarters to assist their compatriots. At the same time it became known that shooting had started in Larnaca, too.

The spreading of the fighting induced the Greek side to order extensive security measures on 23 December. Members of the *Organosis* and the paramilitary of Lyssaridis and Sampson were appointed Special Constables. Lyssaridis and roughly 100 men were ordered to occupy and defend the area around the Ledra Palace Hotel. Sampson and 41 fighters were sent to the defenders of Omorfyta as reinforcements. In Nicosia there were again wild shootings, killing 10 people and wounding 20. Despite heavy exchanges of fire nobody was killed in Larnaca and Famagousta.

The three Guarantor Powers demanded an immediate cease fire and resumption of the talks about changes to the constitution. These moderate tones were accompanied by shriller ones in Ankara when Inönü spoke about an impending holocaust and conferred with the General Staff. On 24 December Foreign Minister Erkin alleged that in Cyprus genocide was taking place. In Nicosia the British and American diplomats organised a meeting between Makarios and Küçük at the Paphos Gate. A cease fire was agreed upon which, unfortunately, was not kept. The Turkish paramilitary installed machine guns on minarets and fired on everything moving. The Greek police returned the fire from flat roofs of the higher buildings of the Greek area. When in Omorfyta some houses inhabited by Greeks were taken, Makarios permitted the arming of the Greek paramilitary from government stores.

By 20.00 hours the counter-attacks had begun in Omorfyta. As an attack on the Turkish position was hopeless without heavy weapons these were improvised: A bulldozer moved forward with its shovel lifted, followed by three lorries driving backwards with Sampson's paramilitary on the flatboard behind sandbags, wildly firing at everything. By noon of 25 December Omorfyta had been conquered. During these fights horrible excesses happened: paramilitary, running amok, murdered women and children, plundered and destroyed Turkish property and took hostages. It was this action which made Sampson known as a pathological killer of Turks. The number of deaths rose to 20, and there were dozens of wounded. Allegedly 700 hostages were taken. Makarios was horrified by the brutal excesses of the irregulars of the *Organosis* and Sampson's troop.

An especially abominable murder happened in the suburb of Kumsal about one kilometre north of the Ledra Palace Hotel deep in the Turkish controlled area: There killers wearing masks forced their way into the house of an army doctor of the Turkish contingent living there with his family. They shot his wife, and the three small children in the bathroom. A visitor was wounded and his wife who had hidden in the toilet, was shot through the door. To this day the precise sequence of events is not clear and there are inconsistencies which raise doubts about the real identity of the killers. Most Turkish Cypriot authors have no doubt that the killers were Greek Cypriots, but there are serious publications stemming from Turkish Cypriot authors who speak of a TMT provocation to spur the Turkish contingent into action. However this may be, some time later the family house was made into a "Museum of Barbarity" which still exists.

Christmas Day 1963 began with a Turkish show of force when in early hours three fighter jets thundered at low-altitude over the roofs of Nicosia. A little later rumours were heard that a Turkish invasion fleet was on its way to Cyprus. At 10.15 hours, at an extraordinary meeting of the NATO Council, the representative of Turkey announced that Turkey would act unilaterally and send troops to Cyprus if by a joint action of the Guarantor Powers the situation could not be brought under control. The other members pressed for moderation and the Americans vetoed any action if American weapons were used. In the following days there were intensive diplomatic contacts to master the crisis. UK Foreign Minister Butler suggested a joint intervention of the Guarantor Powers. Finally, it was agreed that British, Greek and Turkish forces in Cyprus should form a Joint Truce Force under the command of General Peter Young which would supervise the cease fire. Makarios agreed after some hesitation. In the evening of 26 December the British began their patrols through the old town and along the front line. Their landrovers were decorated with the Union Jack and the occupants armed. In the morning of 27 December 1963 the first British troops moved between the fighting parties and occupied their positions. Continuous radio announcements pointed out that the British troops patrolled the town with the connivance of the Cypriot Government and appealed to the public to support them. Though some shots were still fired the situation calmed down noticeably.

General Young's mission was to keep up the cease fire. But he interpreted this order extensively, thus changing the Peace-Keeping-Mission into a Peace-Making-Mission. He set up teams consisting of one British, one Turkish and one Greek officer of which the Briton had to speak Greek or Turkish. If a riot occurred somewhere on the island one of the teams flew there and saw to it that a violent clash was avoided. The Greek and the Turkish officers were influencing their respective communities. Young's idea was right because Peace-Keeping-Operations only preserve the status quo, separate the fighting parties but do not resolve the conflict. Patient sensitive mediation offered the chance for reconciliation. The 1963 Christmas unrests had damaged the relationship between the two ethnic groups but had not destroyed them irreparably. The actions of Young and his team opened a window of opportunity for reconciliation. The question was whether it would remain open long enough to lead to real reconciliation.

On 28 December 1963 Commonwealth Relations Minister Duncan Sandys flew to Cyprus to support the mission of general Young politically. In the morning of 29 December he met Makarios, Küçük and the ambassadors of Greece and Turkey. It was agreed to set up a political committee which would meet daily in order to work out agreements for the cease fire and reestablish cooperation between the two sides. On 30 December the two opponents withdrew from the frontline, which from now on was the Green Line because it had been drawn on the map with a green pencil. The next day both sides released their hostages and prisoners together; 545 Turks and 26 Greeks. 69 people had been killed, among them 49 Turkish Cypriots. 30 Turkish and 4 Greek Cypriots were missing. Most of the refugees returned to their homes but TMT took care that many Turkish Cypriots did not return to their mixed villages, but remained in Nicosia or settled in villages inhabited by Turks only in the north of the island. Thus, the relocation program of the 50's respectively Denktash's partition plans, were realised. In an interview with *Le Monde,* Küçük said that the island had to be partitioned along the 35th Parallel. The Turkish Cypriots wanted a state of their own which would remain independent or join Turkey.

Though it was clear that all involved would meet in a few day at a conference in London, Makarios tried to create a *fait accompli*. On 28 December he sent a telegram to the heads of state of the most important states with the exception of the Guarantor Powers announcing that he would withdraw from the Treaties of Guarantee and Alliance unilaterally. On 29 December Kyprianou said that the majority should rule in Cyprus while the rights of the minority would be protected and the two Treaties would be cancelled. On 1 January 1964 Makarios made it known over the radio that he withdrew from the two treaties. Sandys put such massive pressure upon Makarios that he revoked his statement, announcing that he only intended to do that.

The Conference in London began on 15 January 1964. The Greek Cypriots had agreed to steer a tough line: they wanted the abolition of the two Treaties and the reduction of the rights of the Turkish Cypriots to the status of a minority. The Turkish Cypriots wanted the partition of the island and a reallocation program for their compatriots. The Turkish Government wanted security for their kinsmen on the island and the Greek Government continued good relations with Ankara. As all participants stuck to their positions, the British recognised rather quickly that the conference would find no solution. As the tensions on Cyprus were mounting again a renewed clash and an intervention of the two mother countries seemed possible. Thus the conference was very close to failure. It was clear that in this case the Government of Cyprus would bring the case before the UN.

London was afraid that in this case the existence of the British bases would be called into question. As London did not want to give them up because of its obligation in CENTO, considerations began whether on could not involve NATO. On 22 January London proposed to Ankara and Athens to send a NATO-peace-keeping-force to Cyprus. Athens and Ankara agreed and so did the Turkish Cypriots, but Makarios rejected this. Athens put pressure on him to accept the proposal because it would surely have led to a restoration of the *status quo ante* i.e. led to a stable situation in Cyprus. There is reason to assume that this would have led to peace on the island. This would have restored the mutual trust of the two communities and thus opened the way to an amicable revision of the Constitution, also wanted by the Guarantor Powers. The NATO proposal offered a new chance to again find conditions for peaceful cohabitation. The question was whether the Greek Cypriots would accept this proposal or insist on going to the UN Security Council.

NATO-Plan and Ball Mission
So far the US Government had held off on the Cyprus question and left the initiative to the British. But now American diplomats in London recognized that the British Government was

not very keen on getting into a predicament again in Cyprus in an election year. The British would be glad if they could dump the Cyprus Problem on the UN. As the Americans were afraid that the Soviet Union could interfere, a discussion began about a greater American engagement in Cyprus. Secretary of State Rusk hesitated but consented finally that Undersecretary George Ball should look after this question and this he did until 1965.

In the following weeks Ball was in constant contact with the three Governments involved and developed the following plan: A NATO-peace-keeping force with American participation would be sent to Cyprus for three months. Athens and Ankara would undertake to refrain from any unilateral intervention and agree to the appointment of a mediator from a third country. This infuriated the British because it amounted to saying that they had followed the wrong course. They recognised that they should go on carrying the main weight, that a solution was not at hand and the Americans were only conditionally ready to engage themselves. In view of this situation they saw to it that the American plans found their way into the public eye. The aim of this manoeuvre was probably to provoke Makarios to reject the American proposal or force the Americans to take over the Cyprus Problem or dump it on the UN.

Thus substantial elements of the plan appeared in the press on 30 January 1964 but the British hypocritically declared themselves ready to accept the plan as it stood. The Greek-Cypriot press had already denounced the plan when the first rumours from Greek sources about a NATO solution had circulated. Makarios was of the opinion that if troops were sent to Cyprus it should be UN troops having a mandate to defend the island against attacks from outside. However, he avoided a clear statement. On the same day the Soviet Union warned the West in a letter to the UN Secretary General U Thant not to interfere in internal affairs of Cyprus.

Ball was not impressed by these manoeuvres and continued his effort to make Athens and Ankara accept the plan. He assumed that the leadership of the Greek and Turkish Cypriots was under the remote control of the mother countries. He was right in the case of Küçük, as had been proved in the past, but in the case of Makarios it was the other way round. He steered a totally independent course which he had often forced on the mother country. Ball and the State Department did not understand at that time that a solution without Makarios could not be found and Makarios rejected Ball's plan: a Peace-Keeping Force had to be subordinated to the UN-Security Council.

The State Department was of the opinion that Ball should fly to Cyprus and "give the old bastard [Makarios] absolute hell." Although the British began to doubt the wisdom of Ball's plan and began to seek for alternatives, and the Soviets warned against an intervention of NATO, Ball insisted on the implementation of the NATO solution. Between 9 and 11 February Ball visited London, Athens and Ankara to inform himself about the position of the Governments there. On 12 February Ball appeared in Nicosia. What followed was a typical example of American brute force diplomacy which brought about the opposite of what it intended.

When Makarios insisted at their second meeting to submit the case to the UN and Clerides rejected Ball's plan with stringent reasons, Ball threw a tantrum and fell out of his diplomatic role: He told off Makarios and his Ministers and described in lurid details the consequences if they persisted in their cruel and reckless conduct. He threatened that the US would lift no finger if Turkey invaded Cyprus. Ball did not grasp some friendly gestures of Makarios' and misinterpreted them completely. His remark that Clerides and Papadopoulos were fanatical and over the edge and had some Communist colouration in their background proved that the responsible US services did not have the slightest idea about Cyprus. Ball's attack that the Greek side was out to massacre Turkish Cypriots had nothing in common with reality: at the time of Ball's visit there were some minor violent incidents between the two communities but these were far from being massacres.

Still in Cyprus, Ball thought about declaring publicly that the failure of his mission was caused by Makarios, but Rusk rejected this. Now Ball suggested that one should pre-empt Makarios by going to the UN Security Council before him and propose to set up an international peace-keeping force. The American Delegation at the UN seized this suggestion and contacted the British. It was agreed that the British, supported by the Americans, should file an expedited application for an urgent meeting of the Security Council the very moment when the Cypriots became active in the UN. Under normal circumstances everything should have run smoothly but due to a faux pas on the part of the new British Commissioner, Makarios learned about the British-American plot.

Makarios felt deceived and rang up the representative of Cyprus at the UN, Rossidis, and asked him to go straight to the Security Council and ask for an urgent meeting in order to preempt the British appeal. Rossidis should base his appeal on an impending Turkish invasion. Rossidis did what he was told but his appeal was filed after the British one. At the meeting of the Security Council on 15 February it was decided to debate the matter in the afternoon of 17 February. Although Ball developed some ideas about how to prevent a UN peace-keeping force, one of the three States involved raised objections; therefore nothing came about. Thus the NATO plan was off the table and Ball's mission had failed.

Cyprus at the Security Council
Makarios wanted two UN resolutions: In the first the Turks should be requested to respect the sovereignty and territorial integrity of Cyprus and refrain from any aggression. The second should set up the UN peace force with the task to restore peace and order, prevent separatist situations and defend the island. At the same time the Treaties of Guarantee and Alliance should be declared void. Clerides told Makarios that the first resolution stood no chance of being accepted but Makarios insisted on trying it.

UN Secretary General U Thant proposed that the three Guarantor Powers together with Cyprus should submit a plan to station a peace-keeping force on Cyprus for three months, the commander of which would be responsible to the Secretary General. This force should secure the peace and prevent further inter-communal clashes. Additionally a mediator should be appointed. The Security Council would appeal to all members of the UN to respect the independence and territorial integrity of Cyprus. Although Clerides explained to Makarios that in view of this proposal the Cypriot one did not have a chance, Makarios, however, insisted on a trial. Obviously Makarios' gambler's nature had won over sober reason and the Cypriot delegation went to New York to fight for the resolution with tied hands.

After several days of a war of words in the Security Council beginning on 17 February 1964, it became clear that Clerides had been right because the resolution submitted by Cyprus did not have the slightest chance. On 24 February it was obvious that there would be a peace-keeping force and a mediator. The still existing differences were related to the text of the preamble. When on 26 February a text was presented which had the chance to get a majority of the members of the Security Council, Denktash sent a letter to U Thant in which he told totally exaggerated horror stories. The vehemence of these unqualified attacks and the exchange of polemic arguments during the debates made some delegates hesitant to support U Thant's plan because they were afraid that the result might be a war and they began to look for noncommittal formulations. Accordingly a resolution that was neither fish nor meat seemed probable.

In the afternoon of 28 February Denktash was allowed to speak to the Security Council as a private person. For two hours he did his best to prove that Greeks and Turks could not live together in Cyprus. He presented inflationary figures, quotes taken out of context, half truths and manipulated facts in the style of a virtuoso pettifogger and polemicist against Kyprianou and Makarios. He painted a black and white picture of the horrors in Cyprus enriched with his typical cynicisms and sarcasms. The Cypriots used this speech as a pretext to refuse his return to Cyprus. Denktash went to Ankara and there he worked for the Foreign Ministry.

During the following days the haggling about the text of the preamble continued. On 4 March the text of Resolution 186(S/5575) was available. It demanded that all states refrain from threats or application of violence against the territorial integrity and political independence of each state. The states should omit everything that could worsen the situation or endanger international peace. A Peace-Keeping Force would be formed and a moderator would be appointed. Naturally all states involved tried to present the resolution as a result of their negotiating competence but in reality everybody was disappointed with the result. The Cypriot delegation had in vain tried to ensure that Turkey was mentioned in the resolution *expressis verbis* as the country which threatened the territorial integrity and sovereignty of Cyprus. Likewise, it did not succeed in charging the peace force with the defence of the island. Further, it could not get rid of the two Treaties; on the contrary they were corroborated by entitling the Guarantor Powers to accept the proposals of the mediator or not. The Resolution strengthened Turkey's right of co-determination in all questions regarding Cyprus. On his way to a unitary Cyprus with a majority and a minority, Makarios had not been able to proceed one step.

By the Resolution of 4 March 1964 a UN-Peace-Force came into being which became part of Cypriot history under the name of UNFICYP. The Resolution had estimated the operation to last for three months. At the moment of writing these lines UNFICYP has been in Cyprus for 45 years.

Makarios and Georgios Papandreou

From the Greek parliamentary elections on 3 November 1963, Georgios Papandreou and his Centre Union had emanated as the strongest power but as a coalition with the left (EDA) was out of the question he formed a minority Government and prepared new elections on 16 February 1964. From these he emerged with an absolute majority. Even during his first government he had tried to get Makarios under control with the help of Foreign Minister S. Venizelos. In a letter of 29 December 1963 Venizelos strongly criticised Makarios' unilateral actions but Makarios did not even think of respecting the leadership of the "National Centre". As Papandreou's Government resigned on 31 December 1963 and a service government took over to prepare the elections, Makarios did not even pay attention to the letter of the Foreign Minister who had resigned as well: without even informing Athens he made the effort to get rid of the Cyprus Treaties which we described earlier.

Therefore Venizelos developed the idea to replace Makarios with Grivas. This idea was rejected by the Greek Cabinet but met with great interest on the American side especially from the CIA, as George Ball tells us. Grivas himself tried to organise his return to Cyprus by asking a friend to mention him as a possible C.-in-C. of the armed groups in Cyprus but the service government did not show any interest. When Papandreou again became Prime Minister on 19 February 1964 he showed himself determined to discipline Makarios. On 25 February he requested closer cooperation from Makarios. It was unacceptable for the Greek Government to learn from the press what Makarios had done or was planning. In other words, Papandreou formulated here clearly the doctrine of the claim for leadership of the "National Centre" (Athens) to which the periphery had to subordinate itself.

Makarios' answer was a paradigm of his ability to allegedly agree to demands but at the same time to reject them clearly. He stated that it was his aim to abolish the Cyprus Treaties so that the people of Cyprus could exercise their right of self-determination. In Papandreou's thinking this meant enosis which he, too, was struggling for. For Makarios this meant unfettered independence of an independent Cypriot state. His aim was so cleverly formulated that

Papandreou did not understand it. Papandreou did not answer because he did not grasp that Makarios had rebuffed him and continued with his self-reliant policy.

Continued civil war

Although the fighting had almost stopped during the conference in London in mid-January 1964, small shooting incidents happened. When the Conference ran into a stalemate unknown persons exploded a bomb again at the Bayraktar mosque which immediately increased the tensions between the communities and led to shootings at the demarcation line and in some mixed villages without deaths, fortunately. After that the shooting incidents and the taking of hostages moved to the countryside. The focus of the new round of incidents was around Paphos. Further shootouts followed in the Tillyria at the bay at Morphou and in the village along the northwest coast. In remote villages in the countryside a feeling of insecurity, even anxiety, spread which reminds one of *La Grande Peur* in the early phase of the French Revolution. The Greek police began to steer a tougher course against the Turkish "insurgent". TMT on the other side saw a chance to prove that Greek and Turkish Cypriots could not live together. Thus slowly the war of the villages began, as Martin Packard called it.

When on 10 February it became known that George Ball would arrive soon this caused new Turkish provocations in order to provoke a Greek overreaction. This time the focus was Limassol. Both sides used automatic weapons and had grenades. The Greek side used bulldozers as improvised tanks to attack fortified strongholds in the streets. It took quite an effort to arrange a cease fire. In a telegram to President Johnson Küçük alleged that 150 hostages had been murdered in Limassol. The number of 150 was totally exaggerated but Ball believed it and he began to discredit Makarios and put pressure on him. The incidents of both sides continued all through February; during the debate in the Security Council, on a slightly reduced scale. In early March a bad incident happened in Ktima where 14 Turks and 11 Greeks lost their lives. In the following days the unrest swept all over Cyprus.

As the incidents of early March 1964 almost exclusively emanated from the Turkish side it seems obvious that these incidents and provocations were planned and coordinated from a central command unit in Nicosia, with the aim of provoking the other side so much that it would retaliate with a big massacre, which in turn would lead to a public outcry in Turkey compelling the Government to intervene. It was hoped that a *fait accompli* might be brought about before the UN-Peace-Keeping Force could stabilise the situation. It is improbable that the initiative for this action was the mental product of Küçük; it rather goes back to Denktash and TMT or even to certain military circles in Turkey. This thesis is corroborated by the evidence mentioned. One cannot prove it by hard evidence but this is in the nature of such things.

However this may be, the fact is that on 12 March the Turkish Government issued an ultimatum to the Government of Cyprus with copies to the Governments of Athens and London threatening the invasion of the island if the assaults on the Turkish community in Cyprus did not end. The siege rings around the villages had to be lifted, the hostages released and the corpses of the murdered be given to the relatives. If this was not done Turkey would intervene on the basis of the Treaty of Guarantee. At the same time it became known that the Turkish Air Force was getting ready for an attack. If there was no cease fire in Cyprus by the evening of 13 March Turkey would intervene.

The Government of Cyprus rejected these accusations. The Turkish ultimatum was an unacceptable interference in the internal affairs of Cyprus. Most of the Turkish accusations were demonstrably false. This was a manoeuvre of the Turkish Cypriot leadership to induce Turkey to intervene in order to create a *fait accompli*. In Washington it was recognised that one had to act quickly to avert a catastrophe. President Johnson urged the Canadian Prime Minister to send the troops earmarked for UNFICYP immediately. At the same time diplomatic moves began to prevent Turkey from overhasty steps.

When the Turkish Government learned of the accelerated transport of the Canadian unit it abandoned the intervention on 16 March 1964 but the Government requested the Turkish parliament, in secret session, grant full authority for a military intervention in case a new necessity arose. Only four deputies abstained from voting. When the first Canadian Blue Helmets arrived the situation quieted for the time being.

During those critical days Makarios was in Athens for the funeral service of King Paul. When the Turkish ultimatum became known Papandreou called a meeting at his house in Kastri, a suburb of Athens, at which Makarios, Foreign Minister Kostopoulos, Defence Minister Garoufalias, the Commander of ELDYK Brigadier G. Peridis, Foreign Minister Kyprianou, Ambassador Kranidiotis and Grivas participated. The military situation was discussed: as Cyprus was far away from Greece *ad hoc* help was difficult. Therefore, it was decided to strengthen the defence of Cyprus by men and material so that it could defend itself successfully. Papandreou thus offered to send additional troops to Cyprus besides the Greek contingent. Makarios returned to Cyprus on 13 March 1964.

As early as February 1964 Makarios and his Cabinet had considered how to meet a Turkish invasion and how to integrate the various armed groups in one military organisation and how to strengthen the defence forces of Cyprus. A National Guard (Ethniki Froura) controlled by the State on the basis of volunteers with a command structure of its own was to be set up. High cost excluded the creation of armed forces based upon compulsory military service. During talks between Kranidiotis, Garoufalias, Grivas and Greek staff officers it became clear that the existing forces, with few exceptions, suffered from severe deficiencies in military training. Strictly speaking everything had to be rebuilt from scratch; officers, especially, were necessary.

After Makarios' visit to Athens a special staff was set up under Grivas within the headquarters of the Greek Armed Forces called EMEK (Eidiko Mikton Epiteleion Kyprou - Mixed Special Staff Cyprus). For political reasons the Greek Government did not want to send Grivas to Cyprus, thus it was agreed with him and Makarios that the retired General Georgios Karagiannis would take over the command in Cyprus. In the second half of March big quantities of weapons and ammunition were secretly sent to Cyprus. At the end of March Garoufalias suggested sending 1,000 to 2,000 well trained mountain troops (LOK) which could later be augmented to 8,000 men. Makarios accepted and saw to it that these soldiers were equipped with Cypriot passports and could enter Cyprus from April on.

The decision for this command structure and Karagiannis meant that the Cyprus Government no longer had any influence on the security policy of its country. Decisions were taken by a committee of representatives of the Ministers of Defence and Foreign Affairs and Grivas. Really questionable was the fact that from now on the defence forces of Cyprus were brought to a militant anti-communist line. Karagiannis and his second-in-command had proved their anti-communism during the Greek Civil War. The officers sent to Cyprus had been educated to become radical anti-communists and there were some who played a leading role in the 21 April 1967 coup in Greece. Thus a conflict potential was created because these anti-communist forces tried to force their ideas on Makarios. They considered his course of non-alignment as treason and they did not understand that Makarios had elegantly solved the problem of Cypriot Communism by integration. The presence of the Greek military weakened the position of Makarios.

In the second half of March the first greater number of UNFICYP Blue Helmets appeared in Cyprus and at the end of the month they officially took over the peace-keeping from the British, thus ending the peace making operation. On 20 April General Karagiannis came to Cyprus for a kind of stock taking. During one of the numerous meetings with Defence Minister

Georkatzis the latter told him that since the unrests, troops of the Turkish contingent had blocked the road from Nicosia to Kyrenia and TMT units had controlled the area from the castle of St. Hilarion to Kyrenia. Indeed, TMT planned to expand the area controlled by it towards the west and the east and link it in the south with the area controlled by the Turkish contingent. In the west TMT wanted to control the road from Myrtou to Kyrenia and in the east that from Lefkonoiko to Kyrenia. Thus a big coherent area would have been created which would have been able to absorb huge numbers of Turkish Cypriot refugees. In principle this was a first step towards the creation of a separate state of the kind which Denktash planned. The Greek-Cypriot side had known these plans since February and was planning counter measures. It was clear that an operation against these TMT positions could only be executed before UNFICYP units appeared in greater numbers. It is not known whether Georkatzis informed Karagiannis about the impending attack against the TMT position. For good or ill Karagiannis was in Cyprus all the time but apparently practiced a hands-off approach although he should have intervened according to the policy of Athens.

In early April there were clashes in the Tillyria on the coast near Kokkina. In this area the local commander of *Organosis* had made himself independent and controlled the region like a war lord, feared by the Turkish Cypriots and his own kinsmen alike. The region was very poor. The locals were a bit backward, wild, aggressive and still believed in vendetta. The former Peace-Making teams had encountered great difficulties enforcing a cease fire. When the work of these teams ended the clashes began promptly and escalated quickly. Blue Helmets intervened and negotiated a precarious cease fire. On 10 April the operation against the TMT positions in the Kyrenia mountains began dragging on all April and widening to the whole region. The Greek paramilitary forces succeeded in pushing TMT back to St. Hilarion Castle but then UNFICYP intervened, moved in between and thus stopped the fighting.

On 1 May Karagiannis returned to Athens and reported. Grivas was discontented with all measures taken for the creation of the National Guard. Obviously Grivas considered only himself capable of mastering such a task. Indeed Grivas had composed a totally illusory time-table for the setting up of the National Guard - on paper: within ten days 12 battalions and after another two months a lot of reserve units should be set up, altogether 8,500 men. Additionally, Grivas wrote a military study on how a Turkish invasion could be repulsed which, however, had nothing in common with reality. The real situation was far more sobering: with great difficulty Karagiannis had managed to set up one battalion by 1 June.

After Karagiannis had returned to Cyprus on 8 May Grivas began to quarrel with everybody in Athens, threatening to resign and only with a great effort was he kept in office. By the end of May he had said to Papandreou that chaos was ruling in Cyprus and only he could install order there. When Papandreou did not answer he declared his resignation as chief of EMEK and demanded permission to go to Cyprus. When Georkatzis signalled from Cyprus that Grivas would be welcome, Papandreou gave in and allowed a visit limited to a few days under strict secrecy. Grivas, however, was resolved to remain in Cyprus.

On 9 June Grivas arrived at Limassol by ship. Already during his first talk with Karagiannis it became clear that Grivas wanted to take over the command and make the National Guard his private army. When after one week Grivas made no attempt to return to Greece, the Greek Government ordered him on 18 June to immediately return on a plane of the Greek Air Force especially sent to Cyprus for him because his presence in Cyprus might lead to a breach between Athens and Ankara. Grivas refused this categorically and demanded to be appointed C.-in-C. of the armed forces of Cyprus. At the same time he arranged that his presence became known in Cyprus. Makarios could not but welcome his return by public tributes and rallies.

Next, Grivas constantly provoked Karagiannis so that at one point the latter declared his resignation but revoked this immediately. No sooner had Grivas heard of Karagiannis'

Plate 25

Grivas and his guerillas in the Troodos mountains

The wreckage of the Hermes plane blown up on 4 March 1956

Plate 26

EOKA terror: Manolis Pieridis killed in a church

EOKA terror: two Britishe victims in Ledra Street

Plate 27

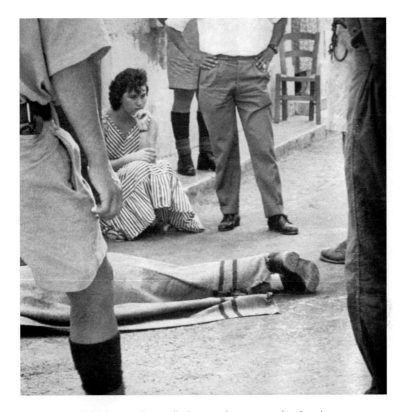

EOKA terror: Drosoulla Dimitriadis mourning her fiancée

Grivas in his workroom on the groundfloor

Plate 28

Grigoris Afxentiou

Afxentiou as a monk

Identity check

Plate 29

Razzia in a village

Gouvernor Hugh Foot

Plate 30

Küçük and Denktaş

Intercommunal clashes: arresting of looters

Plate 31

Intercommunal unrests: use of tear gas by the police

Blown up house: former hideout of Matsis

Plate 32

Barbara Castle and Makarios

Averof and Zorlu

resignation when he occupied an office in the staff building of the National Guard and began to pour out orders ignoring Karagiannis and his Second-in-Command. After two days Karagiannis took Grivas to task. Grivas falsely alleged that the Greek Government had transferred the command in Cyprus to him. From Athens Karagiannis learned that Grivas had demanded this but it had been rejected. At this moment the following forces were in Cyprus: the National Guard under Karagiannis, the Greek contingent under Brigadier G. Pieridis and the illegal infiltrated LOKs counting 8.000 men in August, also under Pieridis' command.

All Greek troops were under the command of the General Staff in Athens. Grivas had no military authority over Greek or Cypriot units; his heart's desire was to become C.-in-C. of all troops in Cyprus with the rank of a Field marshal, thus becoming the second Greek soldier after Alexandros Papagos with this rank. Allegedly Papandreou had promised him that in the case of a war with Turkey he would get the supreme command in Cyprus. In order to push through his claim for leadership Grivas bombarded the Greek Government with letters and memoranda.

On 1 July, Minister of Defence Georkatzis complained about Grivas in Athens, saying that Grivas was deceiving him and demanded that the responsibility for the security of the island should be conferred upon him exclusively. Besides that he was undermining the authority of Makarios. In reaction Athens created a kind of virtual supreme command in Cyprus (ASDAK) and made Grivas chief of it. But Minister of Defence Garoufalias told Grivas that the Greek contingent and the additional Greek troops (LOK) were directly under the command of the Ministry and Karagiannis continued to be the responsible commander of the National Guard. Grivas did not care about these restrictions and from 22 July 1964 he put on airs of a C.-in-C.

In the wake of the unrests in December 1963 about 200 Greek Cypriots had been ousted from mixed villages or had fled on their own. The number of Greek Cypriots who had lived in the Turkish quarters and had left their homes then counted several thousand, but this number was diminished to a few hundred soon because many were able to return to their houses. On the other side Turkish Cypriots left 72 mixed villages and 24 Turkish villages were given up. From another 8 mixed villages most Turkish Cypriots moved away. UNFICYP estimated the number of Turkish Cypriot refugees at around 25,000. The flight movement happened in several waves. The first batch left during the Christmas unrest in 1963 when people fled from the villages in the regions of Nicosia and Larnaca.

About 50 percent of the abandoned villages were left in January. The third wave mainly hit the Paphos district, causing another 18 percent of abandoned villages. In March three and in May two villages were abandoned. In August the attack on Kokkina and Mansura in the Tillyria area caused another flight movement. At first those Turkish Cypriots left the mixed villages where they were a minority but when the Greek Cypriot paramilitary moved into mixed villages with a Turkish majority, many fled. Many refugees fled under orders of TMT. But the majority hesitated to obey TMT's order and only fled when there were assaults by Greek radicals. Many of them hoped that after the end of the fighting they could return. There were cases where TMT activists told the villagers that their village was in the zone of the imminent Turkish invasion and might be bombed. When the number of refugees increased, their maintenance become a problem for the Turkish Cypriot leadership because the refugees had left their homes empty handed. The lucky ones found shelter at the houses of relatives in a Turkish village but many refugees were stranded in the Turkish quarter of Nicosia at the end. There in the vicinity of TOURDYK they felt safe and hoped to find shelter and work.

According to UN information about 55.000 Turkish Cypriots needed food. In June the number of refugees was estimated to be about 16.900 of which 60 percent lived in Nicosia. 1.500 lived in tent camps north of the Capital. 86 villages had accommodated refugees. The Turkish Red Crescent sent 2.331 tons of relief supplies.

By autumn 1964 several big Turkish Cypriot enclaves had come into being. The biggest stretched from the northern suburbs of Nicosia on the left and the right of the Kyrenia road to the first houses of this town. Two other Turkish centres emerged around Lefka and Limnitis in the East and the North of the Tillyria. In the towns there were still the Turkish quarters. The number of Turkish villages had diminished considerably. They concentrated in the West of the island near Polis, in the Southwest at Kouklia, in the Southeast outside Nicosia and in the area of Lefkonoiko and Aigialousa in the Karpasia peninsula. Before the fighting there had been 233 Turkish-Cypriot villages of which 98 were now totally abandoned. Of the 135 villages inhabited by Turkish Cypriots only 20 with a population of 8,000 were in Government controlled areas. The others formed enclaves of varying size.

The December unrests had almost completely destroyed the administration of the Turkish Cypriots and it took until spring 1964 for a new structure to emerge. In Nicosia a General Committee consisting of 13 former ministers, deputies, members of the judiciary and members of the Turkish Communal Chamber was formed under the presidency of Küçük. It was a kind of Government of the Turkish Cypriots. In the capitals of the five districts branches were set up which were in contact with the Turkish Cypriot villages of the district. Additionally, there was a military command structure of TMT which was not completely congruent. TMT was commanded by a Turkish Army General who had the *nom de guerre Bozkurt,* as has already been mentioned. He was subordinated to the Turkish General Staff and kept close contact with the Turkish Embassy in Nicosia.

The American Intervention
After the Ball-mission the responsible officials in the State Department and the US Embassies in Ankara, Athens and Nicosia started an opinion-forming debate. During this discussion ideas were developed which from now on resurfaced every now and then, i.e., an exchange of population between Cyprus and some Aegean island or even the Greeks of Istanbul. The Ambassadors agreed that enosis linked with voluntary emigration of the Turkish Cypriots and some concession to Turkey would be the best solution. In the Foreign Office this idea was brought to the handy formula "enosis cum territorial compensation". The UN mediator, however, the Finnish diplomat, Tuomioja, considered the situation as hopelessly muddled.

In Ankara Foreign Minister Erkin demanded the formation of a federal government or the separation of the island. If the other side would not accept this Turkish troops would land on the island and separate it. In the following weeks there were diplomatic efforts to avoid a crisis but in mid-May it became increasingly clear that the Turkish Government had manoeuvred itself into a stalemate, believing that the only way out was an act of violence. But renewed diplomatic efforts quieted the situation.

There was no evidence that there should be any reason why the status quo, however unpleasant it was especially for the Turkish side, could not be popped up for some time. But by the end of May the Turkish Military had become nervous. They had watched the rapid expansion of the Cypriot armed forces and learned of the dislocation of the Greek soldiers (LOK) to Cyprus despite all efforts to keep it secret. They understood that in a few months an invasion would be a bad affair or impossible. In view of this situation the military pressed for a preventive strike.

But Inönü still hesitated and undertook a final attempt to solve the conflict peacefully by making the National Security Council take the following decision: Küçük should ask Makarios in writing to call a cabinet meeting in its original composition and return to constitutional rule; changes to the constitution were considered possible. Should Makarios reject this the Turkish Cypriots should declare certain areas - the enclaves - as Turkish territory. Then Küçük should ask Turkey to help and Turkey would intervene. This manoeuvre had the characteristics of an alibi because Inönü knew that Makarios would reject the proposal. This, however, was exactly what had been premeditated and when Makarios did reject the proposal on 3 June 1964 Turkey had the desired excuse. Inönü decided to unilaterally intervene in Cyprus and to have this decision blessed by the Cabinet in its meeting in the evening of 4 June 1964.

From various sources the Americans were informed that the Turks were preparing a military intervention. When Foreign Minister Erkin admitted this to Ambassador Hare on 4 June the latter warned Washington. Secretary of State Rusk understood that he had to act quickly and called President Johnson by phone to have his agreement for a sharp message to the Turkish Government to keep them from decisions with catastrophic consequences. Johnson agreed that the Turks should be reminded of their promise to undertake nothing without consulting him. As the prime minister was pressing him, Dean Rusk rang up the Turkish Ambassador and made it clear to him that Johnson was extremely worried.

In Ankara Ambassador Hare managed to have the Turkish Prime Minister fetched from the Cabinet meeting at about 21.00 hours on 4 June. For three hours Hare worked on Inönü and Erkin to call off the invasion. Though Inönü was constantly trying to return to the Cabinet meeting Hare managed to prolonge the discussion. Finally Inönü wanted to know from Hare what he wanted. Hare replied promptly: "24 hours delay". Inönü agreed saying that he would wait for Johnson's reply until 21.00 hours on 5 June 1964 and stressed the need for absolute secrecy.

In Washington Secretary Rusk and two high ranking officials of the State Department had worked out the text of Johnson's letter. When this text was given to George Ball he characterised it as a *"diplomatic equivalent of an atomic bomb"*. Although the text was polished a little during the day, in its brutal directness it is unprecedented. Most probably Johnson never saw the text of the letter which carries his name but he gave his blessing knowing only the letter's tendency.

The letter came to the point immediately: he, Johnson, was extremely worried that Inönü was planning a military intervention in Cyprus. By this he was breaking his promise to consult the US Government first. The intervention might lead to a war with Greece, extremely endangering the coherence of NATO. The use of weapons supplied by the US violated the agreement of 1947. If, nevertheless, the invasion took place and the Soviet Union intervened then Turkey would stand alone. Closing the letter the US side suggested consultations.

Ambassador Hare handed over the letter to Prime Minister Inönü who read it diligently and stated that at some points he did not agree with the content. However, he was prepared to refrain from the intervention and have this confirmed by a Cabinet decision. The public, however, had to be informed that the intervention had been cancelled due to American interference. Obviously Inönü was looking for a culprit but Washington anticipated this by an announcement of its own. Inönü kept his countenance and the Turkish Cabinet took the planned decision. Thus the affair seemed to have ended.

But now an awkward situation developed for Inönü when the content of the letter was leaked to the press. The newspaper *Hürriyet* knew that the Americans had forbidden the intervention. *Miliyet* spoke of a turning point in Turkish-American relations. In the Turkish Parliament the opposition accused Inönü of buckling and tabled a vote of confidence which ended in favour of the Government but the majority was thin (200:2:194). The effect of the Johnson letter on the Turkish policy cannot be overestimated. Johnson's letter was the factor which destroyed the Turkish primal trust in American leadership. Though the letter led to a temporal detente, the real problems were not solved. Within a very short period of time these resurfaced and led to a new inclination to intervene and this the Americans could not stop, as the bombardment of Kokkina in August 1964 showed. The ultimate threat was no longer effective. Looking at the long term effect of the Johnson letter, it can be concluded that it was the beginning of a long alienation process between the US and Turkey and a slow cautious Turkish turning to the Soviet Union to get a kind of rear cover.

As early as October 1964 the Turkish Foreign Minister visited the Soviet Union and in May 1965 Foreign Minister Gromyko appeared in Ankara. In 1965 Turkey prohibited the American reconnaissance flights over the Soviet Union from Turkish soil. In the mid-1970s Turkey was the biggest receiver of Soviet economic aid outside the Eastern Block. From then on Turkey was a conditionally loyal member of the Western Alliance.

The Americans had promised Inönü to engage themselves more in the search for a solution to the Cyprus problem. This meant that they had to develop ideas of their own. Ambassador Belcher in Nicosia was of the opinion that only a unitary Cypriot State was acceptable for the majority of the Cypriots. A partition or federation would prolong the trouble. Ball had a different opinion: So long as Cyprus existed as an independent state it endangered the Western Alliance because a Turkish intervention was threatening constantly. A lasting solution could only be reached on the basis of union with Greece and territorial or other compensations for Turkey. He mentioned Castelorizo, Samos, Chios, Kos or parts of Thrace. Turkish Cypriots who left Cyprus voluntarily should get financial compensations. The realisation of this plan should be transacted by the UN. When Ball presented these ideas to Papandreou in Athens the latter rejected them. Ankara, too, was sceptical.

In mid-June 1964 Washington prepared for the visit of Papandreou and Inönü: Cyprus as an independent State no longer existed in American considerations. Should a solution be found the Government of Cyprus would not participate in the negotiations. Double enosis was the basis for discussion between Greeks and Turks. Of course, there would be some "arm-twisting" to make them negotiate seriously. But the President would "bear down on both of them" so that they would accept further suggestions. After that representatives of both countries should get together with an American (Acheson) secretly and during these meetings a solution should be "hammered out" which would then be presented. One should inform U Thant and Tuomioja that a solution could be found only between Athens and Ankara. Obviously an octroi was being prepared, as in 1959.

Papandreou, who was afraid that the Americans would bring him together with Inönü to force them to a solution, declared himself only prepared to visit Washington after Inönü had left. During the meeting of Johnson and Inönü they agreed the Greek-Turkish negotiations for a solution to the Cyprus Problem should begin on 4 July 1964 in Camp David. On 24 June Johnson and Papandreou met. Though Johnson exerted considerable pressure on Papandreou to participate in the Camp-David-negotiations Papandreou rejected this because in his opinion real negotiations did not make any sense for the time being. He regarded Johnson's and Ball's statement that the Americans would not stop the Turks as a threat, as a kind of ultimatum and felt himself a victim of American arrogance of power, as Senator Fulbright called it. During his last round of talks with Rusk and Ball he wanted to know why the negotiations would not be conducted in the UN. Ball alleged that Tuomioja had suggested that Acheson should back his negotiations. Papandreou agreed.

Ball immediately went to New York to commit U Thant to this line. U Thant rejected Camp David and recommended Geneva. Ball agreed and tried to have Acheson accepted as co-mediator of Tuomioja, which U Thant rejected as well. Acheson would only be accepted as external advisor. Papandreou agreed to U Thant's proposal and thus effectively blocked the American effort to push through negotiations under their aegis for the time being. The decisive question was whether he could continue to do this during the actual negotiations.

The first Acheson Plan

Makarios had watched the talks in Washington and on 27 June he tried to block their possible results: Cyprus was a member of the UN and other states did not have the right to take decisions regarding its future. Even if Greece and Turkey should agree on a solution the Cypriots were not bound by this. The Cyprus Problem was not a dispute between Athens and Ankara.

On 5 July the delegations came to Geneva. The US was represented by the former Secretary of State, Dean Acheson, and the Deputy Assistant Secretary, John D. Jernegan. The Greek Government sent one of its most experienced diplomats, Dimitrios Nikolareïzis, Ambassador in Belgrade. Turkey authorised the chairman of the foreign policy committee of the Turkish parliament to uphold her interests. The British sent an observer. The Cyprus Government decided to boycott the talks.

The negotiations in Geneva began on 6 July with a conversation between Tuomioja and Acheson. The latter wanted to get rid of his passive role and participate actively in the negotiations in order to push through his ideas. Therefore, he asked Toamioja to make Nikolareïzis accept a talk with Acheson. Tuomioja agreed and thus Acheson was in the game. Acheson had read the position papers of the State Department and had arrived at the conclusion that the Cyprus Problem could only be solved if Cyprus disappeared as an independent state. At a preliminary talk with Erim on 11 July the latter accepted the proposal that Cyprus be united with Greece and Turkey receive a huge military base there, and the security of the Turkish Cypriots was guaranteed by a half-autonomous status. From the Turkish point of view this was a first step towards partition.

On 13 July Nikolareïzis had a first talk with Tuomioja: According to his instructions direct negotiations with the Turks were excluded. The Finn said that this could be interpreted as intransigence. The Turks insisted on partition of the island that they called double enosis. They rejected unfettered independence because it might lead to (unilateral) enosis which they rejected. They had postponed their intervention plans but they could revive them if the situation required it in their eyes. But he believed that Turkey would accept enosis, provided her security interests were guaranteed and the rights of the Turkish Cypriot minority secured. Tuomioja recommended that Nikolareïzis should talk to Acheson, who could contribute to a solution of the Cyprus Problem.

During the talks between Nikolareïzis and Acheson the latter repeated practically the arguments of Tuomioja and suggested, additionally, the cession of the island of Castelorizo. Nikolareïzis promised to pass the Acheson's ideas on to Athens. When Acheson spoke with the Turks they presented a map with the details of the future Turkish base. At the first glance Acheson saw that it was far too big to be accepted by Greece. When Acheson pointed this out to them the reply was that a base had to be big enough to accommodate the whole Turkish community there, which would lead to double enosis i.e., the partition of the island. The base needed an adequate harbour to be able to function properly. If this was not accepted Turkey could create the necessary conditions by a military intervention. One day later Erim added: the size of the base had to be proportional to the percentage of the population and thus comprise 20 percent of the surface of Cyprus.

Acheson summarized the proposals submitted so far in writing and gave them to the representatives of Athens and Ankara. Papandreou was prepared to make great concessions regarding the minority. Though it would be difficult to sell the cession of Greek soil to the public, he was ready to cede Castelorizo to the Turks. But the establishment of a sovereign Turkish base was impossible. However, he could imagine a shared base provided the base itself remained under British sovereignty.

When Acheson met again with the Turkish representatives on 20 July these demanded even greater territorial concession, namely an area from Lapithos in the west of Kyrenia to Famagousta i.e., 21 percent of Cyprus. The Greeks showed themselves ready to compromise on the following day. On 22 July during a conversation between Acheson and Tuomioja the latter said that the Greek Cypriots would never accept the establishment of a sovereign Turkish base on their island. Perhaps some Turkish troops could be stationed in the British bases. The Turks rejected this idea but were prepared to accept territorial compensations. When Tuomioja mentioned the idea of a leased base to Nikolareïzis the latter said that this was acceptable.

During the following days the Turks presented further exorbitant demands. Acheson understood that the Turks were stalling and were not ready to retreat from their maximal demands. Until that day secrecy had been kept but on 27 July Makarios came to Athens for consultations. He was informed about the state of affairs and it was agreed that Acheson's plans were to be rejected since they would lead to a partition of the island. The negotiations in Geneva should be abandoned and the case should be brought before the UN. Makarios promised that no military measures would be taken in Cyprus without consulting Athens.

On 30 July Erim declared in Geneva that a leased base was unacceptable, and in Athens Makarios said to the press that he flatly rejected the Acheson plan, it was unacceptable. President Johnson had the feeling of an "awful kick in the pants". The next day Papandreou apologized to the American Ambassador for Makarios' indiscretion, hinting that perhaps a solution without Makarios had to be found. Extreme right wing circles around the former deputy, Nikolaos Farmakis, who were in contact with the Americans said openly that Makarios had to be deposed. They were sure that Papandreou would approve this. In Cyprus N. Sampson and T. Papadopoulos were in close contact with this group. The putschists of 21 April 1967 emanated from this Athens clique. This is the first mention of the enosis-by-putsch idea. It is breathtaking that the Greek Government and the right-wing plotters developed the same idea and the Americans found nothing objectionable in it and followed a hands-off line. Even Ankara was in the picture, as became clear during a talk between Erkin and US-Ambassador Hare on 6 August: The Turkish Government also considered Makarios as the main obstacle to a solution of the Cyprus Problem. His disappearance was the precondition for a bilateral solution, an opinion which was unofficially shared by Hare. The question was when would the negotiation partners find a solution plan on this basis but all of a sudden the negotiations were interrupted: in Cyprus new fighting had broken out.

The fighting at Kokkina-Mansoura

All through the summer small incidents had continued to occur but they had not been disquieting. Both sides had built up a considerable military strength. The police counted 5,000 men and the National Guard 24,000, but in this number the illegal Greek soldiers (LOK) are included. The number of TMT fighters was estimated at roughly 10,000. To this were added 1,700 policemen and 300 Turkish soldiers who had secretly entered Cyprus via Kokkina and another 300 who had been infiltrated in other ways. War material had been brought to the island from Greece via Limassol and from Turkey via Kokkina/Mansoura in the Tillyria.

In order to secure their enclaves the Turkish Cypriots built roadblocks, dug trenches, constructed concrete pillboxes and strongholds surrounded by sandbags. The Government forces countered with similar constructions which often were only 50 metres apart. The Turkish Cypriots would not allow the Greeks to pass and these took revenge by excessive controls and chicanery at their road blocks. In mid-July the situation worsened when the Government produced a list of strategic material for which the Turkish Cypriots needed a special permit from the Ministry of the Interior if they wanted to buy it. Among this strategic material were building materials, cement, construction steel, wire, electric devices, bags, spares for cars, chemicals and fuel.

Until July Red Crescent aid supplies, such as medicaments and foodstuff had reached their destinations without serious problems. But in July the authorities began to collect duties on these. When the Turkish Cypriots refused to pay these only 360 tons of 900 tons aid goods could be unloaded duty-free. Additionally, the Government demanded control over the distribution. Küçük accused the Government of starving the Turkish Cypriots.

In June the Turkish Cypriot paramilitary tried to extend the enclave at Kokkina towards the south but the National Guard stopped them. Later Blue Helmets moved in between the opponents. On 24 July Makarios and Karagiannis visited the area and were content with the situation. In spite of this towards the end of July the Government dispatched troops there. At the beginning of August about 1,500 National Guardsmen with heavy equipment were in the Tillyria. A little later light and heavy artillery arrived. At this point the commander of UNFICYP recognised the deployment but Makarios assured him that nothing would be done without giving a prior warning. On 6 August the deployment was completed. The question arose whether this was a case of scare tactics or the preparation of an attack and Makarios would order it contrary to his promise.

On this evening Grivas returned to Cyprus from visit to Athens. Later the Cypriot Council of Ministers had a meeting in which participated the commanders of the two Greek units, a representative of the National Guard and Grivas. After he had been informed extensively about the situation in Tillyria, Grivas wanted to know from Makarios what was politically wanted, consolidation of the Greek position there or the destruction of the Turkish bridge head. Although there were voices advocating the second, the majority was for the first option. But even consolidation meant a limited military operation, and Makarios pointed out to Grivas that even in this case Athens had to be consulted.

Makarios tried to ring up Foreign Minister Kostopoulos but he was not in his office. Grivas interfered and assured Makarios that a consultation with Kostopoulos was not necessary. However, he would, before giving the order for attack, contact Defence Minister Garoufalias. Makarios apparently relied upon Grivas keeping his word. Perhaps he had nothing against a limited action which would disrupt the Geneva negotiations, but Grivas could not be slowed down. He went to the Headquarters of the National Guard and ordered the beginning of the consolidation operation and the preparation of the general attack on the Turkish bridge head, which should only begin after his explicit order. Instead of trying once more to get in contact with the Greek Foreign Minister Grivas sent a wireless message to the general staff in Athens informing them about his orders. Thus the Greek Government learned about his orders only in the morning of 7 August.

The carrying out of the action itself was typical of Grivas. Instead of entrusting the execution to the experienced and responsible second-in-command of the National Guard - Karagiannis was in Athens - Grivas usurped the command, acted on his own from the green table without consulting anyone, not even the other military commands in Cyprus and without precise information about the true situation and although he had no experience at all to coordinate different units and bring them simultaneously to attack. Among the Cypriot units coming into operation were two Cypriot patrol boats which were to shell the Turkish position from the seaside. In the early hours of 7 August Grivas gave the order for attack without checking whether the units earmarked for attack were ready or even there. The result was that the consolidation operation began late in the afternoon of 7 August. The operation was successful, and the Turkish Paramilitary retreated. In the evening four Turkish F-100 fighter-jets flew over the little town of Polis and fired the aircraft weapons over the sea to demonstrate their strength and fighting power.

When General Karagiannis arrived at the Headquarters of the National Guard in the evening of 7 August he found Grivas in a violent argument with the commander of ELDYK: Grivas demanded that the latter attack TOURDYK, but he refused this without an order from Athens. Turning to Karagiannis Grivas explained that he was attacking Mansoura. Karagiannis wanted to know whether this attack had been authorised by Athens. Grivas replied that the Cypriot Council of Ministers had authorised it. When Karagiannis pointed out that the permission of the Greek Minister of Defence was needed, Grivas replied that those in Athens had no idea, only he could assess the situation in Cyprus correctly. At a meeting of Makarios and Grivas in the Headquarters of ASDAK at 21.00 hours, the latter informed the Archbishop about the situation and they decided to continue the offensive and conquer the area of Kokkina and Mansoura.

Early on 8 August 1964 Karagiannis tried to stop the continuation of the fighting. At 6.30 he ordered his commanders to cancel the action and informed them about the talks in Athens. The atmosphere began to change but at 7.30 it was reported that Grivas had ordered the attack on Mansoura and Kokkina. The Turkish paramilitary retreated to Kokkina, which Grivas ordered to be shelled by the artillery and the patrol boat from the sea. Now a radio message from the Greek Ministry of Defence arrived forbidding any further action. Garoufalias rang up Makarios and asked him to have all actions stopped. Makarios reacted angrily: Garoufalias should himself tell this to Grivas, who was in the combat area. Garoufalias' order was brought to Grivas by a helicopter and reached him around 14.00 hours. Thus Grivas was informed about Athens' position but this did not bother him and he let the attack go on. According to his opinion Kokkina and Mansoura would be taken in an hour, why should one stop the attack? A little later heavy Turkish bombardment began and brought the attack to a standstill.

The Turkish Air Force did confine its bombardment to the combat zone but bombed all villages in the area. One of the patrol boats was set ablaze and had to be beached. In the evening the Council of Ministers met and Karagiannis attacked Grivas heavily. Grivas did not say anything but a little later he resigned as commander of ASDAK. Karagiannis ordered the troops to stay where they were and wait for orders. After the end of the meeting of the Council of Ministers Georkatzis telephoned Garoufalias and explained the situation to him. Garoufalias was horror-stricken by Grivas' behaviour. When it became known that Turkish warships had set course for Cyprus Athens rejected any help. Not even the Greek troops stationed in Cyprus would be allowed to help. It was obvious that Athens had no interest in being drawn into an armed conflict with Turkey .

In the morning of 9 August the Turkish Air Force again bombed the whole Tillyria area up to Polis all day long until the late afternoon. Heavy demolition bombs, Air-ground missiles, Napalm and machine guns were used. The civil population had heavy losses, 53 dead and over 125 wounded. When the fire brigades tried to extinguish the fires they were shot at by the planes. The heavy air raids led to a panic in the Cypriot Government. By noon the Council of Ministers had met and decided to issue an ultimatum to the Turkish Government which was to be conveyed by the American Ambassador to his Turkish colleague: if the Turkish air attacks had not ended by 13.30 hours MET the Cypriot Government would order an all out attack on all Turkish Cypriot villages. It is unclear who gave this order but it can be safely assumed that it was Georkatzis who was ready to order massacres if the bombing did not stop.

Washington was of the opinion that Papandreou should bring Grivas under control. In Athens Papandreou wanted to know from Kranidiotis why Makarios behaved like that. Quietness had been agreed upon; in Geneva important negotiations were going on about the future of Cyprus. Was it possible that the attack on Mansoura was intended to torpedo these negotiations? With this assumption Papandreou was indeed close to the truth. Papandreou was so angry at Makarios that he ordered Grivas to resume his command. Obviously Papandreou did not have the slightest idea about Grivas' real role. No sooner was Grivas back in command of ASDAK when he again showed off as C.-in-C. of all Greek forces in Cyprus. This caused

Karagiannis to declare his resignation as commander of the National Guard. On 13 August Grivas was appointed commander of the National Guard.

In the evening of 8 August the UN Security Council had met at the request of Turkey and Cyprus but postponed any decisions until the following day. On 9 August the Security Council asked Turkey to stop bombarding the Tillyria. Under American influence a resolution was passed demanding an immediate cease fire. The Governments of Turkey and Cyprus accepted the content of the resolution and ordered a cease fire. When on 10 August Turkish reconnaissance flights over Cyprus continued, the Security Council met again on 11 August and asked Turkey to stop these flights. On 12 August the Turkish Air Force stopped them and thus the fighting in the Tillyria came to an end and the negotiations in Geneva could be resumed.

Further Acheson plans
When the talks were resumed on 15 August Acheson recognised that now the Turkish military had the say and tried to steer a tougher course. The policy of *do-ut-des* had ended; one had arrived at either-or. Acheson informed the Greeks about this and the conclusion was that on the path hitherto followed a solution could not be reached. From then on Makarios' course of unfettered independence had to be supported. If Makarios recognised that it was not intended to enforce a solution upon him he would keep quiet until the beginning of the session of the UN General Assembly in order to not to predetermine anything. On 16 August Tuomioja suffered a stroke, and U Thant appointed Galo Plaza as mediator. Thus from now on Acheson played the main role.

The following days were characterised by insecurity, nervousness and hectic activity. Constantly new ideas came into the discussion; alternately highly conspiratorial action scenarios and retreat positions were developed. In Athens Papandreou was in dull ambience. On 17 August he developed a desperate idea in a conversation with UN Ambassador Labuisse: a coup should be organised in Cyprus and enosis immediately declared which would be ratified by Parliament within the shortest possible time. The Americans and the British should keep the Turks quiet. As soon as enosis was achieved Greece would come to an agreement with Turkey. Papandreou was thinking of a 50 km^2 Turkish miliary base in the Karpasia peninsula leased for 45 years. In American sources this enosis-by-putsch plan is referred to as "instant enosis", a nice euphemism, indeed.

Acheson regarded the idea of a coup as good. From Athens Labuisse warned that in the case of the realisation of "instant enosis" the Americans would have to negotiate the agreement with the Turks because Papandreou was too weak politically. London agreed and considered Grivas an adequate successor of Makarios, but London was not ready to participate in the plan; after all Cyprus was a member of the Commonwealth and one could not plot against the head of a member state. Somehow information about these plans had found its way to Cyprus. On 29 August US Ambassador Belcher reported from Nicosia that the island was full of rumours of an imminent coup and murder. Georkatzis who was part of the conspiracy advised Belcher to hit quickly. But as Grivas was not sure whether after a coup he would be prepared to make concessions to the Turks he stepped on the brakes: one did not know how Turkey would react. Thus the enosis-by-putsch option was stopped for the moment.

Now Defence Minister Garoufalias developed a new idea, "unilateral enosis" *(monomeri enosis)*, which, like a surgical intervention would remove the purulent abscess, Cyprus. According to this plan the Cypriot House of Representatives and the Greek Parliament should hold a meeting at the same time. The House should resolve union with Greece and in Athens Parliament would accept this resolve and accept the Cypriot deputies in their chamber. After that the Cypriot Government should resign and the Greek Government take over and be responsible for any further development. Strongest guaranties would be given to the Turkish

Government for the security of the minority in Cyprus and a base granted. The whole action was to be absolutely peaceful. Allegedly Papandreou was enthused by this idea. The Crown Council *(Symvoulio to Stemmatos)* with the King in the chair agreed unanimously. Garoufalias was instructed to "sell" this idea to Makarios. He flew to Cyprus, Makarios listened to his proposals and did not answer. Thus "unilateral enosis" was dead.

In the meantime, Acheson had integrated the new ideas in his plan. The size of the base was now to be 200 square miles and the leasing should last 50 years. On 20 August Ball said that the coup should be realised quickly as Kyprianou was to visit Moscow, which might lead to a Soviet intervention. Thus the "Communist Danger" now became a means of pressure. On the same day Labuisse accordingly asked the Greek Government to stage the coup against Makarios and to accept the Acheson Plan. The only problem Papandreou discovered was the size of the base because it was double the size of the British bases. Nevertheless, he promised to answer the next day.

Ball urged that, if Papandreou did not proceed the King should be approached. The decision had to be taken at once otherwise the plan would not work. He did not understand Papandreou's indecision. It was a matter "instant enosis". Labuisse visited Papandreou once more and the latter declared he had the green light of the Cabinet and was ready to make the deal, provided the Turks guaranteed to stop the deportations of the Greeks of Istanbul. The King expressed himself in this spirit and said that he would be ready to talk to the ERE leadership in this sense. Acheson was enthused and congratulated Labuisse on his success. He had beaten all, but the cold shower came when Acheson spoke with the Turks who rejected the deal of enosis with a leased base. Even when Acheson conjured up the "Communist Danger" the Turks remained stubborn. Acheson recognized that the crux of the matter was the sovereignty of the base because only the latter could be sold to the Turkish public as a kind of partition. Acheson had only one card left, the direct appeal to Inönü.

Inthe afternoon of 21 August Ambassador Belcher warned from Nicosia that the Greek Cypriots would never accept a Turkish military base. From Athens Labuisse let it be knownthat a solution could not be imposed on the Greek Cypriots, who had their own ideas. Turkey on the other hand, would only accept enosis if she received a compensation. Greece could "sell" a base to the Cypriots even against the will of Makarios provided it was not bigger than the British bases. The size suggested by Achseon had the character of partitioning the island. He regretted deeply that an agreement could not be achieved in this way. He hoped that the UN General Assembly would agree to Cyprus' unfettered independence.

When Inönü too rejected the plan Acheson understood that the negotiations had failed and on 22 August he recommended stopping them. But Ball, who was not up to date because of the time shift, stuck to his tough course: the negative Greek answer was unacceptable. Labuisse should exert maximal pressure. Should the deal fail the culprit had to be clear. The King, in connivance with Papandreou and ERE chief Kanellopoulos, was to call Grivas to Athens and tell him, in the presence of the two politicians, that the Greek Government had accepted the American plan and was of the opinion that it should be implemented. Only a quick realisation could save Cyprus from a Communist takeover. Grivas should be made to understand that this was his chance to bring his role as Dighenis to a glorious end.

Papandreou, however, held to his negative answer. But Ball did not give up, though he had to admit that the Geneva negotiations had failed: Cyprus had to be prevented from becoming another Cuba. Therefore, one should tell the Greeks to go on with their enosis plans. If these could be realised quickly the Americans would take over the obligation to keep the Turks, or any other power, from intervening militarily in Cyprus provided the Greeks would enter into negotiations with the Turks about a revision of the Cyprus Treaties immediately after enosis was achieved. Athens should be obliged to lease a military base to the Turks for 50 years, the size of which would be decided in cooperation with NATO. The Turks should be informed about this, hoping that they would accept such a *fait accompli*. Ball's proposal was an irresponsible game because its realisation would have led to a Greek-Turkish clash which could have been stopped only by an American forceful intervention.

On 24 August Kyprianou came to Athens and made it clear that Makarios rejected any kind of enosis linked with territorial compensations. Enosis could be achieved via unfettered independence and the exercise to the right of self-determination. In Nicosia Makarios said that the Cypriots would never accept any territorial cession. One day later Makarios paid a short visit to Athens telling the Greek Government exactly that. Although Papandreou once more tried to enforce the claim for leadership of the national centre at the end of the month, Makarios was not impressed. He answered as late as February 1965. In Washington they continued to develop and discuss possible solution scenarios but it was clear that the Geneva negotiations had failed.

The Cyprus Problem remained unresolved. The danger inside Cyprus had increased because the inner closeness of the leadership of the Greek Cypriots had been called into question by the putsch plans beginning to be made. Makarios began to lose control of the security forces and had to rely more on the popular masses. The animosity between the two communities had increased because of the bombing by the Turkish Air Force and the blockades. Additionally a process of alienation began, leading to hostility between Athens and Nicosia. The planning of a coup d'état against Makarios backfired against Greece because it let those genii out of the bottle which soon got out of control.

1964-1965: THE POST-CIVIL-WAR PERIOD

The return to normalcy
In order to win back the initiative in the discussion of a possible solution to the Cyprus Problem Makarios began a political offensive by giving interviews to many European press organs and TV stations. The interviews were all alike: Cyprus wanted unfettered independence and self-determination. The conflict with Turkey was the result of Britain's colonial policy. He himself did not reject enosis but the Acheson Plan only pretended to realise enosis. In reality it aimed at a well hidden partition of the island. If enosis were realised then the British bases would have to be dissolved. Even in the case of enosis the Turkish Cypriots would have to fear nothing. There was no quarrel with the Greek Government. However, some self-appointed friends of Greece tried to force the Greek Government into solutions which were not in the interest of Cyprus. Rumours about Makarios quarrelling with Grivas and the latter preparing a coup were baseless.

In September Foreign Minister Kyprianou visited the Soviet Union and on 30 September he signed an agreement on Soviet military and economic help. The weapons ordered were delivered from 1965 on. By mid-September 1964 it became known that U Thant had appointed his representative in Cyprus, Galo Plaza, as new mediator and the Brazilian diplomat Carlos Bernardes as Plaza's successor. In September and October intensive negotiations took place about lifting the road blocks and blockades and the delivering of foodstuff to the enclaves. On 26 October the positive result was there: the first convoy accompanied by UNFICYP vehicles went from Nicosia to Kyrenia. In early October Makarios participated in the Conference of the Non-Aligned in Cairo.

Although there continued efforts to weaken Makarios or to apply the enosis-by-putsch plan, Makarios' position had been consolidated so much that he could put pressure on Athens. In the eyes of Galo Plaza he towered above all Greek politicians, he was Mr. Cyprus. How strong Makarios' position was became visible when he began realising some of the 13 points which had triggered the conflict. In autumn 1964 the National Guard slowly became a professional army and many former volunteers were fired. Among those were many fanatical adherents of Grivas who now, together with other former EOKA members, began to organise underground and *parakratos* organisations and propaganda groups and to recruit supporters in high schools, the National Guard and in the Administration. Obviously another underground organisation like EOKA was being built up. This was the beginning of the future EOKA B.

Of course, Makarios was informed about these machinations by the secret services of the Government and on 2 December he met the press and fulminated against a secret organisation of subversive elements. Measures against them would be taken. He had ordered the armed forces not to mingle in politics. Students belonging to such organisations would be expelled from school.

On 15 December the House of Representatives passed a law threatening everyone with two years jail who tried to disturb the order and discipline in the armed forces. Clerides, the President of the House stated that there were foreign agents in Cyprus trying not only to split the population but also the army. He did not mention the name of the foreign power but everybody understood that he meant Greek *parakratos* organisations within the army and the secret service (KYP) which were still working on the realisation of enosis-by-putsch plans. Unfortunately Makarios' verbal attacks did not impress those *parakratos* organisations which began their first bomb assassination attempts in January 1965.

All through autumn Galo Plaza tried his best at talks with all sides to find approaches for an amicable solution to the Cyprus Problem but had to realise that the positions had hardened too much. Turkey insisted on partition or federation or double enosis, which was the same. In December the mandate of the Blue Helmets was prolonged for another three months.

When Turkish Foreign Minister Erkin travelled to the Soviet Union hereby signalling a change in foreign policy, Washington woke up. It was feared that Turkey might steer an even tougher course. Ambassador Hare wrote from Ankara that the Geneva concept - meaning the Acheson plans - was maculation and the only solution was an independent Cyprus. This opinion was shared by Papandreou and Galo Plaza both demanding an independent, nonaligned, demilitarised Cyprus with minority protection for the Turkish Cypriots. Papandreou would accept everything to which Makarios agreed. Even the Soviets would accept this concept because it served their interests.

On 2 December Belcher telegraphed from Nicosia: If one did not want to ruin the relations with Turkey the only remaining solution to the Cyprus Problem was independence but this needed to be defined. Federation as suggested by the Turks meant partition and was impossible. If one tried to force this solution upon Makarios he would trigger another wave of anti-American and anti-NATO hysteria and talk of foreign intervention. No means existed by which Makarios could be pressured, Makarios had more pull because he closed down American monitoring installations. Federation as proposed by Turkey would only lead to war.

Thus at the end of 1964 the Cyprus Problem had reached that status of insolubility which still exists. American intervention by Ball and Acheson had sharpened the problem by propagating those solutions (enosis and double enosis) which were mutually unacceptable to the Cypriot communities. At the same time this intervention dragged the mother countries so deep into the conflict that it was impossible for them to search for a rational solution. The question arose whether it would be possible after a cooling down phase to do so in a more equanimous way. How deadlocked the situation at the end of 1964 was, is shown by the fact that Galo Plaza abstained from making proposals of his own when he submitted his report in March 1965.

The Galo Plaza report of March 1965
By mid-March 1965 Galo Plaza had submitted his report about the state of affairs in Cyprus. It consists of a precise description and analysis of the mental state of all sides and a number of conclusions pointing the way towards a solution, which - strictly speaking - could be achieved even today. The solution should primarily be found by bilateral negotiations between the two ethnic groups. Plaza recognised clearly that Greece and Turkey had interests of their own which they superordinated to those of the two communities. He understood that a return to the *status quo ante* of the Zurich and London Agreements was neither possible nor desirable because this would lead to renewed tensions. The two decisive elements of a solution would emerge from compromises: the Greek Cypriots would obtain unfettered independence and the right to self-determination but simultaneously never applying the latter in order to achieve enosis, which was precisely Makarios' line. In this way the most delicate and potentially most explosive element would be abolished.

The Turkish Cypriots would accept the principle of majority rule but would receive cast-iron guaranties of their rights as a minority which would be supervised and guaranteed by the UN . Cyprus would be demilitarised. The Turkish Cypriots would be autonomous on questions of education, religion and civil status without, of course, questioning the unity of the state. This offered chances of finding new trust between the two communities. With a little goodwill one could have re-established the necessary favourable climate. Those governing Athens agreed and even the British had nothing against this, provided they could keep their bases.

Thus Ankara played the decisive role. If the Turkish Government agreed to the principle developed by Plaza and asked the Turkish Cypriots to cooperate a movement towards a solution would have begun. The radicals of TMT would have lost some of their influence since Denktash was out of the country and the moderates might have gained strength. There is little doubt that in this case a solution might have been possible and this the more so as Makarios had tamed the radicals on the Greek side. But the new Turkish Government was weak in internal politics and had, thus, to distinguish itself in foreign politics, and this it did by sweeping Plaza's proposals from the table.

Plaza was often accused of making proposals that favoured the Greek side but this is unjust. Plaza's report is an effort to find a reasonable sustainable solution for the Cypriots. He deliberately left out the interest of the mother countries because their ideas for a solution boiled down to either enosis or double enosis or federation with territorial separation of the communities, which would certainly have led to war. He recognised the two stumbling blocks of any solution: enosis and the guaranteed rights of the minority. He expected that the Greek Cypriots would renounce enosis and the Turkish Cypriots would give up political equality and be content with the status of a minority with guaranteed rights.

A further accusation was made that even a UN guarantee of the right of the minority would not have been enough because the Greek side, once in control of the whole state would have defied it. This is an assertion without any proof; facts speak in favour of the opposite, i.e that control would have functioned. If one looks at Greece's treatment of its Muslim population in Western Thrace - before the time of the Junta - one can conclude this. This is corroborated by the way the Cypriot Government treated the Turkish minority living then in the Government controlled area. The central question, however, was whether the Government would succeed in regaining the trust of Turkish Cypriots.

Plaza's ideas were reasonable and an attempt should have been made to make them the base of bilateral talks which might have improved them. Makarios should have put a motion to the UN Security Council, thus obliging it to study the content of the report and the attitude of those concerned. A sober analysis leads to the conclusion that here again an opportunity for the solution of the Cyprus Problem was gambled away.

The first missile crisis

As has already been mentioned the Cyprus Government ordered weapons from the Soviet Union. Among these were torpedo boats and anti-aircraft missiles which were to be delivered via Egypt. The necessary experts for the handling of the rockets were to be trained there. The rockets themselves would be brought to Cyprus by a vessel of the Greek navy. The first transport went off without a hitch but then something leaked to the Greek press in Cyprus and on 29 January the Athens newspapers reported the secret transport of weapons to Cyprus.

In early March Ambassador Belcher wrote to the State Department that from a military point of view these SAM rockets were not very important. The real danger was the psychological factor. The State Department was afraid that Turkey might hit spontaneously on a grand scale when she heard about the stationing of the SAMs. Therefore, it was decided to pass on a general warning that Cyprus was importing heavy highly developed weapons. One day later Belcher who already anticipated a general big aircraft attack by the Turkish Air Force, suggested that one should influence the Air Force General to bomb only selected targets after prior announcements. When Labuisse saw this proposal he was horrified.

In order to stop the possibility of initiating a crisis in the run-up, the State Department decided to turn to the Greek Government, which should use its influence to stop Makarios' dangerous game. On 12 March Undersecretary Ball expressed his concern about the Soviet delivery of arms to Greek Ambassador Matsas. The Greek Government passed this on to Makarios but Minister of Defence Georkatzis complained to Ambassador Belcher about the Americans hindering the delivery of Soviet arms to Cyprus. Belcher, however, had the impression of a stick-up and protest was raised to show that Athens could not control the Cyprus Government.

During a conversation between Papandreou and Ambassador Labuisse, the former declared that he was ready to see to it that no further rockets were transported to Cyprus if the US and /or Turkey guaranteed that there would be no more air raids against Cyprus. Ball was prepared to become active in this way provided Papandreou guaranteed that there would be no provocations in Cyprus for at least six months. When Ambassador Hare talked to the Turkish Government in this sense he recognised that the new Government of Ürgüplü had nothing to say, but the military had. The National Security Council, which was dominated by the military, had decided on a tough course. Should there be any "inhuman actions" in Cyprus one would strike. Negotiations with the Greeks about enosis were excluded. If the Americans intervened like in 1964 this would have disastrous consequences for Turkish-American relations. The Americans understood that they had heard the voice of the real rulers of Turkey.

When the Americans informed Papandreou about this he promised to force Makarios to show more flexibility. Labuisse understood that Papandreou wanted peace, indeed, and advised the State Department to interfere and to dissuade the Turks from sabre-rattling. On 21 March Garoufalias flew to Cyprus. In the morning of 22 March the Cypriot Council of Ministers met in secret session, Clerides and Grivas participating. In the afternoon session the Greek Ambassador and the commander of ELDYK participated. Though strict secrecy had been agreed on, some information leaked to the press: For the next six months there would be an armistice in the political, military and economic sector. The national guard would withdraw from certain positions. The status of Cyprus would not be changed during this period. The replacement and exchange of the Turkish contingent would not be hampered. The National Guard would not receive any more heavy weapons. Thus the tension in Cyprus was eased.

When this became known in Cyprus the frustration and bitterness was great. The newspapers spoke of treason and demanded that Garoufalias and Kostopoulos should be brought to court but soon the excitement ebbed away. The anti-aircraft missiles remained in Egypt and some time later Makarios gave them as a present to his friend Nasser. Thus the first missile crisis ended.

The murder of Dervis Kavazoğlu and Kostas Misaoulis

Hardly had this foreign policy crisis ended when another internal one caused another commotion. Already at the Court hearings in connection with the killing of the journalists Gürrkan and Hikmet, Denktash had stated openly that he considered leftists as criminals, and it was self-evident that TMT had the same opinion. In the eyes of those radicals, the Turkish-Cypriot journalist, Dervis Kavazoğlu was doubly guilty because he had written for the newspaper *Cumhürriyet* of Gürkan and Hikmet and he was a well known leader of the left union PEO and a member of the CC of AKEL. In speeches and articles he turned against the separatist policy of Denktash and Ankara's, which in his eyes was chauvinist and racist. Later he wrote for the paper *Inkilapci* and criticised Ankara's policy of partition and advocated peaceful coexistence and cooperation of the two communities. In his opinion the Turkish Cypriot leadership consisted of extremists terrorising their compatriots. In articles, speeches, radio interviews and TV transmissions he constantly attacked the fascist terror methods of the Turkish Cypriot leadership bought by imperialists. TMT reacted by requesting its members to kill Kavazoğlu. More than 100 fanatics allegedly swore an oath that they would kill Dr Ihsan Ali, Devis Kavazoğlu and others working for the cooperation of the two communities. Repeatedly extremists tried to murder Kavazoglu but as he lived in the Greek part of Nicosia it was difficult.

On Sunday 11 April 1965 the TMT killers were successful. By 9.30 Kavazoğlu accompanied by his friend Kostas Misaoulis, also a PEO member, had left Nicosia by car for Larnaca. At the 13th milestone the murderers were waiting and when the car arrived they riddled it thoroughly with automatic weapons. A few hours later a UNFICYP patrol found the murdered men. Dr Ali Ihsan accused TMT of this murder. The Government advertised a reward of 5,000 pounds for the seizure of the perpetrators. The House condemned the murders and the AKEL Secretary General praised the two victims as true Cypriot patriots.

At first the Turkish-Cypriot leadership tried to lay the blame on the Greeks but when the waves of indignation became high, because of this cowardly murder, the Turkish extremists remained quiet, later it was said that Kavazoğlu had only been a Communist ejected by the Turkish community. It was obvious that TMT was out to destroy all relations between the two communities.

Further talks

The radical rejection of the Plaza proposals by Turkey induced Ball to conduct a kind of stock-taking: Enosis could not be achieved without territorial compensations. Should the Greeks undertake something in the direction of enosis without prior agreement with Turkey, the latter would react violently. The US could neither enforce enosis nor restrain the Turks in case of "instant enosis". Labuisse should make this clear to the Greek Government.

On 6 May 1964 the Crown Council met in Athens with Makarios and Kyprianou present. Again the situation and the possibility for enosis were discussed and past models tabled. Papandreou closed the topic by stating that enosis meant war, leading, not to enosis, but to its burial with bloody consequences for the Greeks of Cyprus, Istanbul and Thrace. Enosis could only be achieved by a Greek victory, which was most improbable. Makarios said that he was for enosis but without territorial compensations which would lead to the island's separation. Finally, the Crown Council arrived at the following conclusions: One should try to find a solution in the UN. Galo Plaza should come to Cyprus to talks about the start of new inter-communal negotiations. The blockade measure should be further reduced. A more relaxed climate should be achieved in Cyprus. In spite of these clear agreements the Greek Government under American pressure, began a dialogue with the Turkish Government. In order to foreclose a Greek-Turkish agreement behind his back, Makarios interfered and began to send signals to Ankara that he was ready for negotiations. On 31 May the Greek Cabinet discussed Makarios' policy. Papandreou declared that he would stick to his course and continue the talks with the Turks. Should Makarios obstruct he would break with him. He had told him this. On 4 June the Turkish Foreign Minister demanded 18 percent of the island's surface area, not necessarily on the island itself, but in Thrace. The area's size must correspond with the percentage of the Turkish population in Cyprus. This Papandreou could not accept. He offered a base leased for 99 years which was unacceptable to the Turks.

On 10 June Kyprianou told Ball and Rusk that his Government did not object to a dialogue between Athens and Ankara as long as the Cypriots could decide on their own future and no solution was imposed on them. Makarios did not object to enosis but Athens and Ankara could negotiate on Cyprus, after all Cyprus was an independent state. The Greek Cypriots would never accept a solution leading to separation. Territorial concessions as elements of a solution were out of the question. When Kyprianou wanted to know the American position Rusk answered that he saw no role which the Americans could play at the moment. Ball promised to think about it. Obviously the Americans did not feel like burning their fingers again with the Cyprus Problem.

On 15 July 1965 the Government of Papandreou stumbled over the so-called ASPIDA affair and thus the dialogue between Athens and Ankara ended. Papandreou's overthrow led to the political instability which brought about the military dictatorship of 21 April 1967. For some time it had been clear that Turkey was only prepared to accept enosis if she received substantial territorial compensations either in Cyprus or in Greece (the Evros area or some island in the eastern Aegean sea). The Turkish Government had to consider public opinion in Turkey and the military leadership and besides that elections were due. Thus it would only agree to enosis if the size of the area ceded was big enough to impress the public and the military so that both no longer cared for the fate of the Turkish Cypriots. Should the cession take place in Cyprus it would have meant separation and double enosis as the Acheson plan had intended. Only a strong Greek Government could have survived a cession of land in Greece. The weak Governments after Papandreou did not have this option. The idea that Turkey might agree to enosis without compensation was wishful thinking. As the Government in Ankara understood this they began to think about a federative solution by which the interests of Ankara and the Turkish Cypriots could be assured.

Makarios wanted to keep Cyprus independent. For him, mention of the right to self-determination was pure lip-service to keep the super-nationalists in Greece and Cyprus quiet. Makarios' aim was unfettered independence and the abolition of those treaties which hampered the former. At the same time he wanted to change the partnership between the Greeks and the Turks on the island provided by the Constitution into a system of majority and privileged minority. He did not understand that any tampering with the constitutional basis would lead to a conflict with Turkey. The maximum that Makarios could achieve were some amendments which did not reduce the rights of the Turks but led to a smoother functioning of the Constitution, and even for this he needed the consent of the Turkish Cypriots.

Unfortunately, the supporters of reason were a minority in Cyprus. Whoever advocated it was denounced as a traitor or coward. The adherents of the irrational options had the sympathies of the masses on their side even if these options were extremely unreasonable, as is proved by the dealings of Grivas, who at a certain time believed that enosis could be achieved by simply proclaiming it. The results of these efforts to realise wishful thinking were conflicts between all groups which escalated quickly, drawing the mother countries into it and plunging Cyprus into an abyss.

1965-1977

THE CATASTROPHE:

EOKA B, COUP, INVASION AND PARTITION

1965: continued "unfettered independence" course

The political crisis in Greece since mid-July 1965 had its repercussions on Cyprus because it terminated the Greek-Turkish dialogue, hesitantly begun in May. for good. Makarios considered this a chance to make progress towards "unfettered independence". On 20 July 1965 the Council of Ministers met and passed two bills; one of them a new electoral law which was submitted to the House of Representatives two days later. This law provided for a unitary voting list replacing the hitherto separate lists. As this was against the constitution the leadership of the Turkish Cypriots rejected this proposal. The Greek side, however, did not pay attention to the protests of the Turkish Cypriots and passed the bill on 23 July 1965.

Indeed, the adoption of the new electoral law by the House of Representatives was the first material violation of the constitution by the Greek-Cypriot side. Until then Makarios had confined himself to submitting proposals, thinking aloud, talking about intentions or announcing that the Treaty of Guarantee was no longer valid. All this had been rather noncommittal as it did not contain any legal basis, such as an act of parliament. Of course, there had been de facto deviations from the constitution but not de jure. The electoral law broke the constitution.

The Turkish Cypriot members of the House of Representatives met on 23 July also and passed several resolutions, among them one stating that the decisions of the House were not binding for the Turkish Cypriot community. On 26 July the Turkish Communal Chamber passed a law prolonging the term of office of the vice-president and published it in the Turkish Cypriot Government Gazette. The Turkish Cypriots began to act in a more self-confident manner. From Ankara on 27 July "exiled" Rauf Denktash urgently called on his compatriots to form a government of a Turkish republic on Cyprus. This government should be recognized by Turkey. Negotiations with Makarios led nowhere. These ideas were well known tones of the well known separatist but so far he had never gone as far as demanding a state of his own. Küçük continued to play the moderate: the Zurich and London agreements continued to be valid and could not be abolished unilaterally but they could replace them by negotiations amicably.

Although Athens and London were indignant about Makarios' violation of the constitution they were not ready to intervene. When Ankara demanded the calling of a conference of the guarantor powers they rejected this. Thus on 30 July Turkey appealed to the UN Security Council accusing Makarios of violating the constitution and the UN Resolution of March 1964. The Security Council discussed the Turkish charges and the Cypriot counter-charges on 3, 5, and 10 August 1965. The representative of Turkey at the UN, Eralp, accused the Cyprus Government of creating an explosive situation with the electoral law. It endangered the peace on the island by trying to enforce its ideas for a solution, thus not only violating the constitution but also resolutions of the Security Council. Kyprianou countered accusing Turkey of interfering in the internal affairs of Cyprus. The representative of Greece denied a critical situation in Cyprus; the Turks saw this in a partial way. The British representative admitted that Makarios had violated the constitution and the resolutions of the Security Council. He was trying to unilaterally abolish the treaty of guarantee; the treaties could only be changed with the consent of all partners and until this happened they had to be complied with. The Turkish delegate filed the motion that Denktash be heard. The Security Council agreed and thus on 5 August 1965 Denktash was offered for the second time the possibility to appear before the UN Security Council and to polemicise forcefully.

The resolution of 10 August disapproved of Makarios' unilateral actions violating the resolution of March 1964. The Cyprus treaties and the constitution were operative. Turkey was asked to refrain from any military intervention and the Cyprus government to reestablish law and order on the island. Additionally, the Cypriot government and the two communities were admonished to show more restraint. However, as the resolution of March 1964 had not hindered Makarios from violating the constitution, the 10 August resolution would not be respected by him likewise.

How little Makarios was impressed by this resolution became clear at the end of August when it became known that the Cyprus government had been working on a minority charter for some time. The text leaned on the recommendations of Galo Plaza. The government was ready to have the realisation controlled by UN observers. The Turkish side, however, let it be understood that it would never accept a minority status and insisted on "sovereign partnership" as determined by the Cyprus treaties. On 11 October the text of the charter was published.

The charter consisted of two parts. In the first part the government declared its readiness to apply all basic rights and freedoms of the universal declaration of human rights. All minorities should be autonomous as regards education, culture, religion and civil status and be represented in parliament. The government was ready to have the realisation supervised by a UN controller. The second part contained a detailed human rights catalogue with 24 points, followed by a catalogue of the rights of each individual with a guarantied recourse to the courts. The charter, too, triggered a debate in the UN.

The resolution of 10 August had been much too mild according to the taste of the Turkish government. On 15 September it requested a debate of the UN General Assembly on this topic. In order to win a majority both sides began intensive lobbying activities. On 10 October parliamentary elections took place in Turkey which were won clearly by the Justice Party (*Adalet Partisi*, AP) of Süleyman Demirel with 240 seats and 52.9 percent of the votes. Already on 14 October an official statement said that the Turkish community on Cyprus did not have a minority status and would never accept one. Changes could only be made if all states involved agreed. Should the Cyprus government try and change anything unilaterally Turkey would take reprisals. In Athens prime minister Stefanopoulos replied that actually he wanted to normalize relations with Turkey but this would be difficult in view of these threats and provocations. But by the beginning of November Athens had let Ankara know that one was ready to resume the Cyprus talks.

Just when it looked as though both sides would restart the talks a serious incident took place in Famagusta which became a topic of discussion for the Security Council. On 5 November the Security Council listened to the statements of the representatives of Turkey, Cyprus and Greece who had been invited to the meeting. The Security Council members regretted the incidents and praised the efforts of the UN for a ceasefire and the reduction of the tensions. On 7 November the Council adopted a rather soft-worded admonition in the form of a "consensus" at which one had arrived without voting.

The big Cyprus debate began on 11 Decemeber in the First Committee with a verbal exchange between Kyprianou and his Turkish colleague Çağlayangil. After a drawn-out apologetic historical discourse on the history of Cyprus, Kyprianou wanted to know whether Cyprus as a small state was obliged to tolerate interference in its internal affairs. This was a clever move because it called for the solidarity of all small states and all those states which had minorities, i.e., most former colonies, and these backed Cyprus at once. Çağlayangil presented his point of view, which had little in common with historical reality. He did not notice that he offended the majority of the African and Asian states with his exaggerations, half truths and threats.

The debate dragged on for several days. On 17 December 1965 the First Committee, after a lengthy additional debate on the by-laws, finally voted on the motion which had been tabled by the non-aligned states. The high number of abstentions was amazing. All nonaligned and Greece (47) voted for the resolution and only 6, among them the USA and Turkey, against. When the General Assembly voted one day later the result was almost identical (47:5:54). This resolution (2077/XX) was much more outspoken than the Security Council resolution of March 1964 which had generally appealed to all states to refrain from threats or the use of force in their foreign policy, which had just been a moral appeal. Now these appeals were concretized and linked to Cyprus. Moreover, there was talk of the people of Cyprus and not of the two ethnic communities. The resolution referred to this by mentioning the minority charter and speaking of the rights of the minority thus by implication recognizing the existence of a majority and a minority. The appeal to the member states to respect the sovereignty, unity, independence and territorial integrity was concrete also and practically contained Makarios' demand for "unfettered independence". Makarios' plan had succeeded. The question was now whether this resolution could be turned into practical politics because resolutions of the UN General Assembly were not binding for the states. Nevertheless, for Turkey the resolution was a shock.

The Turkish public was inflamed by the press announcing Cyprus was lost. The leader of the right-wing republican peasant popular party, Alparslan Türkeş, called for an occupation of western Thrace, the Aegean islands and Cyprus. On 19 December Demirel said at a press conference that the resolution was contrary to law and a violation of international treaties. Turkey could not be held responsible for the consequences. The government spokesman made assurances that the Turkish right of intervention still existed and the government would apply it if the treaties were violated. Çağlayangil was even more outspoken: the resolution had not abolished the rights of Turkey. It was legally irrelevant, it was a noncommittal recommendation.

Makarios and the Greek Cypriots regarded the resolution as a great victory. Regarding public relations and morals this was true. But Makarios and the Cyprus government overrated the value of such a resolution. The struggle for such victories in the General Assembly became, and remained, the standard aim of Cypriot foreign policy until the mid-1980s. The numbers of these victories increased and became more impressive. Finally in 1974, after the Turkish invasion, resolution 321/XXIX of the General Assembly was accepted unanimously. Though the tone of the resolutions became more outspoken and demanding, its noncommittal character remained. In the Security Council such victories were impossible because of the veto power of its permanent members. But the victory in the General Assembly affirmed Makarios on his course of "unfettered independence" and of majority and minority. The success of such a course depended on the policy of Athens. As long as Athens aimed at enosis Makarios was obliged to walk the tight rope.

On 31 December 1965 Galo Plaza resigned as UN mediator. U Thant regretted that the situation had led to this.

1966: Renewed interference of the mother countries

Makarios felt affirmed in his course by these resolutions. No sooner had they been passed than he introduced another bill about the reorganisation of the civil service to the House which contained another reduction of the privileges of the Turkish Cypriots and was another violation of the constitution de facto. The US Embassy commented on this sarcastically: apparently Makarios was successively realizing his 13 points. Though the British noticed this they did not get up the energy to protest. Obviously, they were no longer keen on asking for trouble because of Cyprus.

Within the Greek government reactions were divided. Vice-premier and foreign minister I. Tsirimokos recommended continuing the mediation of the UN. Greece should assist this. It would be a mistake if Athens dictated a policy and Nicosia just obeyed. Greece would love to acquire Cyprus but not conquer it. Greece wanted enosis but not against the will of the Cypriots. In a talk with Makarios, Tsirimokos encouraged him to follow an independent policy which led to outbursts of fury by the adherents of enosis in Cyprus and Greece alike. Grivas complained to premier Stefanopoulos that Tsirimokos was playing Makarios' game.

Stefanopoulos, on the other side, believed that Athens was the "national centre" of the Greek world and Nicosia had to subordinate itself. Additionally, Stefanopoulos did not like Makarios for personal reasons and therefore together with the minister of defence S. Kostopoulos he supported Grivas. Both pinned their hopes on bilateral negotiations with Turkey to achieve enosis. According to them the territorial compensation due in the case of enosis should be shouldered by Cyprus. Somewhere in their minds Acheson's ideas of the previous year were still active. They expected Makarios to accept their solution on the basis of the doctrine of the "national centre" without any objection.

In Ankara by the end of February 1966 Çağlayangil had developed new ideas: a solution could only be achieved by acknowledging the existence of two peoples on the island on the basis of a federation safeguarding the rights of the Turkish Cypriots. Independence should be guaranteed internationally; guarantor powers could be the US, France, the UK and the Soviet Union. The guarantee could have the character of the treaty establishing postwar Austria, which excluded union with Germany and guaranteed the rights of the (Slovenian and Croatian) minorities. He was ready to negotiate with the Greek government and Makarios provided they first accepted the federal concept.

By the end of January Çağlayangil had become even more concrete towards Ambassador Hart: the Cyprus treaties could be modified; however, the following four principles were indispensable: 1) no unilateral annexation; 2) acknowledgement of the existence of two ethnic groups; 3) no ethnic group should dominate the other; 4) both ethnic groups must participate in the government. One could talk about the latter's form, be it a federation, a cantonal system or municipal autonomy. He was open to each concept of independence, including double enosis, as long as it did not violate these principles. Turkey was facing big economic problems and the Cyprus problem was threatening her like the sword of Damocles. The relation with Greece should be improved and this could not be achieved without a solution of the Cyprus problem. He would even agree to a UN mediation if the mediator was a European. He hoped that the US would participate in the talks. Obviously the Turkish government was ready to agree to a reasonable compromise. The question arose whether Athens would move, too.

The Athenian government was split. Prime minister Stefanopoulos and his followers aimed at enosis without territorial compensation but with guaranteed minority protection. But this concept was not well thought out and served only to keep the nationalists quiet. Stefanopoulos was in close contact with Grivas, who was planning a coup against Makarios. Foreign minister Tsirimokos was of the opinion that the Cyprus problem was a Cypriot affair. In order to appease the situation Athens should give a guarantee to the Turks that Cyprus would remain independent for ten years. Makarios, however, did not even trust this idea since he was informed about Grivas' plans. Finally on 4 February 1966 the national security council of Turkey stated that should there be a coup in Cyprus to achieve enosis Turkey would intervene militarily. In view of this warning Athens should have steered a very cautious course, indeed.

In mid-February Grivas flew to Athens to have talks on the security of Cyprus. On his arrival he gloated in front of the waiting journalists: the Cypriot army was ready to repulse any Turkish attack, be it from the air or over the sea. "No Turkish soldier will ever put his foot on the soil of Cyprus, the enemy will be thrown into the sea." The Cypriot minister of defence, Georkatzis, did not participate in these talks - he had not been invited. Although Stefanopoulos was informed about Grivas' plans of a coup he decided that Grivas should not only have the command of all armed forces on the island in war but in peace as well, including that of the National Guard. By this the Greek government put all armed forces in Cyprus under its command and deprived the government of Cyprus of control over its own forces.

Makarios protested violently against this. A quarrel began between Athens and Nicosia which dragged on until April. Makarios' position was clear: the C.-in-C. of the National Guard was appointed by the Council of Ministers. He was under the orders of the minister of defence of Greece and was accountable to him regarding organisation, training, discipline and order in the National Guard. At the same time he was the chief of staff. The Greek officers serving in the National Guard were under his orders. Greek military laws were applied regarding disciplinary cases. In all other fields the officers were under Cypriot command. The Cyprus government had the right to dismiss Greek officers but was obliged to inform the Greek government accordingly.

Defence minister Kostopoulos admitted that from a legal point of view Makarios was right, but he had to subordinate himself to the lead of the "national centre". When foreign minister Tsirimokos resigned on 11 April and the international press wrote about Grivas' coup plans and he insisted on being the C.-in-C. Makarios became afraid that the forces under Grivas' control could be used by Athens to enforce the will of the "national centre" upon him. Moreover, this would strengthen the Cypriot supernationalist opposition and the adherents of enosis. Therefore, he decided to build up a counterweight. A special unit of the police would be set up.

During the following weeks preparations for this began. Under strict secrecy the necessary legal basis was created on which this paramilitary force, the future presidential guard, was to be set up. The members were recruited from the police among policemen especially devoted to Makarios. The unit was to be equipped with light and medium weapons which had been ordered in July 1966 from the ČSSR and were successively delivered in autumn, causing quite some excitement.

By the imprudent Greek policy Greek-Turkish relations had reached such an all-time low that the Foreign Office spoke of Turkish sabre rattling. Despite this Tsirimokos had constantly tried to begin a conversation with Ankara. After prolonged diplomatic haggling behind the scenes, which dragged on until May and in which London and Washington and even the UN participated, at the beginning of June bilateral talks began.

By the end of May the new Greek foreign minister, Ioannis Toumbas, had met Kyprianou: the aim of Greece's Cyprus policy was enosis, still. But this could only be achieved by a dialogue with Turkey not within the framework of the UN. The decisive factor was absolute secrecy. They would try to keep the Cypriots informed and if they did not always succeed in this it was not because of ill will. The Cyprus government should see to it that there were no incidents. Kyprianou promised this. Toumbas added that the press in Cyprus and Greece had to be silenced. At two short preliminary talks at the beginning of June, Toumbas and Çağlayangil agreed upon absolute secrecy. The first round of talks, which had an exploratory character, took place in various European towns and was lead by a small team of reliable ambassadors. These talks dragged on and by October it became clear that there hadn't been any progress. For reasons of internal politics both sides could not move away from enosis or taksim and were negotiating secondary problems just to keep the negotiations going but they were not able to come closer to a solution of the main problem.

By November Athens gained the impression that one could approach a solution if the Turks were offered a sovereign military base on Cyprus. Because Makarios categorically rejected the setting up of such an installation Athens conceived the idea that the Turks might get the British Dhekelia base. As this could not be achieved without British agreement London was asked whether the UK would consent. The answer was an elegantly formulated rejection with conditions impossible to meet. Foreign minister Toumbas did not understand this and from now on he was convinced that the British had agreed. It is astonishing that not one of the seasoned Greek diplomats pointed this out to their boss; but this was probably a case of lack of moral courage towards a minister who was a former admiral and as such accustomed to obedience.

In mid-December 1966 Toumbas and Çağlayangil met informally at the conference of NATO's foreign ministers and had a long talk during which it once more became clear that both sides were not ready to move one millimetre away from their respective maximal positions: Turkey demanded independence or a condominium and Greece stuck to enosis. It was agreed that one disagreed but that the negotiations should go on. In his memoirs Toumbas describes this meeting as a great success, saying he achieved a breakthrough on the Cyprus question. But he is in good company since Stefanopoulos and Mitsotakis told similar stories and a great part of Greek historiography concurred. The truth is, however, that in six months of negotiations nothing had moved.

1967: The Greek Junta, Cyprus and the Evros Fiasco

Since 22 December 1966 prime minister Ioannis Paraskevopoulos had been ruling Greece. His service government continued the effort to improve Greek-Turkish relations. But the Turkish government steered a tough course: in January threats were heard that the Turkish armed forces would be ready to intervene at any time. Turkey would never accept enosis, not even with territorial compensations in the form of a NATO base. The Cyprus treaties could not be changed unilaterally. In Cyprus there were two equal ethnic groups; a domination of one by the other was unacceptable. Cyprus could never be unilaterally annexed by any state under any excuse whatsoever. The balance established by the Treaty of Lausanne must not be destroyed.

In view of this situation on 6 February the Greek Crown Council met with the aim of finding a political line on the Cyprus question accepted by all parties to be followed by the service government and to overcome Makarios' resistance to the Greek-Turkish dialogue. At the first meeting on 6 February those present discussed whether they should commit themselves to a common line before Makarios arrived and confront him with a fait accompli. Papandreou advised them not to keep anything secret from Makarios and to lay down the common policy only after listening to his arguments. After a lengthy discussion in the plenary it became clear that all Greek politicians, with the exception of Papandreou and Tsirimokos, were for the continuation of the dialogue with Turkey. Only these two had apparently understood that enosis could not be achieved.

Makarios, too, rejected a continuation of the dialogue; a partition of the island was unacceptable. Since the Turks demanded a cession of a part of Cyprus and this would never be accepted by the Cypriots the dialogue had to end. Obviously Makarios was afraid of another Greek-Turkish *octroi*. The final communique stated vaguely that the Cyprus problem had been reviewed from all sides and the assembly had arrived at the unanimous opinion that this national topic should be followed up.

During a conversation between the Turkish president, Cevdet Sunay, and president Johnson on 3 April 1967 the Turkish position became very clear: good Turkish-Greek relations were of vital interest for regional security. The Cyprus problem had to be solved by peaceful means in order not to destroy the good bilateral relations. In order to achieve this both sides would have to make concessions. Areas with a Turkish majority should have autonomy status. Cyprus should be demilitarised. In order to protect Turkish interests Turkish troops should be stationed on the island. As enosis was excluded he suggested a Turkish-Greek condominium and the abolition of Cypriot independence. Turkey was ready to resume the dialogue as soon as the situation in Greece permitted this.

At the same time there were signals from Ankara to Athens that one was ready to resume the talks. But these came too late because the Paraskevopoulos government had resigned in the wake of another internal crisis in Greece. On 3 April the leader of the conservative ERE,

Panagiotis Kanellopoulos, formed a new government. However, before he could start a new initiative he was toppled by the military coup on 21 April 1967.

As has been stated several times Makarios rejected enosis because in his eyes it was no alternative to independence. But out of tactical motives he had paid lip service to it in order to keep the super-nationalists in Cyprus and the chauvinists in Greece who fanatically demanded enosis quiet. He had been able to steer this course rather successfully because the enosis fanatics were in no position of power. There had been talk about a coup against him by Grivas but as the latter did not receive any green light from the civilian government of Athens the danger had not been too big. But now the radical enosis fanatics within the military were in power. For Makarios the vision of a transfer of the Greek dictatorship to Cyprus was pure horror because he was politically a moderate and a pragmatist, rather in the middle of the political spectrum of Cyprus.

As the new rulers in Athens controlled the armed forces on Cyprus and could organise a coup at any time, Makarios had to avoid any provocation or, even better, to establish a certain amount of confidence with the junta. Such a course had two dangerous points: if the putschist colonels arrived at an agreement with the Turks the end of Cyprus' independence and Makarios' presidency would have come. But this scenario was relatively improbable. The danger emanating from Grivas was far bigger but as long as Athens controlled him it was not too big, since even the military Athens did not want a confrontation with Turkey. But if Grivas disengaged himself from the influence of Athens and began to act on his own this could have disastrous consequences for Cyprus. Thus Makarios was between the devil and the deep blue sea, a breach with the junta, which was demanded by his critics, would have been morally correct but would doubtless have led to an immediate putsch on Cyprus. Thus this course was excluded.

Indeed those putschists belonging to the military developed wild ideas: they were ready to leave a part of the Karpasia peninsula to Turkey and a share in a possible NATO fleet base on Cyprus. As soon as such an agreement was signed by Turkey Makarios and Grivas would be asked to agree to this. If they rejected it Greek troops would take over, enosis would be proclaimed and a month later the Karpasia area would be ceded to Turkey. The civilian putschists on the other hand, wanted to continue the dialogue with Turkey. As in Cyprus many anti-dictatorial elements had assembled, tension rose. Rumours of an impending coup became stronger in summer 1967. By the end of July it had become known that dictator Papadopoulos would fly to Cyprus on 3 August to have talks with Makarios.

Papadopoulos was received in a most pompous way. After a short meeting with the press Papadopoulos, who seemed rather impressed by the reception, was driven to the presidential residence where he and Makarios conferred in private. In the evening Makarios gave a dinner in honour of Papadopoulos to which everybody of distinction had been invited. After the dinner Makarios and Papadopoulos who was overwhelmed by Cypriot hospitality retired and continued their private talks.

On the following day they visited the *Fylakismena Mnimata* (imprisoned graves), the graves of the executed EOKA-fighters in an inner yard of the Nicosia prison. The emotional effect of such a visit in the minds of patriotic Greeks cannot be overestimated. But the main weight was on the dialogue between Makarios and Papadopoulos. It may be safely assumed that during those talks Makarios brainwashed Papadopoulos so thoroughly that he saw things with the eyes of Makarios. Additionally, the pious, if not bigoted, Papadopoulos was involuntarily ready to accept the Archbishop as a natural authority. In the press conference before his departure Papadopoulos announced that enosis should be achieved by peaceful methods and means in cooperation with Makarios. Obviouly Makarios' mental caressing had done the job. From now on the relations between Makarios and Papadopoulos were rather good, with a short exception in 1972.

All summer long the contacts between Athens and Ankara had continued on the ambassadorial level. The Greek proposal that the two prime ministers should meet was accepted in Ankara reservedly. Foreign minister Çağlayangil considered this a window dressing manoeuvre because the Greek side had made no effort to prepare the meeting diplomatically. The explanation was rather simple: the junta did not trust the professional diplomats and thus not even the head of the Turkish department of the Greek foreign ministry was allowed to participate in the preparatory talks. Only three days before the meeting the leaders of the negotiations, among them prime minister Kollias and vice-premier Spandidakis, had themselves informed by the responsible diplomats. Rather quickly it became clear that neither understood what was at stake. They went to the meeting totally unprepared.

The negotiations on 9 and 10 September 1967 were a total fiasco. They demonstrated to the Turkish side how naive, inexperienced and inflexible the colonels were. The only result was the agreement that they did not agree. According to the judgement of a participating Turkish diplomat the whole affair was a farce. The talks at Evros were the end of the second and last effort to solve the Cyprus problem between Greece and Cyprus bilaterally. On 12 September prime minister Demirel stated: the negotiations failed because the Greeks stubbornly clung to enosis as the only solution. This solution could not be accepted because, on the one hand, it would destroy the balance established by the Lausanne treaty and on the other hand, violate the Cyprus treaties which were based on the existence of two ethnic groups. Both were linked to the Greek and the Turkish nations and one could not simply back out but had to search for a solution. If the talks ended an armed conflict threatened. However, a solution had to respect the national honour and for its protection the Turkish nation was ready for every sacrifice.

Makarios reacted to this mess by submitting a plan for normalisation of relations with the Turkish Cypriots which was to be assisted by the good offices of the UN. The government in Athens watched the new course of the Cyprus government with distrust and decided to interfere. On 21 October vice-premier Spandidakis appeared in Cyprus and announced that enosis was the only possible solution. At the Evros meeting the two sides had discussed the future of Cyprus but one had not arrived at a solution, thus the dialogue had to be resumed. One should give the Turkish Cypriots guarantees and make it clear to them that there was a common enemy - Communism. Makarios countered, stating that a solution of the Cyprus problem had to be achieved by an inner-Cypriot dialogue.

After Spandidakis' departure Makarios said in an interview that the 18-month long Greek-Turkish dialogue had failed. A solution could only be found within the framework of the UN and had to be negotiated between the two communities. But Makarios could not bring himself to accept an equal partnership at this point. Makarios' new normalisation policy might have led to a release of tension but now another severe inter-communal incident happened at the village of Kofinou.

The Kofinou Crisis In November 1967

A little southeast of the crossing of the old roads from Limassol to Larnaka and from Limassol to Nicosia is the village of Kofinou, which was inhabited by Turks only. South of the road to Limassol a little more to the west there were two further Turkish villages, one of which was Mari, a village on a mountain ridge above the road. In the middle between these two Turkish settlement centres lies the then mixed village of Ag. Theodoros. Without the existence of this village a Turkish Cypriot enclave could have been established there after the unrest of 1963/4.

During the unrest in 1963 Ag. Theodoros had remained remarkably quiet even after the Cypriot police regularly made patrols through the valley to the village.

When the unrest broke out in 1963 the Turkish inhabitants of Kofinou occupied the police station, ousted the police officers and controlled the traffic on the three roads from then on. Between 1965 and 1966 a TMT force was formed in Kofinou under the leadership of an officer from Turkey. Since early 1967 the leader was a captain with the *nom de guerre* Mehmet. He saw to it that the local Turks did not acknowledge the organs of the state. Friendly contacts with the Greek neighbours in Ag. Theodoros were forbidden. Under his direction a 400 TMT fighter group was built up in these villages. In January 1967 first harmless provocations began which slowly escalated despite conciliatory efforts of UNFICYP. TMT fighters blocked the road to Ag. Theodoros and Mehmet even assaulted blue helmets. It was clear that the aim was the eviction of the Greeks from this village in order to create a homogenous Turkish enclave with access to the sea via the small fishing port of Zygi.

In autumn a battalion of the National Guard was moved to the Greek village of Skarinou but the provocations continued. On 31 October the political and military leaders united in the Cypriot Defence Council decided to act against the road block and to secure the road to Ag. Theodoros. In order to safeguard the road permanently against the attacks of the TMT fighters it was necessary to eject them from their fortified positions on the ridge east and above the road from Skarinou to Ag. Theodoros. The main attack would be launched against this ridge position. It was hoped that the TMT fighters of Kofinou, which lies behind this mountain ridge, would not intervene. The whole operation was to last a few hours because one was afraid of an intervention of the Turkish Air Force if the operation was protracted. However, before those present could fix a date for the operation it became known that Denktash, trying to return illegally to Cyprus, had been discovered and arrested. In view of this new situation the Defence Council decided to postpone the operation.

As we mentioned before, the authorities had refused the return of Denktash in February 1964. In August of the same year, just before the fighting in the Tillyria began, he had tried to enter the island illegally via Kokkina helped by the Turkish military. The fights forced him to give up this effort and he returned to Turkey. Now he had returned without the help of the military. When he was questioned by officers of the Greek military secret service he successfully managed to hide his real plans. During a talk with Clerides it became clear that he wanted to take over the leadership of the Turkish Cypriots. A few days later Clerides heard that the Greek military were thinking of shooting Denktash on the pretence that he was fleeing. Only when Clerides and Makarios exerted massive pressure did the military give up their plan which certainly would have had catastrophic consequences. On 11 November the Council of Ministers decided to exempt him from prosecution for raisons d'état and permit his departure to Turkey. The Turkish government regretted the incident: Denktash had gone to Cyprus without their knowledge and they were ready to accept him back. Thus on 12 November Denktash flew back to Ankara.

On the very same evening of 31 October Grivas had informed Athens about the decisions of the Defence Council. In early November he received a green light for the limited operation, Any intrusion into the village of Kofinou was strictly forbidden. Obviously Athens understood the possible consequences of an attack on a Turkish village. The operation was to begin on 14 November 1964.

At noon of 14 November two police cars, accompanied by armoured cars of the National Guard and infantrymen, drove along the valley from Skarinou to Ag. Theodoros and through the Turkish part of Ag. Theodoros over the bridge to the Greek quarter. Nothing happened, neither on the journey there nor on the journey back. But now Grivas started to provoke: he drove with a greater number of vehicles of the National Guard to Ag. Theodoros but again nothing happened. But when the TMT command in Nicosia heard of it, they ordered their forces near Ag. Theodoros from now on to repulse similar advances. Despite this order, in the morning of 15 November another escorted patrol drove to Ag. Theodoros unmolested.

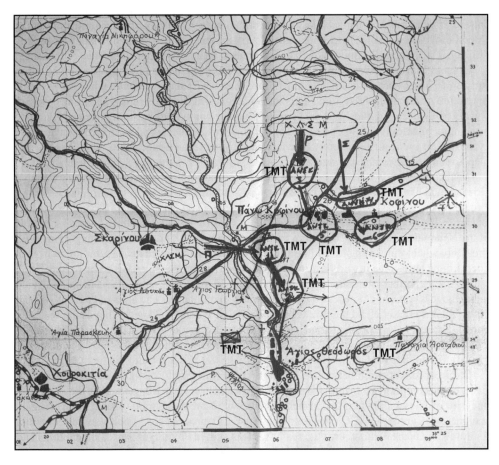

Original sketch of the operations at Kofinou on 16 November 1967

ΧΛΣΜ - χώρος λήψεως στηματισμού μάχης - assembly area of the National Guard; ΑΝΣΚ αντικείμενικος στοχός - operational targets in chronological order; crosses = MG-positions (e.g. near Agios Georgios); small circles = buildings

Now UNFICYP made it clear to the Cypriot government that the provocations sufficed. If these kind of patrols continued violence would erupt soon. And this is precisely what happened when another patrol went to Ag. Theodoros in the early afternoon. Turkish TMT paramilitary fired on the patrol and soon a gunfight began in which the National Guard used artillery and mortars against the Turkish part of Ag. Theodoros. Within a very short time Ag. Theodoros was in the hands of the Greeks: there were 9 dead and the same number of wounded. When the attack on Ag. Theodoros began, TMT fighters from Kofinou intervened by opening fire on the attackers from the mountain ridge near Ag. Theodoros. This caused Grivas to order the main attack, though Makarios had great misgivings. Two companies of the National Guard attacked the positions on the ridge and the village of Kofinou itself. In both cases British UNFICYP positions in between were overrun without any losses of the Blue Helmets. Quickly the National Guard occupied the heights above the valley of Ag. Theodoros north and northeast of Kofinou. In the afternoon the attack on the village itself began though not a single shot had been fired from there. The attack was supported by light tanks, machine guns, mortars and an artillery battery. The fighting was hard and lasted until after 8 pm. 22 Turks were killed and 9 wounded. One National Guardsman was shot and two policemen were wounded. Thus Grivas had disobeyed the orders of Athens which had expressly forbidden an attack on Kofinou.

Upon massive pressure from Athens Grivas reluctantly ordered the retreat from Kofinou early on 16 November. This did not hinder pro-Grivas newspapers presenting the attack on Kofinou as a major military success. This in turn provoked the Turkish side extremely and it countered by accusing the National Guard of having committed ugly atrocities. Both items brought the masses to boiling point and prime minister Demirel was pressured from all sides even from his own party. The government reacted by alarming the armed forces and sent some planes on a low level mission over Cyprus.

As the Americans were afraid of the crisis spreading they demanded that Athens recall Grivas immediately. On 17 November an order to that effect was given. Under normal circumstances Grivas could have been expected to obey and fly to Athens the following day. But the 69-year old bulldog took his time and went on provoking by sending two further patrols of the National Guard to Ag. Theodoros. Obviously he did not grasp that he was playing with fire. Only when prime minister Kollias ordered Grivas on 18 November to return to Athens at once did the latter give in and flew to Athens on 19 November.

In Ankara parliament authorised the government in a secret session almost unanimously to intervene in Cyprus and if necessary in Greece as well militarily. The units of the first Turkish army which were to defend the Straits against a Warsaw Pact attack were moved to the Greek border. Foreign minister Çağlayangil handed a kind of ultimatum over to the Greek ambassador demanding the withdrawal of the troops which were illegally stationed in Cyprus and of Grivas himself. As no date was mentioned in the note there was room for diplomatic manoeuvres.

During a conversation between US Ambassador Hart and foreign minister Çağlayangil a five points compromise formula was worked out: Turkey would guarantee the territorial integrity of Cyprus. Ankara and Athens would withdraw their troops which were illegally stationed in Cyprus. UNFICYP would supervise this process for which it would obtain a reinforced mandate. The security forces of Cyprus should be reorganised as mixed units and the paramilitary units dissolved. The inhabitants of Kofinou should receive indemnities. The safety of the Turkish Cypriots should be safeguarded. The government in Ankara agreed to this formula but in Athens the foreign minister had resigned and the new one, Panagiotis Pipinelis, was not yet fully oriented. Therefore Athens did not react. Only on 22 November did he signal readiness for talks after the Americans had pressured him.

As the Greeks did not react the Turks continued with their military preparations for an intervention. The air force continued its daily reconnaissance over Cyprus. A great part of the navy was deployed to Mersin. On 23 November American observers on the spot gained the impression that Turkey was close to an attack. News about this reached Cyprus, where the defence council ordered a kind of mobilisation. On 22 November the British High Commissioner informed Makarios about the five-points-plan. Makarios reacted positively but had some reservations.

In London the government understood that a Turkish invasion was imminent but decided to keep out of everything. Foreign minister George Brown said that the Turkish attack was not aimed at the government of Cyprus but against the Greek troops. The UK had no defence agreement with Cyprus and was not obliged to do anything if the Cyprus government appealed to her in case of a Turkish invasion. Obviously the British guarantor power was seeking a way out, shirking its responsibility.

In Washington a team of State Department experts discussed possible ways out of the crisis. The undersecretary responsible for the Near East suggested sending a high ranking trouble-shooter as a personal envoy of the President to Ankara and Athens and possibly to Nicosia. Foreign Secretary Rusk considered this a good idea and submitted it, accompanied by a list of possible candidates to President Johnson. The latter agreed and chose the former Secretary for Defence Cyrus A. Vance who had a name as an efficient troubleshooter and who was fully trusted by Johnson. Vance was charged with averting a Greek-Turkish war by all means.

Between 23 and 28 November Vance performed shuttle diplomacy between Ankara and Athens. Ankara insisted on the immediate withdrawal of the Greek division from Cyprus. Athens wanted a simultaneous reduction of the Turkish mobilisation. Both sides bid high but at the end a compromise was found: the withdrawal of the Greek troops would begin immediately and be finished within 45 days. The Turkish deployment in Thrace and the preparations for the invasion would be stopped at the same time. Both things were done and by 16 January 1968 the Greek division was withdrawn. UN Secretary General U Thant was informed about it. Now Makarios had to be pushed to accept it.

Vance's negotiations with Makarios vividly resembled those of 18 February 1959 in London. Makarios bargained for each iota. Finally, Vance in co-operation with U Thant managed to outwit Makarios so that he agreed. Outwardly there were no winners or losers. Vance had avoided the international press, the Greek press was under censorship and the chauvinist outburst of the Turkish press was not noticed due to the language barrier. As Vance himself admitted, the fact that there was a dictatorship in Greece helped him a lot. Under democratic conditions the concessions Greece had to make would have been difficult to achieve. Vance's success in this mission was owed to his discretion, his integrity, his reservation and most of all to the assistance of the State Department and the White House. Additionally, he was helped by the fact that neither Greece nor Turkey really wanted a war.

The Greek political leadership understood that enosis could not be achieved via bilateral negotiations. Due to miserable preparations, one had suffered a diplomatic defeat at the negotiations on Evros and now one had to accept a massive weakening of one's own position. But the colonels did not totally give up the idea of Cyprus' union with Greece: in their eyes the main obstacle had been Makarios, if he could be removed from the scene perhaps one could find a bilateral agreement with the Turks. When later Makarios granted asylum to enemies of the junta these ideas became an obsession, as we shall see.

The moderates in the leadership of Turkey could be satisfied because they had pushed through their demands: Grivas was away and the Greek division was being withdrawn. The hawks, of course, would have enjoyed seeing the case closed for good by annexing Cyprus. The withdrawal of the Greek division strengthened the self-confidence of the Turkish Cypriots the leadership of which became more intransigent. They recognized that Makarios was not able to enforce his will upon them and thus they took the first step towards a state of their own by forming a "Temporary Separate Turkish Administration" with a kind of constitution by the end of December 1967.

If one analyses this result from the point of view of Makarios one discovers positive and negative items. The most positive result was that Grivas who had triggered the crisis by his irresponsible behaviour, had been forced to disappear from the scene. The withdrawal of the Greek division, on the one hand, weakened the defensive strength of the Greek Cypriots but, on the other hand, the danger of a coup against Makarios was considerably reduced because quite a number of officers sympathising with the junta had to leave the island. The reason for worrying was the fact that most of the officers of the National Guard belonged to the Greek army and thus the junta still had their fingers in the pie of Cypriot internal affairs. Therefore, Makarios demanded total demilitarisation. As he could not achieve this he had to proceed with the building up of the police in order to form a counterweight. Makarios' independence course was strengthened. For most of the Greek Cypriots enosis considerably lost its attraction because of the dictatorship in Greece. Enosis was a dream which was slowly fading. The question was now whether Makarios would manage to convince the Turkish Cypriots of his new course.

The Americans, on the other side, had ignored the independence of Cyprus and had focused on the Greek-Turkish talks, believing they could enforce their results upon Makarios. Now they were obliged to recognise that Makarios was the head of an independent state. Therefore they decided to assist the UN in their effort to make the two communities negotiate a solution.

The inter-communal talks in 1968
With the creation of the "Temporary Separate Turkish Administration" the Turkish Cypriot leadership created facts which put Makarios under pressure to act: the Turkish side declared that this "constitution" was nothing new, only a kind of stock-taking of the situation but in reality this was the first step in the direction of a federative solution. Makarios' first reaction was a statement on 12 January 1968: the solution to the Cyprus problem could only be searched for in the framework of the feasible, not always that which was wanted. With this statement the adherents of independence and the moderate adherents of enosis could identify themselves because enosis had only been postponed to a distant future.

But before Makarios could initiate a new policy he had to have himself elected president once more because his term was over. Makarios remained rather noncommittal in his election campaign statements, which infuriated the radical adherents of immediate enosis. Among them were the Bishops who asked him by the end of January to resign as president if he had to accept a solution excluding enosis forever. Makarios succeeded in quieting the rebels by promising them that he would never accept such a solution. Against Makarios ran the psychiatrist, Takis Evdokas, who was supported by the adherents of Grivas and the sympathisers of the junta. This in turn caused AKEL to appeal to its members to vote for Makarios. The result of the elections of 25 February 1968 was an overwhelming victory for Makarios (94.45 percent of the votes). 93.45 percent of those entitled to vote participated in the election.

But it was not only Makarios who looked for a new legitimation by elections. On 20 January Küçük announced that the Turkish Cypriots, too, would go to the polls on 25 February to elect the vice-president because it would be unconstitutional if only the president were elected. Küçük declared that he would run for the office. The former judge of the Highest Court, Mehmet Zekia, announced his candidacy, too; he was supported by TMT. However, on 27 January he withdrew his candidacy after heavy pressure from Ankara. Ankara wanted to avoid a split in the Turkish community and was afraid of new unrest if Zekia were elected. As there was no other candidate the actual casting of the votes was waived and the Turkish-Cypriot election supervisor declared Küçük elected.

U Thant signalled that he was ready to support the inter-communal talks. In the following weeks the government removed most of the control posts so that the Turkish Cypriots could move freely in the areas controlled by the Greek Cypriots. The Turkish side, however, stuck to its control of the enclaves and did not allow any transit. On 12 March Makarios submitted some proposals for a solution which, though they contained some positive elements to overcome the separation, would have reduced the Turkish Cypriots to a privileged minority. Obviously Makarios was not able to move on this question. Nevertheless, U Thant was able to state in June 1968 that tensions had eased.

In April Makarios even accepted the return of Rauf Denktash as chief negotiator of the Turkish Cypriots in the future talks. Makarios had gained the impression that Denktash, too, wanted a compromise solution and, indeed, foreign minister Çağlayangil had instructed him accordingly. But the Turkish Cypriots were split: there were the moderates who were supported by Dr. Ihsan Ali and the future founder of the Republican Turkish Party Ahmet Berberoğlu and, at this point, by Denktash as well as the Turkish government. But there were those super-nationalists and separatists fixed on separation of the island who were closely linked with the TMT leadership. The higher leadership of TMT consisted exclusively of Turkish staff officers, known as the "Pashas".

As in all critical questions the consent of these officers had to be obtained; it was the Turkish General Staff which controlled Turkish policy in Cyprus and to a much lesser degree the government. The Cyprus problem was a "national" problem which was decided by the National Security Council of Turkey, in which the military had the say. Though this mechanism was not visible during the upcoming negotiations, Denktash had the difficult task of also convincing the pashas by the results of the negotiations and via them to induce the chauvinists of TMT to make concessions. This task was made more difficult by the fact that TMT developed itself into a state within the state with a leading elite and loyalties of its own.

The first round of the inter-communal talks took place in June/July 1968. The two sides had agreed that Clerides and Denktash should lead the negotiations. The first topic was possible changes to the constitution. Clerides and Denktash knew each other since they had attended the same secondary school and both had studied law at Grey's Inn. Despite all political differences they respected each other and even during the most massive arguments they never said anything which they might have regretted later. Both had a distinct sense of humour which they preserved until old age, as the author can confirm from his own experience.

The negotiations began on neutral soil in Beirut on 3 June. The two agreed that they would represent their communities and not the government or the provisional administration. Quickly they complied that the Zurich agreement contained clauses negative for both sides. They concurred to speak openly. Denktash gave to understand that the Turkish side was ready to revise certain articles of the constitution provided their status as an independent political group remained. But they were ready to abandon certain constitutional rights of government level if they got greater local autonomy in turn. Therefore they had to talk about the local administration; Clerides agreed immediately because in all advanced democratic systems decentralisation of power towards greater local self-administration existed.

At their next meeting on 24 June at Ledra Palace Hotel, Clerides and Denktash agreed that they would meet twice each week at their homes. The next meeting would take place on 27 June at 10 o'clock in the house of Denktash, who was responsible for the lunch as well because they wanted to continue their talks in the afternoon. On 28 June Clerides informed Makarios about the state of the negotiations: Denktash was ready to accept the Greek demand that the seats in the house of representatives should be divided proportionally according to the size of the community. Denktash accepted abolishing the separate majorities on budget questions and he regarded Denktash's counterclaim that the government finance the Turkish educational system as acceptable. Denktash's offer to agree to distribute the civil service posts proportionally between the two communities met an old Greek demand as well. Equally acceptable was a united judiciary. Clerides recommended accepting Denktash's offers. Makarios, however, was of the opinion one should not commit oneself. At the further negotiation Denktash urged a quick solution because he was under pressure from the hardliners.

In August the negotiations paused and the Greek Cypriot side used this to inform Athens secretly about the results achieved so far. Foreign minister Pipinelis agreed with almost everything. On 29 August Clerides assessed that Denktash had accepted the following changes to the constitution: abolition of the veto of the vice-president, reduction of the number of Turkish deputies to 20 percent according to their proportional part of the population, abolition of the separate majorities on budget bills, financing of the education by the government, joint election of the speaker of the house and his deputy (one being a Turkish Cypriot), reduction of the Turkish share in the civil service and in the security forces to 20 percent, united higher judiciary, abolition of the Cypriot army. The Turkish side expected as quid pro quo the election of the local administration instead of appointment, the administrative aggregation of Turkish and Greek villages regardless of their geographic distribution. There were more details which Clerides considered acceptable.

Thus Denktash had almost fully accepted all 13 of Makarios' demands. The only thing he rejected was to have his people made a minority. He wanted to preserve the partnership in some way and keep the guarantee of Turkey in force which was understandable in view of the past. On 29 August Clerides informed Makarios about this and urged him to agree. Had Makarios agreed, a solution could have been found in summer 1968. But Makarios radically rejected the pooling of villages. He agreed that the proposed autonomy rights of the local administration posed no problem but they had to be kept under control of the ministry of the interior. Clerides had negotiated in vain.

Makarios' motives for his rejection are complicated: he wanted a unitary state controlling everything. His reservations against Turkish autonomy at the lower level were not caused by his fear that this might be a first step towards partition, but because he admittedly suspected that the moment the Turkish Cypriots received local autonomy the Greek Cypriots would demand the same rights, and thus they would loose control over the base altogether. At the same time this is an indicator of Makarios' claim to absolute power. Makarios wanted to make the Turkish Cypriots a privileged minority but he was not ready to grant them any political autonomy. The only concessions he made were his normalisation measures and these aimed at the breaking up of the enclaves. This aim was another reason why he vehemently rejected the pooling of villages because this would have caused the opposite of what he wanted. Obviously Makarios tried to apply the same negotiation tactics which he had used successfully with the British in 1956 and 1960 and with the Americans in February 1964 and at the end of 1967.

On 13 August 1968 an event took place in Greece which pushed the interest in the inter-communal negotiations aside. On that day a Greek by the name of Alexandros Panagoulis tried to assassinate dictator Papadopoulos, but did not succeed. During the ensuing police investigation it was found out that the Cypriot minister of the interior, Georkatzis, was involved in the plot. After a lot of haggling between Nicosia and Athens, searching for a face saving solution, Georkatzis resigned after Makarios had promised him that he would call parliamentary elections in January 1969 and thus pave Georkatzis' way back into power. Since Makarios did not keep his promise because of pressure from Athens, he alienated Georkatzis and a great part of the moderate former EOKA members. The resulting frustration made Georkatzis develop, to a certain degree, inimical feelings towards Makarios. But his real loss of power was much less than one could expect because he continued to control his networks inside and outside the state apparatus. He continued to be well informed of all developments and to have his fingers in many a pie. Moreover, many policemen were personal henchmen since EOKA times and had been appointed by him. Since Makarios did not call elections, the party-forming process slowed down and the inter-communal talks came to the fore again.

The second round, too, which lasted from the end of August to January 1969 was charac-terised by a constructive spirit. Denktash continued to be ready to reduce the share of power

Plate 33

Released EOKA internees

Grivas pacing a guard of honour at Athens airport

Plate 34

Karamanlis, Grivas and Mrs. Grivas

London Conference: Makarios speaks to the press

Plate 35

Makarios' return to Nicosia in 1959

Memorial of the liberation struggle

Plate 36

Makarios, Gouvernor H. Foot and F. Küçük signing the Cyprus Treaties

Old man greeting the first soldiers of ELDYK

Plate 37

Makarios and Küçük welcome the first soldiers of TOURDYK

Minister of the Interior Georkatzis and Makarios

Plate 38

1963: *Sampson with captured Tukish flag in Omorfita*

Grivas visiting the National Guard: "The enemy into the sea."

Plate 39

The Cabinet welcomes Grivas: Polykarpos Georkatzis, Renos Solomidis, Tassos Papadopoulos, Georgios Grivas, Makarios, Andreas Arouzos, Patroklos Stavrou

A village in the Tillyria bombed by the Turkish Air Force

Plate 40

Turkish Cypriot fighters in St. Hilarion castle

Makarios visiting Greek Cypriot fighters near St. Hilarion

at government level but wanted to strengthen the local autonomy considerably. Makarios' tactic, to keep everything pending and decide nothing, began to appear counterproductive because it enabled the Turkish side to continuously table new and bigger demands regarding the local autonomy. Clerides tried to convince Makarios that one had to concede a certain amount of autonomy to the Turks. In his opinion the organisational structure of the local administration should be included in the constitution, thus securing them constitutionally so that the majority could not change it unilaterally. When Clerides recognised that he could not persuade Makarios he offered to resign as negotiator and president of the house in his desperation. Makarios rejected this, too.

Clerides was annoyed by the situation and said this rather bluntly: the Greek side - he meant Makarios - behave like children who always asked for that what they could not get. The decisive thing, however, was that the Turkish Cypriot leadership cooperated at government level. At the local level they could settle their matters alone, after all. By and by this separation would play an even lesser role provided the mutual trust was reestablished. Denktash, too, was pressured by the hardliners of his community and had to give in by necessity. Although the Greek government tried to bring Makarios to a more flexible course, they failed for similar reasons as the Turkish government when they tried to prevail against the hardliners in the army. From December 1968 onward Clerides' and Denktash's room to negotiate became more and more narrow.

However, the talks in autumn 1968 also offered, indeed, a chance to find a solution. Clerides was a pragmatist who advocated the independence of Cyprus and a partnership with the Turkish Cypriots. Denktash, too, was steering a pragmatic course then and was ready for a solution. For him the security of his people had absolute priority. He wanted to keep the degree of equality granted by the Cyprus treaties but he was ready to shift them to the lower level and realise it in the form of local autonomy. Clerides, on the other hand, was prepared to accept this with the aim of overcoming the separation in the long run. Since the government in Ankara had the parliamentary elections in mind it was ready to accept any solution provided the Turkish Cypriots agreed with it. The Greek government, as well, wanted a solution to get rid of the annoying problem. But the negotiators had no *carte blanche*. Clerides had to consider Makarios' position and Denktash that of his hardliners. It may be safely assumed that the Turkish military had their hands in the game and strengthened the hardliners thus hindering the Turkish government from fully supporting Denktash and forcing the hardliners to compromise. The decisive factor, however, was Makarios. Had he given up demanding the minority status of the Turkish Cypriots a solution would possibly have been found in winter 1968/9. Thus at the end of the second round of the inter-communal talks there remained - once again - a lost opportunity, one of many.

Murder and Putsch Plans of the National Front 1969-1970
Makarios' tactical manoeuvre to promise Georkatzis early election made it clear to the other politicians that they had to act, because the elections had to take place in 1970 at the latest. Until then AKEL was the only well organised party. It had been founded in the early 1920s as KKK (Kommounistiko Komma Kyprou - Communist Party of Cyprus). After the unrest in 1931 it was prohibited, like all other political groups. When during WWI the repression was reduced Ploutis Servas founded AKEL (Anorthotiko Komma tou Erganzomenou Laou - Progressive Party of the Working People) which soon replaced KKK.

Makarios did not like the idea of founding parties. The Patriotic Front (Ethnikofronon Parataxis) was no party but a kind of clientelistic network of persons dependent on him, not following a course of their own and active only before elections. In Makarios' eyes parliamentarians were transmission belts for his ideas. Despite that, he agreed when Clerides informed him that he intended to set up a conservative party together with P. Georkatzis and T. Papadopoulos. On 5 February 1969 it was founded under the name of Union Party (Eniaio Komma). In order to be able to continue his *divide-et-impera* policy Makarios encouraged other political grandees to found parties, too, of which only the Socialist Party of V. Lyssaridis (EDEK) succeeded.

On the right fringe of the Greek Cypriot society these manoeuvres were watched with distrust. In the eyes of the adherents of Grivas and other former EOKA followers the founding of parties was treason to the national cause because parties supported Makarios' independence course and hindered enosis. It was decided to set up a secret armed organisation, the EM (Ethniko Metopo - National Front) according to the EOKA model. Even some of the Bishops supported this enterprise. The aim of the EM was enosis which was to be achieved by bombs. A few, who were especially radical, went as far as planning to assassinate Makarios. It was dangerous that the EM had adherents in the security apparatus.

The leadership of EM soon came under the control of those Greek secret service officers who served in the National Guard, the Greek embassy in Nicosia and in ELDYK. It was self evident that all these officers were radical anticommunists and many very close to the junta. A few such as, e.g., the commander of the Cypriot Commandos (LOK), Colonel Dimitrios Papapostolou had participated in the coup of 21 April 1967. These officers took over the lead of the EM groups, supplied them with weapons and even facilitated the hiding of members in the ELDYK camp if the Cypriot police were on their heels.

The EM led a leaflet war, threw bombs and organised assassinations. The police could not achieve much against them since EM sympathisers in their own ranks warned their friends of planned actions. In the beginning Makarios did not take the EM seriously because he did not recognise their real aims. Only when a strategy paper was leaked to him did he understand the danger: they wanted to kill him, take over power, partition the island and realise double enosis. This idea fatally resembled the enosis-by-putsch plan of the previous years. Behind this plan stood the chief of the Greek Military Police (ESA), Dimitrios Ioannidis, who hated Makarios. On 28 August EM was outlawed, which led to a cessation of bombing and assassination attempts. In October, however, when another series of attempts began the government declared a kind of state of emergency in Cyprus which permitted the use of the National Guard against the terrorists. In the following weeks EM came under pressure.

In January 1970 Makarios visited Tanzania, Zambia and Kenya. In Nairobi the American ambassador warned him that there would be an attempt on his life at the airport in Nicosia on his arrival. Makarios did not take this warning seriously but when he met dictator Papadopoulos in Athens on 17 November he informed him about it. Papadopoulos condemned the activities of EM in an interview with the Cypriot radio. Indeed a fanatic adherent of enosis, a Cypriot student named Adamos Charitonos, had already planned an attack in Athens. Behind this fanatical student was LOK commander Dimitrios Papapostolou who had been in Athens in early January and had allegedly given the student his own gun for the assassination attempt. He had advised him that in case of arrest he should say that he had acted at the instigation of Georkatzis. When Charitonos objected that Georkatzis would defend himself against this charge Papapostolou allegedly answered that a dead man could not deny anything. Obviously Papapostolou did not only plan to kill Makarios but also Georkatzis, who was informed about the activities of the colonel by his net of informers.

In February 1970 the measures taken against EM became more and more effective and therefore Makarios did not take seriously another serious warning which came from the US embassy in Nicosia this time. According to this information an attempt on his life would be made within the next two weeks. Via AKEL channels the Soviets had heard about it as well and the news agency TASS claimed that a small clique of reactionary Greek officers was planning a coup in Cyprus. Indeed, such plans had been developed by staff officers in the National Guard and LOK under the lead of Papapostolou in cooperation with EM for quite some time. The basic concept was an enlargement of the EM plan of autumn 1969: assassination of Makarios, takeover by the military and then double enosis. A precondition of the success of the plan was the death of Makarios. Apparently the miliary left the assassination task to EM. They planned a coup to take place by the end of May. On 27 January 1970 the final version of the putsch-plan was finished which scheduled the coup for 28 May 1970. However, in order to be successful a precise time management and cooperation of all involved was necessary and this did not work because EM made its assassination attempt on Makarios as early as 8 March.

Since Makarios was always surrounded by bodyguards when he appeared in public it was difficult to get close to him. Therefore the killers decided that they would shoot down Makarios' helicopter. It was known that on 8 March 1970, as every year, Makarios would fly to Machairas monastery to attend the memorial service in honour of Afxentiou. Well targeted rumours about an attempt there caused a concentration of personal guards and police forces. As the flight would begin at the Archbishopric in the old town of Nicosia the inhabitants of that area were informed about the time of the departure by the newspapers, as usual. The assassins had taken two positions: on the flat roof of the Severis Library of the Pancyprian Gymnasion opposite the Archbishopric and on the flat roof of an apartment building further south. If the first group did not succeed in bringing down the helicopter and left the firing range the second group was to open fire.

When the helicopter with Makarios on board started shortly after 7 o'clock and had ascended ten metres the first group began to fire with a machine gun. The pilot was hit in the abdomen but he managed to land the helicopter on an unbuilt plot nearby. Makarios had not been hurt and residents of the area transported the pilot with a car to Nicosia General Hospital. The killers fled. When Makarios was still in the hospital suddenly colonel Papapostolou showed up with his private car though he should have been at Machairas supervising the security measures. Makarios became suspicious and refused to take a ride in the colonel's car to the Archbishopric alone and ordered a prison warden, who happened to be around, to join him. Then Makarios decided to take Papapostolou's car to the Archbishopric. The latter urged Makarios to go to the Presidential Palace on the outskirts of the town in order to talk over the radio. Makarios rejected this and made Papapostolou drive the car himself while he and the "body guard" sat in the backseats. Apparently Makarios understood that there he would be exposed to an attack by LOK members; the LOK camp was only a few kilometres away.

Makarios sent for his official car which was conducted by his brother. When it arrived Papapostolou climbed into the car, assuming the role of a body guard. Shortly before Makarios left for Machairas he ordered that Georkatzis be questioned and his house searched. This lead to the wildest rumours and even wilder conspiracy theories which circulate in Cyprus to this day. According to these rumours Georkatzis was behind the assassination attempt. The truth is much simpler: Georkatzis knew a lot about the activities of EM, the Greek officers and above all about Papapostolou.

After a failed effort to leave Cyprus on 13 March Georkatzis arranged a meeting outside Nicosia in the evening. Georkatzis was afraid of being killed by Papapostolou or his henchmen because he knew too much about their activities. In order to avoid this he had only one option: to threaten Papapostolou with dangerous revelations and these could logically only be revelations about the putsch plan. It may be safely assumed that Georkatzis did have certain pieces of information but not enough to frighten Papapostolou when he confronted him with them. Therefore they agreed to meet again the following day.

This meeting, however, was postponed to 15 March 1970. In the evening of 14 March Georkatzis received from one of his men the plan of the May coup d'etat which had been provided by a Cypriot officer on the staff of the National Guard. The file was copied and brought back. Georkatzis gave the copies to a trusted person (Patatakos) ordering him to hide them in a safe place.

In the morning of 15 March Georkatzis instructed Patatakos to hand over the copies to Clerides who should pass them on to Makarios if something happened to him at the meeting with Papapostolou. Georkatzis was to meet Papapostolou outside Nicosia in the evening. When Georkatzis and Patatakos approached the meeting place they saw a car with parking lights on at some distance. Georkatzis reduced speed and got ready to enter a farm track on the left. He asked Patatakos to leave the car and wait for him. Patatakos said that driving there was dangerous. Georkatzis replied that he would not stop and would drive towards the forest if he did not see Papapostolou. Patatakos left the car. As Georkatzis stopped he must have seen Papapostolou otherwise he would have driven on. A few seconds later Georkatzis was executed. He was just 40 years old when he died.

Wild speculations exist in Cyprus about this murder. Dependent on the political sympathies vastly different opinions can be heard. A sober analysis, however, leads to the conclusion that the assassins must be sought among those Greek officers remotely controlled by ESA chief Ioannidis and whose local resident was Papapostolou. The analysts of the US embassy in Nicosia came to the conclusion that some Greek officers were behind the affair who were malcontent with the moderate course of the junta leadership and wanted enosis. These officers were controlling, via the Greek Intelligence Agency (KYP) channels, the EM. They intended to overthrow Papadopoulos by starting a diversionary operation in Cyprus. The premature action on 8 March by EM forced them to postpone their plans, but as the events in 1974 showed clearly they were not given up.

According to his instructions Patatakos gave the copied documents to Clerides who passed them on to Makarios. Makarios recognised that he was facing a dilemma. If he acknowledged the plan as genuine he had to throw Papapostolou and his clique out of Cyprus. This would lead to a confrontation with Athens ruining his good relations with Papadopoulos,; the junta would close its ranks around Ioannidis and strengthen the forces under his influence. Therefore he declared at a press conference on 17 March that he considered the document a forgery. He did not believe in the rumours that Greek officers were involved in the assassination of Georkatzis. These rumours served only to undermine the psychic unity between people and army which was one of the main pillars of the Greeks of Cyprus. These were nice words intended to distract attention from the truth. Later Makarios even accepted the allegation that Georkatzis had been mixed up in the assassination attempt on him.

Even when DER SPIEGEL reported details of the plan calling it *Hermes* plan Makarios stuck to the language ruling even during the interview with this magazine in early April. There he said that the attempt on his life had been made by Greek Cypriots and denied that a foreign finger had pulled the trigger. He did answer a question about the assassination of Georkatzis. Since then the putsch plan has been called *Ermis* plan in the Greek literature.

The trial of the would be assassins of 8 March was a farce. Two of the six defendants were not even charged because, allegedly, there was not enough proof. The other four shifted the blame to Georkatzis. Nevertheless, they were sentenced to 14 years in prison. But they served only two years because Makarios exercised Christian charity and pardoned them.

The successful removal of Georkatzis encouraged Papapostolou to go plotting. Now he tried to bring the Bishops on his side and sponsored the creation of a youth organisation of EM. When new attempts on Makarios were made on a great scale the state hit back. Mass arrests were made and the leaders were brought to court; 22 were jailed. In January 1971 Makarios pardoned them, which proved to be a major mistake because many of them joined EOKA B later on. In June 1970 Papapostolou left Cyprus for good.

Further developments 1969-1971

The rest of the year 1969 and the following two years were rather quiet in Cyprus. The inter-communal negotiation continued and between August and November 1969 there was a third round. As in October 1969 there were parliamentary elections in Turkey and in July 1970 in Cyprus the talks were interrupted. The fourth round began in September 1970 and ended in September 1971.

In the third round Clerides and Denktash discussed local autonomy. Denktash wanted to have it included in the constitution. His aim was the horizontal administrative pooling of the Turkish Cypriot villages in groups even if they lay far away, as well as the establishment of a hierarchical structure to the highest level. The character of this concept was federal or even con-federal but not territorially. Based on one's experience of the Turkish Cypriot enclaves one could interpret this as a first step to ethnic separation of the island. No government could accept such a proposal without abdicating as government, the amount of power lost would have been unbearable. On the other hand, it was understandable that the Turkish Cypriots wanted auto-nomy. If a reasonable balance could be achieved a peaceful prospect was possible for Cyprus. Clerides considered the pooling of villages as harmless; this could even be realised on the basis of existing laws (*Improvement Areas Law*). For him the decisive points were the responsibilities of the local administration and because on this question he did not see any difference in opinion between Denktash and himself, he was ready to accept a hierarchy up to the district level, as Denktash had originally proposed.

But Makarios and his ministers rejected this because they believed that the Turkish Cypriots would give way a bit when. Makarios and foreign minister Kyprianou repeated in and outside Cyprus over and over again that further concessions were excluded. A government based on partnership with local autonomy was out of the question for them, they wanted a central state with guaranteed rights for the Turkish Cypriot minority. In Makarios' eyes partnership was the first step to federation.

In December 1969 Denktash submitted a reasonable compromise solution. He was ready to drop the demand for a hierarchically structured local autonomy and to return to the status quo ante when the village councils were elected by the inhabitants and not appointeded. Thus the central stumbling block for a solution was removed. Now talks about Makarios' 13 points could have started; Denktash declared himself ready to compromise. Clerides' tactics were also suitable to pave the way to a solution; again a chance for a solution appeared on the horizon. When Clerides informed Makarios about this he appeared pleased by the concessions Denktash had made but then he put forward new additional claims. Makarios' gambling nature took over. He did not see that he was heading towards a shipwreck. Clerides was not allowed to make further concessions and fought a forlorn battle.

On 21 April 1970 elections were fixed for 5 July and on 29 May Makarios dissolved parliament. Precisely ten years after the first elections the second took place. Of the 263,858 persons entitled to vote 200,141 went to the polls, i.e. 75 percent. 35 deputies were to be elected. AKEL became the strongest party (79,665 votes, 40.7 percent) but won only 9 seats because it had nominated only 9 candidates. It would have been easy for well organised AKEL to put up a candidate in each constituency, thus becoming the strongest party not only in votes but in mandates as well and therefore the strongest power in parliament. But this would have led to a unification of all other parties against it and the Western countries, especially the US, would have seen Cyprus threatened by the Communist menace. This might have led to an intervention. In view of this AKEL exercised wise self restraint, stepped into the second row and accepted that the votes for AKEL in constituencies without an AKEL candidate were lost. It knew that this was a loss which was compensated by the close cooperation with Makarios by a long way.

Clerides' *Eniaio Komma* received 26.11 percent and won 15 seats. *Proodeftiki Parataxi* had 18.28 percent and 7 seats. EDEK of Lyssaridis got 13.74 percent and 2 seats. T. Evdokas' DEK won 10.04 percent but no seat since it had not got a majority in one constituency. Additionally, two independent candidates were elected.

In the meantime negotiations between Clerides and Denktash had continued. On 6 July they had finished a document containing all points in which they agreed and disagreed regarding the executive, legislative, judiciary, civil service, police, human rights and local autonomy. The Athens government advised Makarios to make some concessions in order to arrive at a solution soon. But Makarios remained intransigent. He made concessions only on secondary problems which were not worth fighting about. In the decisive questions he was not ready to yield at all.

The Turkish government, also, pressed for a continuation of the inter-communal negotiations. In view of Makarios' intransigence Denktash had actually intended to resign as negotiator, seeing that Makarios did not move at all and thus recognizing that the negotiations would fail. But when he visited Ankara the foreign minister told him to continue the dialogue. Obviously Ankara and Athens were cooperating on this question.

At their first meeting for the fourth round on 21 September 1970 Denktash complained that he had made concessions on the 70:30 relation, the veto of the vice-president, the security forces, the separate majorities, the election of president and vice-president etc. but the Greek side had not moved at all. Nevertheless, the two agreed to go on negotiating. By mid-December Denktash submitted a compromise on the question of the hierarchy structure of the autonomous administration. Clerides inwardly agreed with it and when he reported to Makarios he strongly recommended accepting Denktash's proposal. He warned him that one day Ankara would consider the talks useless and finish them. Should there be any incidents a Turkish invasion could take place. Makarios was not impressed and instructed Clerides to reject Denktash's proposals at their next meeting on 21 December 1970. Makarios was not ready to accept a partnership, not even in the limited version suggested by Denktash. He wanted the Turkish Cypriots to be politically a minority.

In his memoirs Clerides bitterly states that the solution offered by Denktash and rejected by Makarios was better by far than the so-called High Level Agreement which Makarios and Denktash signed in 1977, and the catastrophe of 1974 would never have happened. There remains the sad statement that, once again, an opportunity to solve the Cyprus problem was gambled away.

In the second half of February 1971 there were constant student riots which grew such proportions that on 12 March the army intervened, forcing Demirel to resign. Nihat Erim became the new prime minister and Osman Olcay foreign minister. In early April it was announced that Denktash would go to Ankara to talk with Erim. Clerides and Denktash decided to interrupt the talks until the latter's return. The new Turkish government advocated a tougher course. Via the German ambassador Makarios was informed that if he continued to reject compromises the negotiations would be terminated.

On 27 April 1971 Denktash submitted his package solution in the form of a long letter. After listing his hitherto concessions he presented his ideas on self-administration: there had to be a central self-administration authority. The subordination of the local autonomy administration under the District Commissioner was not acceptable. He expected that the Greek side, also, would make concessions. His aim was to modify the constitution in such a way that it would function again and not prepare the way for enosis. Then a list followed with all concessions made by him which practically were Makarios' 13 points of 1963. Finally, he expressed his hope that the Greek side would show itself to be a bit generous.

From here on until the official end of the talks on 20 September 1971 the talks were making progress. Makarios obliged Clerides not to make any concessions. Denktash presented himself as flexible. In August he stated that he had accepted all 13 points of Makarios and even some additional ones. During the negotiations he had aimed at the security of his community, never at partition of the island. The wish for local autonomy did not mean the creation of a state within the state. Denktash went into the details which showed clearly that on most questions the two sides were very close, with the exception of autonomy. Clerides' answer was a repetition of the well known positions of Makarios. He stressed that the Greek side was aiming at a permanent solution, that partnership did not mean collective but proportional equality. He had nothing against a functional federation but he rejected a central organ of local autonomy. The arguments of the two protagonists were going in circles. The negotiations had reached a dead end.

The negotiations continued until July 1974. The Turkish Cypriot side was flexible and in 1972 Clerides and Denktash found another compromise solution. But Makarios rejected it, again. Later Clerides blamed himself that he had not resisted Makarios and resigned as negotiator, but as such a move would have caused harm to Makarios he couldn't do it. Thus the negotiations continued until the coup of 1974.

Before we continue describing further developments we will throw a glance at a rather bizarre affair which has haunted the literature on the subject. On 2 June 1971 NATO foreign ministers met in Lisbon. During this conference foreign undersecretary Palamas and foreign minister Olcay came together. Allegedly a secret agreement was made between Greece and Turkey to divide Cyprus. This allegation was made for the first time during a conference in Washington in February 1975 but neither then, nor later, was it scientifically proven. Nevertheless, this story was taken up by many authors, repeated and even enriched with new details, of course, without giving any verifiable source. This conspiracy interpretation of the Lisbon talks proved to be penetrating and persistent. In reality the two foreign ministers agreed to exert influence on the respective communities to continue the talks and press for more flexibility. Should the talks fail Ankara and Athens would reopen their dialogue.

Indeed, Papadopoulos urged Makarios in a letter of 18 June to be more accommodating towards the Turkish Cypriots, after all, they had accepted the 13 points. Should the talks collapse because of Makarios and a crisis occur Athens would leave him out in the rain. Makarios was not impressed and counterattacked by leaking the letter to the press which promptly denounced Papadopoulos a traitor of Hellenic ideals accusing him of sacrificing Cyprus to the Turks. Makarios himself protested against the threat. The press wrote that Makarios had allegedly said that he had outlived 13 prime ministers of Greece and he would survive a fourteenth as well. When Athens reminded him of the national centre's claim of leadership Makarios answered on 4 August officially by a cautiously worded letter to Papadopoulos. Principally he agreed with the claim but he rejected that Athens had the final word on the Cyprus question if the national future of the Greek Cypriots was at stake. Obviously Makarios wanted to avoid a breach. At the end of August he suggested a meeting with Papadopoulos in Athens.

These talks took place on 3 and 4 September. The local self-administration was the main topic of the talks. Makarios vehemently rejected the appointment of a Turkish minister for these affairs because this would lead to separation. He preferred the status created by the treaty of Zurich. Papadopoulos and Makarios agreed that in view of the political and military situation enosis was excluded. Cyprus had to remain an independent sovereign state which was governed by the majority with the privileged minority. But these talks, too, did not bring about a result on the question of autonomy. It was decided that the inter-communal talks should continue. The personal relationship between Makarios and Papadopoulos remained strained. At the end of the visit a meaningless communique was published.

1971-1974: ON THE WAY TO THE CATASTROPHE: EOKA B

The way into the crisis 1971-1972
As will be remembered, Grivas had been ordered back to Greece following the Kofinou crisis in November 1967 and the junta had put him under quasi house arrest. In 1969 he began to make plans for the establishment of an underground organisation which should topple Makarios and bring about the union of Cyprus with Greece. Though these ideas were similar to those developed by EM, Grivas did not want any connection with it and kept his distance. When EM was smashed in 1970 he told his supporters in Cyprus to recruit its members for the future EOKA B. (B stands for the Greek letter Vita which is at the same time ordinal number II).

On 1 April 1970 the anniversary of the beginning of the EOKA struggle Grivas waged war against the Cyprus government at a big rally. In Cyprus the pro-Grivas newspaper *Patris* began to agitate against Makarios. In autumn and winter preparations began for Grivas' return to Cyprus. A new hiding place was prepared. First hideout-places and weapon depots were built in the Pantadaktylos mountains. Armed groups were set up. Adherents of Grivas began with enthusiasm the new struggle for enosis. At private meetings and in discussions there was talk about a new epos of EOKA and one came to the conclusion that only an armed struggle against Makarios could save enosis.

On the 1971 anniversary of the beginning of the EOKA struggle Grivas delivered another speech in which he announced that he was, once more, ready to fight for enosis. In Cyprus Grivas' activities had been watched suspiciously. There were thoughts about whether one should allow him to return legally to keep him under control. However, on 29 July a letter from him was read at the congress of the Cypriot student organisation in Athens in which he insulted Makarios and called the students to armed resistance. Grivas was now 73 years old but had not become one brass farthing wiser, as this speech proves. He could not refrain from showing off at times. The consequences did not interest him. But with this speech Grivas terminated any possibility of cooperation with Makarios.

On 28 August Grivas managed to abscond from the control of the Greek secret police and go on board a Kaïki which brought him to Cyprus. On 31 August he went ashore near Pissouri, west of the British Akrotiri base. His return had been organised by him and his friends alone. The often heard allegation that ESA chief Ioannidis had been involved cannot be proved. On the contrary, the Greek government was rather shocked when Grivas' arrival became known because it was afraid of a conflict with Turkey.

No sooner had Grivas arrived at his new hideout than he began pouring out orders which he wrote down in his diary like in the days of the first EOKA: The name of the new organisation was to be EOKA B. Section commanders were to be appointed. He ordered the setting up of two death squads consisting of five men each of which should operate independently and get their orders directly from him. He demanded a detailed report on the preparations made so far.

EOKA B was structured according to the centralised conspiratorial model of EOKA A. Grivas was the chief who controlled everything. There was no staff only aides de camps. Grivas divided Cyprus into sections and appointed section commanders. The most important sector was Limassol where EM, too, had its main weight. Each member of EOKA B - with the exception of old fighters of EOKA A whose oath was regarded as still valid - had to swear a solemn oath on the holy Trinity. It said that the aim of the organisation was enosis. Members owed absolute allegiance to the leader and promised to keep the organisation's secrets if questioned . The members would honour the weapons given to them and never surrender them to the enemy. Whoever broke his oath would be executed. Again Grivas succeeded in recruiting many young people, abusing their youthful idealism.

In the beginning EOKA B, too, suffered from a scarcity of weapons. A few of the old fighters had kept their weapons from the time of the liberation struggle but these were few. Thus Grivas ordered raids on weapon depots of the National Guard but these were well guarded as a rule. Occasionally there was a collusion between members of the National Guard and EOKA B by which Grivas' adherents could steal a greater number of weapons. Sympathisers in ELDYK found ways to accord weapons to EOKA B. Later Kalashnikovs were bought in Lebanon and smuggled to Cyprus. Another problem was money. EOKA A had been financed by the church but this source of money was no longer prolific. The building up of the organisation was slowed down so much that it made a real appearance only as late as 1973.

All through autumn 1971 Makarios made an effort with declarations and interviews to keep Grivas from burning the bridges behind him and beginning the armed struggle. This would only lead to civil war and self-destruction. At the same time, however, Makarios began to take measures against the armed groups. As he could not rely upon the National Guard or the police he decided in November to set up a special police unit, the so-called *efedriko* (reserve). Grivas was not impressed by Makarios' appeals nor by the concrete counter-measures. In November 1971 he founded a political front organisation, the ESEA (Epitropi Syntonismou Enotikou Agona - Committee for the Coordination of the Struggle for Enosis). Grivas regarded himself in the possession of the panacea of truth and as he did not succumb to self-doubts, in his hideout his ideas hardened and gained a programmed character. He wanted to purge the nation of all antinational elements and this he would achieve by a coup d'état and the elimination of Makarios.

As neither the National Guard nor the police was ready to cede any weapons to the *efedriko* Makarios ordered weapons from the ČSSR which were delivered in January 1972, brought by secret ways into the country and stored in safe places. Of course, this was observed by EOKA B and some members complained about this to the Greek ambassador, Panagiotakos. He informed Athens. Palamas reacted strongly and demanded that the weapons should be given to the National Guard. Makarios, of course, rejected this.

On 9 February a crisis meeting took place in Athens during which the situation in Cyprus was discussed. It was decided to send a diplomatic note to Makarios demanding the immediate handover of the weapons to UNFICYP, the forming of a government of national unity and the recognition of the authority of Athens as the national centre to whom Nicosia owed obedience. Orally Panagiotakos should request that Makarios should quit politics. Grivas, too, should be made to leave Cyprus. In order to avoid possible irritations from the Turkish side Athens informed Ankara about these measures.

On 10 February 1972 Panagiotakos visited Makarios and gave him the note. After reading out the text of the note he pulled a slip of paper out of his pocket and read the text of the verbal note asking Makarios and Grivas to withdraw to private life. Panagiotakos' attitude during this scene showed that he enjoyed playing the proconsul of Athens. Makarios understood that he was fighting with his back to the wall for his political survival. He knew he needed allies and the backing of the people. If he succeeded in winning both he would have new room for political manoeuvring. His first reaction was to bring the Americans on his side: he would reject the note but he was ready to hand over the weapons to UNFICYP provided Grivas left Cyprus and dissolved his armed groups. Additionally, he was ready to reshuffle his government, but only if the impression was avoided that he did this on orders from Athens.

Panagiotakos, on the other hand, tried his best to blacken Makarios with the Americans as a friend of the communists. Makarios was a nobody who had forgotten that Athens was the centre of the Greek world whose order one had to obey. If he did not comply with the demands of Athens there would be a popular upheaval during which he would be killed. He, Panagiotakos, had asked him to resign and leave the country. If he did not obey he would have to bear the consequences. Grivas, on the other hand, would obey orders.

While on 12 February 1972 the Cyprus government sat, Panagiotakos gave a press conference during which he made known the content of the note, adding arrogantly that this was no invitation to a dialogue. Athens did not expect an answer but execution. The government had to be reshuffled and adherents of Grivas integrated. If Makarios rejected the demand he would bear the responsibility for the consequences. On 14 February the text of the note was given to the press in Athens. In Nicosia it became known that Makarios and his government were not ready to accept the demands of the note. The rejection was made in a factual way because one did not want to add fuel to the fire. Nicosia was set on mediation. Panagiotakos began to row back: he regretted that some of his statements at the press conference had been misunderstood.

In order to obtain the support of the Americans Makarios started a brilliant tactical manoeuvre on 14 February. He made Clerides come and had him informed by the chief of the Cypriot secret service of an allegedly impending coup which should take place the following day. He instructed him to inform the Americans about this and beg for an immediate intervention of the President of the US in Athens in order to stop the coup. Clerides complied and informed ambassador Popper: the Cypriots would fight against a coup and there would be bloodshed. President Nixon should intervene and stop Athens. As Popper knew Clerides' personal integrity he passed the message on to Washington, characterising it as credible.

In Washington this message caused a meeting of the Special Actions Group with security advisor Henry Kissinger in the chair. Though there were some doubts whether a coup was really planned, those present agreed that one could not let Clerides down. Kissinger informed Nixon. Nixon ordered ambassador Tasca to visit Papadopoulos and make it clear to him that the US government was against an overthrow of Makarios and demanded a categorical assurance that nothing would happen. This was done and Papadopoulos assured that neither the Greek troops stationed in Cyprus nor the officers serving in the National Guard would do anything against Makarios or his government. By 17.00 hours Popper had informed Clerides about this and the latter passed it on to Makarios.

Historians, adherents of conspiracy theories, believe that, indeed, a coup was imminent and insinuate that the Americans were involved but produce not one verifiable proof. The fact is, however, that a coup would not have suited Athens' policy. Athens wanted peace on Cyprus and no anger with Turkey. It is exactly the effort to remove Makarios and Grivas from the scene which argues against the coup thesis. The aim was to remove the bone of contention. The formation of a government of nationalists should overcome the differences in the conservative camp. Of course, there were a few officers who would have loved to carry out a coup but they did not yet have the say.

It is known that in Nicosia there had been rumours about an imminent coup for several days and it cannot be excluded that these were used by Makarios' people or had even been disseminated byem. Makarios knew that the Americans would not have intervened because of the Athens' demand for his resignation. Therefore the rumours were inflated to an imminent putsch. The trick functioned, the Americans intervened in Athens and the Greek government was forced to postpone their plan to get rid of Makarios for the time being. Apparently, Makarios was de facto under American protection. By his rude behaviour and diplomatic bumblers Panagiotakos himself had made sure that these tactics were successful. This interpretation is corroborated by the fact that he was already giving in. Makarios had successfully managed to extricate himself from a hopeless situation.

The rumours had alarmed the population and induced mass rallies on 14 and 15 February. One day later Makarios declared that each trial to enforce a solution would be rejected. Panagiotakos left Cyprus on 17 February for good. The crisis was over and Makarios the victor of this first round in the quarrel with Athens. But no sooner had the crisis been overcome than a new attack began.

Panagiotakos had even incited the Bishops of Kyrenia (Kyprianos). Kition (Anthimos) and Paphos (Gennadios) against Makarios. Kyprianos hated Makarios because he had been elected Archbishop in place of him. Anthimos and Gennadios had been elected with Makarios' backing and had been on his side during the first years of the republic. But after the events of 1967 they had fallen out with him and since 1972 all three had been inimical to him. On 24 February they requested a meeting of the Holy Synod. Makarios agreed. Now both sides began to gather supporters. In early March it was obvious that the Bishops wanted to overthrow Makarios as president and as Archbishop.

When on 2 March the Synod met, a huge number of clerics protested against the behaviour of the Bishops. Makarios opened the session by giving a survey of the situation created by the Greek diplomatic note but the Bishops were not interested in this. Kyprianos demanded that Makarios resign immediately because canon law did not allow him to have a secular office. Though Makarios had been informed that this demand would come up he exploded and allegedly roared against them so loudly that he was heard in neighbouring offices. He accused the Bishops of having assembled illegally and of conspiring against him. Archbishop Ieronymos of Athens told him over the phone that the Greek government did not demand his resignation as president, let alone his deposition as Archbishop. Makarios should tell this to the members of the Synod and ask them to refrain from any public statement. This was done and thus the rebellion was curbed for the time being. A little later Makarios reminded the Bishops that the Archbishop had always been ethnarch as well. Their reproach had thus been baseless.

At the same time he told Athens that the weapons had been put under the control of UNFICYP. He was ready to accept the claim for leadership of the national centre but then followed a flat rejection: If Athens steered a course which would not be accepted by the Greek Cypriots, their opinion would have priority because they would have to bear and live with the consequences. Papadopoulos insisted in his answer on Athenian primacy but stressed that he would appreciate a return to the status quo ante. Thus the conflict was ended.

Makarios knew that EOKA B was a deadly danger. If it united with his enemies in the National Guard the situation in Cyprus would become critical and this the more so as he could not trust the police and the organising of the *efedriko* had become difficult because the weapons earmarked for it had been put under the control of UNFICYP. In view of this situation he tried to find an arrangement with Grivas. Through an intermediary he contacted Grivas and suggested a meeting. After quite some haggling about security questions and discussion themes on 26 March 1972 the historical meeting took place in the house of a niece of Makarios. The house was secured by EOKA B gunmen, the neighbouring house by Makarios' security forces. Makarios and Grivas arrived punctually.

The talks lasted for almost two hours. As they took place behind closed doors there were no witnesses and no minutes. The only reliable sources about what was talked about are some letters by Grivas and Makarios but they only allow a vague reconstruction of the topics discussed. According to them Grivas demanded from Makarios to stop his present Cyprus policy and to come out in favour of enosis. Moreover, Grivas allegedly asked Makarios to resign and suggested an election campaign on the basis of self-determination/enosis. Makarios rejected this since it would lead to partition and double enosis. Obviously the meeting had no results.

In an order of the day Grivas announced that he was ready to cooperate with everybody who fought for enosis, even with the devil. He was now 74 years old and even if his strength was waning he was ready to fight against all enemies of enosis. On this he had sworn an oath. Grivas' letters were highly emotional, pathetic and histrionic and reminded one of his appeals of the EOKA A struggle. He was convinced of his historic mission and incapable of recognising a rational alternative. The consequences for Cyprus and his people did not interest him. It was Grivas' old egocentric attitude of *après moi le déluge*.

In early April Athens let it be understood that one would appreciate a return to the old friendly relations. In order to achieve this certain ministers and high ranking officials, who had a negative influence on the bilateral relations, had to be dismissed and replaced by persons of mutual confidence. Foreign minister Kyprianou and a few others hindered this. On 3 May Makarios announced a cabinet reshuffle. On 5 May 1972 Kyprianou resigned. On 15 June the cabinet reshuffle took place. Ioannis Christofidis became the new foreign minister. But none of the new ministers was an adherent of Grivas. Thus the crisis between Athens and Nicosia ended.

The EOKA B Terror 1972-1973

In 1972 there were almost no armed incidents. Grivas was busy with staff work for his takeover. In September his people managed to smuggle weapons and munitions worth $ 486,000 from Lebanon to Cyprus. In comparison with the small quantity which had found its way from the depots of the National Guard and other sources to EOKA B, this was an enormous increase in firepower. In December the US embassy estimated that Grivas' force counted a few hundred well-trained and well-equipped fighters ready for action. They considered these groups capable of making attempts on the life of members of the government, blowing up telecommunication facilities and the airport. In January 1973 it became clear that the attacks would begin soon. The question was only whether these attacks would happen before or after the presidential elections on 8 February.

In his hideout in Limassol Grivas produced scores of orders, appeals and proclamations. Towards the end of the non-bloody actions he praised the victories and assured that enosis would be achieved. His forces were able to attack at random. The enemy, i.e., Makarios, and the Cyprus government had to be beaten mercilessly. A brilliant victory was on the horizon like Aurora. Military lyrics about the brave Greek soldiers followed.

The attacks by EOKA B caused Makarios to search for rear cover in Athens. Therefore on 24 January 1973 he sent the new foreign minister, Ioannis Christofidis, to Athens and he managed to persuade Papadopoulos to make a public statement in favour of Makarios. In a radio speech Papadopoulos made it known that the Greek government did not support Grivas' activities in any way. Grivas was not bothered. In February 1973 he began to plan a coup for July 1973. This operation received the code name Apollo. First EOKA B would attack and the National Guard would follow up. The Apollo plan was meticulously worked out as if done by a staff; sub-plans carried names like *kenavos* (flash) und *seismos* (earthquake). There were plans for the takeover in certain towns and villages. Certain Greek officers of the National Guard were fully briefed.

This episode shows, on the one hand, how well entrenched the circles of the Greek para-kratos around Ioannidis were, since they could defy the orders of Papadopoulos and, on the other hand, how far the National Guard had been infiltrated so that Grivas' plans to cooperate with it during his coup were not unreal. The leadership of the police still was on Makarios' side but the middle ranks which had been appointed by Georkatzis bore a deep grudge against Makarios and were open to the insinuations of those Greek officers. The question arose whether Makarios would succeed in building up the *efedriko* in time so that he could smash EOKA B before Grivas started his coup.

In March 1973 the rebel Bishops tried once more to force Makarios to resign. This time, however, Makarios was prepared and he hit back. He called an enlarged synod together in which the Patriarchs of Alexandria and Antiochia and some other high prelates participated. The Synod found the rebel Bishops guilty of schism and defrocked them.

In April the first bomb attacks of EOKA B began which caused some deaths. As the Americans were afraid of a big crisis they warned the staff of the National Guard by informing them of concrete Turkish invasion plans. This caused Grivas to stop his coup plans temporarily but already in July he ordered new bomb attacks and the planning of the assassination of Makarios. But now the *efedriko* responded efficiently. Lots of EOKA B members were arrested. Grivas retaliated with more bombs but Lyssaridis' paramilitaries paid them in their own coin. A minister was kidnapped by EOKA B. Civil War was close by.

This caused Papadopoulos to interfere via the radio: he condemned sharply Grivas' enosis-course. The solution to the Cyprus problem would be found in the local inter-communal talks on the basis of an independent state. Grivas reacted indignantly and appealed to the radicals in the Athenian junta to overthrow Papadopoulos. In the following weeks Grivas undertook a media offensive against Papadopoulos, slandering him in a most ugly way. On 7 October 1973 an attempt on Makarios' life was made by a bomb operated by remote control which miscarried.

Grivas had not been informed about this action and when he heard about it he believed that it had been a hoax by the government. He ordered an investigation and when he discovered that EOKA B of Limassol had been behind it he fell silent. This in turn made Makarios continue his accusations and point out that Grivas' silence was a confession of guilt. Grivas couldn't say anything against this because otherwise he would have had to admit that he no longer controlled his followers.

On 20 October 1973 the new Greek prime minister, S. Markezinis, stated that the inter-communal dialogue had to be resumed and a solution found to which the Cypriots would agree. He did not intend to enforce a solution on Cyprus. Obviously Grivas could not expect any help from the Greek government and EOKA B would remain under continuous pressure from the *efedriko* and be more and more weakened so that the danger emanating from it would be lessened. Without any help from outside EOKA B, also, would suffer from the same erosion process which had led ESEA to decide to continue the struggle for enosis with peaceful political means. The change to Markezinis meant a certain liberalisation of the regime which unfortunately changed the balance of power within the junta and the takeover by the radicals around Ioannidis.

Ioannidis, Kissinger and Cyprus 1973/4

In summer 1973 Papadopoulos had reached the summit of power. He was regent, prime minister, minister of defence and foreign relations. No Greek politician had ever had such an amount of power in the 20th century. But with this concentration of power Papadopoulos isolated himself from his colleagues, and his enemies waited for an opportunity. His liberalisation measures provoked the radicals. Though Papadopoulos noticed that the opposition grew, he did not recognise where the real threat was. The real danger came from the frustrated officers in the army. These were colleagues of Papadopoulos in the higher hierarchy of the junta but these would only act if he made serious mistakes or got into conflict with middle rank army officers. But these middle ranks, majors and colonels were decisive as had been proven by the coup on 21 April 1967. If these turned away from him and allied with the radicals it would become dangerous. This happened when Markezinis announced the holding of elections because they would have ended the random access of the military to funds of the state.

At the end of October the radicals around Ioannidis decided to overthrow Papadopoulos and to assume power. On 14 November a spontaneous student unrest of the polytechnic began and when police lost control on 17 November the military suppressed the unrest by force. Ioannidis interpreted this as a declaration of the bankruptcy of the regime. But the student unrest did not trigger the new coup as has been written over and over again; perhaps it accelerated it. The coup of the radicals took place on 25 November 1973 copying exactly the model of 21 April. Papadopoulos was put under house arrest. The commander of the first army corps, Faidon Gizikis, became president. Adamantios Androutsopoulos, who had been minister of finance and interior under Papadopoulos became prime minister. Ioannidis did not take over any office. He preferred to pull strings from behind. The Americans were not involved in the changeover although this had been asserted many times.

In the days before the coup, i.e., between 14 and 19 November the annual seminar of the *Center for Mediterranean Studies of the American Universities Field Staff* took place in Rome. The "seminario tis Romis" is also part of those legends entwining Cypriot history as is the Lisbon agreement. According to public opinion of Greece and Cyprus this seminar was a sinister American conspiracy which sealed the fate of Cyprus. In Greek newspapers one could read that the Americans allegedly gave the Turks the green light for their intervention in summer 1974. The adherents of conspiracies in history saw the CIA at work there.

In this annual seminar graduate American political scientists met, among them postdocs, who study problems of the Mediterranean countries. These students specialised in one country, visited it for some time to study its problems. Then they wrote a research paper on their findings. Already in the past there had been a course on Cyprus and Denktash, as well as Clerides, had spoken to the students visiting Cyprus and had answered their questions. But in 1973 there took place a kind of seminar within the seminar. There were the usual events for the students but at the same time high calibre Cyprus specialists in politics and economics from the US, the UK, Greece, Turkey and Cyprus met to discuss possible solution perspectives of the Cyprus problem. Clerides and Denktash had come from Cyprus. These meetings were not open to the public.

Thus the seminar had the character of a meeting of a think tank comparable to the British Chatham House. It was an independent discussion forum where specialists of different origins presented their opinions. The results were made known to the desk officers responsible for Cyprus in the various foreign ministries. It is, however, unknown whether these pieces of information found their way up to the top to those who took the decisions or not, though this is doubtful. By no means was the "seminario tis Romis" a sinister American conspiracy.

For Cyprus the change from Papadopoulos to Ioannidis spelled disaster. Papadopoulos had practised realpolitik in the case of Cyprus. In February he had been fuming against Makarios and demanded his resignation but he had quieted down and returned to his previous course: independence and solution of the problem by inter-communal negotiations. He knew that any attempt to push enosis would mean war with Turkey ending in a Greek defeat and, at least, separation of Cyprus if not annexations by Turkey. Ioannidis did not have a clue about this and he was not adaptive,as his behaviour had shown in the past. This meant that the smallest case could induce him to intervene in Cyprus and this would lead to a catastrophe.

But this, however, was not the only change which would influence events in Cyprus. In September 1973 Henry Kissinger became Foreign Secretary. Scarcely in office, his attention was absorbed by the following events between October 1973 and June 1974: The Yom Kippur war, his trip to Moscow, his first journey to the Near East, a new visit to China, the Geneva conference, the shuttle diplomacy in the Near East and finally the energy crisis caused by OPEC and the constantly worsening Watergate scandal. Indeed, during the first six months of 1974 the Watergate crisis reached its climax. Practically, the US was without a government. Kissinger took over the role of the president. In view of this situation and Kissinger's engagement in world politics it is scarcely astonishing that Greece and Cyprus were not topics for him until March 1974.

In February 1974 the desk officer responsible for Cyprus, Thomas Boyatt, noticed that something was brewing there. Boyatt, who spoke Greek fluently, had been first secretary at the US embassy in Nicosia from 1967 to 1970. From 1971 to 1974 he was director of the Cyprus branch of the State Department. Since late 1973 and increasingly in 1974 he noticed that the radical forces of the junta, of KYP and in the military were supporting those forces in Cyprus who wanted to topple Makarios and achieve enosis. From personal experience in Cyprus he knew that this would lead to a Turkish invasion.

In view of this he wrote a message to be sent to Ambassador Tasca instructing him to go to Ioannidis and say to him in plain language that the US was against any action in Cyprus. Boyatt's superior, however, rejected the text and Boyatt rewrote it in more moderate form. But at the next level of the State Department it was disapproved of again. In the meantime Ambassador Tasca had received an invitation to a hearing of the Foreign Affairs Committee of the House of Representatives and appeared in Washington. In order to harmonise his testimony with the ideas of the State Department a meeting was held on 20 March 1974 in the presence of Kissinger.

This was the first time that Kissinger had concerned himself with Greece and Cyprus since he had become Secretary of State. His questions proved that he did not have a clue about what was happening. Finally Tasca arrived at the crux of the matter: in Greece there had always been a "foreign factor" intervening in Greece's policy. At the moment the US was this factor and so deeply involved in Greek politics that even non-intervention would be interpreted as intervention in favour of someone, in this case Ioannidis. Tasca wanted instructions about what he should answer to the questions of the Congressmen. Kissinger could not or would not take a decision. After further discussion it was agreed that the decision should be postponed and the present policy continue. Tasca should keep a low profile in Athens. Kissinger was not interested in this topic because he was making world policy and did not recognize that in Cyprus something unpleasant was brewing. A warning, as in March 1972, would have been overdue.

Boyatt, however, did not give up. At several meetings in the State Department in April he warned that Ioannidis was preparing something in Cyprus. But each time his warnings fell on deaf ears. It was obvious that Kissinger's hands-off-the-junta policy worked and produced anticipatory obedience among the higher echelons of the State Department.

On 7 May Kissinger met Gromyko in Cyprus in the framework of his mediation between Syria and Israel. Makarios played the perfect host and Kissinger gained the impression that no crisis was around the corner. Exactly at this time further warnings reached Kissinger but he ignored them. He rejected an intervention in Athens, after all one could not mingle in the internal affairs of an ally.

In June, too, warnings arrived constantly. Ioannidis said openly to Tasca and his CIA liaison man that Makarios had to be knocked off. Finally on 29 June a rather watered down version of Boyatt's original message of February, intended to stop Ioannidis, was sent to Athens. But Tasca was on leave and the deputy chief of mission charged a female diplomat with this task. Later it was found out that this woman did not go to Ioannidis directly but had the message conveyed by a third party. One can imagine how little such a demarche impressed the ESA chief, conveyed to him by a woman. Boyatt's rescue effort failed because of the incompetence of the Athens embassy.

Indeed, Ioannidis did not pay any attention to this mild warning. But in order to prevent a last minute tougher intervention Ioannidis assured the Athens CIA chief that the Greek government would do nothing against Makarios. This was passed on to Washington where everybody was leaving for the weekend without worrying. Due to the time shift the Americans learned as late as the early morning hours of 15 July that the coup had begun in Nicosia.

In a great part of Greek and Cypriot historiography Henry Kissinger is blamed for the coup. For these historians the coup is an American conspiracy with the Athens junta to topple Makarios. Kissinger himself asserts that he was not informed and therefore did not intervene. On the one hand, this is wrong and, on the other, it is an assertion designed solely to avert the claim of his real responsibility. Makarios annoyed him and therefore he allowed things to run, Makarios, after all only a stumbling block, was to be removed. Had Kissinger been aware of the real consequences, namely the armed Turkish intervention, he would probably have intervened.

But at that time he was occupied with Near Eastern politics and conducted grand diplomacy. He believed he could run the State Department from his plane, trusting that from there he would be warned of critical situations. He overlooked that he himself had prevented this by his own attitude on the Cyprus question. The upper echelons of the State Department practised anticipatory obedience, i.e., they behaved as they thought Kissinger expected them to behave, they left him alone. There is another point which should not be neglected: Henry Kissinger's arrogance. He believed that with his high intellect he could see through each problem but in this case he stumbled over his own inability to understand the stupidity and narrow-mindedness of the brain of a Greek military policeman. He considered it impossible that someone could commit such a lunatic deed as Ioannidis did. But unfortunately this was reality. Kissinger did, indeed, understand very little of Cyprus and Greece.

This chapter would not be complete if we did not register Kissinger's behaviour against Boyatt, with his cumbersome warnings. Kissinger deposed him from his office and sent him on leave. After that he had him participate in a qualifying training programme. During the hearings of the House of Representatives Boyatt contained himself and Kissinger thanked him by making him chief of the US mission in Santiago. This was the reward for not having blackened Kissinger in Congress.

The Countdown to the Coup, January-August 1974

The change from Papadopoulos to Ioannidis had been welcomed by EOKA B frantically. Grivas announced the end of the cease-fire which he had ordered when the Markezinis government had taken over. Now he ordered an offensive against Makarios and his "regime". Members of the government and of the security forces, policemen, and especially Makarios, should be killed like lightening. A motorised rapid deployment force should be set up which should support the attacks of the partisans. All this was pointless. The original aim, enosis, had been lost, was out of sight. In December assassination attempts began but before these could assume big proportions Grivas died of a heart attack on 26 January 1974.

In order to make a gesture to his adherents the government ordered a three day national mourning period during which Grivas lay in state in the open air in the garden of the house where his hideout had been during the EOKA A struggle. A general amnesty was proclaimed for all EOKA B crimes. The prison doors opened and EOKA B inmates were set free. Whoever came out of his hideout and handed over his weapons was free. As the funeral service was held by the three rebel Bishops nobody from the government or the official church appeared.

In Cyprus Grivas is venerated as the leader of the struggle for independence by many of the bourgeois camp. His role during the German occupation of Greece in WWII is as unknown as his activities in post-war Greece when he was one of the main organisers of the *parakratos*. Both things do not interest the Cypriot because these activities did not concern Cyprus. The perception is reduced to the EOKA A time and for this he is elevated in the "pantheon of the immortals". The fact that more Greeks died than British soldiers is repressed as are his later activities, though these triggered the Tillyria bombardment and the 1967 Kofinou affair played a major role in the inter-communal civil war. For many years people never talked publicly about EOKA B. The image of the "hero of the struggle of liberation" outshines the dark chapters of his biography, though these had more influence on the fate of Cyprus than the liberation struggle.

After Grivas' death, inside EOKA and ESEA a struggle about his succession and the future course began. The radicals wanted to continue the course of terror, the moderates end it. In May 1974 Ioannidis intervened and put the remnants of EOKA B under his control. During this time Greek foreign policy sailed into heavy weather in connection with the beginning of the Aegean conflict with Turkey. In order to restore the prestige of the regime by a success in April, Ioannidis began to talk about an action against Makarios. At a meeting of the junta it was decided to do something against Makarios but only after a thorough check.

In the meantime, the *efedriko* inflicted heavy blows on EOKA B. Police interrogations proved Greek officers of the National Guard were behind it and these were directed from Athens. Their aim was the disposal of Makarios and the seizure of power in Cyprus. When in March 1974 the junta tried to infiltrate EOKA B members as officer cadets into the National Guard the first clash appeared because Makarios rejected this. Moreover, he used the opportunity to try to purge the National Guard of all officers who had close relations with EOKA B, thus trying to get the National Guard under his control. In view of EOKA B's weakness and the escalation of the Aegean conflict Makarios obviously felt strong enough to risk a clash with his opponents in the National Guard.

In May and June tension between Athens and Nicosia rose. At a meeting of the military and the civilian junta leaders it became clear that the chief of the General Staff, Bonanos, and foreign minister Tetenes as well as prime minister Androutsopoulos tried to stop Ioannidis: Bonanos explained that the details of a move in Cyprus had to be analysed scrupulously. President Gizikis and Androutsopoulos agreed. But Ioannidis did not answer because he continued to dwell on the topic behind the backs of the others in personal talks with trusted officers in Greece and Cyprus.

Ambassador Kranidiotis warned Makarios that a coup was imminent. Makarios, however, did not believe it because Ioannidis had not dared to do it so far and now he could not succeed because he, Makarios, would clear the situation in the National Guard. He would demand the removal of all Greek officers and replace them with Cypriots. In mid-June the junta met again. Cyprus was the main topic. Ioannidis said that Makarios was a catastrophe for Cyprus and Greece and therefore he had to cease exerting political and ecclesiastical power and had to be removed. Androutsopoulos agreed. Bonanos tried to gain time: before one proceeded to topple Makarios one should analyse the possible reactions of Turkey. Greece was not yet ready for an armed confrontation. President Gizikis did not utter one word but Ioannidis rejected Bonanos' arguments: in Cyprus all eventualities had been planned. Bonanos realised that Ioannidis had acted behind his back. He was so depressed by the course of developments that he allegedly thought of resigning but did not do it, with the usual excuse in such cases - he wanted to prevent worse developments.

In the meantime Ioannidis had ordered the rest of EOKA B to start assassination attempts. This they did but the *efedriko* hit back and by the end of June 1974 EOKA B was practically smashed. In the eyes of Ioannidis EOKA B was finished; the coup would have to be executed by his own people in the National Guard and ELDYK. Extremely infuriated, he ordered them to proceed with the preparations for the coup. In this situation Makarios, who totally misinterpreted Ioannidis' psychology, decided to provoke a breach between Athens and Nicosia in order to get rid of the threat. Probably he expected that in view of the charges against Ioannidis he would take cover and risk nothing but Ioannidis reacted even more aggressively.

On 1 July 1974 the Cypriot Council of Ministers decided to reduce service in the National Guard from 24 to 14 months. By this the number of active soldiers and consequently the officers necessary would be considerably reduced. Thus the danger originating from the National Guard could be lessened and it would offer an opportunity to get rid of the pro-junta officers. But now Makarios committed a tactical error: instead of sending these "superfluous" officers noiselessly back to Greece within the framework of the restructuring process Makarios made this public by sending a letter to Gizikis on 3 July 1974 and giving it to the press at the same time.

This letter was a kind of settling of accounts with the junta and contained a list of all "sins". In the past it was claimed that this letter triggered the coup against Makarios which is utterly wrong because a putsch had been decided on in early June. The final decision for the coup was taken on 2 July, the day when Makarios wrote the letter, by Ioannidis and Bonanos. It would take place on 15 July under the lead of brigadier Michail Georgitsis. When Georgitsis voiced his concern about a Turkish intervention Bonanos and Ioannidis reassured him: he need not be afraid as they had assurances that there would be no intervention by anyone because they had "rear cover". Both did not mention where the rear cover would come from but Georgitsis received the impression that the Americans were meant. They agreed to meet once more the following day to discuss the details of the realisation of the coup and this they did. The discussion was not very productive because they did not have enough information about the situation in Cyprus.

In the following days Makarios received numerous warnings about an imminent coup but he did not take them seriously. He was in contact with people in Athens who all had one thing in common: they were not involved in the conspiracy. Obviously Makarios did not perceive the real power structure, he did not try to contact and influence Ioannidis. The latter, however, watched Makarios' effort to find a peaceful solution closely and allowed the persons whom Makarios addressed to negotiate freely, thus, Makarios received the impression that he was conducting real negotiations. Practically, he became the victim of self-deception and a highly refined distraction manoeuvre organised by Ioannidis.

But Ioannidis was no strategist but a tactician. He was the typical narrow minded regular officer with no knowledge beyond his metier, the military police and the secret police. He wanted to topple Makarios because he hated him and wanted enosis. About the possible consequences of his actions he probably never thought once, believing that the Turkish government would not intervene. Unconsciously he naively relied upon the *xenos paragontas*, the foreign factor, internalised by him, too, i.e., the Americans who had intervened twice when it had become dangerous in the past. As there had been no protests against his course by them he probably interpreted this according to this logic as an approval. Ioannidis did not understand that such a policy would lead to partition. Because not one general had the civil courage to stop him fate, took its course. On 13 July the putschists met at the ELDYK headquarters and fixed the beginning of the coup on 15 July 1974 at 8 o'clock.

1974: COUP, INVASION AND PARTITION

Coup and Countdown to Turkish Intervention, 15-19 July 1974
At 8 o'clock on 15 July 1974 Makarios received a group of the Greek-Orthodox Youth of Cairo in the presidential palace. Suddenly shots were heard and a member of the presidential guard informed him that armoured vehicles and a tank were firing at the palace. The ten guardsmen defended the building as well as they could. Makarios and the children took cover in the corridor of the palais where they were safe. When the eastern wing of the palace began to burn it became clear they had to flee. Makarios and his attendants left the building through a garden door and

followed a path down to the bed of the river Pedaios. The remaining guardsmen brought children down to the basement, where they were secure.

Makarios' flight in a commandeered car led over the eastern slopes of mount Troodos to the presidential summer residence near Platres and ended at Kykko monastery. In the meantime the putschists occupied strategic key positions in Nicosia which partly were strongly defended . In late afternoon they controlled practically all Cyprus with the exception of the Paphos region. Paphos, indeed, was another world. The 17 Greek officers stationed there had not been privy to the coup plans and on 15 July they were on regular duty. When the first news about the putsch arrived in Paphos loyal policemen arrested them. Members of EDEK and AKEL called for resistance. Villagers of the whole area streamed to Paphos to defend democracy. The para-military of Lyssaridis united with the police. The police handed out weapons to those ready to fight. By noon the town was under the control of the followers of Makarios. The proprietor of the local radio shop managed to bring a VHF transmitter on air. This station, "Radio Free Cyprus", appealed to the people to resist the putschists.

In Kykko Makarios heard the transmissions of "Radio Free Cyprus" and went to Paphos. Over the radio he spoke to the people and called for resistance. Thus the story of Makarios' death disseminated by the junta was proved a lie. Georgitsis ordered an advance of the National Guard towards Paphos.

In Nicosia Georgitsis ordered a henchman named Kombokis to try and find a successor for Makarios. When the potential candidates learned that Makarios was alive they rejected the offer. The only person keen to get the job was Nikos Sampson. Kombokis accepted him. Kombokis, not a very intelligent person, did not grasp what mischief he was making with this decision. In the afternoon he organised the swearing-in of Sampson as president by the defrocked Bishop Gennadios. The decision to make Sampson president was the greatest possible mistake of the putschists. Since the times of EOKA A he had been known as a pathological killer and during the 1963 Christmas unrest he had acquired the doubtful reputation of a Turk eater (tourkofagos) who had murdered at least 20 Turkish Cypriots. Sampson was an egomaniac with a sadistic disposition of the worst kind. Without him a peaceful solution might have been found, with him it was impossible: his appointment was the greatest possible provocation for Ankara.

The news of the coup in Cyprus reached the Turkish prime minister Ecevit on a flight from Ankara to Afyon. He came to the conclusion that the coup meant enosis in disguise and he had to intervene. After his return to Ankara Ecevit informed the military about his conclusion. They told him that they had fully elaborated plans for an intervention. In the evening the national security council of Turkey met. It was decided that the intervention would take place on 20 July 1974 and that the political leadership would prepare and cover it by suitable diplomatic mea-sures in London. At the ensuing meeting of the council of ministers the majority agreed but doubted whether the guarantor power, Britain, would participate. After the end of the meeting at 3 a.m. on 16 July 1974 Ecevit went to the General Staff and signed the orders for the armed landing and the occupation of a bridgehead in Cyprus. The preparation for the invasion of Cyprus had begun.

In Washington Henry Kissinger was woken in the early morning of 15 July by the news about the coup. A female staff member of the National Security Council gave him a memorandum in which the opinion was expressed that Ankara would not move. At the meeting of the Special Actions Group at 10.15 undersecretary Sisco supposed that the best thing would be to wait and see. A war between Turkey and Greece should be prevented and the Soviet Union be kept from taking advantage of the situation. The coup in Cyprus was an internal affair of the Greek community. As Kissinger himself had no better idea he fell in line with Sisco. When in the afternoon the news of Makarios' survival came in Boyatt proposed to help restore the Archbishop to his office. When Kissinger was informed about this proposal he rejected it but spoke of a Clerides-solution. This idea originated from the Cypriot ambassador in Washington whose brother had become Sampson's foreign minister on that day.

Kissinger did not consider the advice of the experts on this question. He was of the opinion that the US should steer a hands off course and act only if one's own previously defined interests were affected. The prerequisite for the functioning of such a policy was that all involved played the game according to these rules of power politics and acted rationally. Kissinger did not understand the fact that these rules were not applicable in this part of the world. Neither Greece nor Turkey had pursued an independent policy but had always waited for the "foreign factor"' guidelines. Both countries were American client states and were accustomed to interventions if the Americans did not agree with the course of events. If no directions were given this was interpreted as approval.

Kissinger's policy of maximal flexibility resulted in the opposite - a policy of absolute non commitment which everybody could interpret at random. In this way wrong, or rather no, signals were sent to those who were waiting for such signals from the Americans and now assumed that the signals they received from somewhere were American ones. Kissinger's policy of non-interference meant that he no longer controlled the development, giving free reign to it and thus accelerating it in a direction which the Americans had tried to prevent for years. Of course Kissinger's personal animosity played a role as well. Good relations with Turkey were more important to him than those with Greece. Besides that Kissinger could not conceal his attitude that as a former Harvard professor he was brighter than everyone else.

In Cyprus 16 July 1974 began with fights near Paphos between the adherents of Makarios and the putschists. When tanks arrived from Nicosia Makarios understood that the struggle was lost. He went to the camp of Dutch blue helmets nearby. From there he was taken by helicopter to the British Akrotiri base and from there he flew in a British plane to Malta.

The putschists now controlled the whole island The media then spoke about high losses on both sides. In 2000 a reliable source mentioned 43 dead on the side of the defender. 30 National Guardsmen were killed and so were 18 civilians. 8 Greek officers lost their lives. Sampson erected a terror regime under which chiefly AKEL and PEO members suffered. Now old accounts could be settled and political opponents be humiliated. The right wing fanatics could live out their hatred against communists.

In Ankara Ecevit strove hard to safeguard the pending intervention domestically and interna-tionally. In the morning of 16 July he called all party leaders to a meeting and informed them about the developments. They agreed that he should try to make the British cooperate on the basis of the treaty of guarantee. Therefore the Turkish ambassador in London went to the Foreign Office and suggested consultations with Foreign Minister Callaghan. In the Foreign Office they immediately understood that the Turkish government aspired to a joint military operation on the basis of the Treaty of Guarantee in order to restore the *status quo ante*. Callaghan declared himself ready for talks after 17 July.

Ecevit had given his military guidelines for a limited military intervention: a bridgehead was to be formed on the island which would give the Turkish Cypriots access to the sea and establish a balance of power. As soon as this was achieved the further developments would depend on the then existing situation. The military prepared a double-stage plan. At the end of the first phase diplomacy should get a chance. If nothing came about on this level the military operations would continue.

In Washington the Special Actions Group met again and it became clear that Kissinger still did not grasp the real situation. He believed that the imminent Turkish intervention had the purpose of restoring Makarios. Internationalisation of the present conflict had to be avoided as well as recognition of the Sampson regime. Further discussion proved that Kissinger was insecure and avoided decisions. Finally he asked his people in Athens and Ankara to find out in which direction things were moving.

In Athens during a talk between a CIO liaison man and Ioannidis it became clear that the latter had not the slightest idea that a catastrophe was looming. According to him, contacting Ankara was not necessary as enosis had not been proclaimed. But one would soon talk to the Turks. This conversation once more proved the total incompetence and narrow-mindedness of Ioannidis. He did not understand that in the eyes of the Turkish government with the coup against Makarios, who was the guarantor of Cypriot independence, he had made a decisive step toward enosis, and his tactical manoeuvre not to mention it for the time being was a transparent trick by which no Turkish government would be taken in. If Ioannidis did not contact Ankara this indicates that, unconsciously, he relied upon the Americans who would, as in the past, restrain the Turks. But as they did not do anything to stop the government in Ankara, matters ran their course.

On 17 July 1974 two important conversations took place in London. In order to prepare for these Callaghan asked the Defence Ministry whether it would be possible to restore Makarios forcefully. The answer was positive. In the early afternoon Prime Minister Wilson and Makarios met. The content of their conversation is unknown. The result of the meeting between Makarios and Callaghan was the demand that Athens should respect the treaty of guarantee and withdraw the Greek officers from the island.

In the evening Ecevit, Wilson and Callaghan met in 10 Downing Street. Ecevit demanded the return to the *status quo ante*. Otherwise Turkey would intervene militarily, even unilaterally if necessary. Turkey did not want to act alone but in cooperation with the second guarantor power, Britain. In order to avoid greater bloodshed and a confrontation between Greece and Turkey the UK government should allow the Turkish troops to go ashore through the British bases. Should the UK government not co-operate he would act unilaterally. Wilson rejected the use of the bases for this purpose but suggested calling a conference of the three guarantor powers. At the same time he informed Ecevit that US undersecretary Sisco was on his way to London.

Ecevit disapproved of the conference proposal. The decisive thing was that the Turkish Cypriots got access to the sea. He hoped that the British would not object to this and would persuade the Americans not to repulse it either. Obviously Ecevit was still fearing an American veto. Callaghan replied that he would consider this proposal but had doubts that he could support it. It was obvious that the British tried to extricate themselves from their responsibility as a guarantor power and tried to pass the buck to the Americans. After the end of the meeting Ecevit informed his military in Ankara that there would be no change in the plan and preparation for the intervention should continue.

At about the time when Wilson spoke with Makarios in Washington, the Special Actions Group met. After a survey of the situation it was decided to send Sisco to London for talks with Makarios, Ecevit and the British government. Now Kissinger grasped that the only peaceful solution to the crisis was the return to the *status quo ante*. But he did not want Makarios back and stubbornly insisted on Clerides. If Makarios returned to his office he would move towards the eastern block. Should the Athens government collapse the Greek Left would assume power. When Nixon agreed to the Sisco mission Kissinger instructed him as follows: He should accomplish a six months acting presidency of Clerides. After that elections would be called in which Makarios could participate. In the meantime the inter-communal negotiations should continue and a new agreement should be negotiated. A Clerides presidency would enable Athens and Ankara to find a face-saving solution. These instructions, once more, proved that Kissinger did not have the slightest idea about Cypriot political life and did not heed warnings. In order to enable Sisco to realise these instructions Sisco should have been entitled to exert pressure but Kissinger sent Sisco with empty hands on a "mission impossible".

On 18 July Sisco arrived in London. During his meeting with Callaghan the latter stressed that the Americans should put pressure on the Greeks. The Greek officers should be withdrawn otherwise a Turkish landing would occur. Should the Greeks interfere the Turks would beat them. He doubted, however, whether American pressure could bring the Greeks to act but without such pressure they would not move at all. According to his instructions Sisco replied that the most important thing was to gain time. He supported the British idea of convening a conference of the guarantor powers. One should seek a package solution. The withdrawal of the Greek officers had to be a part of it as soon as Clerides was installed as president. Callaghan did not agree with most of Sisco's proposals. One should exert maximal political pressure on Athens. He could even imagine a naval blockade in order to stop the transport of Greek supplies to the putschists in Cyprus. The return of Makarios had to remain an option. Sisco said he would fly to Athens on 19 July. In the meantime one should try to convince the Turks that time was necessary.

At noon Sisco and Ecevit met. The only source of the content of this conversation is a meagre *Editorial Note* in *Foreign Relations*. According to them Ecevit made tough claims: Makarios had to be brought back, the Greek officers withdrawn and the Turkish presence on Cyprus strengthened. After lunch Sisco and Callaghan searched for elements of a package deal. When Sisco and Ecevit continued their conversation the latter made even tougher claims bordering on partitioning of the island. They agreed to continue the conversation in Ankara on 19 July. Despite Ecevit's tough demands Sisco believed that Ecevit still leaned towards a peaceful solution and begged him therefore not to move before he arrived in Ankara on 19 July. He wanted to sell the British proposal of a tripartite conference to the Greeks and to Ecevit the presidency of Clerides as a peaceful way out of the crisis. He did not realise that the die had already been cast.

Ecevit had prepared the Turkish intervention in the most perfect way: he had consulted the second guarantor power and had proposed a common action which had been rejected. Thus he had the right to act unilaterally. Though the Americans had sent a high ranking diplomat he had not exercised a veto à la Johnson. Ecevit's promise to wait until Sisco's arrival was not more than a polite gesture. He knew that Athens did not move and was not ready to accept the Turkish demands. Thus from the Turkish embassy he informed Ankara about the results and gave the green light for the intervention.

While in London the talks were moving towards their end, in Washington the Special Actions Group met. Kissinger theorised about how to keep everything pending in order to arrive at negotiations. The US should not take any position which obliged them to anything.

On 19 July a deep helplessness prevailed but the censored Greek media continued to describe the coup as a spontaneous action of the Cypriot armed forces which had gone off without a hitch. The Greek readers learned neither anything about the tough reactions outside Greece nor about the rising tension with Turkey. When Sisco arrived in Athens Ioannidis had gone into hiding and only after some considerable time was it possible to find him. Sisco confronted him with the Turkish war threat but Ioannidis did not grasp anything. With a great effort Sisco succeeded in wresting two tiny concessions out of him. Sisco realised that things were moving rapidly towards partition. He asked for Kissinger's consent if he tried to stop Ankara by applying pressure. Kissinger rebuked him sharply: one should not commit onself to anything but remain flexible. He should not exert any pressure on Ecevit but talk to him in a friendly way. By this Sisco's trip became truly a "mission impossible".

During his flight from London back to Ankara Ecevit developed the propaganda concept of selling the military intervention to the world public, namely as a peace operation. In the early hours of 19 July Ecevit conferred with the military: a bridgehead had to be gained, big bombing was excluded because there were too many tourists on the island. At 8:30 a.m. he gave the mission order. The invasion fleet consisting of five destroyers and 31 landing crafts with 3,000 soldiers aboard hoisted anchors at the harbour of Mersin and at 4 p.m. began moving towards Cyprus. The first wave was to go ashore at 6.30 a.m. on 20 July 1974. During the night the fleet encountered one of those fishing trawlers full of antennas flying the Soviet flag. Questioned about what to do Ankara replied that the fleet should not worry about it. This incident proved that the Soviets were informed about the movement of the fleet and wanted to get a closer picture. The bulk of the fleet was moving at a snail's pace, because of the slow landing crafts, towards Kyrenia.

News about the impending Turkish invasion reached Athens from various sources. Ioannidis did not take the warnings seriously: The Mehmets (memetides) did not have the heart to risk anything, they were just bluffing. When the BBC correspondent in Athens, David Tonge, was informed from the BBC head office that the Turkish fleet had left Mersin he passed this news on to Athenian ministries and to the General Staff. The answer was: he should not worry. Every two or three years the Turks were in the habit of setting out to sea to breath the fresh Mediterranean sea air and then returning. The only possible comment in this case is the classical aphorism of Publilius Syrus: *Quos deus perdere vult, dementat prius.* (Whom God wants to destroy, he first makes mad).

In Ankara the political and military preparations of the invasion proceeded smoothly according to plan on 19 July. Sisco arrived late at 22.45 p.m. in Ankara. Ecevit made him wait until 1.45 a.m. of 20 July. The first talk ended without any result after a short time. Sisco went to the US embassy. There he found a message from Kissinger: he totally disapproved of the Turkish course of action. Now the Clerides solution had to be pushed through and he expected the Turks to cooperate. Sisco replied that Athens and Ankara rejected this. Sisco went again to see Ecevit and tried to sell him Kissinger's proposal. Ecevit told him that it was too late, the fighter jets would start in a few minutes. Sisco returned to the embassy.

About the same time when Sisco and Ecevit talked Kissinger was informed that the Turkish invasion fleet was on its way to Cyprus. But the Turks had assured that there would be no war with Greece if the Greeks did not shoot first. He informed Sisco, who had arrived in the embassy in the meantime, and instructed him to keep the Greeks from intervening and to push the Clerides solution through. When Sisco replied that the Greeks and the Turks rejected this solution Kissinger was at the end of his tether.

Kissinger's hands off policy had led to the catastrophe and now he assumed an attitude as erstwhile Pontius Pilatus washing his hands and trying to find a scapegoat to whom he could attribute the guilt. In the five days of the crisis he had not once looked more closely at the problems at issue but had persisted in the Clerides solution. He had sent Sisco with empty hands on a "mission impossible" and not grasped that Ecevit meant business. Kissinger had acted irresponsibly, if not wantonly negligently, and had not made one serious effort to stem the tide. Kissinger's behaviour was characterised by arrogant ignorance, superficiality and incompetence and his personal dislike of Makarios; insinuating conspiracy activities would be a total misinterpretation.

The Turkish Intervention (Attila I), 20-22 July 1974

Already during the night from 19 to 20 July every now and then concrete warnings came from the Cypriot coast radar which were passed on to the high command in Athens. The answer was unbelievable: they should watch the development but the Headquarters were of the opinion that the Turkish fleet movements were a part of a naval exercise. In Cyprus among the officers of the National Guard rumours spread that a Turkish landing was imminent. Spontaneously some of them went to their headquarters. After some time a major showed up and told them: *"Gentlemen keep quiet. Nothing will happen. Those above (Athens) assure us that the Turks were conducting a simple exercise."* Sisco would see to it that nothing happened. The major ended: *"There are no problems. Go to sleep, gentlemen."* The officers returned to their units and did what they had been ordered to do.

The question arises why had the chief of the general staff, Bonanos, heeded the warnings of the previous days and not taken any measures of precaution and why had he ordered not to be woken because of any information about Turkish fleet movements? Logic leads to the conclusion that he ruled out an invasion, interpreted the fleet movements as empty political threats as in the past and relied upon the Americans who would keep the Turks from serious enterprises. Sisco's visit may well have reassured him in this view.

For Ioannidis' behaviour there exists no reasonable explanation. Since 15 July he had been quasi petrified. He had given himself over to fatalism and the naive belief that the Americans would straighten it out. Accordingly, Ioannidis was totally bewildered when he heard that the Turks were intervening militarily. Allegedly he said that he could not believe this, it had to be a lie. His was the reaction of a man for whom a world collapses. It is, however, astonishing that he had dominated Greek politics to this very point.

Because of the order to go to sleep only very few troops were near the landing place near Kyrenia when the Turks attacked. Many units were still in the area of Nicosia where they had been needed for the coup and the subsequent repressive measures. When the Turkish air force began to bomb military targets at 5 a.m. most of the soldiers were asleep. Thus the Turkish landing west of Kyrenia near Pente Milia took place against almost no resistance. The parachutists who jumped around 6 a.m. north of Gönyeli met little resistance, as well. There was no resistance because the commander of the National Guard was waiting for the green light from Athens. But Athens urged restraint. The chief of staff of the National Guard, who had a permanent telephone line to the General Staff in Athens was waiting for orders which did not come. In desperation he held the telephone receiver out of the window so that those in Athens could hear the explosions of the bombs and understand that the Turks were doing exercises.

In Athens from 8 a.m. on the war council was in session. It was determined that they could not do much for Cyprus. The decisions taken referred to the security of Greece. When the chief of the navy suggested sending the Greek fleet to Cyprus Bonanos rejected this because the Turks, after all, attacked only Cyprus. This meant that he was ready to forsake the Cypriots. Not even the Greek submarines which were close to Rhodes were ordered to sail to Cyprus. But, at least, the council, two and a half hours after the beginning of the attack, allowed the National Guard to shoot back.

When the units of the National Guard began to move to the destined positions the Turkish air force attacked them on the march in such a way that they arrived at their destination places rather shattered and only conditionally operational. The same happened to the artillery units. Indeed, there was no functioning plan for the defence of Cyprus. Since the withdrawal of the Greek division the staff of the National Guard had not managed to work out a new realistic concept for the defence of the island. Probably the staff officers had been more absorbed by the planning of the coup. Though some units managed to stop the Turkish advance to the west the Turks had landed in three places successfully without any losses. The bridgehead west of Kyrenia had been established successfully.

The National Guard undertook a rather successful night attack but after daybreak the Turkish air force pushed the attackers back. The command of the National Guard, consisting almost exclusively of Greek officers, failed all along. Instead of taking action in view of the landing by Turkish troops they waited until the landing was a fait accompli. The attacks by the air force continued all day long on 20 July. There was "collateral damage", of course: the Nicosia psychiatric hospital was bombed and many patients were killed.

While Cyprus was being attacked Henry Kissinger was in California visiting Nixon. Now, when he finally understood that the situation was dangerous, his main concern was not Cyprus but the Soviet Union because he was afraid the Soviets might intervene. His instructions for the Special Actions Group showed that he was not yet ready to counter Turkey. The UN Security Council, on the other hand, passed unanimously resolution 353(1974) calling on all states to respect the territorial integrity, independence and sovereignty of Cyprus, to declare a ceasefire, to end the military intervention, to withdraw all foreign military personnel except the legal contingents, begin trilateral negotiations to restore the constitutional order and to cooperate with UNFICYP.

In New York Makarios would not exclude the suspicion that the invasion had been schemed between Athens and Ankara. The Swiss *Neue Zürcher Zeitung* turned this suspicion into a fact: *"Makarios talks of a collusion of Athens and Ankara"* and maintained that *"Turkey and Greece acted in secret connivance in order to achieve the partition of the island and to get rid of him. The result of this action will be the partition and the allotting of one part to Turkey and the other to Greece. The stupid coup organised by the Greeks opened the door for Turkey."* Rarely can the beginning of a conspiracy theory be localised so clearly.

Sunday 21 July 1974 was rather hectic on all levels of action. Late in the evening of 20 July information had reached Ankara that a Greek ship convoy was on its way to Cyprus. The General Staff decided to dislocate three of the five destroyers protecting the landing place near Kyrenia towards the west. Further information confirmed the existence of the convoy and increased the impression that the Greeks were sending reinforcements to Cyprus and that a Greek-Turkish war threatened which would be fought out in Cyprus. Reports about attacks of the National Guard on the enclaves created the impression in Ankara that the Greek Cypriots were slaughtering the Turkish Cypriots. The High Command ordered the acceleration of the sending of reinforcements to Cyprus, above all tanks. At 4.30 a.m. on 21 July the Turkish air force began the new attacks, which this time were unlimited; everything was bombed; "collateral damage" did not matter.

Sisco, who was still in Ankara, tried to talk the Turks into accepting a ceasefire. But Ecevit rejected this: he had lost all confidence in the Greek side. In Cyprus unarmed Turkish villages had been attacked and the inhabitants massacred. Greek officers had participated in this and in the attacks on TOURDYK and Athens was sending reenforcements to Cyprus in a convoy. If the convoy did not return it would be sunk. Sisco was horrified: If the ships were sunk this meant war. Athens had threatened to leave NATO and to declare war on Turkey if the intervention did not end within 48 hours. A ceasefire must be announced at once. Ecevit replied that Turkey would not back off in response to threats. Only if the convoy returned could trust be restored and an atmosphere created in which talks would be possible. In the meantime Turkey would follow her peace operation to its end.

At 10 a.m. the three destroyers *Adatepe*, *Kocatepe* and *Fevzi Çamak* received the order to sail west to intercept the convoy when it approached the restricted area and make it turn round. At 11.30 a.m. another order conveyed told the captains of the destroyers to open fire on all Greek ships in the restricted area.

In Athens Ioannidis wanted war. The military, however, were against it but they did not dare to say this clearly and found excuses. In the course of the morning they brought themselves to agree to a cease fire. Prime minister Androutsopoulos informed US ambassador Tasca accordingly and added that there were no Greek ships in the vicinity of Cyprus. The US ambassador in Ankara, Macomber, informed Ecevit accordingly. But Ecevit did not trust the Greek promises: the Greeks would fool the US and Turkey, the Greek convoy was close to

Cyprus and would land soon. The Turkish forces had the order to fire at the ships of the convoy as soon as they entered the restricted area. Even a telephone conversation with Kissinger could not convince Ecevit that the ships were not Greek. Kissinger replied that no one would blame Ecevit if he sank his own ships.

In the meantime the three Turkish destroyers were sailing along the west coast. The pilot of the reconnaissance plane discovered that two ships of the alleged Greek convoy were Italian vessels and wondered where the convoy had remained. Moreover he discovered the three Turkish destroyers. He reported this to his control centre but they did not pass this information on to the high command. In the meantime, the high command ordered the air force to attack the convoy. When the pilots of the three attack squadrons saw the three destroyers in the area they reported they were sure that these were Greek vessels and attacked. On board the destroyers it was believed that the attacking jets were Greek ones and fire was opened on the attackers. The anti-aircraft fire convinced the pilots in their belief that they were attacking Greek ships. At the first attack *Kocatepe* was directly hit in the funnel, which set the ship ablaze.

Incompatible communication systems of the navy and air force led to a catastrophe: *Kocatepe* was hit once more and when it was about to explode was given up by its crew. The two other destroyers were able to withdraw north rather badly crippled. The Turkish navy had 53 dead. When at the seat of the government the message came in that the Greek convoy had been stopped and a Greek destroyer had been sunk those present were jubilant. At the High Command horror spread when the tragic error was understood. In the beginning the military tried to conceal the sinking but when the first survivors were fished out of the sea by foreign ships they had to admit the sad truth.

In Athens the argument between the hardliners and the moderates had gone on. When beseeching cries for help came, Androutsopoulos and Ioannidis ordered the confiscation of the huge car ferry *Rethymnon* in order to send troops to Cyprus. Fortunately for the passengers the journey from Piraeus to Cyprus takes one and a half days and when in the night of 22 July the ferry approached Cypriot waters it was called back because in the meantime a ceasefire had been agreed upon. The air transport of a commando unit in the night of 22 July ended in a disaster. As the defenders of the airport had not been informed the landing aircraft were shot at and 33 commandos died by friendly fire.

At about the same time the Special Actions Group met with Kissinger in the chair. He stated that a cease fire was urgently needed but Ecevit was trying to postpone this. Apparently he had to be pressured. Then Kissinger spoke about the time afterwards: a presence of the Greeks in Cyprus was against American interests, in contrast to a Turkish presence which was highly desirable. In Greece an overthrow of the regime was imminent. He was afraid the new government would be friendly to the Soviets. Thus a cease fire had to be achieved quickly.

Kissinger rang up Ecevit and pressed for a cease fire at 4 p.m. (Turkish time). Ecevit replied that he could not stop the army before it had reached secure positions. Kissinger said that the time was enough for that and reinforcements could be brought to Cyprus even after the cease fire. Ecevit promised to discuss the matter with his general staff. Obviously Kissinger was inviting Ecevit to disregard the future armistice.

In Athens they were still reluctant to agree to a cease fire which might humiliate the Greek side. Finally it was agreed that the Americans should announce that the governments in Ankara and Athens agreed to a cease fire in accordance with the resolution of the UN Security Council of 20 July. Thus it became clear that on 22 July 1974 at 4 p.m. the guns would fall silent.

In the morning of 22 July the Turkish army disembarked massive reinforcements including a number of tanks. With these it succeeded in conquering Kyrenia and created a connection with the Turkish enclave north of the Kyrenia mountains. Athens and Ankara agreed the peace negotiations would take place in Geneva. At 4 p.m. the cease fire came into force and at 5 p.m.

Ecevit announced that the town and district of Kyrenia had been occupied and would remain Turkish from now on and give the Turkish Cypriots access to the sea. The Turkish military presence was irreversible. Then he claimed that on Cyprus something was happening which could be characterised as a genocide.

Ecevit's claim was a part of a campaign beginning now which was to justify the further Turkish intervention aiming at the partition of the island. The atrocity propaganda was a mano-euvre to impress journalists from abroad and distract their attention from the violations of the armistice which were a part of the preparations for the second phase of the Turkish operation called Attila. The intervention for the alleged restoration of the *status quo ante* changed its character and became an invasion to partition the island.

While the Turkish reinforcements were going ashore, in Athens the government gave itself over to fatalism. In Cyprus the Sampson government and the leadership of the National Guard still had some illusions. They had not been informed about the cease fire negotiations and interpreted the arrival of the Noratlas transport planes with the commando unit as the beginning of Greek aid. The government controlled radio began to pour out nationalistic tales: the great hour of union with Greece had arrived. Until 10.30 a.m. Sampson was convinced that militarily everything was running smoothly. By 10.45 a.m. the chief of the National Guard, Georgitsis, told him to formulate the text of the proclamation of enosis. Sampson went to work and wrote down a bombastic declaration. At this moment Sampson heard about the continuation of the Turkish landing. Sampson called Gizikis and asked for help. The answer was procrastination. Obviously the military leadership in Athens was resolved to avoid everything which might draw them into a war with Turkey.

At 4 p.m. the armistice was in effect but this did not mean the end of the fighting. This was enabled by the fact that only a cease fire had been agreed and nothing else. Thus the Turkish invasion forces continued to improve its positions. The number of victims of these three days is frighteningly high. On the Greek Cypriot side on 20 July 145, on 21 July 37 and on 22 July another 42 people were killed. On 23 July, the day after the cease fire, 26 persons were killed when the Turkish forces attacked the airport. Among the dead were 75 civilians, 72 conscripts, 65 reservists and 5 soldiers by profession as well as 5 volunteers. ELDYK lost 47 soldiers. According to the official announcements of the Turkish General Staff there had been 57 dead, 242 were missing and 184 wounded. In this number the dead of *Kocatepe* are not included. Denktash said later that on the Turkish Cypriot side 44 civilians and 126 TMT fighters were killed.

During the Turkish advance there were numerous cases of human rights violations by the Turkish army, carefully examined and documented by the commission of the Council of Europe in September 1975. According to this report there were numerous cases of murder of civilians and prisoners of war, raping of women, ill treatment of captured civilians and soldiers, and extensive plundering. News and rumours about these outrages horrified the population in such a way that when the Turkish army continued its advance on 14 August panic broke out and people dropped everything and fled to the south to save their lives.

In Washington Kissinger was to meet Makarios on this day. At a meeting of the Special Actions Group he expressed the opinion that the Turkish position was now weaker than before the invasion. When his advisors tried to explain that the Turks were expanding their positions he ignored this. Obviously Kissinger was still not yet fully briefed. At the end of the conversation he said in a self satisfied way that they had mastered the crisis excellently and he had to congratulate them.

The meeting of Kissinger and Makarios in the afternoon of 22 July was characterised as private. On no account did Kissinger want to receive Makarios as president of the Republic of Cyprus because this might prejudge something, Therefore the State Department had announced that Kissinger would meet Archbishop Makarios. Announcing this the State Department spokesman let it be understood that in their eyes Makarios was responsible for the situation and not the junta in Athens. The conversation itself was fruitless because Kissinger stuck to his opinions. He continued to dislike Makarios and to believe that a Clerides solution would have been better. For geopolitical reasons he considered Turkey more important than Greece and therefore he had nothing against Turkey strengthening its forces in Cyprus and circling her position.

Armistice Violations and the First Geneva Conference, 23-31 July 1974
Although the armistice went into effect at 4 p.m. on 22 July the Turks continued to advance towards Nicosia airport early on 23 July. As they were intruding in an area under UNFICYP control a clash threatened. In order to prohibit this now and forever the airport was put under UN control.

In Athens the change of power took place. Ioannidis was brought down by the military, and Konstantinos Karamanlis became the new prime minister. Seven long years of dictatorship were over. In Nicosia the representative of the UN Secretary General urged a change of power, as well. The president of the House of Representatives, Clerides, declared himself ready to deputise for Makarios as acting president as the constitution prescribed it. But the Greek military demanded that Sampson confer the presidency on Clerides in order to deprive Makarios of his powers and have Clerides sworn in by Bishop Gennadios. Clerides was of the opinion that the swearing in of an acting president did not have any constitutional consequences and had himself sworn in so that Sampson disappeared more quickly. In a radio speech afterwards he announced that Sampson had resigned and he had taken over as acting president, according to article 36 of the constitution. Thus in Cyprus, too, dictatorship ended.

Clerides at once contacted Makarios who assured him of his support. Clerides wanted to extend the armistice concluded between Greece and Turkey to the Cypriot communities. In order to achieve this he went, accompanied by UN representatives, to Denktash's home in northern Nicosia. Denktash and Clerides agreed that the bloodshed had to end because the two communities would have to live together. Clerides offered the return to the treaties of Zurich and London as Makarios had proposed. Denktash said that the Turkish government would decide about this. He would consult Ankara and inform Clerides in two or three days about the answer. This he did and four or five days later he informed Clerides that Ankara rejected this proposal.

On 24 July 1974 it became obvious that the Turkish army intended to occupy the airport. The commander of UNFICYP, the Indian General Prem Chand, knew that if he retreated this would lead to massive loss of face of the Blue Helmets and therefore he ordered his troops to resist. UN Secretary General Kurt Waldheim aligned himself with him and ordered the defense of the airport. In between it became known in New York, Washington and London that a clash between UNFICYP and the Turkish army was threatening. Waldheim rang up Ecevit and explained the situation. Ecevit appeared badly informed but he promised to make an effort to find a peaceful solution. A little later prime minister Wilson called Ecevit and made it clear that the British would intervene. He ordered reinforcements to be flown to Cyprus and dislocated an RAF squadron with 12 Phantoms to Akrotiri. The British soldiers were placed under the orders of UNFICYP. The planes would intervene if called by the British blue helmets.

Ecevit understood that he had to withdraw. He called Wilson and told him that the Turkish troops would not attack the airport. Waldheim found a face saving way out of the crisis for Ecevit. The courageous behaviour of Prem Chand and Waldheim had prevented another catastrophe. The airport remained under UN control and closed. The UN had the airport repaired so that the weekly UN plane could start and land but it was impossible to find an agreement for a reopening

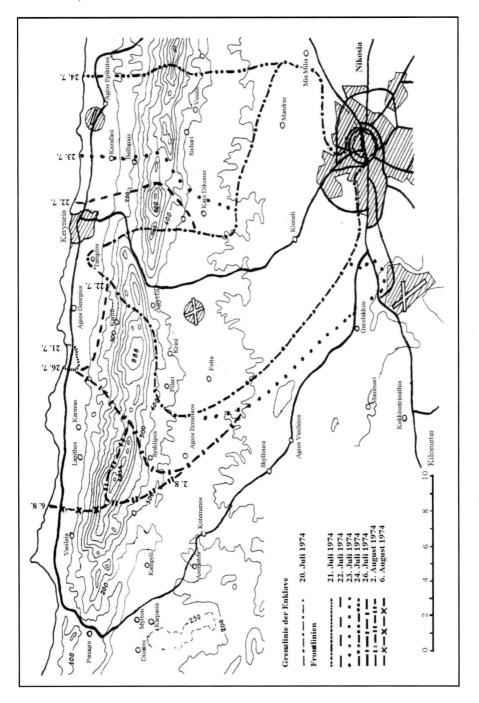

Attila I: Violations of the the Armistice; border of the enclave and frontlines with dates

of the airport for civilian usage. For the past 35 years there have been many efforts to achieve this but each time one side or the other found a a problem with the negotiations concerning the reopening. Thus Nicosia International is still closed.

In contrast to the airport of Nicosia there was no intervention of the Blue Helmets when the Turkish forces broadened the bridgehead of Kyrenia to the west and east. On 1 August they controlled 43 kilometres of the coast and all roads from the coast to the Mesaoria plain. Their strength had risen to 30,000 men with 240 tanks and 400 armoured vehicles. The Greek speaking population of this area was systematically expelled.

UN resolution 353 of 20 July had asked the UK, Turkey and Greece to begin negotiations for the restoration of peace and constitutional conditions. The change of power in Athens, however, delayed the beginning until 25 July. The negotiations were tenacious because the Turkish side was not ready for concessions. As in 1969 the basic decisions about Cyprus were taken by the three guarantor powers without asking the Cypriots. The Turkish side managed to bypass resolution 353. This resolution had demanded that all foreign troops with the exception of the legally stationed contingents should be withdrawn. Now this was turned into the vague formula that the withdrawal would take place "in a timely fashion" and in phases which meant that Athens accepted the presence of Turkish troops even after the end of the conflict. The second important success of the Turkish negotiation technique was the acknowledgement of the existence of two administrations on the island. Thus a first step towards a future bizonal federation was taken.

Finally, the Greek foreign minister, Mavros, scored an own goal by demanding that Clerides should represent the Greek Cypriot side at the next round of the Geneva negotiations. His Turkish colleague, Güneş, retaliated by nominating Denktash as negotiator of the Turkish Cypriot side. Thus Makarios was excluded from the future negotiations. This, in fact, violated resolution 353, too. At the same time Denktash's position was upgraded. In order to return to constitutional conditions the conference was to continue on 8 August, representatives of the Greek and Turkish Cypriot side participating. On 31 July the conference adjourned until 8 August.

In Washington on 29 July Kissinger and Makarios met for another talk. Makarios complained that Turkey was violating the armistice and continued to advance. Kissinger denied this. Makarios demanded that Kissinger play a more active role. Kissinger replied that he could not meddle in the Geneva negotiations and mentioned the Turkish troops. Makarios answered that he was afraid that Turkey intended to leave them in Cyprus until a future solution and the negotiations to find this could take many years. Kissinger agreed. The talk ended with Kissinger making noncommittal statements. It was obvious that Kissinger had no interest at all in committing himself more deeply. He still wanted to let things develop provided this development did not run contrary to American interests. The Turkish government recognised this wait and see policy and reacted accordingly.

Meanwhile, Clerides was fighting on two fronts: internally he had to try to disempower the hot-heads in the camp of Makarios and of EOKA B as well as the adherents of the junta. Externally, on the other hand, he had to try to stop the continuous violations of the armistice and the military buildup in Cyprus by Turkey. Although the number of Makarios' supporters was huge they were weak because they had been disarmed by the coup on 15 July. Their opponents, i.e., EOKA B, the henchmen of Sampson and of the junta were armed. But successively Clerides managed to get things under control.

In view of the constant violations of the armistice and the widening of the bridgehead Clerides understood that soon the Turkish offensive would be resumed. The National Guard would not be able to stop another Turkish advance in the flat Mesaoria because it had scarcely any tanks left, no anti-tank weapons and no anti-aircraft systems. In addition, the morale of the troops had sunk to an absolute rock bottom, reinforcements from Greece could not be expected as Karamanlis had made it clear during a telephone conversation with Clerides. Therefore Clerides tried to explore the attitude of Kissinger and Callaghan in case of a further Turkish advance and came to the conclusion that both sides would do nothing concrete. In his desperation he addressed the representative of the Soviet Union on 26 July. The reply was negative. This story shows clearly two things: first, the extent of Clerides' despair which induced him, a staunch conservative, to search for help from the Soviet Union. On the other hand it is proof of the cautiousness of Soviet foreign policy after the Cuban Missile Crisis. For this effort, however, Clerides was sharply rebuked by Kissinger who somehow had learned about it.

The Second Geneva Conference, 8-13 August 1974
The second round of the Geneva negotiations began in a rather frosty atmosphere. During the official opening no word was uttered. The delegations took their seats, had themselves photographed by the journalists and left the hall immediately in order to begin the talks in another room. After two hours the first session ended. Callaghan, who played the moderator, was content that he had managed to avoid a breakdown of the conference on the first evening. They agreed that on 9 August there would be bilateral talks and that the plenum would meet again in the evening of 9 August.

In Washington on this day president Nixon resigned and Gerald Ford was sworn in as the new president. In Geneva the Turkish foreign minister, Güneş, presented himself as an extremely intransigent hardliner. Clerides was afraid that he would demand a bizonal federation and informed Makarios accordingly. Makarios still rejected this thus narrowing Clerides' room for manoeuvring massively. During bi-lateral talks Güneş let it be understood that he would accept only a bi-zonal federation. By late afternoon Callaghan heard from London that the Turks would continue their offensive as late as 20 August, no matter whether results had been achieved in the meantime or not. According to this information the Turkish troops were to occupy an area beginning 5 miles east of Morphou and ending at the harbour of Famagousta. The operation would last 18 hours. Should no satisfactory result be achieved at Geneva the troops would move further west behind Lefka.

Callaghan was indignant about the duplicity of Güneş and more so because the latter had assured him in the morning that the Turkish forces did not intend to enlarge their bridgehead any more. Callaghan said to an American diplomat that this was unacceptable and the UK would react militarily in case of doubt. The American tried to quieten him stating that this certainly was only a contingency plan but he would inform Washington.

In the morning of 10 August Denktash told Callaghan proudly that the Turkish quest for bi-zonality went back to him. Should regional autonomy not be accepted it could happen that the Turkish army would march to Famagousta. After all it had not come to Cyprus for a soccer match. Callaghan made the consequences of such an action clear to him, after all Britain was one of the guarantor powers.

During the subsequent talk between Callaghan and Waldheim they agreed that UNFICYP should make a stand against a further Turkish advance. Waldheim was certain that the Turks would not attack the Blue Helmets; this had been proved by their behaviour in connection with the attack on the airport. If they reinforced UNFICYP quickly so that it gained a convincing deterrent strength the Turks would refrain from an attack. Callaghan promised to send additional troops. He was impressed by Waldheim's upright attitude. Waldheim, on the other hand, obviously did not expect any objection by the US.

Later Callaghan, Mavros and Clerides discussed an article which was published by *Milliyet* on this day. The article contained a map with a dividing line stretching from Lefka to Famagousta. According to this map the area alotted to the Turkish Cypriots covered 30 percent of the surface of Cyprus. In the article one read that Ecevit demanded a unitary republic consisting of two autonomous parts with armed forces and a parliament of their own. Clerides said that this article depicted the Turkish aims accurately. He was ready, however, to accept functional federalism but no geographic separation. All agreed that the content of this article corresponded with reality. To that American Callaghan said that he was not ready to allow the Turks a breach of the armistice because the consequences for Cyprus would be disastrous. He was in favour of real deterrence and not of bluffing.

In the afternoon the plenum met. Rapidly it became clear that the Turkish side was not ready to make any concession. Callaghan considered it reasonable to give an explicit warning to the Turks. He told journalists that British reinforcements were on their way to Cyprus. The British troops would not hesitate to open fire if the Turkish forces advanced. The British troops would support the Blue Helmets of UNFICYP. The British press met the expectations of the foreign minister and committed the expected indiscretion and reported about the reinforcements.

Güneş, on the other side, knew that the conference would have no result and began looking for a convenient excuse for letting the conference fail. In Ankara Ecevit and a representative of the foreign ministry bluntly stated to the American and German ambassadors that forced would be applied in order to achieve the solution desired by Ankara.

In Washington Kissinger did his best to teach President Ford his view of things: In his opinion the British government was only steering a tough course because elections were imminent. Callaghan was rather inexperienced. He himself had spoken on the phone to Ecevit, who was a former student of his, and told him that the US would be bemused by a new use of force. He would convey this to Ecevit in writing, as well. When Ford wanted to know whether this letter would keep the Turks from using force Kissinger intimated that the Turks were not the problem but the British. Though this was a perfidious argument it worked since Ford told him to continue in this sense. He might try and quieten the British. In his letter to Ecevit Kissinger admonished him mildly to show a little more restraint and suggested the forming of cantons as a solution. This proposal was as unacceptable to Ecevit as Clerides' functional federation. Ankara wanted bi-zonality.

On 11 August extensive troop movements were reported from Cyprus. It was obvious that the Turkish side was preparing a military operation. Ecevit said to the American ambassador that he would think about Kissinger's proposal but factually the countdown to Attila II had begun. In Geneva Güneş was waiting impatiently for the secret message of this in order to blow up the conference. By a misunderstanding the message was delayed and reached him late. For the rest of the day Kissinger conducted appeasement policy towards Ankara which reminds one of that applied by Chamberlain. Callaghan considered those gentle tones wrong. If one intended to achieve something with the Turks one had to use clear hard language. However, during a talk between him and Güneş, the latter expressed himself so ambiguously and spoke of a cantonal solution that Callaghan gained the impression the Turkish side was not yet ready for military action.

On 12 August Güneş submitted a proposal of his own which even contained a map. The paper called Cyprus a bi-communal independent state consisting of an autonomous Greek and Turkish Zone containing 6 Turkish and 2 Greek districts. The Turkish main district would be delimited in the west by the Kyrenia-Myrtou-Skyloura-Gerolakkos-Nicosia road. In the east the delimitation would follow the road from Nicosia to Augustine and then the side roads over Genagra, Maratha, Styloi to Famagousta. There should be autonomous districts near Lefka, Polis, Paphos and Larnaca as well as one on the Karpasia peninsula which in general would be a Greek district. The size of the Turkish-Cypriot district would be 34 percent of the total. The details of the boundaries should be fixed later. The area of the Turkish main district had to be cleared of the troops of the Greek contingent, the National Guard and all paramilitary within 48 hours.

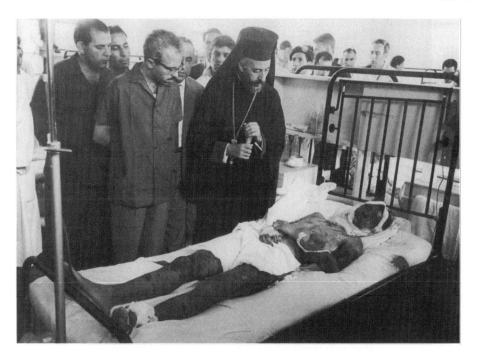

Georkatzis and Makarios visit wounded

Turkish Cypriot refugee camp in the Kokkina enclave

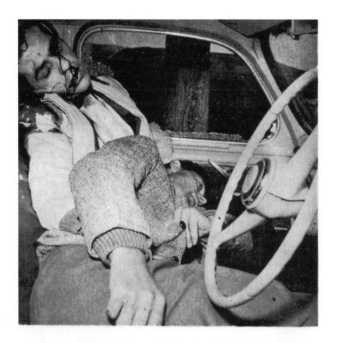

Murdered unionists: Dervis Kavazoglou and Kostas Misaoulis

Papadopoulos, Makarios and Grivas

The intercommunal negotiations 1970: Clerides, Osorio Tafall and Denktash

1970: assassination attempt on Makarios, inspection of the shotdown helicopter

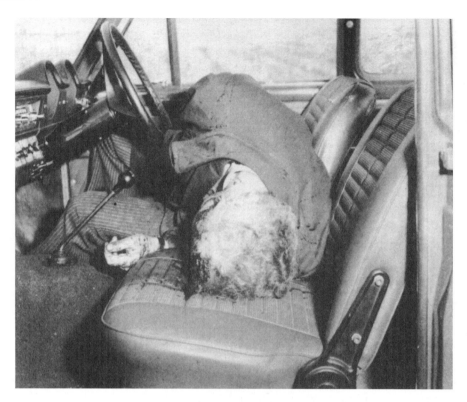

15 March 1970: the murdered Georkatzis

Colonel Dimitris Papapostolou

15 July 1974: tanks of putschist National Guard moving to the centre of Niosia

15 July 1974: the burned down Presidential Palace

15 July 1974: the coup's leaders, in light uniform Michail Georgitsis

15 July 1974: Putschist Nikos Sampson and his press officer Spyros Papageorgiou

16 July 1974: Makarios in the British base of Akrotiri

Attila 1: the first wave of the Turkish invading troops wading ashore

Attila 1: advancing Turkish unit

Güneş told Callaghan that this proposal had the blessing of the Turkish government. The conference should bring about a decision about his proposals and the next morning the leaders of the two Cypriot communities should present them as their solution. This was a kind of ultimatum. Even Kissinger recognised this when he was confronted with it but he did not know what to do against it. Obviously, his hands off strategy had led Cyprus into the catastrophe. Waldheim now, too, retracted: should the Turks really attack he would order the Blue Helmets to retreat. Güneş insisted on his ultimatum: the Greeks had one day to decide.

Although in the morning of 13 August Clerides submitted an alternative proposal he knew that he stood powerless before a classic dilemma. No matter how he decided, a part of Cyprus would come under the control of the Turkish army. The question was only how much force would be applied. If he wanted to avoid a catastrophe for the Greek Cypriots in the form of a forceful eviction there was only one way out, to accept the bi-communal and bi-zonal solution, i.e., Güneş' proposal. But even then he could not be sure whether the population movement would take place in an orderly fashion so that they could take their movable property with them. But he knew that Makarios rejected a federal solution. As Mavros had been ordered by Karamanlis to accept nothing which Makarios rejected, the only solution was to convince Makarios and make him yield by pressure from the Greek government. This meant that Mavros and Clerides would first have to convince Karamanlis to accept the bitter reality and then in a joint effort persuade Makarios to change his mind. This needed a postponement of 48 hours. At the same time Clerides knew if he accepted Güneş' ultimatum, in Cypriot history he would be considered as the traitor who gave a big part of the island to the Turks without fighting. Any further political career would have been impossible after that. Moreover, by agreeing he would supply the Turks with a legal alibi which they could and would use as a justification in the imminent UN debate.

Callaghan demanded that Güneş concede these 48 hours to the Greek side. Güneş rejected this but promised to consult Ankara. Callaghan appealed to Kissinger to insist upon a delay of two days. Kissinger did this but in such a weak way that Ecevit only promised to think about it. When Kissinger spoke about this with Ford it became clear again that Kissinger still regarded the Turks with sympathy. The British had caused the mess by weak crisis management. He saw no American reason why the Turks should not obtain one third of the island. Kissinger again played a piece of realpolitik 19th century style and the guilty ones were the British.

The last round of the Geneva negotiations began at 7 p.m. as Güneş had procrastinated. Meanwhile Güneş had been informed by Ecevit that he should protract the conference until 2 a.m. of 14 August. Shortly after, the attack in Cyprus would begin. Thus the last round was shadow boxing. Güneş played a cruel game. He knew that Clerides wanted to move but could not before Makarios consented. Mavros was in a similar situation. Both underwent this ordeal hoping that Güneş or Ecevit would concede them the 48 hours. Both knew, and so did Callaghan, what was at stake and they fought against the threatening doom hoping they could avert it. Güneş played with them. He denied that any military action was planned but rejected a postponement. Clerides went as far as assuring Güneş that he would study his proposals with an "open mind". Güneş kept the conference going until 2.25 a.m. of 14 August 1974. Precisely half an hour later at 5 a.m. Cypriot time (3 a.m. MET) the new bombardment began by the Turkish air force. The first target was the radio station in the west of Nicosia.

A few moments before the end of the conference Clerides asked Callaghan whether the British would stand on the sidelines watching the Turkish attack, doing nothing. Callaghan promised to bring the case to the UN Security Council. Callaghan, who had originally been pugnacious and had shown his teeth in the case of the airport, avoided now taking a clear position *coram publico* and repeating his honourable stand. Certainly Güneş registered this behaviour with satisfaction because it reduced the risk of the Turkish attack to almost zero. The few lightly armed Blue Helmets were not dangerous. The answer to the question whether a tough attitude on the part of the British could have prevented the Turkish side from attacking must remain speculative but there are many arguments in favour of it.

Callaghan's change of course was caused by Kissinger's attitude. On 12 August Kissinger had made him understand that the US rejected any British military intervention even within the UN. Kissinger's pressure bought off Waldheim's courage, as well. Alone the British did not want to act because the memories of American behaviour during the Suez crisis were still vivid, when the US had actively stopped the British attack on the Egyptian fleet, and were present even with Labour politicians. For Henry Kissinger the Turkish action now beginning was the sword stroke which cut the Gordian knot of the Cyprus problem apart. In reality he fastened the knot even tighter and made it impossible to untie it.

The Turkish Invasion (Attila II), 14-16 August 1974

The Turkish plan envisaged three directions of attack: the 39th division was to occupy the area north of the Nicosia-Famagousta road, i.e., the northern Mesaoria plain. The 28 division was to carry through an analogous operation in the western direction towards the enclave of Limnitis. Other units were to conquer the airport and the area of the ELDYK camp. The forces of the attackers were far superior to those of the defenders. The strength of the Turkish troops amounted to 40,000 soldiers, about 160-200 tanks, 200 armoured troop carriers and 120 heavy artillery pieces. The Turkish air force dominated the air space totally. The soldiers of 25 battalions of the National Guard were badly equipped infantrymen. Additionally, there were 11 worn-down Russian T-34 tanks and 70 light infantry guns.

Actually the Turkish units could have achieved their aims on the first day of the attack but they advanced very slowly to give the Greek populations the opportunity to flee. Indeed, the Turkish advance caused an avalanche of refugees. When at 6 p.m. on 16 August the second cease fire agreement came into effect the Turkish army had occupied almost 37 percent of Cyprus. Now they could establish an ethnically homogenous federal state. A further advance would have been counter-productive because in these areas there lived too many Greeks who could not all be expelled. Similarly the Turkish government was not interested in double enosis because this might create a possible threat by Greece from the south, from Cyprus.

The area of Varoşa south of Famagousta became a special case. On the one hand, Varoşa was the new town of Famagousta inhabited only by Greek Cypriots and on the other hand, it was the island's hotel town stretching to the southeast along the coast. The plan of Attila II provided for the occupation of Famagousta and its harbour but not of Varoşa. However, when the Turkish army advanced the Greek inhabitants of Varoşa also fled to the British base of Dhekelia. For three days after the conclusion of the armistice Varoşa was a no-man's land patrolled by Swedish Blue Helmets. After three days a Turkish patrol occupied the empty town. But as the occupation of such a big area after the conclusion of the armistice might have caused major anger it remained unoccupied. The town and hotels were surrounded by barbed wire and the whole area has been uninhabited until today. Varoşa is a ghost town.

In Athens Karamanlis threw a tantrum because of Ecevit's behaviour. Only with a great effort could the Greek military keep him from taking imprudent military aid measures which certainly would have led to war. His decision, however, to leave the military part of the NATO alliance met with general agreement; politically, Greece remained a member of the alliance. This measure on the one hand was intended to quieten the Greek public and show that the government was doing something and on the other to exert pressure on the Americans: the re-nationalisation of the Greek armed forces tore a considerable hole in the southeastern flank of NATO. Though this decision is comprehensible it was imprudent because by it Athens abandoned the possibility of influencing the development via the NATO Council. Indeed, the

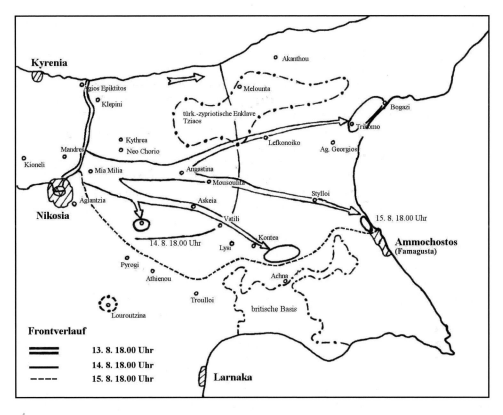

Advance of the 39th Division towards the East with frontlines

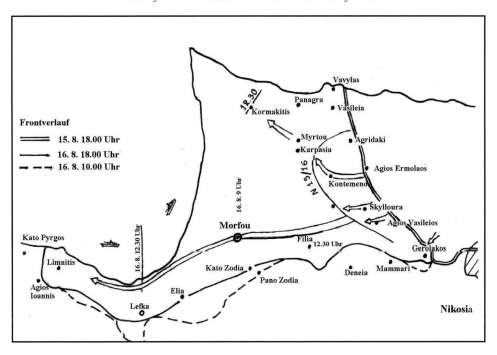

The advance towards the West with frontlines

Greek representative at NATO HQ contented himself with reading a dry declaration instead of requesting a NATO intervention.

In Washington Kissinger decided to stick to his policy. He considered the proposal to cut down American military aid to Turkey as total nonsense. He still saw no need for action because in his opinion things developed in such a way that American interests were not affected. A few weeks later the US Senate Committee for Refugee Questions came to the conclusion that the US government had a pro-Turkish tilt.

The Turkish advance toward Morphou and Famagousta made ten thousands flee. Already during Attila I there had been massive human rights violations and murders. Information and rumours about them caused the Greek Cypriots to flee from the advancing Turkish army on foot or by whatever vehicle they had. Many of these refugees were completely destitute. 180,000 refugees were straying over the roads and fleeing south or were camped in the security of the British base of Dhekelia. To feed, cloth, medicate and house them was a herculean task, the enormity of which one can only understand if one realises that each third Greek Cypriot had lost his home. In Germany after the end of WWII each fifth person was a refugee. Luckily it was summer and camping in the open air was possible. Many found refuge in empty school houses or in hotels or apartments evacuated by tourists.

On 1 September 200,000 refugees were counted but when things calmed down about 24,000 people returned to their villages and apartments near the demarcation line. Thus in November the number of refugees was 179,000. In September relief organisations looked after 182,000 and in November 135,000 displaced persons. Later another 3,000 refugees were added who were allowed to move to the south because of negotiations. About 23,000 Turkish Cypriots fled to the north; it is not known how many were directly evicted. About 17,000 were transferred after negotiations, 9,000 of them through a British-Turkish agreement. They had been stranded in the Akrotiri base during the fights. Another 8,000 were allowed to migrate to the north as a result of the inter-communal negotiations in Vienna in August 1975. These were the Turkish Cypriots who had lived in the base prior to the invasion. Altogether about 71,000 Turkish Cypriots went north.

The losses of those three days fighting were again high: 140 civilians, 90 National Guards-men and 104 members of ELDYK were killed. The official report of the Cypriot government speaks of 877 Greek Cypriots who lost their lives during Attila I and II. According to the Tur-kish general staff 250 soldiers fell and 500 were wounded. The number of missing is unknown.

As in all wars war crimes and atrocities were committed in operations Attila I and II but in both cases one has to be extremely careful with the evaluation because some of them existed only in propaganda. However, it can be safely stated that during Attila I the Greek side com-mitted no war crimes. In contrast the Turkish army did commit such crimes during both opera-tions in the area controlled by it. The Turkish Cypriot journalist Sevgül Uludağ who researched these problems for many years reports numerous massacres of Greek Cypriots which were partly committed by Turkish Cypriots. On the Greek Cypriot side, too, crimes were committed not by soldiers of the National Guard but by EOKA B fanatics who had been armed in the aftermath of the coup against Makarios. There were two main areas of these outrages, namely three villages northwest of Famagousta and Tochni on the road from Nicosia to Limassol near Chirokoitia.

The real dimension of the murders becomes evident if one looks at the number of the so-called "missing persons". The term "missing person" comprises several groups of missing. One must differentiate between missing civilians and missing prisoners of war. The first were murde-red during the invasion. A great number of the latter were killed when still in Cyprus, others were killed in POW-camps in Turkey. On 6 April 1996 Rauf Denktash revealed half of the truth in a radio interview: during the advance the Turkish army handed over prisoners of war who were hindering them to Turkish Cypriot paramilitary units and these killed the prisoners. This may be so but only partly because there were signs of life of many of the missing persons from Turkey. Obviously Denktash tried to exculpate Ankara.

Only recently have reliable numbers become available. According to them on the Greek Cypriot side 1,468 and on the Turkish Cypriot side 502 persons were missing. 229 of the latter have been missing since the 1960s and 229 since 1974. Between 1975 and 1979 the UN General Assembly passed three resolutions dealing with this topic and demanding that those involved set up a committee to solve this humanitarian problem. At the end of the inter-communal negotiations between 1977 and 1981 it was decided to found the Committee on Missing Persons in Cyprus (CMP) which was done. But until 2004 almost nothing happened. Only when the UN Secretary General appealed to both sides to begin with the exhumations, identify the remains and give them to the relatives in 2007 did the first "archaeological" excavations and DNA analyses begin. Until autumn 2009 the remains of 562 individuals had been found in 290 mass graves and 345 DNA analyses made and the remains of 172 identified individuals had been given to their families. However, there are indications of mass graves in military off-limits areas of the Turkish army in Cyprus which are inaccessible for the excavators of the CMP. It is high time that those responsible gave way.

This humanitarian action, however, is confined to Cyprus. Whether Turkey will ever officially admit that quite a number of Greek Cypriots disappeared in captivity may be doubted. The fact is that many of them were registered as prisoners of war by the ICRC or by the Red Crescent but did not return when the official exchange of prisoners took place. For some of these missing prisoners even photographs and messages exist which were sent from Turkey.

The first phase of operation Attila could be justified by the treaty of guarantee and the right derived from it of unilateral intervention in Cyprus in order to restore the *status quo ante*. However, with the downfall of the junta in Athens and the change of power in Cyprus to Clerides on 23 July 1974 and the offer by him, or rather Makarios to return to the treaties of 1960 there was no longer any legal justification for the continuation of the intervention. During the first phase to a certain degree, Ecevit had the sympathies of the world public opinion on his side because he was cracking down on the putschists under the remote control of the Athens junta. But when the junta fell from power and Greece was re-democratised and Clerides replaced Sampson the sympathies turned round: from now on the sympathies were on the side of the Greeks and the Greek Cypriots.

However, neither the general staff nor Ecevit understood this. Obviously one wanted to use the weakness of the Greek side and create *faits accomplis*. The second attack was a clear violation of International Law and an act of aggression. In order to avoid future trouble with minorities one resorted to the means of provoking mass flight and expulsion. Ecevit and the military did not understand that by this act they destroyed the reconciliation between Greeks and Turks established by Venizelos and Atatürk by the treaty of friendship and poisoned the Greek-Turkish relationship for decades.

Ankara could pursue a course of realpolitik in 19th century style because at the head of the US there was a personality who also acted in the manner of Metternich or Bismarck or even Machiavelli. For Kissinger, Turkey, because of its geopolitical and geostrategic position in the Cold War, was so important that he was ready to overlook everything provided it did not bother American interests. His policy towards Cyprus led to a deep alienation of Greece, Turkey and the two ethnic groups there. By assisting the Athenian junta during the first phase and after the change of power giving Karamanlis the cold shoulder during the second phase he created the matrix for a militant anti-Americanism which paved the way for Andreas Papandreou, whom he hated.

Following the invasion the American Congress - against the advise of Kissinger - imposed an arms embargo on Turkey which certainly was ethically correct but politically imprudent as the Americans lost a leverage. A threat to impose an embargo might have made an impact but this weapon was blunted when it was applied and Turkey did not care. Quite the opposite happened it imployed the embargo as a lever against the Americans. And the struggle for the lifting of the embargo absorbed a lot of Kissinger's strength because he was very sensitive to Turkish threats.

The Greek Cypriot leadership contributed to the negative development. Had Makarios been ready to accept the Turkish Cypriots as politically equal partners and had he not treated them as a minority Cyprus would not have encountered this catastrophe. Clerides had understood this for a long time but Makarios had blocked it and relied upon the UN to avert the worst. But the UN turned out to be a paper tiger when it became critical. The only ones who could have stopped the Turks were the Americans, but these, according to a UN diplomat speaking to DER SPIEGEL, feigned death. For chancellor Helmut Schmidt Attila II was an imperialist invasion. The victims of these games of power politics were the Cypriots, whose island was partitioned.

1974-1977: ON THE WAY TO STALEMTE

The pile of shard, 17 August to 10 September 1974

Clerides was faced with enormous tasks. 36.3 percent of the country was occupied. 70 percent of the agriculturally used area was gone. Industry had suffered the same loss. Most of the tourist centres were in the occupied area. He had to try to save by diplomacy what could be saved. He had to boost the economy, get the refugee problem under control, restore law and order by disarming the irregulars and securing the demarcation line with the still existing military forces.

At the session of the Council of Ministers on 17 August Clerides proposed radical emergency measures. The 8-hour day for the civil service was abolished and the civil servants were ordered to be in their offices from 7 a.m. to 7 p.m.. Saturday and Sunday were normal workdays. Nobody between 17 and 60 was allowed to leave the country except with a special permit. Mortgages on properties in the occupied areas were frozen. State assistance should save the refugees from distress but this help was limited so that the refugees would look for work. In the industrial sector generous state assistance should encourage the refugees to rebuild their enterprises, shops and service centres. All fallow private and public land was to be cultivated, the government supplying the necessary machines. In order to reduce the number of people without work and to bring foreign exchange into the country construction workers would be allowed to work in the Arab states. The old Larnaca military air field was to be used as an airport and modernised. It is still running.

Kissinger's policy led to massive protests in Greece and Cyprus during which he was called a murderer. This angered him so much he steered an even tougher course regarding Greece and Cyprus. He felt confirmed in this when on 18 August, after a demonstration in Nicosia, shots were fired at the US embassy and the ambassador killed by a ricochet. Clerides apologised in due form and Kissinger accepted the apology but told Clerides that he would wash his hands of Cyprus if the agitation against him continued in Athens and Nicosia. Clerides was not impressed by this but criticised the American policy rather openly.

During the following days there were efforts to resume the Geneva negotiations. But on 20 August Denktash intervened stating to the press in Ankara that he would found an independent Turkish Cypriot state if negotiations were not resumed quickly. One day later he was even more precise: if the Greek side would not negotiate there remained only two solutions: federation with extensive autonomy or total partition of the island and formation of an independent state. There would be a population exchange. Greek land property in the north would be sold with adequate compensation or leased. They had begun to build up an administration of their own. They would issue their own passports, found a bank and introduce the Turkish Lira as their currency. He was ready to talk with Clerides about humanitarian problems but in peace talks the guarantor power had to participate. Obviously the Turkish side was heading towards a loose confederation.

On 22 August Makarios intervened in the discussion from London: in an interview he underlined that there could not be any negotiations as long as the Turkish troops had not been withdrawn to the 9 August cease fire line. The new talks should take place in New York under the auspices of the UN in the presence of Security Council members. A partition of the island would destroy the state of Cyprus. A federal solution was out of the question since it would be a first step towards division. Obviously Makarios still did not understand the real situation but his attitude again reduced Clerides' room for manoeuvring considerably.

During a conversation between Clerides, Karamanlis and other members of the Greek government Clerides said that militarily speaking the situation was hopeless. They discussed whether they should negotiate with Turkey or not and which demands they should put forward. Soon it was clear that the only realist was Clerides, who judged the situation correctly. He was convinced that Turkey would never withdraw her troops to the ceasefire line of 9 August. Therefore this demand should not be made a precondition for the negotiations. One should act quickly because there was the danger that the Turks would form a government of their own in the occupied area. Mavros had an illusion: the pressure exercised by the UN, the FRG and the Soviet Union would make the Turks withdraw, therefore they should wait. Karamanlis considered this unrealistic. Clerides said that no diplomatic manoeuvre would prevent a federalisation based on a geographic separation; he was ready to cede 24 percent of Cyprus to the Turks. If they had accepted the geographic separation in Geneva their situation would be much better. He had been afraid of the reaction of the public but he should have accepted the separation in Geneva. There would never be a solution except a federation with geographical separation. Karamanlis agreed.

Nevertheless, Karamanlis back-pedalled when he stated his preconditions for negotiations: return of the refugees under secure conditions and pullback of the Turkish forces to their positions of 9 August. Under these preconditions he was ready to enter into a dialogue with Turkey, a federal solution with a geographic separation would not be excluded provided there was no population movement.

The question arises why Karamanlis resolved to accept this bad compromise though he agreed with Clerides. The decisive point probably was his anxiety that Makarios might accuse the Athens leadership of national treason. In view of the fact that there would be general elections in autumn this would have been dangerous, indeed. Additionally, he dreaded the responsibility and humiliation of negotiations under such unfavourable conditions, and he feared the reactions of the radical military which had not yet been brought fully under control. They might use a "humiliation" as a pretext to make another coup. Moreover, one should not forget that Karamanlis was "tainted" by the Zurich and London agreements which had been signed during his first rule. Instead of trying, together with Clerides, to reduce the damage, he preferred to avoid a confrontation by this, hardly courageous way and stay away from the negotiations. Lastly, again an opportunity to find a reasonable solution was lost.

On 25 August Clerides stated three conditions under which he was ready to negotiate with the Turks: the Turks had to be disposed to make serious territorial concessions, the Turkish troops should agree to *"a phased total withdrawal"* and the refugees should be allowed to return. If Varoşa were given back the situation on the refugee sector would be eased and the climate generally improved. Obviously, Clerides was trying to build a golden bridge for the other side. If it had reacted positively the population exchange would have been a fact, also, but it would have been on a voluntary basis and thus legitimised and the accusation of expulsion would have been removed. The territorial concession in the area of Varoşa was realisable. The demand for a total phased withdrawal of the Turkish troops accompanied by a demilitarisation of the island was not at all illusionary. Clerides' proposal was based on the do-ut-des principle and was realistic. He believed that if he and Denktash negotiated alone they would find a solution quickly. He was certainly right but unfortunately ever since then all decisions have been taken in Ankara.

Even when UN Secretary General Waldheim tried to call a conference it became obvious that Ecevit only wanted a continuation of the Geneva negotiations and rejected any internationalisation. He and Denktash aimed at securing the status quo by international law. Kissinger, on the other side, was not ready to exert pressure on Ankara to participate in an international conference. Implicitly, this would have meant that he backed the Greek proposal and since the demonstrations he was peeved at the Greeks. Although there were direct negotiations between Clerides and Denktash on humanitarian problems, of which many were solved, these did not bring about the conference.

On 9 September 1974 the former US ambassador, William Tyler, appeared in Athens to acquaint the Greeks with the ideas of Kissinger: the anti-American demonstrations had to stop. Tyler suggested a package deal linking the Cyprus conflict with the Aegean conflict. The proposal to solve the two conflicts by package deal once more proved total American ignorance of the real problems. The Aegean conflict was a bilateral problem without any connection with the Cyprus conflict. The idea that Greece might make concessions in the Aegean to gain concessions by Turkey in Cyprus was absurd. Tyler's tone, on the other hand, was that of a typical American proconsul in a client state asking for obedience by threats. Finally Tyler stated that the US was not guilty of the developments because no mistake had been made. Karamanlis rejected Tyler's demands in a dignified way: Greece was ready to accept a federal solution, but a solution humiliating his country or an unacceptable one for the Greek Cypriots he would not agree to.

Thus 25 days after the end of Attila II it was clear that there would be no Geneva III. Things could move again onlyif Makarios accepted a solution on the basis of a bi-zonal federation. But we shall see now that Makarios bet on the wrong horse by trying to turn history back with the help of the UN.

Efforts to mend the fences, September-December 1974

Makarios and the Cyprus government intended to bring the Cyprus problem to the UN General Assembly. They hoped that it would clearly rebuke Turkey as there was no veto there and this the more so as the non-aligned states and the Warsaw Pact states had an overwhelming majority. It was even considered possible that the General Assembly would officially condemn Turkey as an aggressor, thus inducing the Security Council to a tougher course, perhaps even one of sanctions against Turkey. Additionally, such a resolution would boost the morale of the Greek Cypriots. In order to prepare this action as well as possible Makarios gave numerous interviews and visited the non-aligned countries of the Mediterranean.

From 30 October to 1 November the General Assembly discussed the Cyprus question at five meetings. On 1 November 1974 the General Assembly passed unanimously resolution 3212 (XXIX), which had been submitted by nine non-aligned states. The resolution requested that all states respect the sovereignty, independence, territorial integrity and the non-aligned status of Cyprus and to refrain from any intervention. It urged the speedy withdrawal of all foreign troops. The future constitutional order was exclusively an affair of the Greek and Turkish

Cypriots. Bi-communal negotiations should be continued under the aegis of the Secretary General with the aim of finding a mutually acceptable political solution. The refugees should return and both sides should take the necessary measures for this. The Secretary General should provide humanitarian aid and all sides were to cooperate with UNFICYP. The resolution demanded less than the resolution of the Security Council but it sounded good, impressed the Cypriots and obliged nobody to anything. Thus even the representative of Turkey did not abstain but voted for it. During the following years the passage of such resolutions became a meaningless ritual repeated over and over again and effecting nothing

In Cyprus during those weeks acting president Clerides came under pressure from the adherents of Makarios. In the past their leaders had had direct access to Makarios and had wielded power and were discontent now. The adherents of the junta, on the other side, hoped that he would return soon, proclaim an amnesty and save them from trial and punishment. Finally, the mass of the simple adherents of Makarios wished his return because they believed he would find a way out of the misery. The leaders of both camps began, in an unholy alliance with the defrocked Bishops, to agitate for the return of Makarios. They claimed Clerides impeded the return of Makarios and he would achieve the return of the refugees to their homes. Clerides was allegedly working for partition and only Makarios could prevent this.

The true motive for these ugly manoeuvres was the fact that Clerides and Denktash were making progress in their talks. As early as September political topics had been touched on. Denktash had hinted that in case of a moving back of the demarcation line Morphou could become Greek again and Varoşa could be opened for the return of the refugees. On 20 September he wanted to know whether Clerides was authorised to sign a possible agreement. Clerides signalled readiness for concrete negotiations and submitted a seven-point solution plan. Obviously, Clerides needed a free hand to negotiate but at this moment Makarios announced his imminent return. Clerides knew that in this case the negotiations would fail because Denktash had made it clear that he would not negotiate with Makarios.

Clerides informed Karamanlis about this situation and stated that if Makarios returned he would resign from all posts. Karamanlis was appalled. After all, he agreed with a bi-zonal solution provided the Cypriots accepted it and Turkey made some territorial concessions. But in view of the general elections in Greece, in Cyprus everything should be kept pending until then. In a public declaration Karamanlis rejected a resignation of Clerides. At the same time he put pressure on Makarios: the situation in Cyprus was tense and Makarios should declare as soon as possible that he backed Clerides unreservedly. If Makarios rejected this he would distance himself from him publicly.

As Makarios was preparing his speech in the UN General Assembly on 1 October and there was a meeting with Kissinger on 2 October he took his time replying. On 2 October he called Clerides and asked him to remain in office. On 3 October Makarios sent a message to the people of Cyprus: he alone would decide when he would return. He would come to a decision after the UN debate. In the meantime the Cypriots should support Clerides, who had his absolute confidence. Clerides declared himself ready to stay in office.

On 6 November Clerides decided to tackle the problem head on. In a speech he stated that a return to the *status quo ante* was unreal since Turkey would never accept it. The only solution was on a federative basis. Whoever believed that the UN could achieve a solution to the Cyprus problem was politically naive. When his opponents attacked him, therefore, he added: whoever claimed that one could negotiate a solution other than a federal one on the basis of a geographical separation was mocking the people. The Turkish Cypriot press lauded Clerides and Denktash called his attitude realistic and constructive.

During the talk between Kissinger and Makarios on 13 November Kissinger gained the impression that Makarios was making friends with a federal solution on the basis of cantons. On 17 November Karamanlis won a sweeping victory in the parliamentary elections. Despite this he hesitated to prevent Makarios from returning. Clerides understood that a Makarios returned would undermine his position as a negotiator with Turkey. Therefore he wanted a document signed by Makarios and the Greek government containing the parameters of a solution. He rejected negotiations if at the end Makarios could refuse to accept the solution found.

On 20 November Clerides flew to London for talks with Makarios. There the British government had made it clear to Makarios that they considered a bi-zonal federation as the only possible solution. But Makarios continued to have illusions. He believed that Kissinger would pressure Turkey into accepting a multi-cantonal solution. For him such a solution seemed acceptable provided the central government had real power, a Greek Cypriot majority, and no veto by the Turkish Cypriots neither in the legislative nor in the executive power. Clerides contradicted him: even at the Geneva negotiations Kissinger had demanded a bi-zonal federation and continued to do so. Makarios was not impressed by Clerides' arguments and stuck to his opinion.

On 22 November Makarios said to Callaghan that he was prepared to accept a multi-regional federation. The refugees had to return and the Turkish troops had to be withdrawn. Callaghan was sure that the Turkish side would accept only a bi-zonal federation. He did not even mention Makarios' demand for a withdrawal of the Turkish troops. According to Callaghan the real danger was that Turkey considered the status quo as a solution. Makarios said that he would return to Cyprus in early December.

On 29 November 1974 Makarios and Karamanlis and representatives of both governments discussed possible solutions. Clerides stressed that the Turks accepted only a bi-zonal federation which might even have the character of a confederation and nothing else. The Güneş plan with its cantons was dead. Denktash had told him that the Turks were ready to reduce their portion of the surface of Cyprus to 25 percent. The UN could not help. The Americans were for a bi-zonal federation and not ready to support a cantonal solution. Callaghan as well as the Eastern Block states and the Europeans also were for a bi-zonal federation. Makarios, however, clung to the vague statements of Kissinger.

When the conference continued in the evening of 30 November it became evident that the Greek side was for negotiation on the basis of a geographically separated federation with any number of cantons. Clerides and foreign minister Christofidis agreed with this. T. Papadopoulos gave himself over to wishful thinking and Kyprianou leaned towards Makarios' opinion. It was decisive whether Makarios would move or not. But Makarios stubbornly remained with his demand for a multi-regional federation with many cantons. Karamanlis distanced himself: the dialogue had to take place between the Greek and the Turkish Cypriots. Clerides warned that the negotiations would reach an impasse. Moreover, he had information that Ankara would soon begin to bring Turks from the mainland to the island. Makarios did not want to understand that one could not bargain over a fait accompli.

Clerides knew Makarios and did not trust the oral agreements at the end of the negotiations in Athens but insisted on written instructions binding Makarios as well. The Greek foreign ministry submitted a memorandum in written form which was handed out to Makarios. He found so many points to which he could not agree that the memo had to be overhauled two times. According to him they should bargain for each iota.

Clerides was given the following instructions for the negotiations with Denktash beginning on 19 December: The aim of the negotiations was the creation of a multi-regional federation on a bi-communal basis with a strong central government. The area given to the Turkish

Cypriots should correspond to their proportion of the population, a maximum of 25 percent. In analogy to this percentage an equivalent percentage of refugees should be allowed to return. The cantons should be established where Turkish villages already existed. The canton between Nicosia and Kyrenia should reach the sea. The other demands were similarly unrealistic.

Makarios had forced his ideas on the negotiations almost entirely. With these instructions Clerides was sent to the negotiations with his hands tied. There remains the question of why Clerides accepted this game. He knew that Denktash trusted him to a certain degree and nobody except him was able to cope with Denktash's negotiation skills. He knew that the Turks would never negotiate with Makarios. If someone was able to wrench something from the Turks it was he. Possibly he believed that Makarios might develop the necessary insight when confronted with concrete questions. Besides that, Clerides' sense of duty was big enough to try to save what could be saved even on this mission impossible. On 7 December Makarios returned to Cyprus. The population gave him an enthusiastic reception.

In December Clerides and Denktash negotiated the terms of their new round to begin in January. Makarios did not even think of giving Clerides some leeway at the negotiations. In order to achieve this he established a so-called National Council which united all leading personalities of Cypriot politics. This council was to have an advisory function only but due to its high-caliber composition it was clear that it would have great weight. Clerides was to report on his negotiations with Denktash to this council every two weeks. In January 1975 Makarios reshuffled the cabinet. With the exception of two, all ministers appointed by Clerides were dismissed. From now on Makarios was again controlling everything.

All autumn long the Turkish army did its best to finish the ethnic cleansing in the north by expelling the Greeks who had remained. The methods applied went as far as forceful eviction. In order to slow down this process the Greek authorities did not allow the 8,000 Turkish Cypriot refugees, who were camping in the British base of Akrotiri, to move north. As long as these refugees remained in areas at least indirectly controlled by the Greek Cypriot administration it was possible to exert pressure on the Turkish side to treat the Greeks still living on their side more carefully. Besides that, as the government propagated the return of the Greek Cypriot refugees, moving these Turkish Cypriots to the north would have been counterproductive.

The Turkish refugees lived in tents and the British authorities would have been obliged to look after them in the approaching winter. Therefore London and Ankara made a deal: Turkish planes would fetch the refugees from the military airport of Akrotiri and fly them to Adana from where they would be brought by boat to northern Cyprus. In the second half of January this action was realised. Allegedly 9,400 persons were flown out. The governments in Nicosia and Athens protested and there were demonstrations. But on 5 February 1975 Callaghan declared this dubious proceeding a humanitarian action.

The final relocation of the populations took place in August on the basis of an agreement. 8,033 Turkish Cypriots were brought by UNFICYP to the north. 130 remained at 22 different places in the south and around 1,500 in the Kokkina enclave. 934 Greek Cypriots applied for their transfer to the north. 790 applications were accepted and 379 received a permit but only 346 really went north. 430 family members were allowed to go north. Generally, the agreement was not kept very well. Only 500 children of the 1,400 living in the north were able to go to the three schools. Only eight teachers returned and five others received a permit. In order to open further schools 23 teachers were ready to go north but were still waiting for a permit in late 1975. A team of doctors was rejected because their families did not want to join them. The last Greek doctor left the north in October 1975. From then on the Greeks were forced to use the Turkish health service.. In a number of villages there was no priest and as no cleric liked to go north this remained so. The freedom of movement in the north was greatly restricted and visits by relatives in the south were not permitted. In later years the living conditions of the Greek Cypriots in the north became even worse as the author can testify on the basis of his own experience.

Although Clerides and Denktash strove for reciprocity in their negotiations about humanitarian problems this did not keep Denktash from deepening the partition. In early February it became known that he was aiming at a confederation but kept Turkey from making this public. His constitutional proposals of 13 February prove this: the constitution had to provide a bi-communal and bi-regional federal state. The laws of the central government should not interfere in the internal matters of both federated states. The central government should have only so much power to enable the state to function. All other competences should remain with the federated states. All jobs in common institutions had to be filled with equal representation, thus creating equality *de jure* and *de facto* and domination by one side would be excluded.

On the same day Denktash created a *fait accompli*: in the morning the council of ministers and the parliamentary assembly met and passed a resolution saying that it was the aim of the Turkish Cypriots to unite with the Greek Cypriots in a bi-regional federation. But until then the autonomous Turkish Cypriot administration would restructure and reorganise itself as a secular federated state. The legislative assembly of the autonomous state would be reformed into a constituent assembly. A second resolution appointed Denktash president of the federated state. With this a separated state was proclaimed in northern Cyprus. Although all sides, with the exception of Turkey, condemned this step nothing happened.

Denktash's and Ankara's use of the term federation is deceptive. They did not want a federal solution but aimed at a loose confederation with autonomous constituent states. If from now on the Turkish side spoke of a federal solution or a federation it meant a solution on the basis of a confederation. Occasionally there has been talk of a solution according to the Swiss model. Apparently it is not understood that the *Confoederatio Helvetica* is a federation despite its misleading name. According to constitutional law Denktash's step was a separation. But seen from outside, on the basis of international law Cyprus remained one state. The step to full secession was taken in 1983 when Denktash proclaimed the "Turkish Republic of Northern Cyprus" which was recognised by Turkey only.

Despite these manoeuvres, in April 1975 negotiations between Clerides and Denktash began in Vienna under the auspices of UN Secretary General Waldheim. Soon it became apparent that on orders of Ankara Denktash was not negotiating seriously but only pretended to do so. How intransigent the Turkish side had become was proved when on 8 June a referendum was held on the constitution of the new Turkish Cypriot federated state. A second round of talks in Vienna was equally inconclusive. Makarios wanted to finish them but Athens insisted that they should continue.

In the meantime the conference of Helsinki (CSCE - Conference on Security and Cooperation in Europe) was prepared. On 18 July the Turkish government tried to prevent the participation of Makarios by a highly refined manoeuvre. It made Denktash submit his earlier made proposal to form an interim government once more. Thus the internationally acknowledged government of Cyprus was to be replaced by a new one lacking recognition and thus not being able to participate in the Helsinki conference. Clerides immediately understood what was behind this proposal and rejected it. Ankara demanded a decision by the CSCE about who was to represent Cyprus. On 19 July 1975, the anniversary of the beginning of Attila I, the chief of the Turkish General Staff announced that Turkey would build up a fourth Army near Izmir which would defend the Turkish coast against eventual Greek attacks. This army would not be subordinated to NATO.

On 21 July Makarios said that he would travel to Helsinki. Two days later the Human Rights Commission of the Council of Europe confirmed the legality of the Cyprus government. On 24 July Clerides rejected Denktash's threat that the Turkish Cypriots would not recognise Makarios' signature under the CSCE treaty. Denktash had suggested that he and Clerides should go to Helsinki and sign instead of Makarios. This was a clear effort to gain official recognition of the "TRNC" through the backdoor. On 28 July Makarios flew to Helsinki. Before his departure he said at a press conference that he did not expect anything from the negotiations in Vienna. Despite this Clerides travelled to the next round with Denktash to Vienna.

At the opening of the CSCE conference on 30 July 1975 in his opening speech Karamanlis reminded attendees that exactly one year ago the troops of a member of the conference had occupied part of the territory of another member, thus violating all ten principles which the conference had worked out. The Greek government had thought of leaving the conference but other members had promised to take care of the Cyprus problem. But now one was in the final phase of the conference and he had to observe that the situation in Cyprus had not changed the slightest bit. If the principles of the CSCE, among them the principle of non-interference in the affairs of other states were not complied with this would damage the European security irreparably.

During a meeting between President Ford, Kissinger and Karamanlis the latter stated that he was ready to accept the Turkish wish of a bi-zonal federation provided that the size of the Turkish area was about proportional to its part of the population, i.e., 2 or 3 percent higher than the 18 percent. The Turks could have any constitution. He would help to enforce this.

At his talks with prime minister Demirel and foreign minister Çağlayangil, Kissinger told them that the Greeks wanted a solution. Makarios and Karamanlis accepted a bi-zonal federation. Makarios would agree to a 25 percent share of the territory, For Karamanlis the question of the refugees was linked with the territorial one. Regarding the future competence of the central government he was ready to accept each Turkish proposal. Karamanlis had not specified the territorial size but gave to understand that he could not enforce too big a one for reasons of internal politics. If Demirel was flexible he could achieve everything he wanted. But Demirel remained evasive.

On 31 July Makarios spoke to the conference. He accused Turkey of violating the ten principles of the last act of the conference. Turkey would sign it and continue to violate it exactly in the same way as she had done in the case of the UN General Assembly resolution. However, before Makarios spoke Demirel and his delegation had left the room. According to them Makarios had no right to speak there. Later in the day Turkey declared that she considered the final act of Helsinki as not binding in the case of Cyprus.

The reason for Demirel's hard attitude is to be found in the embargo which the US Congress had imposed on Turkey as a consequence of Attila II. As long as this was not abolished Demirel would continue his hard line. Even when the French foreign minister Sauvagnargues and his German colleague Genscher intervened the Turks did not move for the time being.

In order to prepare the talks in Vienna Denktash submitted proposals for the responsibilities of the future central government. The elements mentioned there are still characterising the discussion to this day. Two states were to be formed which would unite in a federation. They should only cede those powers to the central government which were absolutely necessary for its functioning. The two federate states should be absolutely equal, forming a condominium. The federal government should have the responsibility for foreign policy, federal banking, the stock market, currency, the federal budget, the federal court, post and telecommunications, the health service and other things. These proposals clearly show that Denktash was aiming at a confederation. If they had been realised the *status quo* would have been the solution. During the talks in August and September 1975 it became obvious that Denktash had come with empty hands. Things might move again only when the embargo was lifted. Thus from now on the inter-communal talks were controlled by factors from outside Cyprus.

The international efforts to get the Cyprus negotiations going again continued in autumn 1975. Especially Sauvanargues and Genscher did their best to influence Ankara in this direction. After long diplomatic haggling they succeeded: At the NATO summit on 11 and 12 December 1975 the foreign ministers of Greece and Turkey, Çağlayangil and Bitsios, began to talk again. Çağlayangil dropped all preconditions for resuming the negotiations which he and Denktash had made. He accepted that the territorial problem should be discussed first because this influenced the number of refugees who might return to their homes. As will be remembered, the return of the refugees was Makarios' priority and he was ready to accept the cession of 25 percent of the ground.

They agreed on a package deal, the so-called Brussels agreement: the three topics, territory, federal structure and competences of the central government, would be discussed. None of them could be finalised alone, only as part of the package. Both governments would influence Denktash and Clerides to strengthen their good will. The Turkish side would not submit territorial proposals but the Greek side would state first which territories it expected the Turkish army to evacuate. This had been agreed to with Makarios. The negotiations should not last two or three days as hitherto but last longer. When progress would be achieved mixed commissions of lawyers might advise the negotiators. In order to guarantee the success of the talks absolute secrecy was agreed. Bitsios had constantly informed Makarios about these talks.

The Brussels Agreement opened the way towards a solution because even Makarios had agreed to it. To interpret it as a kind of NATO solution, as was done in the past, is not accurate. The concept was developed by the NATO powers France and Germany and it was realised within the framework of NATO but it was no NATO plan. Only once a NATO solution had been aspired to, namely in 1964 when a NATO peace-keeping force was to be sent to Cyprus. The Brussels Agreement offered, indeed, a chance to find a solution to the Cyprus problem.

On 14 December the director general of the Greek foreign ministry, Ioannis Tzounis, came to Nicosia on behalf of Karamanlis in order to brief Makarios about the negotiations in and the agreement of Brussels. At the meeting Makarios, the Greek ambassador, Michalis Dountas, and foreign minister Christofinis took part but Clerides had not been invited. This made him suspicious. Clerides had, indeed, reason to be suspicious because Dountas asked him whether he would object if Tassos Papadopoulos and Michalakis Triantafyllidis were appointed as advisors. The term advisor was a euphemism; they would really be supervisors or watchdogs of the hardline nationalists with whom Dountas sympathised.

The militant camp (*machitiki parataxi*) of the hardliners was headed by Vassos Lyssaridis who was far more influential than the size of his small party (EDEK) leads one to assume. He stood for a "fighting realism" based on a "triptych of the national salvation" the elements of which were internationalisation, utilisation of any foreign help and the struggle of the people. His ideas about the realisation of the latter were adventurous, indeed. Concessions were excluded for him because they would only sanction the injustice committed by the Turks.

The other hardline members of the National Council, i.e., Takis Evdokas, Spyros Kyprianou and Tassos Papadopoulos, had similar intransigent views . For them the only solution was a return to a modified *status quo ante*. Clerides' *realpolitik* bordered in their eyes on treason and they, also, rejected Makarios' slow approach to reality based on insight caused by necessity. The only astonishing thing was that Makarios did not make an effort to curb the hardliners. Probably he shied away from a direct confrontation because it would have shown how weak his own position was.

The appointment of the two "advisors" was absolutely counterproductive. Some months before Clerides had managed to reject Denktash's "foreign minister" Çelik as advisor. By this he had avoided an upgrading of the "Turkish Federated State" and not allowed Denktash to sneak out of his responsibility as a negotiator. If the Greek "advisors" participated in the negotiations Çelik could no longer be rejected and Denktash would get his chance to withdraw from the negotiations and shift the talks to a lower level where no decisions could be taken and thus procrastinating would be possible. It is unknown who made Waldheim reject the direct participation of the "advisors" in the negotiations. Makarios, however, accepted.

On 28 January 1976 Makarios informed the National Council about the Brussels Agreement which he knew in all details and had accepted. He agreed that the Greek side submitted its territorial proposals first provided the Turkish side committed itself to present its counter-proposals within a reasonable time. The National Council, however, held onto its opinion that the Turks should move first. Finally they agreed to Clerides' compromise proposal: he would suggest to Denktash to submit his proposals simultaneously. The National Council decided further that Clerides should not discuss the structure of the future republic and the competences of the future government before an agreement had been achieved over the territorial question. This decision ran counter to the Brussels Agreement which envisaged a package deal.

With this decision the Greek Cypriot hardliners had successfully torpedoed the Brussels package solution However, if the package was untied Denktash would be enabled to pull the constituent elements apart or block them. Strictly speaking, they undermined Clerides' position in the negotiations and ruined with their demands - once again - a realistic chance to solve the Cyprus problem. In the following days it became clear that now Denktash was stalling. Finally it was agreed that the negotiations would be resumed in Vienna on 17 February 1976. The astonishing thing is that Makarios avoided taking a clear position.

On the way to Vienna Clerides and his "watchdogs" visited Karamanlis. He made it clear to them that the negotiations were a Cypriot affair. The Greek government had opened the way to them with the help of the Europeans, especially of the French and the Germans. It was not his intention to force his opinion on the Cypriots but time was working against them. Clerides hinted that Karamanlis should exert pressure on Makarios. Since the Greek prime minister was not ready to do this it was clear that the Vienna talks would fail. The National Council had imposed a course upon Clerides which would lead to failure. It is doubtful, however, whether Karamanlis would have succeeded in enforcing a change of course if he had tried. He had done his duty and by the Brussels Agreement he paved the way towards a package solution. If the Cypriot leadership did not want to take this road and remained in their old position they would be responsible for the failure. Clerides should have resigned at this very moment.

The negotiations which began on 17 February 1976 soon got into an impasse because Denktash behaved intransigently and Clerides could not move because of the decisions of the National Council. On 19 February the end of the negotiations was at hand. In this situation Clerides sent a teletype to Makarios. He reminded him of his instructions and stated that Denktash was constantly having recourse to the Brussels Agreement according to which the Greek side had to submit its territorial proposals first. The multi-regional concept demanded by the National Council had been rejected at the last round of negotiations. In Brussels it had been agreed that the territorial proposals should have a regional character and a bi-zonal basis. According to Waldheim, it was now time for the Greek Cypriots to submit their proposals. If this was not done the Turks could not be blamed if the talks failed.

As his "watchdogs" stuck to the course laid down by the National Council they rang up Makarios. Makarios was evasive and avoided a decision: Clerides should decide in conformity with his "advisors". He would accept their decision. As the two "watchdogs" stubbornly stuck to their opinion the negotiations - strictly speaking - had come to an end. Clerides, however, knew that in private Makarios agreed with him, as had been proved by his behaviour at the National Council meeting at the end of January and during the telephone conversation. But Makarios did not have the stamina necessary for a chief of a state and a government to enforce a course which he considered right against an opposition. He had bowed out in the National Council and now again and left the decision to the three in Vienna though he knew that two of them were radically against the Brussels Agreement. Probably he hoped that Clerides would react as he did.

Indeed Clerides took a lone decision. At the next meeting with Denktash on 20 February 1976 he suggested that the territorial proposals should be exchanged within six weeks. He himself would submit his proposals first and Denktash would hand over his ten days later. Denktash accepted. They agreed to keep this absolutely secret. The published communique spoke of substantial talks about territorial and constitutional matters. It had been agreed to exchange written proposals within six weeks. The next round of talks would be in May. Thus by Clerides' moral courage a breakdown of the fifth round of talks was avoided.

This gentlemen's agreement meant that Denktash, or rather Ankara, would have been obliged to show their colours by the end of March and state clearly which territorial concessions they would be ready to make. But this was precisely what Denktash and certain other forces in Turkey did not intend. If, however, they had not submitted their proposals, there would not have been a sixth round of talks and Turkey would have been blamed. Therefore, Denktash in connivance with Ankara developed a plan to avoid this and at the same time delay the talks for many months. In the middle of March an indiscretion was committed and leaked information about the Vienna gentlemen's agreement reached the Turkish Cypriot press. The Greek Cypriot press jumped on this "news" and spoke about a secret deal between Clerides and Denktash unknown to Makarios. Obviously, the hardliners of each kind tried to harm Clerides and to torpedo the negotiations. Clerides denied having concluded a secret agreement.

In order to compromise Clerides definitively, Denktash alleged in an interview with the correspondent of the *Times of London* that he had the future proposals of the Greek Cypriots in his hands. On 24 March Clerides had allegedly given them to him. The journalist believed this story and did not crosscheck it. He did not understand that Denktash used him to compromise Clerides and told this story innocently to the Government Spokesman in the south. In reality Clerides had given nothing to Denktash. But this fake story was the opportunity the hardliners had been waiting for. At a joint session of the National Council and the Council of Ministers Clerides was confronted with it. He reacted indignantly and refused to defend himself against such absurd trumped up charges

On 7 April Clerides resigned as negotiator of the Greek side. The National Council and the Council of Ministers accepted his resignation on 8 April. The new negotiator became Tassos Papadopoulos. Thus the only moderate Greek Cypriot politician who had led the inter-communal negotiations for nine years was out of the game. From now on the hardliners controlled the course. Denktash reacted immediately and refused to negotiate with the former EOKA activist Papadopoulos and nominated Umit Süleyman Onan, who had been speaker of the Turkish parliamentary assembly, as the new negotiator of the Turkish Cypriot side. One day later Denktash announced that he would not recognise Papadopoulos as representative of the Greek community but he was ready to negotiate with Makarios. Thus Denktash had successfully downgraded the inter-communal negotiations and they could be postponed *ad libitum*. Only if Makarios was ready to accept Denktash as negotiator at eye level and negotiated with him would any new movement be possible.

Denktash's intrigue would never have been crowned with success if the Greek Cypriot hardliner had not "assisted" him. Clerides had not only been a match for Denktash during the negotiations but often more than that. The hardliners achieved a Pyrrhic victory because only

Clerides' course of *realpolitik* offered a chance to find a solution to the Cyprus conflict. Strictly speaking the hardliners supported Denktash's separatist policy. It is an irony of history that exactly eleven months later Makarios arrived at that solution policy which Clerides had been proposing constantly. But then it was too late. If Makarios had sided with Clerides at those meetings of the National Council and of the Council of Ministers the history of Cyprus would have taken a different course, perhaps for the better. But one cannot exclude that Makarios was not unsatisfied about Clerides' resignation because from then on he again controlled things.

In contrast to the majority of the Greek Cypriot leaders Denktash practised *realpolitik* to perfection. He did not even shy away from using indecent means if he could accomplish his interests. His intrigue against Clerides torpedoed the Brussels Agreement as well. Denktash wanted his own state. The maximal compromise was a confederation. He could only achieve this aim if Clerides was out of the game. Thus an unnatural coalition of hardliners of both sides successfully ruined the Brussels package deal.

The High Level Agreement and the Death of Makarios
In April 1976 both sides presented their proposals in written form. The Greek proposals were a kind of wholesale retreat to positions of the beginning of the Vienna talks. All those advances and concessions Clerides and Waldheim had arduously wrenched out of Denktash were brushed aside. The hardliners tried to realise their own ideas, though it was clear that Denktash would never accept them. Denktash's counter-proposals proved that he continued to aspire to a confederation. On 22 April T. Papadopoulos complained to the UN representative that Denktash had signed as president of the Turkish Federated State. This state was not recognised by anyone. Denktash's proposal to form an interim government aimed at undermining the internationally recognised government of Cyprus. His proposals were not compatible with the UN resolutions. The Turkish side had no interest in constructive negotiations and tried to protract them in order to gain time for consolidating the situation created by force. On 5 May Umit S. Onan replied in the same unqualified way and this kind of exchange of opinions continued until June. On 27 May at the first meeting of Papadopoulos and Onan only humanitarian questions, such as the missing persons, were discussed. The inter-communal negotiations were de facto interrupted.

Clerides had resigned as negotiator but he was still president of the House of Representatives and as such the deputy of Makarios. Moreover, he was the chief of the biggest party in Cyprus (Eniaio Komma - Unified Party). On 17 April AKEL demanded his removal from the post as president of the House. On 29 April the House passed a motion that in the next elections the majority vote system would be applied. Obviously Clerides' opponents were resolved to oust him and his party from parliament. Indeed, if the other parties united against Clerides' party it would not have a chance to win even one seat. Makarios understood this very well and when Clerides continued to criticise Makarios' struggle of long duration (makrochronio agona) the latter gave the green light: on 5 May the anti-Clerides-parties voted for a motion of censure against Clerides. The result was a stalemate.

In early May the parties reorganised themselves in view of the impending elections. The *Proodeftiki Parataxi* and the *Eniaio Komma* dissolved. On 12 May Spyros Kyprianou announced that he would form the *Dimokratiki Parataxi* (Democratic Front). Two years later this party was renamed *Dimokratiko Komma* (DIKO). On 15 May Clerides made it known that his new party would be called *Dimokratikos Synagermos* (DISY, Democratic Rally). He became president and T. Papadopoulos his deputy. In the following weeks the election campaign began. When Clerides criticised the course of the other parties in the Cyprus question T. Papadopoulos distanced himself. When it became clear that Democratic Front, AKEL and EDEK cooperated Papadopoulos left DISY on 23 June. By this move Papadopoulos managed to remain in the political game. On 16 July Clerides and the deputies of his party resigned their seats and on 22 July the rump parliament unanimously elected T. Papadopoulos president of the House.

In the elections of 5 September 1976 the united anti-Clerides parties won 71.2 percent of the votes and 34 of the 35 mandates. T. Papadopoulos, who ran as an independent candidate, gained the 35th seat. Clerides' DISY received 24.1 percent but not one mandate. On 20 September Spyros Kyprianou was elected president of the House.

On 20 June presidential and parliamentary elections had taken place in the north of the island. Rauf Denktash gained 41,059 votes, i.e. the absolute majority; his rival, Ahmet Midhat Berberoğlou, of the *Republican Turkish Party* (RTP) received 11,869 votes. Thus Denktash had already been elected president in the first vote. Denktash's party NUP (National Union Party) won 30 seats, the *Communal Liberation Party* (CLP) 6 and the *Populist Party* (PP) and the RTP each 2. On 3 July Denktash was sworn in.

In summer and autumn the Greek-Turkish conflict over the Aegean came to the forefront and pushed the Cyprus conflict aside. In November Athens and Ankara agreed on talks in Berne which led to no result. As in the US the presidential election campaign was absorbing the attention of the public, Kissinger kept a low profile because he did not want to clash with the Greek lobby. On 2 November 1976 Democrat Jimmy Carter was elected president. Thus it became clear that from the end of January 1977 the US policy towards Cyprus would change. On 3 November the Assistant Secretary of State for European Affairs, Arthur Hartman, suggested in a memorandum sending a fact finding mission to the three capitals. In December the three ambassadors should come to Washington in order to brief the future president about the situation of the Aegean and the Cyprus conflict. After that one should consult the important European allies and finally one should talk with the floor leaders in Congress. If a consensus was achieved a special emissary should be sent to Cyprus for talks with Makarios and Denktash and brief both about the course of the US Administration.

In fact Hartman suggested a joined diplomatic action which might have a chance of success if realised in the way he suggested. But Kissinger intervenedone last time and ordered the memorandum to be retained until the transfer of office negotiations in January 1977. This was done and therefore precious time was wasted because thus the Clifford Mission began as late as February 1977. Apparently Kissinger did not begrudge his successor a tiny chance of a success.

In mid-December 1976 Makarios said in an interview that under certain conditions he would accept a federal solution. But such a federation had to secure the unity of the state. He would not accept a solution which would lead to partition. A basic precondition for him to accept a separated Turkish Cypriot administration would be freedom of movement, settlement and property. This statement caused Denktash to write a letter to Makarios on 9 January 1977 in which he stated his readiness to meet the Archbishop in the presence of UN representative de Cuellar to talk about the problems pending.

Clerides advised Makarios to accept the proposal because otherwise Denktash would have accused Makarios of torpedoing possible negotiations, which would certainly have made a bad impression on the international opinion. On 27 January the first meeting of Makarios and Denktash since Christmas 1963 took place in the presence of de Cuellar.

Makarios made it clear that he was addressing Denktash in his function as representative of the Turkish Cypriot community and not as president of the Federated Turkish State. Denktash countered that he, too, did not recognise Makarios as president of Cyprus. Both agreed that a package deal would be the best. Makarios complained that whenever Denktash spoke about a federation he meant a confederation. Denktash denied this vehemently. Talking about the territorial aspect Denktash spoke about areas and Makarios about an allotment of 20 percent. Denktash demanded 32.8 percent which allegedly was the equivalent of the land owned by Turks. Makarios hinted that he would be ready to accept 25 percent. Denktash insisted on his number. Then discussion turned to the freedoms. Denktash was ready to grant freedom of movement to the Greek Cypriots but did not specify this. He was ready to accept the right of settlement but only to a degree which did not endanger the federation. A limited number of refugees could return to their homes but not all. Denktash's statements proved that he wanted two loosely joined states and maximal separation.

Makarios and Denktash agreed that the inter-communal negotiations should continue. Denktash stressed that they themselves could intervene if the talks stalled. Makarios agreed. De Cuellar suggested another meeting on 13 February in the presence of Waldheim in which the negotiators might participate. Makarios and Denktash agreed.

On 27 January Makarios informed the National Council about this. At two further meetings on 2 and 8 February it became clear that the hardliners were still against a resumption of the talks if Denktash did not accept their preconditions. The discussion assumed features which resembled those Clerides had encountered before the departure to the last Vienna round. But Makarios was not impressed and autocratically decided that the negotiations would be resumed.

On 12 February 1977 Makarios and Denktash met Waldheim. After a four-hour talk the following formula which became known as the *High Level Agreement* of 1977 was accepted by all:

1.   *We are seeking an independent, non-aligned, bi-communal Federal Republic.*
2.   *The territory under the administration of each community should be discussed in the light of economic viability or productivity and land ownership.*
3.   *Questions of principles like freedom of movement, freedom of settlement, the right of property and other specific matters, are open for discussion taking into consideration the fundamental basis of a bi-communal federal system and certain practical difficulties which may arise for the Turkish Cypriot community.*
4.   *The powers and functions of the Central Federal Government will be such as to safeguard the unity of the country, having regard to the bi-communal character of the State.*

With this agreement Makarios made a cautious step towards recognition of reality. By the first sentence he bid farewell to the unitary state as provided by the 1959 constitution and accepted a future bi-communal federation. The bi-communal character of the state was nothing new because this had been included in the constitution, as well as independence. The only new item was the statement that the future republic would be non-aligned, but even this was not really new because it was a description of the political praxis. The only really new thing in this first phrase was the commitment to a federation.

In the second sentence the principle of the hitherto demanded proportionality between population and size of area was given up in favour of economic considerations. The mentioning of land ownership was a concession to the Turkish side and at the same time formed the maximum of the Turkish land quota. It was the starting point for the negotiations.

In phrase three the freedom of movement and settlement as well as property were acknowledged but possible modifications and curtailing dependent on the federal system and on the constraints on the Turkish Cypriots' side were accepted. Point 4, finally, decided that the competences of the future central government had to be big enough so that the unity of the country was preserved. This meant that the future republic would have a federal and not a confederal character. Makarios' concessions meant that he realised the necessity of giving up certain positions which could not be held any longer. His agreement to a federation was such an insight.

The republic established on this basis would have been independent, non-aligned and bi-communal. The term bi-zonal is found nowhere *expressis verbis*. But everybody in Cyprus is convinced that this agreement provided for a bi-communal and bi-zonal federation. The explanation for this is rather simple: As Denktash narrates, Makarios wanted to avoid a greater clash with the hardliners and therefore asked Denktash to agree that this provocative term would be left out in the published text. Denktash agreed. It was a matter of a verbal agreement, a gentlemen's agreement. Denktash's account is confirmed by the text itself because in paragraph 2 the *"territory [...] of each community"* is mentioned and not *territories* (plural). If cantons had been discussed the text would have contained the plural, territories. Additionally, on 16 February 1977 Waldheim allegedly said at a press conference that both sides meant a bi-zonal federation even though in the text a bi-communal federation was mentioned. Clerides confirms that Makarios accepted bi-zonality when he talked with Denktash and even agreed that the Greek side would submit its territorial proposals first accompanied by a map, but did not say this when he reported to the National Council and the Council of Ministers.

The High Level Agreement was a reasonable step towards a solution on the basis of a bi-communal and bi-zonal federation. The only thing which can be criticised is the fact that it came about a year too late. Nevertheless, until today it is the basic feature of all solution proposals.

On 23 February 1977 the former US Secretary of Defence, Clark Clifford, arrived in Cyprus as the personal envoy of President Carter. Earlier he had visited Athens and Ankara. Makarios informed him about the gentlemen's agreement with Denktash. Clifford suggested that the Greek side should present its proposals first including the territorial proposals accompanied by a map. Makarios agreed. Thus Makarios had finally arrived at the status of the Brussels Agreement after one full year. The negotiations would continue and the Greek side would submit its proposals first.

At the meeting of the National Council and the Council of Ministers Makarios forced his new course on the hardliners who were protesting vehemently. At the second meeting they repeated the same stereotyped arguments again and again. Makarios no longer paid any attention and decided that the proposals of the Greek side should be worked out and a map be drawn delimiting an area of about 20 percent. On 16 March 1977 Makarios informed Waldheim by letter that the Greek Cypriot side would submit its proposals, including a map, at the next Vienna meeting. Waldheim informed Makarios that Denktash, too, was ready for substantial negotiations. He would not submit a map but he was ready to discuss the Greek one.

Thus in March 1977 one had arrived at the same point where Clerides had given up exactly one year before. The discussion in the Councils had shown that the hardliners were still in the majority. Their motives ranged from obstinate harping on about principles and fixation on hatred against the Turks, from lack of moral courage to opportunism. The only person with a clear view was Clerides and it was tragic that he was no longer the negotiator because T. Papadopoulos was but a hardliner and not nearly as good a negotiator as Clerides. Makarios had finally brought himself to accept reality. But the question was whether he could control the negotiations.

The sixth round of the Vienna talks was different: they were no longer talks between the two representatives of the two communities in the presence of the UN Secretary General. Now, besides the two negotiators, the two advisors of each side participated. Gentlemen's agreements like those Denktash and Clerides had concluded were impossible. Though Papadopoulos presented the bi-zonal map at the first meeting on 31 March, his written solution proposals regressed behind the High Level Agreement. The meetings themselves were a rather unproductive exchange of well known arguments. After eleven sessions Waldheim gave up totally unnerved, and adjourned the talks for mid-May 1977.

As Makarios on 3 April 1977 had had a light heart attack, stocktaking of the negotiation by the two Councils was delayed until early May. On 21 April 1977 President Carter introduced a bill in Congress which practically terminated the arms embargo against Turkey. On 2 May Waldheim regretted in his report on the sixth round of the Vienna talks that despite all efforts the talks had failed but they would be resumed.

On the same day the National Council and the Council of Ministers met with Makarios in the chair. Makarios was pessimistic about the future of the talks: the Turkish side was using delaying tactics and was ready for any concession but there was no alternative. He had expected this result. Even when the talks were resumed in May nothing moved.

On 20 June the National Council and the Council of Ministers met again. Makarios spoke about his recent talks in Athens and London. They decided to continue the effort to internationalise the Cyprus problem: one would bring it before the UN General Assembly. Other initiatives would be welcome but these could not replace the UN. The convention of an international conference would be approved but only after the debate in the General Assembly. But one should see to it that no confusion occurred. One should begin with the accompanying enlightening campaign as soon possible. On 22 June Kyprianou opened the new offensive by accusing Turkey of intransigence. An exchange of blows via the press followed. As there was a government crisis in Ankara Denktash could hit back at random. On 29 July he threatened with a unilateral declaration of independence. During the last days of July he spoke of settling mainland Turks in Varoşa. The situation in Cyprus was hardening.

In the evening of 2 August Makarios did not feel well and asked his guard to call his doctors. A little later his personal physician (V. Lyssaridis) and two cardiologists arrived at the archbishopric. At 22:45 p.m. Makarios' heart stopped beating. The cardiologists succeeded in getting it to beat again by electroshock. However, at 4:45 a.m. on 3 August Makarios lapsed into a coma from which he never awoke. He was 63 years old.

After his first heart attack Makarios had selected his burial place: on a wooded height above the Kykko monastery. On Monday, 8 August, the official obsequies took place in the Ag. Ioannis cathedral near the archiepiscopal palace. Tens of thousands had come to Nicosia to pay him their last farewell. After that the coffin was taken through Nicosia on a gun carriage to the road towards Troodos. After its arrival at Kykko it was entombed on a height called *Throni Panagias tou Kykkou* (Throne of the Holy Virgin of Kykko) above the monastery. The tomb reminds one of an antique hero's tomb. An era of Cypriot history which had been shaped by Makarios had come to its end.

On 5 August it became clear that the acting president, S. Kyprianou, would be the only candidate for the be-election of an interim-president due in September who would lead the country until the regular presidential elections in February. Denktash used the occasion to state that in his opinion the death of Makarios offered a chance to overcome the separation. He did not want to say something negative about the dead Makarios but from a political point of view he had contributed substantially to the genesis of the Cyprus problem. What mattered now was that the new leader should heal the wounds. In his eyes Kyprianou was the wrong person. A day later he added that each successor to Makarios would be recognised only as the leader of the Greek community. Should this leader be proclaimed president of Cyprus this would mean the end of the inter-communal talks. Thus it became clear that from now on the hardliners would have the say.

NEGOTIATIONS AND NO RESULT

So far the narrative has followed the four volumes of my "Geschichte der Insel Zypern". The survey following now leans on my book *Frieden in der Ägäis? Zypern - Ägäis - Minderheiten*, which was published in 1989 by Romiosini. It described, among other things, the presidencies of Kyprianou and Vassiliou. The present summary is amended by information accessible now. The closer the description comes to the present, however, the more sketchy it becomes because even a historian of contemporary history needs some chronological distance in order to arrive at sound judgements. The analysis concentrates on the questions why it has not been possible to find a solution during the 32 years after the signing of the High Level Agreement in 1977. Internal developments in Cyprus will only be referred to if they are relevant for this process.

1978-1987: The Kyprianou Presidency

Finally, in April 1978 the Turkish Cypriots submitted their proposals for a solution which contained nothing new. The future state was to be a confederation, still. The territorial border corrections were minimal. The Greek Cypriot side rejected the proposals as unacceptable. In July Kyprianou quarrelled with T. Papadopoulos and removed him from the negotiator post. In November 1978 the UN General Assembly in resolution 33/XV demanded the immediate withdrawal of all Turkish troops; 110 states voted for the resolution, 48 states, among them the EEC states, abstained and only 4 voted against. Kyprianou and the hardliners were delighted and regarded this as a reinforcement of their policy of long-term struggle.

In November 1978 Washington, Ottawa and London jointly presented a twelve point comprehensive framework plan for solution of the Cyprus problem. The proposals were realistic and could have served as a basis for the opening of discussions for a solution. But Ankara as well as Nicosia rejected them. Ankara because they did not meet its expectations and Kyprianou was of the opinion that a plan of the Western powers could not became a basis for inter-communal negotiations because it would be a priori pro-Turkish. But, above all, it did not contain the right of the refugees to return and was curtailing the rights to settlement and property. Kyprianou pinned his hope on internationalisation and long-term struggle within the UN. Clerides considered the plan suitable as a basis for negotiations.

All the time Waldheim was making efforts to get the inter-commual talks into gear again. Finally, he succeeded in bringing Kyprianou and Denktash together in Nicosia on 18 and 19 May 1979. Observers did not expect anything from this meeting and thus were flabbergasted when Kyprianou and Denktash signed the following ten-point agreement:

1. *It was agreed to resume the intercommunal talks on 15 June 1979.*
2. *The basis for the talks will be the Makarios-Denktash guidelines of 12 February 1977 and the UN resolutions relevant to the Cyprus question.*
3. *There should be respect for human rights and fundamental freedoms of all citizens of the Republic.*
4. *The talks will deal with all territorial and constitutional aspects.*
5. *Priority will be given to reaching agreement of the resettlement of Varosha under UN auspices simultaneously with the beginning of the consideration by the interlocutors of the constitutional and territorial aspects of a comprehensive settlement. After agreement on Varosha has been reached it will be implemented without awaiting the outcome of the discussion on other aspects of the Cyprus problem.*
6. *It was agreed to abstain from any action which might jeopardize the outcome of the talks, and special importance will be given to initial practical measures by both sides to promote goodwill, mutual confidence and the return to normal conditions.*

7. *The demilitarization of the Republic of Cyprus is envisaged, and matters relating thereto will be discussed.*
8. *The independence, sovereignty, territorial integrity and non-alignment of the Republic should be adequately guaranteed against union in whole or in part with any other country and against any form of partition or secession.*
9. *The inter-communal talks will be carried out in a continuing and sustained manner, avoiding any delay.*
10. *The inter-communal talks will take place in Nicosia.*

This program exceeded the High Level Agreement only on three points: The Varoşa problem was to be solved preferentially so that a large number of the refugees could return. The demilitarisation of the island would solve the security question. Union with another state or secession were prohibited. The other clauses were vaguely formulated and in order to concretise them extended negotiations and a lot of good will would be necessary, as had been proved in the past. If the good will was missing the negotiations would end soon.

Though the negotiations began on 15 June 1979 they were had already been interrupted on 22 June. Both sides accused one another of being responsible for the breakdown. The Greeks wanted an immediate solution to the Varoşa problem but the Turks were only ready to accept this within the framework of a general solution. Denktash accused the Greeks of departing from the High Level Agreement of 1977 trying to replace bi-zonal by bi-communal. Thus the talks had reached a dead end again and Kyprianou could continue his policy of internationalisation.

As before, in November 1979 the usual Cyprus debate of the General Assembly took place which ended in a resolution with a text which was almost identical to those of the previous resolutions. The text demanded the immediate resumption of the inter-communal negotiations and asked the Secretary General to assist this and report about his efforts in March. In mid-December 1979 The UN Security Council unanimously passed a resolution requesting both sides to have talks on the basis of the 10-point agreement. After three months of efforts to bring the inter-communal negotiations into gear again Waldheim wrote in his report of March 1980 that there were three reasons why his efforts had failed: The Turks wanted a state of their own which should be linked by lose confederation with the Greek one. They were of the opinion that the security of their community was guaranteed only on the basis of a territorial separation. They would only be ready to negotiate if the Greeks dropped a part of their demands. This meant that from now on the Turkish side would steer an intransigent course. On 9 August the inter-communal talks began again under the aegis of Hugo Gobbi, Waldheim's special representative. There were twenty meetings but no results.

Meanwhile the fiscal policy of the government caused growing tensions within the unofficial coalition of Kyprianou's DIKO and AKEL. In May 1980 AKEL attacked Kyprianou's policy on the Cyprus question and accused him of lack of courage. A cabinet reshuffle in September was to stabilise the situation. In May 1981 general elections took place. As the quarrel between the parties had not been arranged there were no election coalitions. Therefore four parties entered parliament: AKEL (12 seats, 32.79%), DISY (12 seats, 31.89%), DIKO (8 seats, 19.50%) and EDEK (3 seats, 8.17%). Thus AKEL had become the strongest power and Kyprianou could rely only on 12 of the 35 deputies but because of the presidential system this was of no great importance.

In the north elections, too, took place on 28 June 1981. Denktash's NUP lost 12 seats and won only 18 of the 40 mandates. The Communal Liberation Party (TKP) of Alpay Durduran reached 13 (8) seats and the left Republican Turkish Party (CTP) increased its numbers of seats from 3 to 5. Denktash reemerged as victor out of the presidential elections which took place on the same day but he received only 53 % of the vote, previously 76 %. Alarming was the entry of a party which was voted for mainly by mainland Turks who had immigrated to Cyprus, although it won only one seat.

By mid-August the inter-communal negotiations had been resumed. Earlier that month the Turkish side had submitted new proposals which in fact were largely the old ones. The ideas of a rotating presidency and equal representation in all federal organs were new. The autonomy of the federated states was to be expanded to the control of the air and sea ports. Kyprianou rejected the proposals: he was ready to accept a federation but not confederation or two states because this would mean separation. In November 1981 Waldheim submitted a plan of his own which envisaged a federation with an executive of 4 Greeks and 2 Turks, a two chamber legislature and territorial partitioning. The president and his deputy coming from different communities should be elected by all Cypriots. The negotiations continued but on a low level and thus there were no constructive developments

This was not astonishing because Kyprianou stuck to his internationalisation course and Denktash was waiting for an opportunity to proclaim a state of his own. Additionally, there were political changes in the mother countries. Since September 1980 Turkey had been ruled by the military. From now on the newly formed National Security Council, which was controlled by the military took over the decision-making about Cyprus and has continued to do so to this day. Turkey's Cyprus policy became a part of the national policy above party politics. From now on strategic and security considerations of the military played a major role. In October 1981 Andreas Papandrou and his PASOK won the parliamentary elections. Since the new Prime Minister appreciated the Soviet proposal to call an international Cyprus conference as good, the policy of internationalisation was strengthened and Athens, the "national centre", participated in it from then on.

In February 1983 presidential elections took place in Cyprus. Kyprianou received 56.53 percent of the votes. His rival candidate, Clerides, gained 33 percent of the votes and Lyssaridis got 9.53 percent. Without the support of AKEL Kyprianou would not have been reelected. The AKEL leadership knew that nominating candidate of its own, which might have obtained a relative majority in the first ballot, would have been counterproductive because it would have revived old anti-communist fears. It might have called into question the many years successfully establishing party members in the state apparatus. The reason for Lyssaridis' high vote was the support by A. Papandreou.

On 13 May 1983 the UN General Assembly passed a comprehensive resolution which, among other things, demanded the immediate withdrawal of all occupation forces. Denktash fired back declaring that this resolution was an act of aggression against the Turkish Cypriot community. By the end of the month it became known that he intended to have the word "federal" removed from his state's name by a decision of his parliament so that it became equal to the Greek state. Afterwards one could decide about federation or final separation. On 15 June 1983 the UN Security Council passed a resolution asking the Cypriot communities to resume the negotiations. On 17 June the parliamentary assembly in the north voted for the holding of a referendum on independence. In order to prevent Denktash from taking precipitate steps the new UN Secretary General, Perez de Cuellar, intervened and demanded that Denktash postpone his separation plans. The military in Ankara supported this.

On 8 August 1983 de Cuellar attempted to induce the conflicting parties to have talks. His representative in Cyprus, Hugo Gobbi, handed a memorandum over to them. This memo did not conatin a plan but two models for a solution regarding the construction of the executive and the legislative as well as proposals for the territorial apportionment. The Cypriot leaders were asked to make it clear by 15 September whether they were ready to continue negotiations on this basis. AKEL and DISY under Clerides agreed. Lyssaridis and the Archbishop were against it. Kyprianou was not able to commit himself. Foreign Minister Nikos Rolandis was in favour of an agreement but when he could not prevail he resigned on 21 September. Georgios Iakovou, who was ambassador in Bonn, succeeded him.

On 21 September Kyprianou had talks with Prime Minister Papandreou and President Karamanlis. After they applied some pressure on Kyprianou it was decided to accept de Cuellar's proposal unreservedly. On 30 September Kyprianou informed the UN Secretary General accordingly. Because of Kyprinou's belated answer Denktash, too, could take his time. Finally, he gave a negative answer. When he noticed, however, that his rejection provoked extremely negative reactions he suggested a meeting between him and Kyprianou to de Cuellar. If Kyprianou rejected this he reserved his right to proclaim a state of his own. For tactical reasons Kyprianou told de Cuellar that he accepted this summit meeting provided it was well prepared. He agreed that de Cuellar should convene such a meeting.

Meanwhile, Denktash had started another action which showed clearly that he was striving for a state of his own. He requested that the Council of Europe accept representatives of his pseudo state, which was rejected, of course. Thereupon Denktash demanded that the two representatives of the Republic of Cyprus at the Council be withdrawn. This demand was again accompanied by a threat of a unilateral declaration of independence. So far these threats had been verbal diatribes but when the military in Ankara were engaged with the preparation of elections on 6 November he thought he could act. He announced that he would soon get down to action.

On 14 November 1983 Hugo Gobbi returned to Cyprus. De Cuellar had instructed him to prepare the summit meeting between Kyprianou and Denktash. The following day Gobbi visited both and gave them letters from de Cuellar with proposals for the meeting. Denktash made his parliamentary assembly meet and resolve the establishment of the independent "Turkish Republic of Northern Cyprus". He declared his readiness to further negotiations about the establishment of a "real" federation, but at the same time the "President" of the new state declared that there was no chance to challenge the new statehood. Thus the clause of the High Level Agreement signed by Makarios and Denktash about the unity of the country had become obsolete. The Government in Ankara pretended to be surprised by this step. Whether this was true is unknown but it soon recognised the new state.

On 18 November the UN Security Council declared the unilateral declaration of independence void and appealed to all states not to recognise any other Cypriot state but the Republic of Cyprus only. The states complied with this and thus no state, with the exception of Turkey, has recognised the "TRNC". The Commonwealth summit, the EU, the European Parliament and others condemned Denktash's course of action. Even the superpowers agreed in their condemnation of the secession, but this did not abolish it.

In January 1984 Kyprianou submitted a framework for a comprehensive settlement of the Cyprus problem. The basic prerequisite for a solution was the total demilitarisation of Cyprus. After the withdrawal of the Turkish occupation troops all the other troops, even the legal contingents, stationed there should be removed and the Cypriot National Guard and the so-called Turkish Cypriot forces dissolved. An international force under the aegis of the UN should take over the safeguarding of the island against internal and external threats. The independence, territorial integrity, unity and non-aligned status of Cyprus should be safeguarded by an international treaty of guarantee. But neither Greece nor Turkey should be guarantor powers.

Cyprus should become a federation. The basis of all agreements should be the UN Resolutions, the High Level Agreement of 1977 and the 10-point plan of 1979. 25 percent of the territory of the island should remain under Turkish Cypriot administration. In the central executive the Turkish Cypriots would have a share of 30 percent but no veto right. Regarding the legislature the plan offered two alternatives with mechanisms to solve conflicts. There was a catalogue of the federal powers proving that the central component of the federation was rather strong. Finally, the plan demanded the rights to movement, settlement and property.

Though this framework plan contained substantial concessions, Denktash rejected the territorial concessions as too small and demanded that Turkey had to remain a guarantor power. Despite these obstructions de Cuellar and Kyprianou continued their efforts to bring the talks into gear again. On 16 March Denktash and de Cuellar met and the latter demanded that Denktash should give his opinion on Kyprianou's plan. Denktash promised to do this but delayed his reply and on 10 April announced that in August a referendum would be held on a new "constitution" of northern Cyprus. De Cuellar was alarmed and therefore sent his special representative, Hugo Gobbi, for consultations to Cyprus. Arrogantly Denktash denied de Cuellar's right to submit any proposals. Denktash even demanded the dismantling of the Republic of Cyprus as a precondition to negotiations for another meeting with Kyprianou. At the same time he made it known that on 17 April Ankara would accredit an ambassador in north Cyprus and expected the posting of a "TRNC" ambassador in Ankara. A reply to the Kyprianou plan was not even mentioned.

Provoked in this way the Government of Cyprus appealed to the UN Security Council. On 11 May 1984 the SC adopted resolution 550/84 which condemned the secessionist actions of Denktash and requested the Secretary General to intensify his undertakings to attain a solution. Therefore de Cuellar again contacted both sides and after long pre-negotiations, during which Denktash in a tricky way tried to upgrade his "Government", the two delegations met de Cuellar in Vienna, separately, in August. The Secretary General gave both sides a working paper containing a series of points which could provide the basis for later negotiations and demanded that both sides submit their replies by 10 September 1984.

Both sides reacted positively and the negotiations, now called proximity talks, were resumed in New York on 10 September 1984. De Cuellar separately negotiated with the two delegations. In October and November 1984 there were further rounds of these indirect negotiations without any result. In January 1985 further fruitless meetings followed because Denktash torpedoed them deliberately by ultimately demanding that the paper which de Cuellar had updated regularly after these rounds should not be discussed but signed.

In early April de Cuellar made another effort He sent a document, which became known as *"single consolidated draft agreement"*, to both sides. In this paper the Secretary General had merged the main positions of all previous documents. Kyprianou accepted it as a basis for discussion. At first, Denktash did not reply but affronted the Secretary General by holding a referendum on the constitution of his state (5 May) and presidential elections (9 June). In July and August Denktash explicated his position even more clearly: both communities had to be absolutely equal. The two states had to be separated like the two Germanies. The guarantee by Turkey was indispensable and in order to safeguard this, Turkish troops of considerable strength had to be stationed in Cyprus.

Despite this intransigent attitude of Denktash, de Cuellar tried his best to get the talks under way again. After several meetings with representatives of the Cyprus Government and Denktash in summer and autumn 1985 it was decided to continue the talks on a lower level in Geneva. The aim of these talks should be to work out a text of a framework plan, acceptable to both sides. Parallel to these negotiations Nicosia made another effort to obtain international support. On 2 September 1985 the summit of the Non-aligned, assembled in Luanda, called on Ankara to withdraw its occupation forces and on Denktash to recall his secession. On 13 September the European Parliament condemned Denktash's actions. In October the Commonwealth summit denounced it.

On 8 December 1985 parliamentary elections took place in the Republic of Cyprus. Clerides' DISY received 33.56 percent of the votes and became the strongest force (19 seats). Kyprianous DIKO gained 27.65 percent and 16 seats, and AKEL 27.43 percent and 15 seats. EDEK won 11.87 percent but no seat. The failure of Lyssaridis' party was due to a shift of Papandreou's support from EDEK to Kyprianou, whose party was thus spared a collapse of votes. Nevertheless, from now on Kyprianou had to rule against a parliament in which the opposition had a majority.

In January 1986 the Soviet Union submitted a plan for a solution of the Cyprus Problem within the framework of an international conference. As this proposal corresponded with similar ideas in Nicosia and Athens it was acclaimed there. Ankara, however, did not want to listen to this proposal and Denktash reacted angrily: an intervention of the superpowers in the internal affairs of Cyprus would not serve the interests of the island.

Meanwhile further negotiations between the two sides had taken place which, apparently, had led to a certain convergence of the positions. Thus at the end of March 1986 de Cuellar submitted a third *draft framework agreement*. Basically it did not differ much from the previous proposals except in the chronology of its application. In a first phase de Cuellar wanted to solve the territorial and the constitutional problems. After this was achieved the Turkish troops should be withdrawn.

After intensive consultations with Athens the Cyprus Government rejected this plan since it was afraid of renewed interventions if Turkish troops remained on the island; the Turkish Prime Minister Özal had declared that the rights of the Turkish guarantor power were not negotiable. Additionally, the proposals regarding the three freedoms of movement, settlement and property were considered unsatisfactory. Alternatively, Kyprianou demanded an international conference on Cyprus or a summit meeting with Denktash where the open questions should be discussed. Prime Minister Özal, however, was of the opinion that Turkey should reevaluate its policy if the Cyprus problem was not solved soon. Denktash, stubbornly, refused to participate in any conference prior to a recognition of his state.

Obviously, Ankara had decided to steer a tougher course. Özel's "state visit" in northern Cyprus in early July and the temporary closing of the borders of northern Cyprus may be regarded as elements of this new policy. The increase of the occupation troops to 35,000 soldiers and an intensified settling of mainland Turks in Cyprus point in the same dirction. By the end of 1986 40,000 settlers had been brought to Cyprus, thus increasing the Turkish proportion of the population of Cyprus to approximately 38 percent. This policy was continued for many years. This immigration and the emigration of a huge number of Turkish Cypriots caused the latter to become a minority in their own country, today.

Though the efforts to make progress on the Cyprus question continued in the second half of 1986, the Aegean conflict which flared up then substantially pushed the Cyprus conflict into the background. Although in 1987 Nicosia continued to collect statements of solidarity these remained declarations on paper and contributed little or nothing to the solution. The only substantial progress was the approach to the EC. By mid October the treaty on customs union was signed and in December came into force. During his government Kyprianou had obtained so many resolutions that one could have papered all the walls of the Presidential Palace, as an insider was complaining then, but he had not come one step closer to a solution. Among those governing then the anxiety was widespread that a wrong decision might be taken. In the Greek Cypriot community frustration spread but also the readiness to rethink the situation. Contrary to this attitude Denktash and his supporters supported the status quo.

1988-1993: The Vassiliou Presidency

On 14 February the first round of the presidential elections took place. Kyprianou got 9.22 percent of the votes, Clerides 30.09 and the entrepreneur Vassiliou, who did not belong any party, 27.29 percent. Thus Kyprianou was out of the race. In the run-off ballot on 21 February AKEL supported Vassiliou who defeated Clerides with 51.63 to 48.37 percent.

After his election Vassiliou declared that he would work for a rapprochement of the two communities and for honest cooperation. He announced that he was ready to meet Denktash without any preconditions, but he did not accept Denktash's demand that the two "presidents" should meet. When he was sworn in he suggested a meeting between him and Özal. Then he presented his concept for a solution to the Cyprus problem: withdrawal of all Turkish troops and settlers, respect for the rights of the citizens to free movement, free settlement and property. The refugees should be allowed to return. International guarantees should exclude any unilateral intervention. Talks were useful provided they were not considered an end in itself. In order to solve the international implications the calling of an international conference under UN aegis appeared necessary. If a solution was found the result should be submitted to the people who would decide in a referendum.

The foreign ministry in Ankara rejected the wish to meet Özal. The correct addressee of such a proposal was Denktash. Since the relations between Athens and Ankara had been improved considerably by the encounter of Özal and Papandreou in Davos in January and by Özal's visit to Athens in June 1988 and as the US, too, supported the resuming of the talks Ankara exerted pressure on Denktash so that he agreed to a meeting in Geneva on 24 August 1988. During that meeting the two sides decided to begin new negotiations on the basis of the agreements of 1977 and 1979 without any preconditions whatsoever. Although Denktash remained intransigent during the negotiations in autumn and continued to speak of the two peoples in February 1989, Vassiliou submitted comprehensive proposals for the creation of an independent, territorially integral, non-aligned federal republic.

The negotiations continued in spring 1989 but did not achieve any result. In July de Cuellar submitted a "set of ideas" which he considered as "food for thought" for a possible solution in September. The Greek side did not agree to all proposals contained in the set but was ready to accept them as food for thought. Denktash rejected them sharply and doubted the right of the Secretary General to submit such proposals. The negotiations, however, continued without any result.

In February 1990 de Cuellar organised a meeting between Vassiliou and Denktash in New York. Quickly it became obvious that Denktash wanted to torpedo this round, too. He demanded that the term "community" was considered a synonym of "people" and that each of the two peoples on Cyprus had a right to self-determination and, implicitly, to secession. Thus Denktash left the ground of the 1977 and 1979 agreements which he himself had signed. De Cuellar declared the negotiations as finished and demanded that the Security Council act.

On 12 March 1990 the Security Council demanded Denktash, in resolution 649/1990, continue the inter-communal negotiations and show respect for the UN resolutions and the agreements of 1977 and 1979. On 4 July 1990 the Government of Cyprus applied for membership of the EU. Ankara and Denktash reacted irascibly and the latter broke of the negotiations. In October 1990 the Turkish Prime Minister paid a state visit to northern Cyprus which was a clear provocation of the Secretary General.

In June 1991 de Cuellar made a final effort to get the Cyprus problem moving by suggesting negotiations about the territorial problem and the return of the refugees. The Turkish side rejected this and demanded that its right to secession should be acknowledged, thus invalidating the agreements of 1977 and 1979. The UN Security Council rejected this and insisted on the validity of these agreements. InDecember 1991 de Cuellar submittted his final report of his efforts to reach a solution to the Cyprus problem, underlining that maintaining the status quo was no solution.

In April 1992 the new Secretary General, Boutros Boutros Ghali, submitted an enlarged version of the "set of ideas" which might serve as a basis for further negotiations. The Security Council endorsed Boutros Ghali's initiative by resolution 750/1992. New proximity talks between Vassiliou and Denktash in the presence of Boutros Ghali, began in June. When in the second round, which began on 15 July things began to materialise Denktash began to drag his feet for a full week. This led to a meeting between the five permanent members of the Security Council and Denktash on 24 July where the five made it clear to Denktash that they stood behind Boutros Ghali's proposals. Although Denktash talked after this intervention it soon became obvious that he was pretending to negotiate because he was evasive or used excuses. On 14 August Boutros Ghali had enough; he adjourned the negotiations and reported to the Security Council. The SC, in turn, demanded in its resolution of 26 August that a solution had to be found by the end of the year.

In October the talks were resumed. In November 1992 Boutros Ghali stated officially that Denktash had hindered an agreement by constantly submitting new demands and withdrawing earlier undertakings. As presidential elections were looming on the horizon the talks were adjourned.

1993-2003: The Clerides Presidency

Since in the first round of the elections Vassiliou reached only a relative majority of the votes, a second round was necessary on 13 February 1993 from which Clerides emerged with a tiny majority as victor. In May Clerides and Denktash began new talks about confidence building measures under the aegis of Boutros Ghali in New York. As Boutros Ghali had recognised that whenever he submitted a comprehensive proposal Denktash would raise objections he presented a concrete deal: the airport of Nicosia would be released for use and could be used by both sides. In return Varoşa was to be given back to its Greek owners. This was a proposal according to the principle of *do ut des*. But Denktash managed to reject even this mutually advantageous proposal and torpedo other confidence building measures. When the talks were adjourned to give Denktash the possibility to confer with his people in northern Cyprus Denktash let it be known that he would not return to New York. He wanted to negotiate with Clerides directly.

In early January 1994 parliamentary elections took place in northern Cyprus which brought a more liberal government to power. In February 1994 new negotiations began which again led nowhere because on the Turkish side the good will was lacking, as Boutros Ghali wrote. In August Turkish intransigence reached its climax: Denktash made his parliamentary assembly revoke its prior "resolutions" regarding a federation and insist on a loose association of two sovereign states. In October another effort to find an agreement failed because Denkatsh insisted on the prior recognition of his state.

Even when in early 1995 President Clinton intervened and his Undersecretary Richard Holbrooke tried to get substantial negotiations into gear he failed. There were further efforts later in the year but they failed, as did analogous ones in 1996. In December 1996 Clerides suggested a total demilitarisation of the island but this proposal was turned down by the Turkish side as well. In 1997 the UN Secretary General started another initiative which again failed. But now massive pressure by Ankara was added to Denktash's intransigence: Ankara openly threatened to intervene militarily if the Republic of Cyprus brought the S-300 anti aircraft rockets onto the island which it had bought from Russia . In February 1997 Clerides met the new Secretary General, Kofi Annan, in Davos and informed him about the situation.

On 9 June 1997 Kofi Annan, who was forcefully supported by the Americans, called on Clerides and Denktash to begin direct negotiations. The first round of these talks took place in

Troutbeck near New York from 9 to 13 July. The representative of the Secretary General handed a paper over to them which contained the previous proposals for a solution which had been submitted by both sides. This paper was to be the basis for discussion of the next round which was to begin in August. Denktash and Clerides agreed to meet in Nicosia by the end of July to discuss humanitarian problems, primarily that of the "missing persons". On 6 August, however, Turkey and the "TRNC" signed an agreement which threatened to annex northern Cyprus in the case the EU continued its accession negotiations with the Republic of Cyprus. Obviously, Ankara believed that the EU would shy away from a conflict with Turkey and would stall the talks.

Despite these threats the next round of talks between Denktash and Clerides began at Glöion-sur-Montreux on 11 August. The UN representative submitted some new papers. Clerides accepted them although he had some caveats. Denktash, however, behaved in an obstructive way: he rejected any discussion of the Cyprus problem as long as the accession negotiations continued. At the end of the conference at Glion Clerides stated that they were there where they had been when the talks began. The UN blamed the Turkish Cypriot side for the failure. The EU was not impressed by the Turkish threat and decided in December that the accession process of Cyprus would begin in March 1998. An annexation, however, did not materialise.

On 15 February 1998 Clerides was reelected president of Cyprus. In March he suggested to the EU that representatives of the Turkish Cypriots should participate in the accession process. The EU considered this a good idea and agreed. Denkatsh, however, rejected any kind of participation in the accession negotiations. On 30 March the accession talks began. Until December 1999 nothing moved in the field of the inter-communal negotiations. On 3 December a new round of the proximity talks under the aegis of the Secretary General began. These negotiations continued with a few interruptions until November 2002 without any result. On 11 November 2002 Kofi Annan submitted a first plan for a comprehensive settlement of the Cyprus problem. Clerides criticised a few points and suggested changes. Kofi Annan had these integrated into the plan and in December 2002 he submitted a second revised version.

In February 2003 presidential elections were scheduled in the Republic of Cyprus. Clerides was now 84 years old. He had served his country for 44 years. His health was ailing and he was tired as he writes in his memoirs. He knew that he would scarcely survive a third term of office and thus decided not to run for office once more. He informed his party, the UN, and the Greek Prime Minister, Kostas Simitis. All three begged him to stand for election once more and only for an interim period because only he could bring the negotiations to a positive end. Clerides told them that there was no constitutional basis for this. Finally, it was agreed that he would run for an interim period of 14 to 16 months. But for this the support of AKEL was needed; this party, however, rejected this proposal. Nevertheless, Clerides ran for office stating clearly that he would stay only for an interim period.

At the elections on 13 February hardliner Tassos Papadopoulos who was supported by DIKO, EDEK, and AKEL, was elected. There is little doubt that besides Clerides there was no one capable of leading the negotiations to a positive end. He was known for his ability to compromise. He was a conservative and a pragmatist. Ideological stubborness was alien to him. He had the astuteness to find a reasonable mutually acceptable solution. The change of government in Turkey to prime minister Erdoğan caused a thaw in northern Cyprus and Denktash was rapidly losing his power. If Clerides had stayed President a few months longer there would have been a solution for sure. The change to hardliner Papadopoulos added another lost opportunity to the long sad series.

Due to the short time distance the ensuing development can be described only in a rather sketchy way. The Annan Plan, as it was called now, was enriched by further elements which made it increasingly ugly, not only in the eyes of the Greek Cypriot hardliners. On 24 April 2004 two separate referenda were held. 64 percent of the Turkish Cypriots voted for the plan and 75 percent of the Greek Cypriots voted against it. From 1979 to 2004 the Turkish Cypriot side had blocked a solution but now the Greek Cypriot side did the same thing. Until the spring of 2008 there was no movement at all due primarily to Papadopoulos' intransigent attitude but also to the growing anxieties of the Greek Cypriots in general about the possible consequences in the case the plan was realised. But the year 2004 had also a positive event: Cyprus became a member of the EU. Thus its existence as an independent state was secured.

At the presidential elections in February 2008 for the first time in the history of Cyprus an AKEL chief ran for the highest post in the state and won. The new President, Dimitris Christofias, and his Turkish Cypriot colleague emanated from the trade union movement and like each other. For the first time since 1974 two politicians are in power at the same time who want a solution. Both are full of good will and if they had been left alone they would already have achieved a solution. But both have to overcome strong resistance. Talat's room to negotiate is rather narrow because he needs Ankara's *placet* for each decision, and in Ankara Cyprus has become the apple of discord between the Government and the military on the question of who has the final say in Turkey. Additionally, Talat must struggle with a government controlled by the Turkish Cypriot hardliners. Christofias, as well, has to consider his hardliners. Finally, Ankara's inclination to concession has decreased considerably because its chances of an EU entry are rather slim.

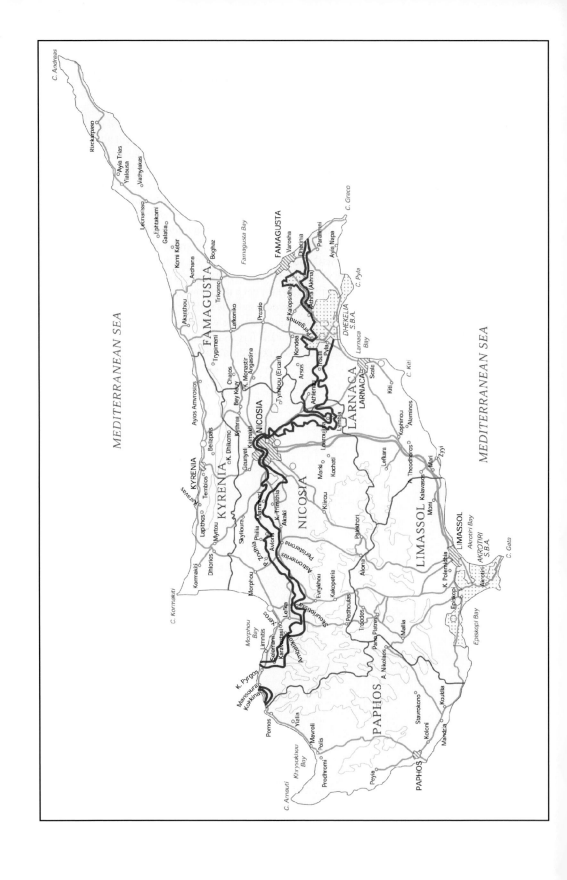

Plate 51

Attila 1: the destroyed village of Gerolakkos

23 July 1974: Acting President Clerides

Plate 52

Geneva Conference: The three foreign ministers Güneş, Mavros and Callaghan

Attila II: Turkish goverment propaganda

Plate 53

Attila 2: war marks in the Green Line in the old town of Nicosia

Attila 2: a Turkish tank arrives at Atatürk Square in northern Nicosia

Plate 54

Attila 2: These five National Guardsmen were taken prisoner by the Turkish Army. A Turkish soldier offers a cigarette to one of the prisoners. According to Denktash few moments later they were shot by a TMT officer. In 2009 their remains were exhumed by CMP and identified and given to their families.

Attila 2: exhumation of a Turkish Cypriot mass grave

Plate 55

Attila 2: a young woman fleeing, probably in Nicosia

Misery of the refugees

Plate 56

19 July 1974: Makarios addresses the UN Security Council

29 July 1974: Makarios meets Kissinger

Plate 57

12 February 1977: after signing the High Level Agreement, only Denktash seems satisfied

Funeral procession: Makarios' coffin on the gun carriage

Plate 58

Rauf Denktash and Glafkos Clerides about 2000

Georgios Vassileiou, Glafkos Clerides and Dimitrios Christofias

Select Bibliography

Chapter 1

Adams, Thomas W. *AKEL: The Communist Party of Cyprus* (Stanford: Hoover Institution Press, 1971)

Alastos, Doros *Cyprus in History. A Survey of 5000 Years* (London: Zeno, 1955)

Attalides, Michael *Cyprus. Nationalism and International Politics.* (New York: St. Martin's Press, 1979)

Crouzet, Francois *Le Conflit de Chypre* 2 Vols (Bruxelles: Emile Bruylant, 1973)

Dischler, Ludwig *Die Zypernfrage* (Frankfurt: Alfred Metzner, 1960)

Georghallides, George S. *A Political and Administrative History of Cyprus 1918 - 1926, with a Survey of the Foundations of British Rule* (Nicosia: Cyprus Research Centre, 1979)

- *Cyprus and the Governorship of Sir Ronald Stors: The Causes of the 1931 Crisis.* (Nicosia: Cyprus Research Centre, 1985)

Hill, George *A History of Cyprus*, IV, *The Ottoman Province, The British Colony 1571-1948* (Cambridge: CUP, 1952)

Kelling, George Horton *Countdown to Rebellion. British Policy in Cyprus 1939-1955* (New York: Greenwood Press, 1990)

Kyrris, Costas P. *History of Cyprus* (Nicosia: Lampousa, 1996)

Reddaway, John *Burdened with Cyprus. The British Connection* (London: Rustem, Weidenfeld & Nicolson, 1986)

Richter, Heinz A. *Geschichte der Insel Zypern 1878-1949* (Möhnesee: Bibliopolis, 2004)

Tzermias, Pavlos *Geschichte der Republik Zypern* (Tübingen: Francke Verlag, 1991)

Chapter 2

Barker, Dudley *Grivas. Portrait of a Terrorist* (London: Cresset Press, 1959)

Byford-Jones, W. *Grivas and the Story of EOKA* (London: Robert Hale, 1959)

Foley, Charles & W. I, Scobie, *The Struggle for Cyprus* (Stanford: Hoover Institution Press, 1975)

Hatzivassiliou, Evanthis *Britain and the International Status of Cyprus, 1955-59* (Minneapolis: University of Minnesota, 1997)

Holland, Robert *Britain and the Revolt in Cyprus 1954-1959* (Oxford: Clarendon Press, 1998)

Nicolet, Claude *United States Policy Towards Cyprus 1954-1974. Removing the Greek-Turkish Bone of Contention* (Mannheim & Möhnesee: Bibliopolis, 2001)

Purcell, H. D. *Cyprus* (London: Benn, 1969)

Richter, Heinz A. *Friede in der Ägäis? Zypern -Ägäis - Minderheiten* (Köln: Romiosini, 1989)

- *Geschichte der Insel Zypern 1949-1959* (Möhnesee: Bibliopolis, 2006)

Stefanidis, Ioannis D. *Isle of Discord. Nationalism, Imperialism and the Making of the Cyprus Problem* (New York: New York University Press, 1999)

Stephens, Robert *Cyprus. A Place of Arms. Power Politics and Ethnic Conflict in the Eastern Mediterranean* (London: Pall Mall Press, 1966)

Tzermias, Pavlos *Geschichte der Republik Zypern* (Tübingen: Francke Verlag, 1991)

Chapter 3

Bitsios, Dimitris *Cyprus. The Vulnerable Republic* (Thessaloniki: Institute for Balkan Studies, 1975)

Choisi, Jeanette *Wurzeln und Strukturen des Zypernkonfliktes 1878 bis 1990* (Stuttgart: Franz Steiner, 1993)

Clerides, Glafkos *Cyprus: My Deposition.* Vol. 1 und 2 (Nicosia: Alithia, 1989)

Crawshaw, Nancy *The Cyprus Revolt. An Account of the Struggle for Union with Greece* (London: Allen & Unwin, 1978)

Drousiotis, Makarios *Cyprus 1974: Greek Coup and Turkish Invasion* (Möhnesee: Bibliopolis, 2006)

Foley, Charles *Legacy of Strife. Cyprus from Rebellion to Civil War* (Harmondsworth: Penguin, 1964)

Harbottle, Michael *The Impartial Soldier* (London: Oxford UP, 1970)

James, Alan *Keeping the Peace in the Cyprus Crisis of 1963-64* (London: Palgrave, 2002)

Kadritzke, Niels & Wolf Wagner *Im Fadenkreuz der NATO. Ermittlungen am Beispiel Cypern* (Berlin: Rotbuch Verlag, 1976)

Ker-Lindsay, James *Britain and the Cyprus Crisis 1963-1964* (Möhnesee: Bibliopolis, 2004)

Kyriakides, Stanley *Cyprus. Constitutionalism and Crisis Government* (Philadelphia: University of Pennsylvania Press, 1968)

Markides, Diana Weston *Cyprus 1957-1963 from Colonial Conflict to Constitutional Crisis. The Key Role of the Municipal Issue* (Minneapolis: Minnesota Mediterranean and East European Monographs, 2001)

Nicolet, Claude *United States Policy Towards Cyprus 1954-1974. Removing the Greek-Turkish Bone of Contention* (Mannheim & Möhnesee: Bibliopolis, 2001)

O'Malley, Brendan and Ian Craig, *The Cyprus Conspiracy. America, Espionage and the Turkish Invasion* (London: Tauris, 1999)

Polyviou, Polyvios G. *Cyprus. In Search of a Constitution* (Nicosia,1976)

Richter, Heinz A. *Geschichte der Insel Zypern 1959-1965* Band 3 (Mainz: Rutzen, 2007)

Stearns, Monteagle *Entangled Allies. US Policy Toward Greece, Turkey, and Cyprus* (New York: Council on Foreign Relations Press, 1992)

Stegenga, James A. *The United Nations Force in Cyprus* (Ohio State UP, 1968)

Stephens, Robert *Cyprus. A Place of Arms. Power Politics and Ethnic Conflict in the Eastern Mediterranean* (London: Pall Mall Press, 1966)

Tzermias, Pavlos *Geschichte der Republik Zypern* (Tübingen: Francke Verlag, 1991)

Xydis, Stephen G. *Cyprus: The Reluctant Republic* (The Hague: Mouton, 1973)

Chapter 4

Asmussen, Jan *Cyprus at War. Diplomacy and Conflict during the 1974 Crisis* (London: Tauris, 2008)

Birand, Mehmet Ali *30 Hot Days* (London, Nicosia, Istanbul: Rustem, 1985)

Hitchens, Christopher *Cyprus* (London: Quartet Books, 1984)

Ioannides, Christos P. *In Turkey's Image. The Transformation of Occupied Cyprus Into a Turkish Province* (New York: Caratzas, 1991)

Purcell, H. D. *Cyprus* (London: Benn, 1969)

Richter, Heinz A. *Geschichte der Insel Zypern* Band 4 (Mainz: Rutzen, 2009)

Salih, Halil Ibrahim *Cyprus The Impact of Diverse Nationalism on a State* (University of Alabama Press, 1978)

Sherman, Arnold *Zypern. Die gefolterte Insel. Der Griechisch-Türkische Zypernkonflikt und seine Hintergründe* (Freiburg: Ahriman-Verlag, 1999)

Sonyel, Salahi R. *Cyprus: The Destruction of a Republic: British Documents 1960-65* (London: Eothen Press, 1997)

Stern, Laurence *The Wrong Horse. The Politics of Intervention and the Failure of American Diplomacy* (New York: Times Book, 1977)

Tatli, Suzan *Der Zypernkonflikt* (Pfaffenweiler: Centaurus, 1986)

Tzermias, Pavlos *Geschichte der Republik Zypern* (Tübingen: Francke Verlag, 1991)

Uludag, Sevgül *Cyprus: The Untold Stories* (Mannheim, Möhnesee: Bibliopolis, 2005)

Yennaris, Costas *From the East. Conflict and Partition in Cyprus* (London: Elliott & Thompson, 2003)

Chapter 5

Pailley, Claire *An International Relations Debacle. The UN Secretary-General's Mission of Good Offices in Cyprus 1999-2004* (Oxford: Hart, 2005)

Potier, Tim *A Functional Cyprus Settlement: the Constitutional Dimension* (Mainz: Rutzen, 2007)

Richter, Heinz *Friede in der Ägäis? Zypern - Ägäis - Minderheiten* (Köln: Romiosini, 1989)

Index

PELEUS

Studien zur Archäologie und Geschichte Griechenlands und Zyperns
hrsg. von Heinz A. Richter und Reinhard Stupperich

Geschichte der Insel Zypern 1950-1959 (2006) 665 Seiten mit über 100 Abbildungen, 32 Phototafeln und einer herausnehmbaren farbigen Faltkarte (41x34 cm), 8°, ISBN 3-933925-79-7, € 49,00

Vol. 37 **Heinz A. Richter**
Geschichte der Insel Zypern 1959-1965 (2007) 644 Seiten mit über 100 Abbildungen sowie und eine herausnehmbare Faltkarte (41x34 cm), 8°, ISBN 3-938646-12-5, € 49,00

Vol. 38 **Tim Potier**
A functional Cyprus settlement: the constitutional dimension (2007) 765 Seiten, 8°, ISBN 3-938646-20-9, € 49,00

Vol. 41 **HeinzRichter**
Geschichte der Insel Zypern 1965-1977 (2009) zusammen 808 Seiten, über 110 Abbildungen, 8 sw Karten, 8°, hard cover, ISBN 978-3-938646-33-5 , € 65

Band 43 **Glafkos Clerides**
Negotiating for Cyprus 1993-2003 (2008) 192 pages, 39 b/w photos, 8°, hard cover, ISBN 978-3-938646-37-3, € 30

Band 48 **Lucie Bonato et Maryse Emery**
Louis Dumesnil de Maricourt. Un consul pour la France (1805-1865) Naples, Messine, Séville, Stettin, Port Maurice, Newcastle, Moscou, Larnaca (2010) ca. 250 pages, 10 pictures, 8°, hard cover, ISBN 978-3-938646-51-9, € 35.-

Band 49 **Heinz A. Richter**
Kurze Geschichte des modernen Zypern 1878-2009
(2010) ca. 290 Seiten, über 100 Fotos auf 56 Tafeln, 8°, hard cover, ISBN 978-3-938646-53-3, € 35.-

Band 50 **Heinz A. Richter**
A Concise History of Modern Cyprus 1878-2009
(2010) ca. 290 pages, over 100 photos on 56 plates, 8°, hard cover, ISBN 978-3-938646-53-3, € 35.-

Can be ordered at Rutzen-Verlag, Am Zellerberg 21, 83 324 Ruhpolding
Fax: 08663 88 33 89; E-Mail: franz-rutzen@t-online.de